W9-BNC-905

The Segregated Scholars

Carter G. Woodson Institute Series

Reginald Butler, Editor

The Segregated Scholars

Black Social Scientists and the Creation of Black Labor Studies, 1890–1950

Francille Rusan Wilson

University of Virginia Press

Charlottesville and London

University of Virginia Press

© 2006 by the Rector and Visitors of the University of Virginia

All rights reserved

Printed in the United States of America on acid-free paper

First published 2006

9   8   7   6   5   4   3   2   1

Library of Congress Cataloging-in-Publication Data

Wilson, Francille Rusan, 1947–

 The segregated scholars : black social scientists and the
creation of black labor studies, 1890–1950 / Francille Rusan
Wilson.

   p. cm. — (Carter G. Woodson Institute series)
  Includes bibliographical references and index.
  ISBN 0-8139-2550-9 (alk. paper)

   1. African Americans—Employment—History—20th
century. 2. African American intellectuals—Biography.
3. Social scientists—Biography. 4. African Americans—
Segregation—History—20th century. 5. United States—Race
relations—History—20th century. I. Title.

  HD8081.A65W55 2006

  331.6'39607300922—dc22   2006028175

Contents

Foreword

The Segregated Scholars profiles fifteen notable black sociologists, economists, and historians who became social scientists between 1890 and 1935, and reveals how they committed themselves to studying the labor and economic inequalities of black workers during a difficult period in the history of American race relations. Driven by a desire to improve the socioeconomic status of black workers, they produced a body of systematic studies that provided an important legacy for subsequent scholarship on the life and experiences of black laborers in America.

Labor studies represented the central intellectual focus of the segregated scholars between 1890 and 1950. Francille Rusan Wilson writes with exceptional clarity in disclosing how this group of remarkable African American academics developed a scholarly literature that describes and analyzes the working and social situations of black workers, and that identified possible solutions to the challenges and problems facing black workers during this period.

Moreover, these scholars were also social activists. As Wilson so clearly reveals, their concerns about the fate of African Americans, including the plight of black workers, led to an active involvement in the creation of and participation in organizations and institutions dedicated to eradicating racial inequality.

Using data drawn from archival research and interviews with three of the segregated scholars still alive when she began her research, Wilson begins her discussion of the work of the segregated black scholars with an examination of the early intellectual life of W. E. B. Du Bois. According to Wilson, Du Bois's pioneering studies, *The Philadelphia Negro* (1899) and *The Negro Artisan* (1902), provided the intellectual foundation for the work of subsequent black labor scholars. Two of the earliest scholars influenced by Du Bois were Robert Wright Jr. and George Edmund Haynes, who conducted research on black workers in northern cities a decade prior to the Great Migration.

However, the period of the Great Migration, from 1910 to 1930, represents the most intense phase of intellectual activity for the segregated scholars. In this period, Wilson features the work and social action of Carter G. Woodson, Charles S. Johnson, Charles H. Wesley, Abram L. Harris, Ida De A. Reid, and Lorenzo J. Green, whose writings focused on the struggles of black workers during the Great Migration. Moreover, Wilson shows how Woodson joined George Haynes at the onset of the Great Migration in not only providing critical analyses of the impact of this massive population movement but also in creating organizations and other institutionalized activity to promote the well-being and study of African American life. Whereas Haynes reorganized the social science programs at Fisk and helped to found the National Urban League, Woodson founded the *Journal of Negro History* and helped to establish the Association for the Study of Negro Life and History. The work of Haynes and Woodson, including the informal networks they created with W. E. B. Du Bois, set the stage for Johnson, Wesley, Harris, Reid, and Greene, whose studies dominated the intellectual discourse on black workers and the Great Migration by the end of the 1920s.

However, despite the notable increase in the number of black social scientists in the 1940s and 1950s, "studies on black workers declined dramatically." Robert Weaver, who later served as Secretary of Housing and Urban Development from 1966 to 1968 under President Lyndon B. Johnson and thus was America's first black cabinet official, was one prominent figure during these decades. According to Wilson, Weaver's book *Negro Labor: A National Problem* (1946), which warned that many black workers in the postwar economy could become permanent economic proletarians unless the government pursued economic policies that promoted full employment, marked the end of fifty years of black social science research on African American workers.

It is important to stress that *The Segregated Scholars* does not focus exclusively on men. Indeed, Wilson provides the first serious interdisciplinary examination of how both race and gender determined the educational opportunities and occupational choices of black women. First, covering the period from the turn of the century to the Great Migration, she examines the research of black female college students, as well as black clubwomen and activists, to demonstrate that African American women were also interested and involved in social science.

Prominent among these women was Ida B. Wells. Although she is well known for working tirelessly to overcome inequality as a journalist, civil rights advocate, woman's rights advocate, suffragist, and community activist, Wilson points out that by using statistics—compiled from court accounts and newspapers—to suggest a causal relationship between the lynching of blacks and white concerns about economic competition from black businesses, she actually preceded W. E. B. Du Bois in the use of social research methods.

Overall, the access of these early female researchers to graduate degrees and salaried positions was severely limited by racial and gender discrimination. The women involved in labor studies during the Great Migration had similar experiences. Wilson brings to life the nearly forgotten intellectual work of Gertrude E. J. McDougald (Ayer), Helen Brooks Irvin, Elizabeth Ross Haynes, Sadie Tanner Mossell Alexander, and Emma L. Shields Penn. These notable women "were twice silenced," states Wilson, "first in their own time by race and gender discrimination that limited their access to advanced degrees and circumscribed their careers, and second in the historical record that has all but erased their intellectual work."

Although a few of these women conducted their own independent studies of black workers, because of the double burden of gender and racial discrimination, their employment was largely restricted to interviewing black working-class women in their homes and in factories, and analyzing and interpreting the results of studies conducted by others.

As I read about these fifteen men and women, I could not help but contrast their situation and work conditions with those of black social scientists today. Many African American social scientists hold positions in American colleges and universities, including elite private institutions such as Harvard, Yale, Princeton, Stanford, Columbia, and the University of Chicago. Except for Abram Harris, who taught at the University of Chicago in the late 1940s, and Ira De A. Reid, the first black professor at Haverford College, the segregated scholars could only dream about positions in America's best colleges and universities. Moreover, many of today's contemporary black scholars have access to research funds and other resources that facilitate their writing and research, as well as reasonable teaching loads and courses that relate to their areas of specialization. This is in stark contrast to the situation of the segregated scholars so ably described in this volume.

But to really appreciate the scholars' accomplishments, we need to look beyond their confinement to segregated institutions with severely restricted resources in which to pursue their scholarship. It is perhaps even more important to understand the broader social environment in which they were working.

Much of the research and social action of the segregated scholars took place during the golden age of racism. The deterioration of race relations in the North, together with the crystallization of Jim Crow segregation in the

South at the turn of the century, were associated with fundamental economic, social, and demographic changes in American society.

This period was characterized by rapid urbanization, industrial strife, internal migration, and disrupted patterns of living, which combined to heighten economic and social anxieties. These anxieties were evident not only in the discrimination and attacks against African Americans, but also in anti-Semitism, and anti-Catholic and anti-immigrant pogroms in the East, and anti-Asian attacks on the West Coast.

In the face of this general anxiety and intolerance, probably the most important factor in the growth of racism and racial conflict in the North was the increased migration of blacks from the South to northern urban centers, beginning in the early twentieth century and especially from 1910 to 1930, the period that marks the Great Migration. Changes in immigration policy following the passage of the 1924 quota law severely restricted immigration from Eastern Europe and virtually eliminated immigration from China and Japan. However, black migration to the urban North continued in substantial numbers. As the research of the Harvard sociologist Stanley Lieberson has shown, the sizable and continuous migration of blacks from the South to the North, coupled with the curtailment of immigration from eastern, central, and southern Europe in the first quarter of the twentieth century, created a situation in which other whites muffled their negative disposition toward the new Europeans and directed their antagonisms against blacks.*

During the first three decades of the twentieth century, racist themes were more loudly proclaimed in public characterizations of blacks. Even northern liberal magazines at that time (for example, the *Nation*, *Harper's Weekly*, and the *Atlantic Monthly*) expressed views supporting white supremacy and postulating the biological inferiority of the black race. Furthermore, scholarly opinion in the biological sciences lent support to racist beliefs. Political scientists and historians reinterpreted the Reconstruction period and the resurgence of white supremacy in the South in a manner supportive of racist apologists.

As Wilson points out in this book, the segregated scholars struggled to offset the racist influence in so much of the writing and scholarship of that time. However, they were the exception rather than the rule. Given the time and social environment in which they worked, we gain an even greater appreciation of their dedication and accomplishments.

*Stanley Lieberson, *A Piece of the Pie: Black and White Immigrants since 1880* (Berkeley, 1980).

Many of the segregated scholars died before the civil rights movement of the 1960s, but, as Wilson notes, they left behind a twofold legacy—an objective body of research on black workers and black life that provided a standard by which subsequent scholars, including African American scholars, can measure their own work; and a "model of black scholars as activists and reformers committed to creating a society that has racial justice and economic equity."

It is indeed fitting that this highly readable and absorbing book brings their remarkable accomplishments back to life.

William Julius Wilson
Harvard University

Acknowledgments

I am grateful and humbled by the generosity and patience of all the people and institutions that have helped me while I wrote, reconceived, and rewrote *The Segregated Scholars*. A collective thank you for setting me on this path goes out again to those who helped with and were cited in my dissertation. I salute all the folk in the ASALH, OAH, and the ABWH who faithfully listened and commented on my presentations and every member of three study groups who read and critiqued my essays on black labor studies and black intellectuals. Special thanks for their detailed commentaries go to Evelyn Brooks Higginbotham, Randall Burkett, Walter Jackson, and Henry Louis Gates of the W. E. B. Du Bois Institute's Study Group on Black Intellectuals; to Lynn Bolles, Taunya Banks, Carla Peterson, and Rosalyn Terborg-Penn of the Black Women and Work Collective; and to Marilyn M. McKenzie, the late Claudia Tate, and Deborah Willis of Jeffrey's Tea Party. Archivists at the University of Pennsylvania, and at Yale, Howard, Fisk, Illinois Wesleyan, and Atlanta Universities helped me find elusive records and photographs as I enlarged the study.

V. P. Franklin, Bettye Collier-Thomas, Jeffrey Stewart, Robin Kelley, Robert O'Meally, Joe Trotter, Mary Frances Berry, and Gerald Horne provided careful and crucial readings of parts or all of the manuscript. The late Armstead Robinson, Nancy Grant, Rhonda Williams, and Herbert Hill lent their intellectual clarity to chapters, and each will be sorely missed in my future projects. M. Melinda Chateauvert, Cynthia Neverdon-Morton, Antonio Holland, Martin Kilson, Michael Winston, Rodney Ross, Adrienne Lash Jones, and Charlotte Holloman shared sources, sent me materials, solved puzzles, and often set me straight. Valencia Skeeter, the staff, and my graduate and undergraduate assistants in African American Studies at the University of Maryland, Kelly Quinn, Heather Lyons, Tammy Sanders, Sara Irwin, Risikat Okedeyi, Lyle Lynk, Adrienne Fudge, Mary Elizabeth Murphy, and Jason Nichols, were indispensable. The steady hand of my editor, Richard K. Holway, and the editorial team at the University of Virginia Press have been very important.

A number of my colleagues have not only read but reread and fed and housed me too. My chair in the African American Studies Department, Sharon Harley, has supported me every step of the way, offering institutional support, leaves, and hosting a women's writers retreat in Martha's Vineyard that facilitated the final revisions. Deborah McDowell gave me a room of my own and a space to write in Charlottesville during a spring break, and my colleague and cousin Adrienne Davis let me move into her place for two summer months. Ribs and a bed in Aisha Ray and Paul Carryon's Chicago home were always available, and when I couldn't get there, Aisha located documents for me. Beverly Guy-Sheftall and Thadious Davis hosted me in Atlanta and Nashville as I searched the archives for materials on women's scholarship and activism. Wayne and Lois Davis lent me their light-filled Philadelphia home to write for weeks on end as they traveled around the globe, and they hosted me during countless research trips. Nell Painter's manifold support of my work as advisor and colleague has sustained me from the beginning to the end.

This book could not have been finished without Norlisha Crawford's painstaking editing and Elsa Barkley Brown's insights, commentaries, and editorial assistance on what we all hoped was the last draft. I am also deeply indebted to Malik Ernest Wilson for going over the final version with great care and to Sara Irwin for her meticulous attention to detail. I can never thank the four of them enough for their tireless attention to *The Segregated Scholars.* After Toni Mortimer's careful copyediting, any remaining errors of fact, interpretation, or punctuation are mine.

My friends and family have kept me reasonably sane. The ladies of the Reading Group give me needed grounding. My dearest friends Karen Williamson and Daphne P. Muse have always had my back through thick and thin. My parents, Georgia Tallier Rusan and the late Thomas E. Rusan, and my godmother, Elizabeth Garlington, have been my guiding lights into the world of their former teachers at Lincoln and Atlanta universities. My two wonderful sons, Malik and Rodney, have grown into manhood as I worked on this manuscript. My spouse, Ernest J. Wilson III, has lived with *The Segregated Scholars* as long as I have, lending his sustaining love and support to this project and all that I do.

The Segregated Scholars

Introduction

The Segregated Scholars and Black Labor Studies

There is only one sure basis of social reform and that is
Truth—a careful, detailed knowledge of the essential facts of
each social problem. . . . Perhaps the most immediate of these
problems is the problem of work.
—W. E. B. Du Bois and Augustus Granville Dill, *The Negro
American Artisan*

*The Segregated Scholars: Black Social Scientists and the Creation of Black
Labor Studies, 1890–1950* is a collective intellectual biography of three inter-
locking generations of black social scientists. It begins with W. E. B. Du Bois's
labor and economic writings in the 1890s and culminates with an account of
the efforts of a young economist, Robert C. Weaver, to use his research to aid
black industrial workers during the New Deal. Their belief that *"the industrial problem is fundamental"* guided black scholars' survey research for five
decades and helped to determine their academic models and their patterns
of mentorship. Robert Weaver was a graduate student in economics at Harvard University when he prefaced a request to Du Bois for advice by stating,
"Indeed I cannot see how a person interested in the economic life of the black
American could hope to escape treating of the Negro worker."[1] Thus, this
study provides a window into how a specific group of black intellectuals mobi-
lized to meet the challenges that black working people faced in the first half
of the twentieth century. This study is both an exploration of the educational
and political networks that produced black labor scholar-activists in successive generations from 1890 to 1950 and a critical assessment of over fifty years
of labor scholarship and economic reform programs they engendered.[2]

   The Segregated Scholars closely examines the world of fifteen representative black sociologists, historians, and economists, from their graduate training through their public careers. The segregated scholars were self-conscious, self-selected, and sometimes contentious colleagues committed to using empirical research to address labor and economic inequalities. The crucial links that fastened this chain of black intellectuals to one another were never merely color or ideological stances; rather, they shared a collective racial consciousness that led them to dedicate their professional lives to efforts to transform or challenge Jim Crow. They frequently came together in specific programs that tried to facilitate or promote the industrialization of black workers, despite the fact that their personal economic ideologies ranged from welfare capitalism to black nationalism to socialism. While many other black intellectuals also believed in racial uplift, reform, or radical change, the segregated scholars' beliefs led them to study black workers and to create a body of systematic studies on a common theme—the socioeconomic status of black workers. The fifteen African American men and women whose lives are detailed here became professional social scientists between 1890 and 1935 because they wanted to improve the economic and social status of their race.

I call this group of black social scientists the segregated scholars, to signify the ironic and dynamic tension between their insistence that as social scientists their absolute objectivity was not only possible but was an essential ingredient in planning any social reforms, and their subjectivity as members of an oppressed racial group who shared all of the public indignities of Jim Crow America with the working-class men and women they studied. Each of the six chapters of The Segregated Scholars is organized around critical periods in the development of black labor studies and focuses on the writings, activism, and interactions between black social scientists and other black and white intellectuals on issues relating to black workers.

Chapter 1, "'To Make a Name in Science . . . and Thus to Raise My Race': W. E. B. Du Bois and the Origins of Black Labor Studies," first re-situates Du Bois within the black intellectual milieu of the American Negro Academy and the Atlanta University Conferences. Black intellectuals had turned to the social sciences to provide answers for problems confronting black people in the decade before Du Bois earned his doctorate and began to systematize black sociological studies. The chapter then locates the foundational literature of black labor studies in Du Bois's investigations for the Department of Labor, his methodological and theoretical essays, and the two works that most affected subsequent black labor scholars, The Philadelphia Negro (1899) and The Negro Artisan (1902).[3]

Chapter 2, "Creating a Cadre of Segregated Scholars, 1898–1912," first brings the reader to the University of Chicago from 1898 to 1908, where, years before the arrival of Robert Park, the sociologist most often credited for initiating studies of black life at the university, the earliest cadre of black social scientists received their initial training, and where they met and were mentored by W. E. B. Du Bois. By 1905, a year that was a geographical and philosophical watershed for black labor studies, two young black scholars, Richard Robert Wright Jr. and George Edmund Haynes, whose studies would self-consciously extend Du Bois's methods, decided to become sociologists; a new coalition was cemented between black and white progressives that would more firmly link social research to social reform strategies; and, at the same time, opposition to social research on black life in general and black labor studies in particular became more apparent both in the academy and in the South. Under Wright and Haynes, pioneering studies of black workers in New York, Chicago, Pittsburgh, and other cities began to fill in the landscape of urban sociology, bringing black labor studies to the North a decade before the Great Migration.

This study also provides the first comprehensive examination of how gender and race affected the educational opportunities and occupational choices of black female social scientists. All of the ten men under study here became productive scholar-activists, and each had a professional career spanning thirty-five years or more, despite Jim Crow. Until the early 1940s, however, black female social scientists were hard-pressed to find more than twenty-four months of salaried work in their profession. Chapter 3, "Black Women, Social Science, and Social Reform from the Turn of the Century to the Great Migration," offers an examination of the research papers of black clubwomen and the research that female college students did to demonstrate that women at the turn of the century were as interested in using social science as were men. The educational climate and gender discrimination of that time limited black women's access to graduate degrees and salaried positions, lowering their incomes and delaying the first master's degrees and doctorates earned in the social sciences for twenty years, compared to their brothers and husbands.

Chapter 4, "Mapping the Great Migration: Black Social Scientists, Social Research, and Social Action, 1910–1930," describes the processes by which six more men join the ranks of the segregated scholars between 1910 and 1930. Carter G. Woodson, who had also been at the University of Chicago at the turn of the century, before earning a doctorate in history at Harvard University in 1912, joined George Haynes as a critical analyst and institutionalizing force at the onset of the Great Migration. Haynes and Woodson reorganized the social science programs at Fisk and Howard Universities, and created the National Urban League (NUL) and the Association for the Study of Negro Life and History (ASNLH), respectively. These two professional and reform organizations, and the informal networks created by DuBois, Haynes, and Woodson, were used to replicate the next generation of segregated scholars, whose labor studies would dominate the discourse by the end of the twenties: Charles H. Wesley, Charles S. Johnson, Abram L. Harris, Ira De A. Reid, and Lorenzo J. Greene.

Chapter 5, "'A New Day for the Colored Woman Worker'? Recovering the Labor Studies of Black Female Social Scientists during the Great Migration," examines four major studies of black female industrial workers and reclaims a portion of the lives of five black female social scientists during the Great Migration: Gertrude E. J. McDougald (Ayer), Helen Brooks Irvin, Emma L. Shields Penn, Elizabeth Ross Haynes, and Sadie Tanner Mossell Alexander. While there have been studies of white female social scientists, mine is the first interdisciplinary examination of social scientists that seriously considers how race and gender determined black women's educational opportunities and occupational choices. Black female social scientists were twice silenced, first in their own time by race and gender discrimination that limited their access to advanced degrees and circumscribed their careers, and second in the historical record that has all but erased their intellectual work.[4]

The Segregated Scholars differs from other, earlier biographies of black scholars in that it is a biographical account of the replication of black social scientists across disciplinary lines.[5] Two of the first blacks to earn doctorates in sociology, Richard Robert Wright Jr. and George Edmund Haynes, have been described more recently as an early historian and the first black economist, respectively, designations that indicate the interdisciplinary nature of their studies.[6] The inner workings of the informal networks and formal institutions that were utilized to create black professional social scientists are related to individual scholars and their studies. In my account, DuBois is important to younger scholars, not just as a scholarly exemplar but also as a mentor who launches the informal network that gives the younger men, such as Wright Jr., recommendations for fellowships, finds jobs for them, and gets their articles published while they are still graduate students. Haynes also used an informal network, of his professors at Fisk, to gain entrance to Yale University in 1903 for graduate school, and he, in turn, sent one of his first students, Charles H. Wesley, to Yale in 1911. When Haynes institutionalized this network in 1910, in the programs of the NUL and courses at Fisk, he was building on the model of five or more years of advice and introductions from Du Bois. The Urban League and its Fellows Program provided employment for the sociologist Charles S. Johnson during World War I, and master's degrees for the economist Abram Harris and the sociologist Ira Reid in the twenties. Woodson's ASNLH, the *Journal of Negro History,* and the Associated Publishers gave black social scientists a professional base that supported their development as scholars and directly assisted younger historians such as Charles Wesley and Wesley's student, Lorenzo J. Greene.

The final chapter, "'A Corporal's Guard' for Negro Workers: Black Labor Scholars during the New Deal and the Second World War, 1930–1950," shows how all three generations of the male segregated scholars were involved in attempts to assist black workers during the Depression. The chapter opens with Woodson and Du Bois offering blistering critiques of the black middle class and calling for a race-based approach to the economic crisis, while Harris was attempting to redirect the mission of the National Association for the Advancement of Colored People (NAACP) toward labor matters. Robert Weaver, a young Harvard-trained economist, made a conscious bid to join the ranks of the segregated scholars by attacking discriminatory wage policies with carefully researched briefs. Weaver's admiration of Du Bois as a social scientist, and his confidence in his own intellectual abilities, echoed twin themes in letters Du Bois had received from the previous generations of young black students: "I would appreciate any further suggestions . . . that your vast experience . . . may prompt. . . . I trust that my future work will compensate you for any inconvenience." Weaver's attempts to make New Deal programs benefit black workers led him into alliances with the most radical and the most conservative of the segregated scholars, Abram Harris and George Haynes, and into research projects with two of the more centrist figures, Charles S. Johnson and Ira Reid.[7]

The predicament of black workers in industrializing America continuously engaged the attention of the African American social scientists, more than any other single topic. As such, the creation of the field is best understood by focusing on the major figures in the development of black labor studies because they established its methods and theories, its patterns of recruitment, and its institutions. I have chosen the segregated scholars included here for several reasons. First, they were selected according to the significance and scope of their labor scholarship. Second, I based my selection of the men by choosing those who had a minimum of twenty years of recoverable relationships with one another so that I could discuss the intergenerational relationships among them. While this approach eliminated a serious consideration of women social scientists from my dissertation, I subsequently became determined to return the pioneering black women social scientists to the historical record, and in doing so explore the factors that shaped their professional lives as well. My first criterion, a significant body of labor scholarship, precluded the inclusion of several excellent male scholars who came of age in the twenties and thirties, such as E. Franklin Frazier and Ralph Bunche, and who were very much a part of the political networks of the segregated scholars but who had little impact on labor studies. I have also not covered comprehensively black social scientists whose studies were important but did not represent new trends in theory or methodology.[8] The second criterion, a pattern of personal relationships that led to public advocacy, led to a decision not to treat in this study independent economic analysts and scholars, such as Horace R. Cayton and Oliver Cromwell Cox, who had much more limited professional interactions with other black academics. The six men of the third generation of black scholars that I do include here provide a cross-section of the most important political beliefs and theoretical approaches of the broader group of scholars whose cooperative efforts continued throughout the half-century studied here.

Black labor studies as a coherent and systematic academic discourse was the most significant result of the collective endeavors of the segregated scholars. As individual analysts, they also had a major impact on other subfields in social science, as well as creating or administering key professional, religious, and reform organizations. W. E. B. Du Bois and Carter G. Woodson laid the foundations for the systematic study of black life and history simultaneously with their development of black labor studies. One of Woodson's first associates, Charles H. Wesley, had published paradigm-shifting studies of the Civil War and of the Caribbean in the decade before his "avant-garde" and "pioneering" *Negro Labor in the United States,* which was hailed as marking the moment when "scientific social research began at Howard [University]."[9] Du Bois, Haynes, and Woodson were the founders of three important and enduring institutions: the National Association for the Advancement of Colored People, the National Urban League, and the Association for the Study of Negro Life and History. As editors, respectively, of *The Crisis* and *Phylon, Opportunity,* the *Journal of Negro History,* and the *Christian Recorder,* Du Bois, Johnson, Woodson, and Wright Jr. reached thousands of readers, within and beyond the academy, with their economic and political commentaries. Johnson and Ira Reid, Charles Wesley and Lorenzo Greene, and Elizabeth

Ross Haynes and Sadie T. M. Alexander were able to influence the organizations their mentors had established: the NUL, the ASNLH, and the National Association of Colored Women. At various times in the thirties and forties, Reid, Johnson, Wesley, and Harris held the faculty positions vacated by their mentors Du Bois, Haynes, and Woodson at Atlanta, Fisk, and Howard Universities, training new generations of black social scientists at these institutions. During the thirties and forties, as Woodson and Du Bois directed their political critiques at Negro education and materialistic elites, two younger, insurgent critics, Abram Harris and Robert Weaver, tried to democratize the NAACP and change the labor programs of the New Deal, in a continuing struggle by black academics to improve the economic status of black workers.

Black women social scientists, such as Helen Brooks Irvin, Emma Shields Penn, and Gertrude E. J. McDougald, had to make the most of their brief opportunity during the Great Migration to earn a salary for studying black women workers, but they nonetheless made important contributions to both labor studies and to the community work of black women, which was guided by their social research.

The Segregated Scholars' focus on labor studies as the central theme among black social scientists between 1890 and 1950 seeks to answer the question of how a black intelligentsia developed both a scholarly literature that described black workers' situation and the institutional structures they used to identify possible solutions to assist black people solve what Du Bois termed their "most immediate . . . problem of work."[10]

Three essays in particular helped shape the questions I posed in the dissertation that began my inquiries into the development of black labor studies. Peter H. Wood's examination of the study of black colonial history during the civil rights movement was my first encounter with the argument that a specific generation of historians can have a collective ethos. V. P. Franklin's study of how early black social scientists challenged the mental testing movement illustrated the benefits of examining black scholars according to a thematic rather than a disciplinary approach. And St. Clair Drake's powerful essay, "In the Mirror of Black Scholarship: W. Allison Davis and *Deep South*," suggested both a collective ethos and an approach that could provide the contextual basis for investigating the world and the works of black social scientists. Although Wood's study is of a different era, its epigraph, "I did the best I could for my day," also introduced me to the nineteenth-century black intellectual Richard Robert Wright Sr. I would soon discover that Wright helped to bring Du Bois to Atlanta University, and that Du Bois, in turn, would mentor Wright's son and namesake, Richard Robert Wright Jr. As I began to realize that black labor studies might offer a central point of reference for understanding the politics and scholarship of black social scientists, this study was born. When I began my research, three of the four segregated scholars still alive, Charles H. Wesley, Lorenzo J. Greene, and Robert C. Weaver, graciously allowed me to interview them.[11] *The Segregated Scholars* is dedicated to the memory of all the scholar-activists in this study, as well as to the enduring ideal of exacting social research that is joined in a commitment to social, economic, and racial justice.[12]

1

"To Make a Name in Science . . . and Thus to Raise My Race"

W. E. B. Du Bois and the Origins of Black Labor Studies

Be the Truth what it may I shall seek it on the pure assumption that it is worth seeking. . . . I am striving to make my life all that life may be . . . with others of my brothers and sisters making their lives similar. . . . I am willing to sacrifice . . . and work for the rise of the Negro people. . . . These are my plans: to make a name in science, to make a name in literature and thus to raise my race. . . . I wonder what will be the outcome?
—W. E. B. Du Bois, diary entry, Feb. 23, 1893

In these words written after a solitary celebration in Berlin where he was a graduate student, the usually abstemious W. E. Burghardt Du Bois, now warmed by wine and liqueur, looked ahead to a life as a scholar and intellectual that was both grounded and bounded by race and ambition. In his twenty-fifth-birthday manifesto Du Bois deftly wove three of the four thick threads of intentionality that, as the timeless virtues of Truth, Duty, and Glory, would become the fabric of modern scholarship on black workers. He would, he vowed, sacrifice individual desire out of his Duty to his race to pursue a Truth that would lead to even greater personal and group Glory.[1] The fourth strand, Purpose, had both a temporal and spatial specificity for Du Bois. It was his sense of purpose that led him to choose the social sciences as the field in which he would endeavor to make his "name in science" and to create the methodological framework for black labor studies.

W. E. B. Du Bois's four ideals—Truth, Duty, Glory, and Purpose—may be more prosaically identified as objective scholarship, collective responsibility, race leadership, and a commitment to racial progress through social reform. These ideals would fully engage Du Bois for the next decade and would also

9

serve as the guiding principles for two successive generations of young black men and women who became social scientists and created the field of black labor studies.

The apparently declining fortunes of black workers at the turn of the twentieth century was a special concern to those black intellectuals such as Du Bois who believed racial progress could be partially measured by the nature and extent of black workers' participation in the United States' rapidly industrializing economy. Obtaining empirical data on black workers was central to Du Bois's overall mission as a social scientist and race man: "There is only one sure basis of social reform and that is Truth—a careful, detailed knowledge of the essential facts of each social problem. . . . Perhaps the most immediate of these problems is the problem of work."[2]

In describing racial progress as his purpose in 1893, the young Du Bois employed the uplift parlance of late nineteenth-century black Americans—"to raise my race." Du Bois and his fellow social scientists' discourse of racial uplift and representation was double voiced, as Nell Irvin Painter, Evelyn Brooks Higginbotham, and Vincent P. Franklin have argued, simultaneously inscribing middle-class blacks' personal commitment to advocate group progress and obscuring the autonomous actions of black working-class people on their own behalf. At the beginning of the twentieth century the social sciences offered Du Bois and other black intellectuals a new weapon in the old battle for freedom and human dignity.[3]

Within a decade of his private pledge, Du Bois had written three books, a dozen monographs, and scores of articles, which laid the groundwork for black labor studies and much of the twentieth century's scholarship on African American life. And as Du Bois had imagined, but would rarely acknowledge, his lifelong quest for Truth and Glory was not a solitary one, but, rather, it was a mission of collective Duty and Purpose with other black intellectuals who were "making their lives similar." Even before Du Bois turned to the social sciences, other black intellectuals were undertaking their own research surveys, collecting data, and were active in professional associations such as the American Social Science Association. The journalist and activist Ida B. Wells gathered and analyzed statistics on lynching and laced them into her fiery lectures, editorials, and books while Du Bois was a graduate student in Europe.[4] The 1893 diary entry therefore provides a window into the multipurposed mission of Du Bois and other educated African Americans who defined themselves as "race men and women" at the turn of the twentieth century. Du Bois's brilliant new use of the empirical methods of sociology would launch the systematic study of black life and labor and give him quite a name in science before he was forty.

In this chapter I focus on the decade between 1893 and 1903, when Du Bois set out to counterpose the clamorous claims of Social Darwinism with a comprehensive social science research agenda. The essential methodological framework for black labor studies was put into place by Du Bois, who used a network of volunteers to help him collect data until his efforts were joined, just after the turn of the century, by several newly minted black sociologists. The early social studies of Du Bois were sponsored and shaped by white social reform groups, the U.S. Bureau of Labor, and Atlanta University. His first sociological investigations, appearing in *The Philadelphia Negro* (1899), monographs for the U.S. Bureau of Labor (1898–1901), and the early Atlanta University Conference studies culminating in *The Negro Artisan* (1902), set, as we shall see, both the standard and the point of departure for the next quarter century of research on black American workers.[5]

Du Bois's Beginnings as a Social Scientist

W. E. Burghardt Du Bois, the self-confident diarist of 1893 was an ambitious lower-working-class orphan from Great Barrington, Massachusetts, whose determination to excel had taken him to Fisk University, one of the best Negro colleges, then to Harvard University and the University of Berlin. In the young Will Du Bois, the Fisk faculty had found a gifted student who was more than willing to take up the mantle of race leadership they were anxious to bestow on their graduates. Between 1885 and 1888 there were fewer than fifty students in the college division of Fisk; most students were in the normal school or were taking high school courses. Students and faculty developed close and lasting relationships. Fisk's classical curriculum, old-school ties, and solid recommendations from Du Bois's professors made it possible for him to gain admission to Harvard. At Harvard, Du Bois continued to have close relationships with many of his professors, who now included some of the most important scholars in America.[6]

The combined experience of his two undergraduate degrees and the first two years of graduate study at Harvard produced a young black man who was chiefly interested in critical inquiry, history, political economy, and writing. At first Du Bois intended to become a philosopher, but he turned instead toward history at the end of his undergraduate years. He studied philosophy with William James, George Herbert Palmer, and George Santayana; American

W. E. B. Du Bois.
(Library of
Congress)

history with Albert Bushnell Hart; and English composition with Josiah Royce. Hart, who exemplified the new professional historian, introduced Du Bois to scientific approaches to history, while James helped move him away from philosophical doctrines dominated by religious thought and toward a modern rationality. Royce and the English professor Barrett Wendell helped Du Bois hone his writing style more firmly into that of the nineteenth-century man of letters, without losing his already unique expressive voice.[7]

The first sociology department in the United States was organized at the University of Chicago in 1892, the year Du Bois left Harvard with a master's degree in hand, to study in Berlin. Harvard in the early 1890s did not as yet offer a systematic program in modern sociology and would not develop a department of sociology until 1931, so Du Bois's sociological training came primarily from his two years in Germany. He had won a combination scholarship-loan from the John F. Slater Fund for two years of studies at the University of Berlin. Du Bois did take an undergraduate course on the ethics of social reform with Francis Peabody, and a graduate course in sociology with a new professor, Edward Cummings, for whom he had little regard.[8]

Sociology and the related notion that empirical research could be used to find solutions to social problems soon captivated Du Bois, but his initial purpose in going to the University of Berlin was to study history and political economy. He studied under Gustav von Schmoller and Adolf Wagner, who gave Du Bois his basic sociological training, and the historian Heinrich von Treitschke. Treitschke was a Prussian nationalist who believed in a strong authoritarian state. Du Bois also attended lectures by Max Weber, who was a visiting professor at the university. Although Du Bois rejected Treitschke's discourses on the inferiority of nonwhites, he was drawn to the nationalistic assertion that strong leaders could mold and raise new civilizations. Schmoller and Wagner both stressed the importance of inductive empirical studies that used economic and historical evidence. Schmoller believed that a careful analysis of society could prompt specific reforms that in turn could engender social justice. Under Schmoller's influence Du Bois now was able to see that being a social scientist incorporated his desire to be a scholar while improving the lot of black people.[9]

W. E. B. Du Bois was obliged to return to the United States in the summer of 1894 without the German doctorate he coveted. Although he had done extremely well in his two years of graduate studies in Germany and had finished writing a dissertation on the southern plantation system, he had not yet met the residency requirement for the doctorate, and his German advisors were unable to arrange an exception to the university's requirement or to persuade the Slater Fund trustees to sponsor the additional required semester. Du Bois returned from Germany with his fare to his home in Great Barrington and two additional dollars. He began a "systematic campaign" to secure a teaching position for the fall.[10]

Racial discrimination and Jim Crow limited the returning Du Bois's job prospects to underfunded Negro colleges whose educational objectives and actual teaching needs did not necessarily match his specialties or goals. He accepted his first offer, a teaching post at Wilberforce University, an African Methodist Episcopal school in Ohio. At Wilberforce, Du Bois's attempts to put his lofty ideals into practice had their first revealing test.

In his writings Du Bois candidly and melodramatically described the three-way misfit between himself—the pure scholar—the denominational politics of Wilberforce's administration, and its often poorly prepared student body. "What business had I, anyhow, to teach Greek when I had studied men? I grew sure that I had made a mistake," he lamented. He was obliged to teach a wide variety of courses, including Latin, German, English, and Greek, to students who rarely met his demanding standards. The conservative bishops and officials who ran Wilberforce were unwilling to have Du Bois introduce courses in sociology or Negro history or to allow physical education or intra-collegiate sports.[11]

Du Bois completed his doctorate at Harvard in the spring of 1895, his first year at Wilberforce. Setting aside his German dissertation, he reworked and extended his Harvard master's thesis on British efforts to end the slave trade. The resulting study closely followed the precepts of his advisor, Albert B. Hart, for heavily documented histories. Du Bois was now the first black person to have earned a doctorate from Harvard University.[12]

Du Bois's plan to make a name in science and raise his race could not be fully implemented at Wilberforce University. His two years at Wilberforce continued and confounded his pleasant memories of student days at Fisk University, leaving him "at once marvelously inspired and deeply depressed."[13] It was at Wilberforce that Du Bois established several important lifelong friendships and first met the Anglican minister and educator Alexander Crummell, who was to provide him with an entree into the black intelligentsia that he would soon personify. Du Bois also met Nina Gomer, a student from Iowa, whom he would marry. While Du Bois was proud to be at an institution run entirely by black people, he was deeply offended that he was not allowed to offer sociology courses under any circumstances. With mounting desperation the young professor renewed his efforts to find a position more commensurate with his goals.[14] In the spring of 1896, when Du Bois was offered a short-term position surveying the black population in Philadelphia's Seventh Ward, he quickly married and moved eastward. Twenty-five years later he would characterize his two years at Wilberforce as a brief delay in his life's plan: "Thus, the third period of my life began. . . . To remain at Wilberforce without doing my ideals meant spiritual death."[15]

Leaving Wilberforce meant that W. E. B. Du Bois could again focus on his ambitious goal to make his name in science and revisit his four ideals. His eighteen-month investigation of Philadelphia's Seventh Ward launched his career in social science and began his adult life as a public intellectual. He began to be pulled into leadership roles in African American professional associations by an older generation of black intellectuals, including Crummell and R. R. Wright Sr. Du Bois was also now in direct contact with prominent white social reformers, such as Carroll Davidson Wright, for the first time, many of whom would become lifelong allies. The early support of Carroll Wright and Richard Robert Wright Sr. enabled Du Bois to deepen his focus on economic and labor issues and gave him the resources and an institutional base from which to conduct socioeconomic research for more than a decade. What made W. E. Burghardt Du Bois truly unique, however, was his ability to synthesize his graduate and undergraduate training and to develop and carry forth a master plan for the comprehensive study of black people in American society. His interim assignment in Philadelphia was but the first step in his larger scheme.

The proposal for a survey of black social problems in the Seventh Ward arose after black voters helped Philadelphia's corrupt political machine defeat a reformist slate. Susan P. Wharton, a wealthy and prominent Quaker on the executive board of the Philadelphia College Settlement, persuaded the University of Pennsylvania's provost, Charles C. Harrison, to sponsor a comprehensive community study. Du Bois's sponsors were interested in a detailed analysis that they could use to design social reforms. "The University has entered upon this work as a part of its duty. . . . We want to know precisely how this class of people live . . . and then having this information and these accurate statistics . . . see what . . . proper remedies may be applied."[16] Du Bois was hired because the sponsors believed that a black male researcher might have more credibility with residents, and the conclusions, which they assumed would emphasize the "social wreckage" of Philadelphia's black community, might have more validity if written by a black person.[17]

The thoroughness of his survey of black life in the Seventh Ward and the extraordinary detachment of his investigative voice was due in part to Du Bois's desire to be recognized for his ability as a social scientist. Du Bois was anxious to shift his attention to the examination of contemporary issues and "determined to put science into sociology through a study of conditions and problems of my own group." He was one of the first American sociologists to move beyond Herbert Spencer's positivist theories of society. Du Bois instead combined the rigorous empirical research called for by Schmoller with detailed surveys, a method that the English reformer Charles Booth had pioneered in his *Life and Labour of the People in London*.[18]

His final report, *The Philadelphia Negro,* provided a comprehensive analysis of black socioeconomic conditions in a major northern city at the turn of the century. Jane Addams's study of the Hull House neighborhood was the only other previous American study that matched Du Bois's in its meticulous mapping and canvassing. It is in *The Philadelphia Negro* that black labor studies commences.[19]

This book presented the first detailed information on black urban occupations, family income, inflated rents, and the problems of female wage earners. Black workers in Philadelphia were limited in the types of jobs open to them and were being crowded out of many of their traditional trades, such as barbering and catering, by newly arriving white immigrants. Black laborers' full participation in the skilled trades, and even in unskilled factory work, was severely curtailed by union contracts barring black members and through gentlemen's agreements.[20] Although Du Bois exhaustively documented the specific effects of racial prejudice on the employment, wages, and occupations of blacks, he would not surrender his firm belief that an individual's will was the chief determinant of his or her fate in life. Du Bois was as much a stern moral taskmaster as his transplanted New England professors at Fisk University and his new icon, Crummell. He was also a Social Darwinist who felt that racism put the hardworking on the same low plane as the lazy: "There are many Negroes who . . . in untrammeled competition would soon rise high in the economic scale, and thus . . . we should soon have left at the bottom those inefficient and lazy drones who did not deserve a better fate. However . . . the law of survival is greatly modified by human choice, wish, whim and prejudice. And consequently one never knows . . . how far this failure to survive is due to the deficiencies of the individual, and how far to the accidents or injustice of his environment."[21]

Du Bois scolded whites for judging all blacks on the basis of black criminals and thieves, but he frequently resorted to simplistic stereotypes. *The Philadelphia Negro* expressed Du Bois's belief that black workers in Philadelphia were not as efficient or as reliable as native white or immigrant workers. Du Bois stated that a black worker was "as a rule, willing, honest and good-natured; but he is also . . . careless, unreliable and unsteady."[22] This was an allegation that he would not simply modify but reject and attempt to wholly discredit in his later labor writings.

Du Bois also offered a descriptive and functional view of black class stratification that differed from Crummell's and Wright's because he equated respectability and morality with the upper classes. Du Bois divided the residents of the Seventh Ward into four grades according to income, moral considerations, and questions of expenditure. At the top were respectable, largely professional families with a nonworking wife and mother in a well-kept home and children in school; next came the respectable working class; then the poor; and, finally, at the bottom, the criminal element. Over the next decade Du Bois's understanding of the dynamic relationship among race, class, and economic interest fundamentally shifted, but his reliance on the value of carefully crafted empirical studies would always undergird his research. *The Philadelphia Negro* set a fifty-year methodological standard by which other black social scientists would measure their own work. We shall see in the next chapter how Du Bois's first protégés, R. R. Wright Jr. and George Edmund Haynes, explicitly modeled their earliest studies of black economic and occupational development on the methods established in *The Philadelphia Negro*.[23] The book is arguably the single most influential work of black social science. Its creation began the sculpting of the terrain of black labor studies.[24]

Du Bois's location in Philadelphia facilitated his reintroduction into East Coast black intellectual life. The most important organization of which he became a part while in Philadelphia was the newly organizing American Negro Academy. The ANA was part of the wave of national black organizations founded in the 1880s and 1890s, such as the Bethel Literary and Historical Association (f. 1881) and the Society for the Collection of Negro Folklore (f. 1890), which combated increased political and economic discrimination. These organizations explicitly attempted to refute charges of black inferiority and promoted original research that stressed the positive contributions of African Americans to the life of the nation. This action signaled a shift by some black intellectuals toward scientific arguments and away from appeals to the morality of whites, an approach that had characterized the abolitionist and the immediate postbellum periods. The ANA provided an audience of critical yet supportive readers of Du Bois's writings on race.[25]

W. E. B. Du Bois joined seventeen other men at the first ANA meeting in Washington, D.C., on March 5, 1897, ten days after his twenty-ninth birthday. At this meeting Alexander Crummell was elected president and Du Bois was made ANA vice president over a number of older and more distinguished founding members in what was a clear signal of approbation of his academic achievements.[26] The older leadership of the ANA turned to Du Bois and other younger members, such as Kelly Miller of Howard University, to supply the intellectual artillery for their assaults on Social Darwinism and to realize their ambitious research agenda. Du Bois had not quite shed his Social Darwinistic tendencies yet; at the ANA's founding he was more conservative, more elitist, and more moralistic than most of the other ANA members, many of whom were clergymen. Membership in the ANA doubtless helped Du

Bois, as he gradually came to accept the leaders' emphasis on nongenetic causes for black social disorganization and their insistence on the need for civil and voting rights for all classes of black people. More significant for understanding the development of black social science and black labor studies as a collective enterprise in the late nineteenth century was the fact that at least two other ANA members, Kelly Miller and R. R. Wright Sr., had already begun to bring modern sociological instruction and research into two of the best Negro colleges, Howard and Atlanta Universities.[27]

Dual factors helped to focus black intellectuals' interest in objective and critical social analyses of black workers. First, black men and women began to conduct social and economic studies partially in reaction to the scholarship that did exist on black social problems. Southern whites' social analyses of black life in particular contained assumptions and value judgments that alarmed and annoyed black readers, and not a few of them began to question the empirical accuracy of these studies. Second, black intellectuals believed that research done by black authors would in and of itself demonstrate that black people were capable of intellectual achievements and undeserving of discriminatory treatment; in other words, black individuals' scientific achievements would inevitably help improve or raise the status of all black people.

Sociological methods were also used by black intellectuals to counter scientific racism prevalent in American social science. The ANA member Kelly Miller's review of Frederick L. Hoffman's "Race Traits and Tendencies of the American Negro" was one of the first social scientific challenges to Social Darwinism published by a black writer in the late nineteenth century, although black intellectuals had been responding in kind to racist attacks for the entire century. Miller's review became one of the best-selling ANA publications. The ANA president Alexander Crummell was thrilled, and he pronounced the review "the most scientific defense of the Negro ever made in this country by a man of our own blood: accurate, pointed, painstaking, and I claim conclusive."[28] Crummell's remark underscored the dual interest of black intellectuals in using sociology to defend black capabilities and to more carefully delineate actual conditions.

Kelly Miller, like Du Bois, was one of a number of black men and women in the 1890s who were independently setting out to study sociology, become sociologists, or to conduct survey research. Miller had studied the classics and mathematics at Johns Hopkins and Howard Universities, and he became a professor at Howard University in 1890, where he began to teach sociology in

Richard Robert
Wright Sr. (From
the Collections of
the University of
Pennsylvania
Archives)

1895, even as Du Bois was rebuffed from introducing it at Wilberforce, placing Howard among the first American colleges to offer sociology courses.[29]

The opening meeting of the ANA placed W. E. B. Du Bois in regular contact with Richard Robert Wright Sr. and Alexander Crummell, important
mentors and exemplars in this self-described third phase of Du Bois's life.
Wright was the president of Georgia State College of Industry for Colored
Youth. He had already begun to undertake his own sociohistorical studies
and was anxious to promote sociology as a tool for racial uplift. Having followed Du Bois's educational career through the newspapers, he often ex-
horted his children and students to aspire to similar academic accomplishments. Wright was also vice president of Atlanta University's board of trustees,
and he was on the lookout for a black sociologist to join the Atlanta University faculty.[30]

The March 5, 1897, meeting of the ANA gave Wright Sr. an opportunity to
observe the young scholar Du Bois at close hand. Du Bois's insistence, in his

reading of his "The Conservation of Races," that races, not individuals, make contributions to world civilization would have resonated a major chord with the slave-born Wright, who was a vocal champion of group advancement. The two men would have surely also discussed Du Bois's ongoing research in Philadelphia. Wright was fighting a losing effort with the trustees and the Georgia state legislature at his school in Savannah to retain college-level courses in the curriculum, but he had significant support for a program of social science courses and research at his alma mater, Atlanta University.

In 1895, while Du Bois was completing his doctorate, R. R. Wright was institutionalizing the growing interest on the part of black college graduates in social research on black urban life by founding the Atlanta University's annual conference on city problems.[31] Although Du Bois never publicly acknowledged his debt to Wright, it is unlikely that he would have been hired at Atlanta University without Wright's blessing, and it is certain that there would have been no Atlanta University Conference without Wright's guiding influence. The Atlanta University conferences began black intellectuals' productive association with the U.S. Bureau of Labor, and they helped the government to become an important sponsor of analytical research on black workers between 1897 and 1906 and again between 1918 and 1923.[32]

R. R. Wright was exceedingly proud that the U.S. Bureau of Labor had agreed to publish charts that displayed the results of the University's study of black health and living conditions in eighteen cities in time for the second Atlanta University Conference, which was held two months after the first ANA meeting. This was the first study of black workers that the Bureau of Labor published, and great stress was placed on the fact that the actual research had been "gathered exclusively by representative colored men and women."[33]

R. R. Wright probably met with the U.S. commissioner of labor, Carroll Davidson Wright, to go over the schedules for publication while he was in Washington in March 1897 for the ANA meeting.[34] The research interests of the two Wrights had been brought together via George Bradford, a wealthy Massachusetts banker who was also a trustee of Atlanta University and corresponding secretary of the new City Conference.[35] Bradford, an 1886 graduate of Harvard College, had arranged for the Harvard sociologist Edward Cummings to design the questionnaires for Atlanta University's first two surveys. Bradford and Cummings then turned to Carroll Wright, former head of the Massachusetts Bureau of Labor Statistics, to publish the results of the second year's study on the physical and social conditions of blacks in cities.

Carroll D. Wright was a pioneer in bringing scientific methods to the study of American workers. The Massachusetts Bureau of Labor Statistics was the first such bureau in the nation, and it is generally credited with making the gathering of labor statistics a scientific, nonpartisan endeavor and extending the scope far beyond occupational and strike data to the home, health, and social life of workers. Carroll Wright believed that labor statistics were a non-sentimental means of confirming the "material, social, intellectual and moral prosperity" of working people. He had overseen some of the earliest economic studies of women and of black workers while in Massachusetts and was central in the planning of the 1890 federal census that was the first to gather detailed occupational statistics by race and gender.[36]

In 1885, shortly after Carroll Wright arrived in Washington, Lucius Q. C. Lamar, secretary of the interior, prevented Commissioner Wright from collecting data on black workers. Lamar, a Democrat from Mississippi, claimed that social research on blacks was too risky politically for Wright's subcabinet bureau. By 1896, when he finally was able to publish statistical studies of black Americans, Carroll Wright had far more clout, but southern politicians' hostility to scientific studies of blacks would continue to have a chilling effect on the collection of all types of federal data on black workers. R. R. Wright was forced to abandon an appointment as a 1900 U.S. census supervisor in Georgia when segregationists opposed his intention to hire black enumerators for half of the positions in his primarily black district.[37]

In early February 1897, before Carroll Wright committed the Bureau of Labor to future studies of black people, he asked W. E. B. Du Bois for advice on the methodologies and approaches that might be utilized. The survey schedules that Edward Cummings had designed for the first two Atlanta University conferences were competent but were unsophisticated and lacked a guiding analytical framework. Du Bois was interested in becoming involved in Commissioner Wright's proposal to design a study "relating to the economic progress of the colored people." Du Bois replied immediately, sending the commissioner a five-page letter and three documents that attested to his skills as a sociologist: a newspaper clipping about the Philadelphia study; blank copies of the six schedules he was using in Philadelphia; and an eleven-page leaflet with extracts from reviews and letters of reference from prominent white academics that Du Bois had printed while he was at Wilberforce. Du Bois began with a direct acknowledgment of what he considered his two strongest points—his extensive sociological training and his racial heritage. "I desire especially to continue my work of historical and statistical investigation into the condition of the American Negro, from the unbiased scientific standpoint. . . . Being a Negro I would perhaps have some advantages in guiding to the true facts, while . . . my training might not be without use."[38] In this letter to Carroll Wright, Du Bois suggested that if Wright had "a half hour of leisure," they could meet to talk about a comprehensive approach to research on black economic life when he was in Washington for the ANA launching. Their meeting might account for the fact that the normally punctilious Du Bois arrived late to the ANA's evening session, where he was to open with a reading of his "The Conservation of Races."[39]

After their separate meetings with Du Bois in early March 1897, R. R. Wright Sr. and Carroll D. Wright independently took steps that would make it possible for Du Bois to set his research agenda for the next dozen years. R. R. Wright helped swing alumni support to hire Du Bois to teach sociology and to lead Atlanta University's urban research conference, and Carroll Wright provided him with research commissions nearly every other summer. Carroll D. Wright asked Du Bois to give him a detailed outline of his research priorities for economic studies of black people. Du Bois's letters to Carroll Wright in the spring and summer sketched out several different strategies but were more concrete and pragmatic than in his fall 1897 formal paper "The Study of the Negro Problems." They revealed Du Bois's genuine intellectual curiosity and willingness to experiment before committing to a single methodological approach. He suggested that it would be most useful to begin with two types of discrete studies, community and social structural, which were designed to test research hypotheses and designs. Plan A proposed community studies that would concentrate on small towns or counties in Virginia, the Carolinas, or Georgia. Plan B was conceived principally as an examination of occupational categories such as black skilled workers and would be done in several cities. Du Bois believed that a number of smaller scale studies would be more useful for establishing methodological and theoretical models than more comprehensive ventures in one location, such as in *The Philadelphia Negro*. Carroll Wright concurred with Du Bois's Plan A and hired him to begin with a community study of Farmville, Virginia. Du Bois's study of Farmville followed the Atlanta University Conference schedules, and it was the second study of black social statistics published in the *Bulletin of the Department of Labor*, and the beginning of a series of eight community studies of black life that the department commissioned from 1897 to 1906. Du Bois completed three of these studies and all followed the basic guidelines that he had set forth in his Plan A. Thus, Du Bois's vision shaped and defined how the federal government would examine black workers before the Great Migration. Du Bois did not abandon Plan B or his other suggestions but used them as he systematically examined African American social structure in his Atlanta University Conference studies.[40]

W. E. B. Du Bois's more theoretical formulation for long-range comprehensive research on black socioeconomic conditions was read at the fall 1897 meeting of the American Academy of Political and Social Science (AAPSS).[41] He hoped that his systematic identification of the possibilities for research on blacks would provoke the interest of white scholars and attract the financial support of major universities, research institutes, and the federal government. Du Bois was speaking to a friendly and sympathetic organization that balanced its increasing domination by academic social scientists with an interest in reform. The AAPSS had had black members since its inception in 1889, and it addressed more black social problems than other predominantly white professional social science organizations.[42] Conservatives in his audience would have easily agreed with Du Bois when he blamed racial segregation principally on black people's failure to reach "a sufficiently high grade of culture and only secondarily on systematic racial subordination." Du Bois argued that black life offered sociologists a unique opportunity to examine the mechanisms of social change and cultural adaptation: "There does not seem to have been awakened as yet a fitting realization of the opportunities for scientific inquiry . . . into the group of social phenomena arising from the presence in this land of eight million persons of African descent."[43]

At the conclusion of his talk Du Bois laid out a program for the broad and systematic study of the history and conditions of American Negroes that should be taken up by black and white universities and scholars. Du Bois hoped that sociological research in the United States would be color-blind, despite the increasing extent of segregation and racialism in the country as a whole. Based on the good reviews of his first two books and certain of the quality of his ideas, he thought that prestigious institutions such as the University of Pennsylvania and Harvard University would be predisposed to do collaborative work. There was in fact no response to his plan from white universities, and this was a source of disbelief, which gave way to disillusionment, and much later to bitterness on Du Bois's part. Initially, however, he was almost too busy to notice white academic institutions' lack of sustained enthusiasm for his ideas. Individual white social scientists and reformers such as Carroll Wright and Jane Addams did lend their support, and he managed to obtain small grants from philanthropic organizations to fund the Atlanta University studies.[44]

Institutionalizing Social Science:
The Atlanta University Studies

The founding of the Atlanta University Conference in 1895 institutionalized social science research as a collective endeavor of black urban intellectuals. The planning and conception of the first two Atlanta University studies by non-graduate-trained researchers predated Du Bois's survey research in Philadelphia. The studies contain, albeit in rough form, the many basic assumptions and methodologies that W. E. B. Du Bois would later shape and give a clear analytical focus during his thirteen years at Atlanta University. Critical to the future development of black labor studies were the painstaking attempts of R. R. Wright Sr. and the conference founders to use empirical research to determine whether there was a causal relationship between the poverty and unemployment in cities and high rates of crime, illness, and mortality, and their rejection of biological determinism. Wright's letter to the attendees at the first conference expressed the desire to obtain reliable indices of black life: "The greatest danger to the real progress of the colored people lies in this sociological condition in the large cities. It is difficult, however, to get the facts. There is very little attention given in the South to the vital statistics of Negroes. . . . The census is neither full nor altogether reliable. The facts . . . must be searched out by conscientious persons specially interested in this kind of work."[45]

The concept and impetus for an annual Atlanta publication series and research conference was led by Wright, the Boston attorney Butler Wilson, and Joseph Smith, a minister from Chattanooga who represented the desire of alumni who lived in the rapidly growing cities of the South and the Northeast to have the university begin a "systematic and thorough investigation of the conditions of living among the Negro population of cities." The Atlanta University Conference framers believed that scientific investigations would provide the statistical data needed to solve "appalling problems before the educated men and women of the race that they and only they alone can and must handle."[46] They wanted to hold their first conference during the Cotton States Exposition in 1895, but twin desires for a careful study and a large audience moved the first conference to the spring of 1896 in a permanent and prominent two-day slot during graduation week. For their first research project, Wright and other alumni sought to gather data to determine the validity of assertions concerning black mortality and disease rates, and of general living conditions in the cities of the South. They were so concerned that the white academy accept their study as scientific and objective that they selected a trustee, the Boston banker George Bradford, to be the corresponding secretary and first editor of the research series. The survey questionnaires were completed by a team of volunteers made up almost exclusively of black college graduates. One of the youngest participants was James Weldon Johnson, a writer and a future executive secretary of the National Association for the Advancement of Colored People, who had graduated from Atlanta University in 1894.

As a result of the first Atlanta University investigation, Wright, like fellow ANA member Kelly Miller, concluded that the urban socioeconomic setting— the environment, and not genetics—was the main cause of black crime and other social ills. Wright told the conference that the first study offered a new and scientific perspective on the interaction of poverty, unemployment, and social disorganization: "The city colored people drift into crime because they are idle and hungry far oftener than because they are purposely vicious."[47] From their inception the Atlanta University studies were concerned with explorations of workers, employment, and the problems of the working classes.

While the Atlanta University findings would serve as a starting point for social research that black Americans undertook, there was not a complete consensus on how to interpret data, and some of the variances in interpretation reflected differing political positions at the turn of the nineteenth century. Not all the conference participants agreed with Wright's interest in socioeconomic factors as explanations for poor health, high mortality, high crime rates, and poor living conditions. Those that rejected environmental causes tended to use class and cultural analyses that emphasized black differences from a hypothetical white middle-class norm. The paper by Eugene Harris of Fisk University, "The Physical Condition of the Race; Whether Dependent Upon Social Conditions or Environment," provides an example of an author who took black people to task for contracting diseases at a greater rate than whites. These analyses suggested that some working-class black people's racial heritage or former slave status was the root cause for their allegedly poor morals or an unwillingness to adapt to the demands of urban life, thereby predisposing them to illnesses such as tuberculosis.[48]

Black women also played a central role in the first two Atlanta University conferences. Three of the six papers at the first conference and six of the fifteen published reports from the second conference were presented by the Atlanta University alumnae Lucy Laney, Georgia Swift King, Rosa Morehead Bass, Adella Hunt Logan, and Selena Sloan Butler. King and the educator

Laney used the second year's meeting to galvanize interest in establishing free kindergartens for working mothers. The kindergarten movement was precisely the sort of practical self-help-style reform the organizers of the Atlanta University Conference hoped to engender. When Du Bois took over in 1898, a regular feature of the conference was a session known as the Mothers Meeting, which was often devoted to exploring the year's research question in relation to the status of black women and children. Thus, the participation of women was central to the development of the conference, and black women actually started the only programs that met identified working-class needs; but, over time, women's participation was increasingly relegated to a separate section of the proceedings. As we shall see, this gender segregation would have important significance for the development of black women as social scientists.[49]

It was important to Wright that a black scholar be brought onto the Atlanta University faculty to represent the intellectual capabilities of black people and to build an enduring social science research program there. Wright, a child of the Emancipation, was a member of Atlanta University's first graduating class, and as a result of a popular poem by John Greenleaf Whittier about a postwar encounter with General O. O. Howard, head of the Freedmen's Bureau, he was also widely regarded as a symbol of the promise and perseverance of his generation. In the poem, Wright was known to be the unnamed "black boy of Atlanta," eagerly studying with other children in a railroad boxcar, who resolutely answered the visiting general's query of "What shall I tell the children up North about you?" with "'General, Tell 'em we're rising!'"[50] Du Bois himself acknowledged the power of the metaphorical "black boy" by beginning the fifth chapter of The Souls of Black Folk, "Of the Wings of Atalanta," with the next to last stanza of Whittier's poem, which asserts that whites were also emancipated by the end of slavery. Now, some thirty years after his meeting with Howard, Wright was facing the challenges of disfranchisement and industrial education in Georgia, and he was determined to select a young scholar who had the social scientific skills necessary to assure racial advancement in the coming century.

Atlanta University president Horace Bumstead was equally interested in bringing Du Bois to the university to duplicate the efforts of College Settlement Association (CSA) programs that he believed were "bringing the highest culture in the land to the lowest need." Bumstead, who was a white northerner, had visited Du Bois and his wife in their Philadelphia home, a courtesy that would have demonstrated to the proud Massachusetts native that the

Atlanta University president would not draw the color line in his contacts with African Americans. Bumstead's strong commitment to the City Conference's research focus had already prompted him to invite the sociologist Samuel McCune Lindsay, Du Bois's erstwhile supervisor in Philadelphia, to attend the second conference in 1897.[51]

The selection of Du Bois by President Bumstead, R. R. Wright, and the Atlanta University trustees could not have been better for the development of social science research on black life, especially for black labor studies. It was from Atlanta University that Du Bois was able to undertake both of the types of the multifaceted research projects that he proposed to the labor commissioner Carroll Wright. Du Bois described his thirteen years at Atlanta University as the time when "my real life work was done."[52]

In Du Bois's letters to Carroll Wright he had emphasized his interest in studying black workers and economic development. He suggested possible studies of black unskilled, skilled, and domestic workers, professionals, and farm and dock workers. Du Bois had also wanted to study the black church as a social institution, the impact of black college graduates on their communities, and to produce a detailed bibliography of literature on the economic status of black people. But Commissioner Wright funded only one plan, the study of smaller black communities. When Du Bois arrived in Atlanta, he set up a ten-year plan of study for the Atlanta University Conference that incorporated virtually all the studies of black economic classes and social structures he had contemplated. Each of these Atlanta University Conference studies was concerned to a greater or lesser extent with issues that black workers faced. Du Bois explained that both his teaching and research involved labor issues: "Chiefly this was because the group in which I was interested were workers, earners of wages, owners of small bits of land, servants."[53] As he worked tirelessly to establish an empirical baseline for studying his race, the labor and economic development of the black masses was in the forefront of his concerns.

Du Bois tended to dismiss and diminish the quality of the two city conferences and research reports that preceded his arrival in Atlanta, but his own reports and annual conferences remained reliant on the same core Atlanta University alumni and an equally loyal cadre of Negro college graduates all over the country for both data collection and conference participation. In his position at Atlanta University, W. E. B. Du Bois had finally joined the "others of my brothers and sisters making their lives similar" in the collaboration he had imagined on that lonely night in Germany.[54]

The Maturation of Du Bois's Thought, 1897–1902

W. E. B. Du Bois's thinking from 1893 to 1903, the critical decade between his training in Germany and the publication of *The Souls of Black Folk*, was shaped by three new influences that caused him to refigure some of his ideas about race, class, and leadership that proved to be critical in the development of black labor studies. First, Du Bois was profoundly affected by the clearly written and well-presented philosophies of race consciousness held by older black anti-accommodationist intellectuals such as Alexander Crummell and William Scarborough. Second, he established important, lasting friendships with progressive black men who were his own age, such as the Atlanta Baptist College president John Hope and LaFayette M. Hershaw, a Washington, D.C., civil servant whose independent research projects were a mainstay of the Atlanta University Conference report series. Finally, Du Bois's personal experience of segregation as an adult in Atlanta and the mounting evidence in his research of the causes and effects of racial oppression created a kind of synergistic mental and emotional reformulation that caused Du Bois to refine his understanding of the linkage between the economic, political, and social status of black people and his ideas on how best to achieve racial uplift and the desired reforms.

Du Bois came to espouse most of Alexander Crummell's political positions, although he met Crummell only three years before the latter's death in 1898. In this reserved and scholarly priest, Du Bois found a black model for his own behavior and ambitions. In a psychological sense Crummell seems to have served as an intellectual father figure for Du Bois, replacing the father he never knew and augmenting Du Bois's romantic picture of his paternal grandfather, Alexander Du Bois.[55] Du Bois recalled his first encounter with Crummell in a poignant tribute in *The Souls of Black Folk*, paying homage to Crummell even as he declared his independence from the nation's most important black political figure, Booker T. Washington: "Instinctively I bowed before this man, as one bows before the prophets of the world. Some seer he seemed, that comes not from the crimson Past or the gray To-Come, but from the pulsing Now,—that mocking world that seemed to me at once so light and dark, so splendid and sordid."[56]

Du Bois updated Crummell's economic arguments, accepted Crummell's concept of black scholars as political activists, and eventually became a mentor to other younger black scholars in much the same fashion that Crummell had for him. Before his association with Crummell, Du Bois planned to become a racial leader, but he had imagined that his leadership would come through the example of his scholarship rather than by personal commitment to a program of action. Whereas his University of Berlin professor von Schmoller and then his association with the CSA had added methodology to Du Bois's notion of scholarship with a social conscience, Alexander Crummell provided an archetype of an activist black intellectual that proved to be very appealing to Du Bois.[57]

Alexander Crummell's strong views on the importance of economic factors in explaining black social disorganization, and his characterization of low moral standards as a class rather than a racial problem, provided Du Bois with an alternative approach to his early views. In this approach, which was also present in the late 1890s in the writings of Kelly Miller and R. R. Wright Sr., Alexander Crummell downplayed the significance of immorality as a factor in black social problems. Crummell argued instead that the poorest blacks were on the same low moral level as the average European immigrant, but unlike immigrants they were also handicapped by political and economic exploitation. Crummell's idea of black self-help began with gaining greater awareness of the economic situation, while Du Bois wanted blacks to improve their behavior before confronting whites. Crummell reasoned that the first order of business was for each black worker to develop an "intelligent impatience at the exploitation of his labor" and the "courage to demand a larger share of the wealth which his toil creates for others."[58] Alexander Crummell was also an earlier critic of industrial education as a panacea for black educational and social problems than was Du Bois. Crummell did not oppose the training programs themselves, but he emphatically rejected the assertions of black and white conservatives that black workers did not understand the work ethic. "One would suppose from the universal demand for the mere industrialism of this race of ours, that the Negro had been going to dinner parties, eating terrapin and indulging in champagne . . . all these 250 years. . . . And then, just now, the American people . . . were calling him for the first time, to blister his hands with the hoe, and to learn to supply his needs by sweatful toil in the cotton fields."[59]

Du Bois's famous political transformation from a casual supporter of Booker T. Washington who persistently tried to land a job at Tuskegee Institute to the leader of the anti-Bookerites was paralleled by a change in the underlying assumptions of his research. Du Bois tended to be far more likely to place primary responsibility on black people's alleged personal moral lapses than the older ANA members or the Atlanta University Conference founders, although in his early studies and essays Du Bois carefully noted the social and economic factors that contributed to black social problems. In "The Conservation of Races" Du Bois had described the rising barriers of Jim Crow in schools, transportation, employment, and even lynching as "pressing but smaller questions" compared to the need for a racial philosophy and self-discipline.[60]

Du Bois had yet to seriously consider the role of these "smaller questions" in producing the alleged sexual misbehavior, crime, and idleness attributed as all too frequent activities among blacks. In Du Bois's view the cultural heritage of slavery, not economic discrimination, racism, or poverty, had prevented blacks from fully developing into a coherent social group with wholesome mores. "The first and greatest step toward the settlement of the present friction between the races . . . lies in the correction of the immorality, crime and laziness among the Negroes themselves, which still remains as a heritage from slavery."[61]

The changes in philosophy in Du Bois's social studies became most noticeable in his writings within five years after he had fully digested the experience of living and working as a black adult in the South. In the 1898 third Atlanta University Conference report, the first produced under his direction, Du Bois included an essay by Crummell on character that ridiculed the materialism of a barely disguised Booker T. Washington. This was a harbinger of Du Bois's more open opposition to Washington five years later in *The Souls of Black Folk*.[62] But Du Bois was not yet ready to make clear connections between employment and social disorganization in his writings. Even though he had lived among and studied black Philadelphians, Du Bois at times seemed oblivious to the situation of people who appeared not to share his values. Atlanta, Georgia, would open his eyes to the complexity of the black predicament. The more closely Du Bois looked at rural poverty and urban underemployment, the more he questioned his assumptions about the character of black workers. Du Bois signaled his analytical change in the conclusions of an empirical research study completed one year before he challenged Washington's political ascendancy in *The Souls of Black Folk*. Du Bois's fifth Atlanta study and the seventh Atlanta University Conference research monograph, *The Negro Artisan*, served as the social scientific basis for his break with Booker T. Washington while firmly establishing black labor studies as a field in which ideology would neither dictate nor dominate empirical findings but, rather, would inform analysis. Du Bois's adoption of social and economic factors as primary rather than secondary factors in understanding black social problems had just as significant an impact on the development of black social science as did his transit from accommodationism to the Niagara Movement's protest actions for black political thought.

For Du Bois, personally, his change of attitude was momentous. Although the change took place over a period of six to nine years, its completeness surprised a number of people. Kelly Miller, a self-described straddler of the line between the conservatives and the radicals, thought Du Bois's new political activities were a waste of time and ignored the fact that Du Bois's more recent research was more in line with Miller's own conclusions. Instead, Miller wondered at what he saw as the transformation of Du Bois from social scientist to social activist: "It is almost impossible to conceive how the author of *The Philadelphia Negro* could have penned the second Niagara Movement Manifesto, without mental and moral metamorphosis."[63] Such a metamorphosis did indeed take place. Du Bois said that his thirteen years in Atlanta led to the "strengthening and hardening [of] my own character. . . . They were years of great spiritual upturning, of the making and unmaking of ideals. . . . Here I found myself. . . . I grew more broadly human, made my closest and most holy friendships, and studied human beings. I became widely acquainted with the real condition of my people. I realized the terrific odds that faced them. At Wilberforce I was their captious critic. In Philadelphia I was their cold and scientific investigator, with microscope and probe. It took but a few years of Atlanta to bring me to a hot and indignant defense."[64]

The Negro Artisan: The Cornerstone of Black Labor Studies

When W. E. B. Du Bois began his 1902 study of black skilled workers, he was ready to integrate six years of research experience with his new political attitudes. In *The Negro Artisan* Du Bois was finally able to pull together the various methodological techniques he had been using separately in the Bureau of Labor, Census, and Atlanta University studies. This resulted in what is, arguably, his best single Atlanta study. Du Bois studied black workers because their situation was central to ongoing ideological debates concerning the role of blacks in American life and because there was general agreement among black intellectuals that their efforts to effect social reforms should begin with the needs of black wage earners.

The Negro Artisan was the first comprehensive study of black American workers as well as the first study that allowed black workers to speak for themselves or that even considered that their opinions might be valuable. It also contains what is apparently the first published research on black children, offering an all too brief portrait of turn-of-the-century working-class home life and occupational aspirations. The design and conclusions of *The Negro Artisan* provided an ambitious benchmark for future scholars in black labor studies. Its format combines a socioeconomic history of black labor with a number of sociological investigations, including nine surveys that detailed the experiences and views of black workers, and an examination of industrial schools. Du Bois's faithful correspondents collected the opinions of black skilled trades persons throughout the United States and the Caribbean, while his Atlanta University students surveyed neighborhoods to determine the occupational preferences of black schoolchildren. Du Bois polled white business managers and owners on hiring practices, and he asked labor unions for information on their membership requirements. In the section on industrial education, Du Bois examined the curriculum, goals, placement records, and budgets of nearly all industrial schools for blacks. Du Bois's method of combining historical and sociological approaches would dominate the writings of black scholars for the next two decades.

One reason that *The Negro Artisan* was a better study than previous Atlanta University monographs was that it fit more neatly into and synthesized the best practices from Du Bois's other research on labor and economic conditions. Du Bois had completed three Bureau of Labor studies that focused on black economic conditions, he was preparing a U.S. Census study on black farmers, and he was active in an American Economic Association committee on the economic status of black Americans. The previous Atlanta University studies had examined businesses, college graduates, and schools. Du Bois now was ready to attempt a multidimensional examination of skilled workers. Undoubtedly, Du Bois's growing personal interest in the political debate surrounding the hiring, training, and competence of black workers contributed to the care he took in the report's preparation.[65]

The methodology of *The Negro Artisan* illustrated both Du Bois's sophistication at asking complex sociological questions and the limitations he faced in getting them answered. Thirty-five Atlanta University Conference correspondents in thirty-two states and Ontario, Canada, Costa Rica, and Puerto Rico sent in general accounts on the situation of black workers in their cities, which were guided by Du Bois's twelve-question survey instrument. They also supplied a short history of black skilled workers and sent in the names and addresses of their leading craftsmen. The thirty-five general summaries were filled with accounts of exclusionary practices by local trade unions, ranging from their refusal to admit black workers, to severe limitations on blacks' access to apprenticeship programs, to city-sanctioned exclusions of black contractors from bidding on public and private construction projects. The accounts conveyed the widespread belief that black workers were experiencing a numerical and proportional decline in skilled occupations in which black men had traditionally held strong positions, such as carpentry, masonry, and bricklaying. These brief surveys and historical accounts were designed to be comparable with Du Bois's more comprehensive study of thirteen hundred black skilled workers in Georgia, but a severely limited budget meant that Du Bois was overly dependent on reports from his volunteers that varied greatly in depth and detail. Several regular conference correspondents, including LaFayette Hershaw and the Harvard graduate William T. B. Williams, added their own independent analyses of workers to their assignments; almost all completed the general surveys, while a few sent in much more sketchy accounts. On his own initiative, Henry Lee of Lemoyne Institute administered Du Bois's questionnaire to 123 skilled workers in Memphis, Tennessee, and was called on to report his sobering findings in person at the 1902 conference. Memphis contractors bitterly complained of being prevented from seeing project blueprints that made it difficult to make accurate bids, and they asked Lee to request that the conference send a black architect to assist them. But the greatest concern of the Memphis artisans whom Lee polled was the small number of younger people who were able to enter the skilled trades.

The content of the reports as a whole clearly indicated that Du Bois's change of opinion on the situation for black artisans followed rather than anticipated an increased level of anxiety by black skilled workers concerning their future. The Memphis artisans expressed their concern using the philosophical language of racial uplift: "No race can be prosperous and progressive without a large number of men who are producing the necessities of life. . . . As a race we *must* do something for the employment of our boys and girls. . . . And every business enterprise established by a Negro giving employment to the Negro youth is a sacrifice for the salvation of our boys and girls."[66]

It is clear from the resolution that the Memphis artisans offered that an emphasis on racial identity and sense of duty to the race as a whole was not exclusive to black intellectuals, nor was a desire for greater black business development limited to the budding bourgeoisie. Almost a decade earlier Booker T. Washington had used a session at an alumni conference at Hampton Institute to gauge the sentiments of his participants on whether black skilled workers, contractors, and small businessmen were losing ground, because an important part of Washington's justification for accommodating segregation was that skilled and professional employment opportunities were possible in the South but more limited in the North. If black craft workers and contractors were facing new barriers in the South, then Washington's argument was undermined. Although they came to differ on how best to combat segregation, both Washington and Du Bois extolled black-owned businesses as a way to circumvent hiring discrimination.[67]

Du Bois also surveyed white trade unions and business managers and owners to gauge their racial attitudes and practices. Replies to his questionnaires on racial policies in organized labor were received from 97 of 108 international unions' in the American Federation of Labor. Over two hundred responses came from the central and state labor federations in thirty states. The unions candid admissions of their discrimination against and exclusion of black workers from their ranks gave greater credence to the often vague and abridged charges of racism in the published reports of Du Bois's regular correspondents. However, for all of its surveys and interviews, a coherent and synthetic review of black trade unionists, in segregated locals or in integrated unions, is missing from *The Negro Artisan*. Subsequent black social scientists followed Du Bois's methodology and analyzed black men and women in organized labor descriptively in terms of their numbers and percentages and only rarely in terms of their subjective individual and group experiences as trade unionists.[68]

After its publication, two union officials took umbrage with Du Bois's charge in *The Negro Artisan* of discrimination on the part of their unions. S. M. Sexton, editor of the *United Mine Workers Journal,* expressed his strong belief that racial hatred in the mines was caused by antiunion black newspaper editors, and he asserted that in areas of union dominance blacks were not disenfranchised or lynched. Sexton's claims regarding the United Mine Workers' racial tolerance had an important caveat: "We gladly accept all races in our Union, but the Chinaman—he drew the line for himself."[69] Sexton's comments pointed to one flaw in Du Bois's analyses, his understatement of the antiunion sentiment among blacks. But Sexton was all too willing to place all the blame for racial discrimination on black newspapers' editorials rather than the frequently racist practices of white mine owners and white miners.

James A. Cable, secretary treasurer of the Coopers International Union, had a methodologically suspect objection to the data on his union. Cable argued that the 8 percent of black coopers in his union was equal to the percentage of white coopers who were organized, and he claimed that discrimination between German and Irish coopers was greater than that between blacks and whites. Du Bois was not much moved by Cable's misuse of statistical evidence because Cable admitted that the white coopers were allowed to establish segregated local unions that effectively prevented black coopers from getting employment in areas where their numbers were small.[70]

For his survey of white southern business managers' attitudes toward black workers, Du Bois secured the cooperation of the *Chattanooga Tradesman* in paying half of the cost to distribute his questionnaire. The *Tradesman's* New South stance supported hiring southern blacks in some skilled and semiskilled positions rather than white immigrants who might favor unions, and had done its own employer surveys on black workers in 1889 and 1891. The *Tradesman's* involvement gave Du Bois a wider and more candid range of opinion than he could have otherwise obtained. White managers who had black workers were satisfied with their performance, and those employers who refused to hire black workers usually attributed their decision to the fear that white workers would object, and more rarely cited unfavorable experiences with black workers. Du Bois's willingness to accept the reports of white business owners and managers at their face value was a curious failure of his otherwise thorough analysis. If white businessmen at the turn of the nineteenth century were so satisfied with black workers, why were black workers experiencing so many economic setbacks in the barely unionized South? Du Bois suggested that regional differences were important: northern white workers were seen as more willing to unite with blacks to maintain wages, while the "southern laborer and employer have united to disfranchise the Negro and make color a caste."[71] The survey of white businessmen's attitudes toward hiring black workers and their largely positive views about black workers' competence became a standard feature of labor monographs, including those that government agencies produced.[72]

The historical section of *The Negro Artisan* fully revealed the extent to which W. E. B. Du Bois had changed his analysis of the black class structure. In *The Philadelphia Negro* Du Bois had stressed the positive role that black house servants played before and after Emancipation. After he moved to Atlanta, however, Du Bois began to argue that the slave mechanic had a more important role in the social organization of black communities. He now asserted that slave artisans comprised a distinct and separate class from house or field slaves and were the authentic leaders of black intellectual life. "Many, if not most, of the noted leaders of the Negro in earlier times belonged to this slave mechanic class, such as Vesey, Nat Turner, Richard Allen and Absolom Jones. They were exposed neither to the corrupting privileges of the house servants nor to the blighting tyranny of field work and had a large opportunity for self development."[73]

Du Bois claimed that in the immediate aftermath of slavery the Freedmen's Bureau cared for the field-hand class, and the house servants "passed easily from half-free service to half-servile freedom." But black artisans passed from the protection of their masters in the resolution of disputes and enforcement of contracts to a far more hostile environment. In Du Bois's analysis, black skilled workers at Emancipation faced three challenges: direct competition from white skilled workers; white exclusionary and violent actions that required racial solidarity or "self-protection" of black workers' jobs, persons, and property; and the technological changes brought by the Industrial Revolution that required new and different sorts of occupations and skills. These three impediments were compounded when Redemption stripped black people of their voting rights and standing in the courts, making lower wages virtually the only means of being competitive in the marketplace with white workers. In his reevaluation of the role of black craftspersons in the nineteenth century, Du Bois suggested for the first time that the loss of the vote produced a significant negative economic and political impact on blacks. Previously, he had argued that allowing illiterate blacks to vote endangered democratic institutions, because it had not occurred to him that disfranchisement might have been the result of the tendency of black voters to make informed choices, decisions that often ran counter to dominant white interests. In *The Negro Artisan* Du Bois asserted that disfranchisement limited black economic opportunity and stifled political dissent. His changing view of black class structures was one aspect of Du Bois's reexamination of the empirical basis for his political philosophy. His critique of the record of industrial education provided another component of a newly framed argument against accommodationism.[74]

The 1902 Atlanta University Conference was addressed by modernist educators and social activists, such as Lucy Laney, and the proponents of accommodationism and industrial education, such as Robert Russa Moton, commandant of Hampton Institute, and Booker T. Washington, principal of Tuskegee Institute. But the conference resolutions and the research report contained an exhaustively detailed and scholarly rebuttal of the basic claims of industrial education as practiced at Hampton and Tuskegee. Du Bois's study of industrial education in *The Negro Artisan* was a low-key, but ultimately devastating, indictment of the entire system of industrial education for black children and young adults. His two main objections to industrial schools were that they were far too costly for their limited results and that they almost always failed to be either industrial or educational institutions.

Although the advocates of industrial education loved to extol the ways in which their students' unpaid work helped to run the schools, Du Bois found that industrial education was far more costly than classical education. He surveyed every black industrial school and their state's superintendent of education on the occupations of graduates, their curriculum, and budget. He discovered that Tuskegee Institute's budget was higher than the combined total of the forty-three schools that the Freedman's Aid and Southern Education Society sponsored, while Hampton's annual budget exceeded the total expenditures for Negro public schools in the state of Virginia. But what had these funds bought? After three decades of operation and over five million dollars of expenditures, Negro vocational schools had trained fewer than one thousand skilled workers. This was less than half of the number of black college graduates that Negro academic colleges produced, and with far fewer resources. Fewer than six in one hundred students at industrial schools actually followed a trade or stayed in agriculture after graduation. Most became teachers, yet because even the best of these institutions—Tuskegee and Hampton—offered something less than a high school curriculum, their teachers were less well prepared than those who had pursued normal school or collegiate programs. Du Bois also found that the so-called industrial schools rarely offered instruction in newer skilled trades and occupations that would have allowed black workers to compete effectively with white workers. Offering these courses might help to solve blacks' exclusion from apprenticeship programs, but Negro industrial schools did not have the facilities or the inclination to train blacks as machinists, boilermakers, or any other of the occupations that were increasingly important but were seen as the white man's prerogative.[75]

Nevertheless, despite the accumulation of withering evidence that Du Bois gathered, he seemed to draw back from an outright condemnation of black industrial schools. Perhaps he still hoped that a school that truly taught the skills that workers needed to compete in industrializing America might be developed. Or Du Bois may not have been ready to burn all his bridges with Washington and Moton, the influential leaders of Tuskegee and Hampton. Du Bois's funding for future studies may also have been at risk because a considerable portion of the funding for his conference came from the Slater Fund, which also gave Atlanta University an annual grant to offer industrial courses.[76]

The Negro Artisan marked an important stage in the maturation of Du Bois's political and economic thought. In the three years between *The Philadelphia*

Negro and *The Negro Artisan,* Du Bois had concentrated primarily on his sociological research and had written short philosophical essays on black life for national magazines.[77] *The Negro Artisan* revealed a considerable transition in Du Bois's attitude toward causality. This monograph was a milestone in black labor studies, and the conference that discussed the concerns of black skilled workers marked a watershed in the controversy over industrial education. Du Bois's famous essay "Of Mr. Booker T. Washington and Others," published in *The Souls of Black Folk,* distilled his political and personal objections to accommodationism, but it is unlikely that Du Bois would have been able to become so vehement a critic of Washington without the empirical evidence from *The Negro Artisan* that industrial education was a deeply flawed system.

The reviews for *The Negro Artisan* in white academic journals and national magazines were largely favorable. The *American Journal of Sociology* said it was "the most excellent study so far of the Atlanta series." *The Nation's* reviewer was surprised that the evidence showed that the American Federation of Labor was "deepening the color line" in recent years. Like many men of his era, the reviewer believed that the pecuniary interests of white workers would overcome their racial prejudice in the long run. Other widely read magazines and newspapers, such as *Outlook,* the *South Atlantic Quarterly,* and the *Boston Herald,* also gave favorable reviews, frequently lauding Du Bois's able scholarship.[78] Du Bois's methodological approach and data were rapidly used by others. In 1905 John R. Commons, the University of Wisconsin labor economist, used excerpts from *The Negro Artisan* in his influential book, *Trade Unionism and Labor Problems.* The state of New Jersey used Du Bois's technique of polling businessmen and labor unions on black workers' competence and admission into unions, but it did not interview any black workers.[79] The most lasting impact of *The Negro Artisan,* however, was its influence on other black scholars. Du Bois's decision to give greater weight to economic and political discrimination than personal behavioral flaws would be repeated in the writings of all the black social scientists who followed him.

The national political climate and intellectual milieu in which Du Bois pursued his reform and research agendas simultaneously supported and sharply circumscribed his endeavors. Black intellectuals sought out the young scholar to join their new professional associations, such as the American Negro Academy, and to join the faculty at Atlanta University. While Du Bois's research agenda was not fully embraced by the white academy, by the time of the publication of *The Negro Artisan* he had been drawn into supportive circles of black intellectuals and white Progressive Era reformers such as settlement home founder Jane Addams. Yet Du Bois never was funded at the level that would have enabled him to replicate the exhaustive detail of *The Philadelphia Negro,* despite extremely favorable peer reviews of his research. Much less prolific and less well-regarded white sociologists received good-paying professorships and substantial research support, while Du Bois, with less than fifteen hundred dollars per year, cobbled together the Atlanta University investigations for more than a decade assisted only by his undergraduate students and race-conscious volunteers.[80]

The foundations of black labor studies were constructed by Du Bois during a time in which his ideas about the interconnection of race, class, and political protest were changing. *The Negro Artisan* served as the social science template, or cornerstone, for the ideological shifts that reached a wider audience in *The Souls of Black Folk.* Even as the thirty-year-old Du Bois was first settling down in Atlanta, a small group of men and women were preparing to embark on their own turn-of-the-century journeys "to make a name in science" as their way of raising their race. In the next chapter, we will follow the education and labor writings of younger black social scientists, especially R. R. Wright Jr. and George E. Haynes, who, with the counsel of Du Bois, who helped to guide their early labor studies, consciously patterned their scholarship after the methodology of *The Philadelphia Negro* and the political analysis of *The Negro Artisan.* In establishing the foundation of black labor studies, Du Bois had not only accomplished his four ideals of 1893 but he had created a body of scholarship that the next generation of black social scientists would augment and extend.

2 Creating a Cadre of Segregated Scholars, 1898–1912

> The acquisition of knowledge on the part of some must result
> in the spreading of intelligence . . . to the many. Our talents
> and possession must be made blessings to our people . . . in
> the financial, intellectual and moral support of every reform.
> —George Edmund Haynes, "The Lamp of Sacrifice"

> When I left for Chicago, an old ex-slave said, "Don't you let
> those white boys up North beat you at anything. . . . I felt that
> I not only represented myself, and the prestige of Professor
> Wright's family, but the whole Negro-American race.
> —R. R. Wright Jr., *Eighty-seven Years behind the Black Curtain*

When George Edmund Haynes insisted that black college students "must
have the recesses of their hearts lighted by the 'Lamp of Sacrifice,'" the
twenty-three-year-old Fisk University senior was echoing W. E. B. Du Bois's
assertion that educated black people's collective duty to make improvements
in the lives of black people far outweighed the pursuit of individual desires.
Like Du Bois, whom he greatly admired, Haynes was in his early twenties
when he avowed that his personal interests should be subordinated to the goal
of racial progress. Haynes urged his classmates to pursue advanced degrees,
arguing that the personal costs of continuing one's education were secondary
to the potential long-term benefits of demonstrating the capabilities of black
people to a skeptical nation. Black men and women who were qualified to get
advanced degrees should "endure the strain and toil of sacrifice," not solely
for themselves but "for the people whom we love, and for the future genera-

tion."[1] The light of George Haynes's "lamp of sacrifice" soon fell on the struggles of black workers who were migrating to northern cities, and he set aside his desire to earn a divinity degree and turned to social science, joining R. R. Wright Jr. as the two most outstanding in a small cadre of black men who became trained social scientists in the first decade of the twentieth century.

Wright Jr.'s deeply ingrained sense of duty to freedmen and women of unmixed African descent was instilled from childhood. He entered the University of Chicago in 1898, when he was twenty years old, five years before George Haynes first set off for graduate studies in sociology, economics, and divinity at Yale University. His family and community expected him to exceed the educational achievements of his remarkable father. Wright Jr. was born two years after the end of Reconstruction, and he was acutely aware that his career would have a symbolic as well as a personal meaning because he was among the "first of the college educated sons of the first generation of educated free Negro Americans."[2] Although he had studied under Lucy Laney, and graduated from the segregated state industrial college that his father ran, Wright Jr.'s success at a northern university would finally "show the white people that a Black boy could learn as well as a white one."[3] In representing the post-Emancipation potential of his race, Wright Jr.'s personal sacrifices could never approach those of the generations born in bondage, but his accomplishments in areas denied to them would validate their faith in education for their children as a means of racial progress. Wright Jr. did not buckle under the added weight of his well-known father's academic and professional achievements, and he turned to social science as a way to directly link his scholarship to reform. While studying with the major figures in early American sociology at the University of Chicago and working on research projects for W. E. B. Du Bois, R. R. Wright Jr. began to chronicle the work and family life of black migrants to midwestern and northern towns and cities. One by one, a cadre formed, with the same sense of purpose and determination to use their research on black workers to advance their chosen field and to advance their race.

In this chapter I examine the social, intellectual, and political forces that guided the education and early labor writings of Richard Robert Wright Jr. and George Edmund Haynes, two pioneering sociologists who extended black labor studies with their investigations of black workers and working-class life in northern cities in the first fifteen years of the twentieth century. They were the pacesetters in the initial cadre of well-trained black social scientists whose exacting research built on the foundations that had been freshly laid by their most important mentor, W. E. B. Du Bois. As we shall see, religion, reform movements, place, and time played a much greater role in the professional development of this cohort than they had for Du Bois. When Du Bois memorably declared that he was "in Harvard but not of it," he was stating that the institutional location was less important to him.[4] But place, in terms of institutional characteristics and community resources, and time, in terms of the coming together of pivotal events, were far more important to the next group of black graduate students. At the turn of the twentieth century the University of Chicago and the surrounding city offered talented young black men such as Wright, Haynes, Monroe Nathan Work, and Carter G. Woodson a more congenial setting, in which they began to realize their intense desire to use their education to improve the status of black Americans. Wright and his classmate Monroe Work began to study sociology and religion with Albion Small, chair of the University of Chicago's sociology department, in 1898, just six years after it was founded. Du Bois had just completed *The Philadelphia Negro,* and he drew the younger men into his research projects, saw that their investigations were published, and introduced them to his circle of white reformers.

The year 1905 was pivotal in the specific development of black social scientists, and served as a geographical and philosophical watershed in the development of black labor studies: Wright and Haynes, whose studies would self-consciously extend Du Bois's methods, decided to earn doctorates in sociology rather than divinity; a new coalition was cemented between black and white progressives that would more firmly link social research to social reform strategies; and opposition to social research on black life in general and black labor studies in particular began to become more apparent both in the academy and in the South. By 1912, the eve of the Great Migration, this cadre of segregated scholars had produced highly original studies of black workers and working-class life in Chicago, New York City, Pittsburgh, and other cities, and was involved in major reform movements in Philadelphia, New York City, Nashville, and Savannah. As important, these disciples of W. E. B. Du Bois began to create programs that would institutionalize the process of producing black social scientists, thereby ensuring a subsequent generation of black labor scholars. But black labor studies moved North even before the steady stream of migrants turned to a flood, pushed out by a hostile political climate a decade ahead of the mass movement.

Black Student Life at the University of Chicago, 1898–1915

Ambitious black students were especially attracted to turn-of-the-century Chicago, with its new and largely unsegregated university and its vibrant black intellectual life. R. R. Wright Jr. sang its praises: "It is new . . . there are few cities . . . where a Negro comes nearer to getting what is his due than in Chicago. What he has done here is then a very important indication as to his capacity for free American institutions."[5] The city and the University of Chicago's early role in developing black social scientists in general and black labor scholars in particular has been neglected because none of the first generation of black social scientists had earned their doctorates at the university or lived in the city during their professional careers. But the three principal elements that would prove necessary for the development of a cadre of black social scientists were first brought together at the University of Chicago in the late 1890s: a pool of qualified black students who were accepted in nonsegregated graduate schools; new models of scholarship and committed mentors; and working relationships with local black and white Progressive Era reformers. After 1906, Philadelphia and the University of Pennsylvania, and New York City and Columbia University, began to offer productive mixtures of the three elements and also became places that would attract, train, and support black social science graduate students.[6]

A fortuitous confluence of factors caused the University of Chicago, which opened in 1890, to immediately attract black students, most of whom were schoolteachers and administrators. The university and the city of Chicago were largely unsegregated, somewhat experimental, and rather exciting. Black students were admitted to the new institution with little fuss. Black college newspapers at the turn of the century regularly reported on, heard from, and praised their alumni who had gone to Chicago to live and study. The university was described as egalitarian not only in terms of race but also was seen as having eliminated class distinctions among the students, a point of no little interest to black students. Atlanta Baptist (Morehouse) College and Spelman Seminary students were told that the University of Chicago "is not a university exclusively of rich men's sons and daughters. . . . The rich and the poor work side by side, in the same classrooms, in the same laboratories. No distinctions of rank or color; blood and brains are the only criteria."[7]

Unlike other universities that required certificates from accredited colleges, entrance to the University of Chicago was by an examination that was held in various easily accessible cities. This procedure facilitated the admission of black students because the majority of Negro colleges were not formally accredited.[8] The University of Chicago also allowed students to take correspondence courses and to partially fulfill its residency requirement for degrees during the summer quarters. These practices assisted black teachers, who could more easily attend summer sessions. Elizabeth Ross, a 1903 Fisk graduate who worked as a high school teacher in Texas, took correspondence courses and spent three summer sessions at the University of Chicago. Her new skills helped her shift from teaching to social work administration and prepared her to conduct research on black women workers during World War I. Carter Woodson earned both a bachelor's and a master's degree at the university in 1908, but he spent only the summer session of 1902 and the 1907–8 academic year in Chicago, having made extensive use of correspondence courses while teaching in the Philippines and in Washington, D.C.[9]

Black college students wanted to study sociology because they believed that it offered a systematic and objective means of identifying social ills and developing programmatic solutions. The Fisk student newspaper warned young people who did not study sociology or understand the science of social organization that they would be lost in the motley throng. "Sociology," the writer argued, prepared students to meet the changing future, teaching them "how to interpret social tendencies and movements and how to recognize the social duties which arise out of conditions and relations."[10]

Black students' participation in summer and regular session courses at the University of Chicago helped to bring sociology into the curriculums of segregated colleges and preparatory schools before sociology courses were offered in white southern universities. Black schoolteachers and clergy enrolled in the summer school to update their education, and took courses in fields that were not offered in Negro colleges. Even a well-established educator such as Lucy Laney, principal of Haines Institute in Augusta, Georgia, took summer courses, at the same time as her former pupils R. R. Wright Jr. and John Hope.[11] Laney, Wright, Hope, and George Haynes subsequently introduced sociology courses at their own schools. When Chicago natives such as Lugenia Burns Hope moved to the South in the early twentieth century, they also introduced social welfare programs similar to those in Chicago.[12]

The relatively less segregated racial climate in the city of Chicago at the turn of the century was an important drawing factor for black students, most of whom were natives of the South. In his book on black life in Chicago before the Great Migration, Alan Spear describes discrimination in Chicago as "unofficial, informal, uncertain."[13] The Arkansas native George Edmund

Haynes had first visited Chicago as a young teenager during the 1893 World's Fair, an experience that helped to draw him back over a decade later to attend summer sessions—despite the fact that he had earned a master's degree from Yale University. The Georgia-born Richard Robert Wright Jr. was initially shocked to see whites working as laborers in the city, and was rendered speechless when the white janitor in his student dormitory instructed him to call him by his first name. Wright promptly decided not to return to the South. Racism had prevented Monroe Work from obtaining desirable teaching positions in Kansas, despite his having the highest examination scores in the state, so he moved to Chicago to get a new start.[14]

Black students at the turn of the century lived and studied in a much more welcoming environment than those who came just one decade later and found that they were barred from living in dormitories. Georgianna Simpson, Mordecai Johnson, and John W. Davis were among those prevented from living in the dormitories, in 1907 and 1911, respectively, while Wright, Work, and Woodson had lived in student housing between 1898 and 1908 without serious incidents. The women's dormitory was the first to draw the color line, four years before the men's, but Simpson—a Washington, D.C., high school teacher—returned almost every summer for the next fourteen years, becoming the first black woman to earn a doctorate. Johnson and Davis, who had just graduated with honors from Atlanta Baptist (Morehouse) College, also persevered, and both later became college presidents. Although the change in housing policy did not go unchallenged, a former dean at the university candidly confirmed to W. E. B. Du Bois in 1914 that black students faced discriminatory treatment at the University of Chicago that she was unable to ameliorate.[15] Beginning with R. R. Wright Jr.'s own 1901 undergraduate thesis, studies of racial housing patterns in Chicago showed that at the turn of the century, blacks were less segregated from native whites in housing than were Italian and other immigrants. Civil rights laws in Illinois ostensibly protected black Chicagoans against discrimination in public accommodations and jobs, but these were not always enforced. Nevertheless, the University of Chicago remained more accessible to black students than most other comparable universities.[16]

Once in Chicago, black students were welcomed by the reform-minded, middle-class black professionals living there, notwithstanding the small relative size of Chicago's black population. In 1900 there were just over 30,000 blacks living in Chicago, then America's second largest city with 1.6 million residents.[17] There were several outspoken black newspapers, a number of reform and uplift groups, and the flourishing Institutional Church, which the African Methodist Episcopal Church (AME) minister Reverdy C. Ransom pastored, and which dispensed social services and promoted social activism. The civic activists Ida B. Wells-Barnett and her husband Ferdinand Barnett, Fannie Barrier Williams and her husband S. Laing Williams, and the Ransoms were among the black Chicagoans with whom black university students developed lifelong associations.[18]

R. R. Wright Jr. and Monroe Work met at the University of Chicago during the summer session of 1898. Both were the sons of freedmen and women, but they arrived at the university via different paths that reflected the heterogeneous life experiences of the first freeborn generation and the varied educational experiences of black people in the late nineteenth century. Born in 1866, Monroe Work narrowly escaped the enslavement that bound his parents and eight older brothers and sisters in Iredell County, North Carolina. Work's parents were poor tenant farmers who moved westward to Illinois and then to Kansas in search of their own land and educational opportunities for their family. Duties on his family's farm in Sumner County, Kansas, made Work's schooling episodic, and he was not able to enter high school until he was twenty-three years old. It took him nine more years of hard work to be able to enroll in a university program. By contrast, Richard Robert Wright Jr. entered the University of Chicago as a twenty-year-old graduate of a fine preparatory school—Lucy Laney's Haines Institute—and the Georgia State Industrial College in Savannah, where his father was the president. His father's political star within the Republican Party had reached its zenith as a result of Wright Sr.'s presidential commission as an Army major and paymaster during the Spanish American War. Work and Wright Jr. represented two extremes in the family backgrounds and personal circumstances of black students at the University of Chicago at the turn of the century. Neither fit the profile of northern black college students from earlier in the nineteenth century, who were either from freeborn middle- or solid working-class backgrounds, as was Du Bois, or were the children of white southern planters and businessmen, as were John Hope and the Grimké brothers.

Wright and Work were among the thirty or so black students enrolled with two thousand other students in the summer term of 1898. The number of black students dropped to four in the fall term, when most of the black students went back to the South to resume their teaching jobs. Wright and Work remained, studying divinity as well as sociology, and they became two of the first half-dozen black men trained as sociologists in the United States. They formed a study and support group with the two remaining students, coaching one another in the four ancient and foreign languages they were expected to have mastered. The four young men also began an informal debating team and gave readings at black churches.[19] Wright and Work got to know each other quite well by working in a university laundry shortly after their arrival, but remembered their most rewarding experience together as being researchers for W. E. B. Du Bois during the summer of 1906.[20]

Graduate Training: Diggs, Work, Wright, Haynes

The first four American-trained black sociologists were heavily influenced by the precepts of the Christian sociology and Social Gospel movements. Each of these four men had been drawn to graduate school with a desire for a career in the ministry and then decided to become sociologists, making them strikingly different from Du Bois in their motivation and their early graduate training. R. R. Wright Jr. and Monroe Work were both licensed African Methodist preachers by the time they entered the University of Chicago in 1898, but they were on the first rung of the ministry. Work had moved to Chicago a few years earlier to attend Chicago Theological Seminary (CTS) in hopes that his theological studies might lead to a better pastorate. Work and Wright's studies at the University of Chicago reflected the close relationships between the faculties of the divinity school and the Department of Sociology under Albion Small. Their courses in sociology, religious studies, and the social gospel reinforced and complemented one another, so Work and Wright did not find they had to choose between the ministry and social science in graduate school. George Haynes began his graduate studies in social science at Yale University in 1903 with the intention of also entering its divinity school, but the choice between service to his race and serving a congregation seemed starker to him, and he chose the former. Haynes then extended his understanding of sociology and psychology by attending summer sessions at the University of Chicago after he left Yale with a master's degree in sociology and economics in 1905.

James Robert Lincoln Diggs, the first black person to earn a doctorate in sociology, had a different graduate school experience and a different career path from Wright, Haynes, or Work, and Diggs did not make a lasting impact on black scholarship. Diggs had a bachelor's and a master's degree from Bucknell University and was already a Baptist minister when he earned a doctorate in 1906 from Illinois Wesleyan University. This was an accredited nonresident degree program with correspondence studies of major sociology texts that took three years and entailed six semester examinations, a doctoral thesis, and a final examination.[21] Although he did not take survey or research methods courses, Diggs's readings in philosophy, sociology, and economics were otherwise comparable to what was expected in resident doctoral programs. The nineteen works listed on Diggs's reading list included texts by philosophers such as Kant, Spinoza, Hume, and Locke as well as social critics and advocates of the social gospel such as Thorstein Veblen's *Theory of the Leisure Class,* Henry George's *Progress and Poverty,* and Washington Gladden's *Social Facts and Social Forces.* The academic sociologists on Diggs's list included Richmond Mayo-Smith's widely used *Statistics and Sociology,* C. Loring Brace's *Gesta Christi,* and the University of Chicago sociologist Charles Richmond Henderson's *The Social Spirit in America.*[22] Diggs became a college president and was an intense political activist who promoted black history and joined the Niagara and the Garvey movements. Although one of the most learned race men of the early twentieth century, Diggs, unlike the cadre of black labor scholars that was forming, did not have the solid grounding in survey research that seems to have kept him from making a major scholarly contribution. The title of his now lost dissertation, "The Dynamics of Social Progress," suggests that he also shared a commitment to racial advancement, via social sciences, with the other younger scholars.[23]

Monroe Nathan Work was the first of the newly forming cadre of black labor scholars to arrive in Chicago and to shift from theology to sociology. He was twenty-nine years old in the fall of 1895 when he enrolled in the Chicago Theological Seminary. One of his professors, Graham Taylor, had just established the Chicago Commons Settlement to teach Christian sociology "from the ground up and not from the clouds down." Taylor had begun one of the country's first programs in Christian sociology at the CTS, and after taking a course with Taylor in 1897, Work quickly became more interested in empirical research than in developing his ministerial skills. His term paper on black people and crime for Taylor's course became the basis for an article published in the *American Journal of Sociology* in 1900. Building on his course work and experiences at the CTS, Work entered the University of Chicago in the spring of 1898 with the express intention of studying sociology and using it as a tool to change black social conditions.[24]

Work's principal advisor at the University of Chicago was William I. Thomas, who taught courses on race. Thomas's rejection of biological theories of race, his arguments for historical and cultural explanations of group differences, and his insistence that prejudice was fear of the unknown resonated with Work and significantly shaped how he began to envision his life's work: "I dedicated my life to the gathering of information, the compiling of exact knowledge concerning the Negro." While still a student at the University of Chicago, Monroe Work started collecting all the empirical data he could find on black life, systematically storing it away in envelopes and notebooks; this data gathering would eventually become a central part of a career as the first comprehensive bibliographer of black American culture.[25]

Work, Wright, and other black University of Chicago students were nurtured not just by the white intellectual community at the university but by the community of black intellectuals and reformers in Chicago. Despite their impecunious finances, Work and Wright had social status as university students and were welcome participants in the many activities of the Reverend Reverdy C. Ransom's Institutional Church. Ransom, a rising star in the AME Church, held both a prestigious pastorate and by 1900 had established the denomination's first urban social ministry, complete with daycare facilities, boys and girls clubs, job training, recreation, and intellectual programs. In this setting, black graduate and undergraduate students at the University of Chicago and Northwestern University met black professionals and working-class leaders. Ransom's Sunday Men's Club sponsored lively discussions on current events, with frequent appearances by prominent black speakers such as Robert S. Abbott, publisher of the *Chicago Defender*. Presentations before the Sunday Men's Club by students such as Monroe Work were arguably their entrée into the black urban intelligentsia.[26]

R. R. Wright Jr. quickly came to see the Institutional Church as a "new venture in religion and social service," which provided him an illustration of his classroom lessons on the social gospel. Ransom offered Wright a model of how a socially conscious and intellectual minister could rise within his denomination, by which Ransom laid the foundation for new social ventures within the limitations of a conservative AME hierarchy. Wright learned from Ransom's example and assiduously copied Ransom in his own career. For his part, Ransom assisted Wright and other AME scholar-intellectuals, such as the labor historian Charles H. Wesley, in their battles with the often balky church leaders.[27]

Ransom began his long mentorship of Wright by encouraging him to become directly involved in the Booker T. Washington–W. E. B. Du Bois controversy over black education. Both Wright and Monroe Work were tapped by Ransom to help with a three-day conference on the black position in America held at the Institutional Church after the publication of *The Souls of Black*

Folk. The centerpiece of the festivities was a well-attended intercollegiate banquet in which Du Bois was an honoree. Wright was the secretary for this event, and Work was on the arrangements committee with Washington's ally, the attorney S. Laing Williams, and the Fisk alumnus and physician A. A. Wesley. The banquet was a not-so-subtle but indirect way for the militant Ransom to demonstrate his disdain for Washington's lack of a bachelor's degree and his controversial views.[28]

The intercollegiate banquet might have been Monroe Work's first meeting with Du Bois, but Work immediately became a part of Du Bois's research projects. In 1903 they worked together on a study of religious activities in Illinois that was incorporated into the eighth Atlanta University Conference on the Negro church. This was the first of much collaboration between Work and Du Bois. Both Work and Wright were asked and agreed to join the militant Niagara Movement. Wright and Work were more moderate in their political views than their mentors, and unlike Ransom or Diggs, each subsequently developed a practical working relationship with Booker T. Washington while maintaining their professional and personal ties to Du Bois.[29]

Monroe Work completed his master's degree in sociology in 1903 with a study on black ownership of real estate in Chicago, confident and proud that he was the first black person to earn this degree. At age thirty-seven and after eight years in Chicago, Monroe Work decided to look for a job in which he could utilize his training rather than go on for the doctorate that could have required at least one or two more years of residence. R. R. Wright Jr. recommended Work to his father, and Monroe Work began teaching at Georgia State College for Negroes in 1903; he soon founded a Sunday Men's Club in Savannah, which developed cultural and social welfare programs and engaged in political actions. Work also developed several research projects on the social conditions of black southerners.[30]

Even though he had decided not to pursue a doctorate, Monroe Work remained influential in the development of social science and black labor studies. He continued to work with Du Bois's Atlanta University studies, contributing several research reports to the 1904 Conference on Negro Crime and preparing a critique of the research that purported to measure the differences in Negro and white brains for the 1906 study of the health and physique of black Americans.[31] In 1908 Work accepted Booker T. Washington's invitation to establish a Department of Records and Research at Tuskegee Institute. For the next thirty years Monroe Work would pursue his goal of compiling a database on black life that would make it "possible to answer in a factual

The Segregated Scholars

manner questions relating to all matters concerning" black people in the belief that "in the end facts will help eradicate prejudice and misunderstanding, for facts are the truth and the truth shall set us free." He collected every possible document, research report, newspaper clipping, book, pamphlet, or article, classified all the material received, and filed it by year for easy retrieval. These regularly appearing databases, especially *The Negro Year Book* and *A Bibliography of the Negro in Africa and America,* were extensively used by scholars, journalists, and students.[32]

Work also continued his personal research that was more directed toward economic and labor issues. He was also a regular participant in professional sociology and history associations. Monroe Work published several articles pointing to the economic, educational, and legal restraints that led black southerners to migrate. In 1917 when the special assistant to the secretary of war Emmett J. Scott received a Carnegie Corporation grant to study black migration, he asked Work to do the research on Alabama, Georgia, and Florida. Work's Department of Records and Research was also responsible for the report's statistical tabulations and compilation of "disturbances," and "economic consequences." In the 1920s Work began a massive study of the effects of migration on farmers and farm laborers. In "Changes in Population and Farm Tenure in Counties of the South by Color, 1880–1920" he gathered data in Alabama, Arkansas, Florida, Georgia, Kentucky, and Louisiana. A 1931–32 Rosenwald Fund grant allowed Work to return to the University of Chicago for one year of postgraduate studies. In the twenty-eight years since he had studied there, Monroe Work had become an important part of the development of black social science in general and black labor studies in particular.[33]

R. R. Wright Jr. began his studies at the University of Chicago with Professors William Rainey Harper and Shailer Mathews, who had a singular effect on his understanding of theology. Harper was head of the Department of Semetic Languages and Literature as well as the founding president of the university. Wright took several courses from Harper on the Old Testament, including Wright's favorite, History of the Hebrew People.[34] Shailer Mathews, professor of New Testament history and interpretation, became Wright's advisor and close confidant as the young man struggled to reconcile his interpretative biblical criticism and history courses with the teachings of his denomination. The Department of Biblical Theology regarded its subject as "an historical science," whose object was to determine "the ethical and religious beliefs of the several prophets, teachers, and writers" of the Bible, a nonfundamentalist stance called the higher criticism. Harper and Mathews intro-

Richard Robert Wright Jr. (From the Collections of the University of Pennsylvania Archives)

duced Wright to critical biblical analysis, evolutionary theory, and the social gospel. His undergraduate minor was sociology, and he had classes with Albion Small and Charles Richmond Henderson, professor of sociology in the University of Chicago Divinity School. Henderson was one direct link between the divinity school and the sociology department. The Department of Sociology chair Albion Small also directed the divinity school's offerings in sociology as a component of the sociology department. At the turn of the century the sociology department had only seven faculty members, yet it was divided into at least four parts: sociology, anthropology, sanitary science (home economics), and divinity. Henderson taught nearly a dozen different undergraduate and graduate courses that ranged from secular sociological topics, such as the family, the labor movement, methods of social ameliora-

The Segregated Scholars

tion, and modern cities, to more social gospel–inspired courses, such as one on the social institutions of organized Christianity. Although Wright credited Mathews for persuading him not to completely give up on his plan to become a minister, his classes with Henderson and his careful reading of Du Bois more clearly shaped his 1901 undergraduate thesis in divinity, "The Industrial Condition of the Negroes in Chicago," a distinctively nontheological study of black workers.[35]

R. R. Wright Jr. eventually became extremely adept in church politics, but his first half-dozen years were difficult. The AME Church's more literal approach to biblical interpretation repeatedly caused Wright to run afoul of his superiors. Monroe Work did not continue to seek pastorates after coming to Chicago because of his discomfort with both the pulpit and the politics of the AME Church. But Wright's father had friends in the modernist wing of AME bishops who interceded on his behalf and urged him to continue his studies whenever he seemed torn between fundamentalism and the higher criticism. Wright needed the intervention of Bishop Benjamin Arnett to be become a full-fledged AME minister after he impertinently corrected his examiner's Hebrew during a Bible examination. Wright's subsequent plan to inject the social gospel into African Methodism by delivering a paper entitled "Sociology and the Bible" at a ministerial conference was quashed until his paper could be read and approved by Bishop Benjamin Tucker Tanner, another old family friend. Tanner informed the would-be censors that it contained "nothing new." Church officials had feared that Wright's paper was about either "socialism" or "social equality," equally dreaded topics to his conservative AME superiors.[36]

While he shifted his educational focus from theology to sociology and back to theology several times, there was never any doubt in Wright's mind that it was his obligation to use his scholarly achievements as foundation stones of enlightened leadership. Like his father, whom he "almost worshiped," Wright Jr. was determined to personally disprove racist conclusions about the intellectual prowess of blacks. Wright Jr. believed that his success at the University of Chicago would be at once an individual, class, and racial achievement in the same way that his father's and W. E. B. Du Bois's educational and intellectual feats were claimed by both educated and uneducated blacks and at the same time remained deeply satisfying to each man.[37]

For ten years after earning his bachelor's in divinity from the University of Chicago, R. R. Wright Jr. would attempt to combine his growing body of research studies and social reform projects with his determination to build his career within the AME Church hierarchy. He believed the church offered positions of leadership and growth to black men that were unavailable elsewhere in American society. In 1901, bachelor's of divinity in hand, Wright was ordained as an AME minister and assigned to a position as instructor of Hebrew at Payne Theological Seminary, which was a part of Wilberforce University in Ohio.

After three mind-expanding years at the University of Chicago and within the black intellectual community he had encountered in Chicago's Institutional Church, Wright found Wilberforce University as restrictive and narrow-minded as Du Bois had seven years earlier. The administration still showed absolutely no interest in offering sociology courses and even regarded with horror any suggestions Wright made that male students might profit from sports and physical education. With recommendations from both Du Bois and Henderson, Wright continued his sociological research by contracting with Carroll Davidson Wright to do a study of the black community of nearby Xenia, Ohio, for the U.S. Bureau of Labor series that his father had started. This project only engendered more suspicion of Wright Jr. by campus authorities. He was warned by church authorities not to get "too theoretical" or "too far above the people" by using a critical approach to biblical texts in his teaching and preaching and to stop doing surveys of black social conditions. Disheartened but unapologetic, he plotted an escape to Germany for graduate studies.[38]

Professor Shailer Mathews helped Wright enroll in the Universities of Berlin and Leipzig to study the New Testament under Adolph Harnich and Bernhard Weiss, in what was more of a rejection of fundamentalist readings of scripture than a turn away from sociological studies. Going abroad for graduate study also fulfilled Wright Sr.'s wish that his son study in Germany as had Du Bois. Wright Jr. did not formally study sociology while he was abroad but extended his study of the New Testament. The battle over higher criticism was at its height, and Wright came to believe that his work had taken place "when Germany was the synonym for intellectual honesty and intellectual effort as applied to the word of God."[39] Wright returned from Germany in 1904 and earned a master's in divinity from the University of Chicago for the studies he began in Germany. He now planned to work toward a doctorate in theology, but turmoil between the divinity and sociology departments that had caused Henderson and others to leave the divinity school and racial disturbances in Chicago made Wright seek a more clearly social gospel approach to his ministry to fulfill his intellectual appetite and satisfy his desire to advance his race.[40]

Wright's movement from religion to sociology partially mirrored events that were happening in Chicago. When Wright returned from Europe he witnessed a bitter and violent labor strike by black teamsters, and he became convinced that sociology would be a more effective method of changing the conditions that led to this kind of industrial violence. The catalyst for Wright was hearing Albion Small preach a sermon based on John 10:10 that stressed that the mission of Christians was to bring forth "more abundant Life." Wright believed that he could finally resolve the contradictions he had found between theology and sociology without having to choose one over the other.[41]

The AME Church assigned Wright to Trinity Mission, a Chicago storefront that had a total of four members. Since almost all of an AME minister's salary was paid by offerings from the congregation, Wright's assignment indicated that he was not much appreciated by church officials who were nonetheless obliged to keep him employed in Chicago while he was in graduate school because of his high-ranking protectors. Wright took this financial liability and turned it into a sociological asset. He immediately made an exhaustive survey of the twenty-five hundred residents and physical environment surrounding Trinity Mission.

R. R. Wright Jr.'s study of the area was a self-conscious extension of the detail found in Du Bois's *The Philadelphia Negro*. Wright's charts and maps indicated the location of saloons, schools, churches, child care facilities, and murders. He discovered that the area around the tiny mission was much more vice ridden and unhealthy than Philadelphia's Seventh Ward, but Wright Jr. reached different conclusions about the motives and character of its black residents. He found that most blacks were not depraved, but, rather, they worked at odd jobs in whorehouses and saloons because the pay was higher than at other places. In fact, the "majority were just poor and made a great effort to be decent." Middle-class blacks had fled the area, leaving poor blacks, and to Wright's surprise, many wealthy whites, co-residents with the prostitutes, numbers runners, and tavern owners. R. R. Wright Jr. delivered his survey results and displayed his charts at a mass meeting on Chicago's social problems at Handel Hall in Chicago's Loop and gained the support of influential white social reformers, including Jane Addams, Celia Parker Wooley, and Mary White Ovington. Wright Jr.'s conclusion was that his neighborhood's social deterioration was neither a sign of racial inferiority nor confined to the black residents: "It was due to the neglect of the city and Christian community which was socially asleep." Wright had turned an unprofitable assignment into a major social survey. Of his experience at Trinity Mission, he wrote that it "completely shifted my interest from the theological to the sociological point of view."[42]

White social reformers, including the wives of the meat-packing industrialists Swift and Armour, joined with black women's clubs to assist Wright with an infusion of funds and volunteers for new programs. The Trinity Mission began to grow. Wright offered a course in Negro history with a textbook of his own making and created a day nursery because his survey indicated that mothers were forced to leave their children home alone when they went out to work. He followed the example of the Institutional Church and created clubs for mothers, boys, and girls. His evening school helped men prepare for the Post Office civil service exam. Wright also claimed he learned how to preach while serving Trinity Mission; but the congregation remained poor and small, and Wright was obliged to work at the Post Office to make ends meet. More important, Wright discovered that he was now more intellectually stimulated by survey research and promoting reforms than he was by New Testament studies, and he resolved to seek a doctorate in sociology.[43]

One year earlier, in 1904, not one of the trio of Monroe Work, George Haynes, and R. R. Wright Jr. seemed poised for a career in the social sciences, despite having earned master's degrees from the University of Chicago and Yale University. Monroe Work, who had studied the most intensively in sociology, obtained a teaching position and slowly became more interested in providing the exhaustive bibliographic record of black life that Du Bois's tenth annual Atlanta University Conference proceedings hinted was possible. George Haynes had earned a master's degree from Yale University in sociology and economics but had then enrolled in divinity school with the intent to become a Congregational minister. A family financial crisis and W. E. B. Du Bois's strong advice against his pursuing a career in the ministry caused Haynes to leave Yale in 1905. R. R. Wright Jr., who would in the coming decade become the most prolific author of the three, had in 1904 just earned a master's degree in divinity. And despite his subsequent secular conversion at Trinity Mission, Wright Jr. did not have the financial means to become a professional sociologist. However, a series of events over the next few years would place Haynes and Wright Jr. at the center of the development of black labor studies and in the forefront of professionalizing and racializing the social reform and social work movement.

The Year 1905: The Hidden Watershed
in Black Labor Studies

The year that R. R. Wright Jr. left Chicago, 1905, was a watershed in the development of black labor studies. The research direction of the black social scientists who joined W. E. B. Du Bois in the twentieth century began to take a definitive shape. Under the guidance of Du Bois, black social scientists and social activists cemented a lasting professional alliance with white social scientists and reformers. This new alliance between black social scientists and white liberal reformers was begun in a special issue of *Charities* that signaled a novel direction in research and fresh implications for black-white cooperative projects that came five years before the founding of either the National Urban League (NUL) or the National Association for the Advancement of Colored People (NAACP).[44] The alliance would provide a long-lasting basis for funding survey research projects, institutionalizing professional training for black social scientists and social workers, and mobilizing social service organizations that could assist black workers and employ the new black professionals.

Before 1905 the vast majority of empirical research on black life was still being conducted by W. E. B. Du Bois and his network of largely unpaid researchers via the Atlanta University annual conference series and the U.S. Bureau of Labor studies of black communities that continued to use the methodological frameworks Du Bois had suggested to Carroll D. Wright in 1898. Beginning with R. R. Wright Jr. and George Edmund Haynes, Du Bois played a central role in expanding the number of black social scientists by assisting them in finding funds for their doctoral research, getting their articles placed in professional journals, and providing introductions to and interventions with their professors and white reformers and philanthropists.

Utilizing the advice and assistance of W. E. B. Du Bois, Wright obtained a fellowship that allowed him to enter the graduate program in sociology at the University of Pennsylvania in the fall of 1905. Du Bois also saw to it that Wright's analysis of black workers' involvement in a Chicago strike was published in the aforementioned 1905 special issue of *Charities*.[45]

In early 1905 Frances Kellor, a young white female sociologist and reformer, wrote to W. E. B. Du Bois asking him to recommend a person who would receive a five-hundred-dollar fellowship at the University of Pennsylvania and "live in a colored neighborhood and investigate for us." Du Bois, thinking of R. R. Wright Jr., replied that he thought he "could find . . . the proper man." Kellor's graduate studies in sociology at the University of Chicago had been underwritten by the philanthropist Celia Parker Wooley, who was a contributor to Wright Jr.'s Trinity Mission. Kellor had also worked closely with University of Chicago professors Charles R. Henderson, Albion Small, and William Thomas, mentors of Wright Jr. and Monroe Work. On Du Bois's recommendation, Wright was contacted by his "schoolmate," who explained that the University of Pennsylvania "was looking for a colored man to take a fellowship in sociology and to do research in Negro American conditions in Pennsylvania, following the work so well done by W. E. B. Du Bois in *The Philadelphia Negro*."[46]

Du Bois followed Wright's progress at the University of Pennsylvania with supportive attention and hired him to work on a research project for the U.S. Department of Labor for several months in the summer of 1906. Du Bois also suggested that one of his wealthy patrons contact Wright, to learn more about blacks in the North, because he regarded Wright as "a very interesting and earnest young man who can tell you a great deal about the situation and answer many questions."[47] Du Bois's active encouragement of Wright's pursuit of a doctorate in sociology did not force Wright to choose between a secular career and an AME ministry because the young scholar was able to get a two-year leave from his presiding bishop in Philadelphia to attend the university and work as a resident at the Eighth Ward Settlement House. This leave gave Wright, who received eight credits for courses he had taken in sociology and European history at Chicago, ample time to complete the University of Pennsylvania's course and residency requirements for the doctorate. Wright majored in sociology and minored in economics and European history and had taken all the required courses and passed all of his written exams by the spring of 1907.[48]

Wright had unsatisfactory experiences with the members of the sociology faculty at the University of Pennsylvania, particularly with his principal advisor, Carl Kelsey—especially when compared to his productive and close association with Shailer Mathews at the University of Chicago. Wright granted that the University of Pennsylvania's sociology faculty, led by Samuel McCune Lindsay, were good methodologists, almost exactly the opposite of the eclectic social gospel approach of his former Chicago professors; but he believed that they were at best woefully uninformed about black life and at worst held racially biased opinions. Wright took three year-long courses on sociological theory and fieldwork with Lindsay, but he felt the most animosity for Kelsey, who had just completed a doctoral dissertation on a study of black farmers.

Although Wright was able to maintain friendly relations with Kelsey, he abhorred his research findings, arguing that Kelsey "knew very little about the real Negro-American farmers" and inferring he had never actually spoken to one. In Philadelphia reform circles, Kelsey played an active role as an expert on black life, but in Wright's bird's-eye view he was a social conservative who was "at heart . . . a segregationist of the gradualist type," a species Wright knew all too well from close encounters in his native Georgia. Wright bitterly resented the fact that wealthy white "welfare dilettantes" considered Kelsey the "local authority on the Negro question."[49] According to Wright, Kelsey made outrageous public comments about black intellectual inferiority and was opposed to black higher education. His proof positive of Kelsey's racist ideology was Wright's contention that Kelsey had stated that no more than a dozen blacks should ever be admitted to northern colleges and that the aim of education should be to "make the Negro the best possible Negro."[50]

In 1905 R. R. Wright Jr. was no longer the reticent young man who had been so surprised with the new racial etiquette in Chicago that allowed black people to speak directly to whites, and he refused to suffer what he considered Kelsey's racial attacks in silence or to concede to his doctoral advisor's point of view: "I contended that, given the same statistics, and the same body of facts, my interpretation of these should be more valid than his, for I knew what it was to be a Negro-American from experience and he did not."[51] Wright may have felt emboldened by the fact that his fellowship was largely independent of his advisor and that he could obtain an AME pastorate or other office, or he may have believed that Lindsay would advise him if Kelsey withdrew his support. In any case, Wright challenged Kelsey's statements about black people so often in one graduate class—probably American Race Problems, in 1906–7—that, according to Wright, Kelsey privately agreed to go over his lectures with him before each class. But Wright's account makes clear that the two men had contrasting views about why they were doing this: "We agreed that he would outline his day's lecture to me before holding his class. Thus he could eliminate what he called the 'emotional areas' and what I called the 'areas of ignorance and prejudice'—that is, those in which there [were] not enough facts to build a valid generalization."[52]

Wright's hostility to Carl Kelsey was based on Wright's insistence that Kelsey let his racial prejudices suffuse his analyses, rendering them less than objective, and on what he considered Kelsey's total ignorance of black life. Although Kelsey had spent one summer in the South doing research for his dissertation on black farmers, Wright charged that Kelsey had never entered a black person's home and, therefore, could not have fully studied the black community.[53] But Wright's hostility was also based on his anger that a man whom he considered his social and intellectual inferior could become an unquestioned authority on black people. Kelsey, an Iowa native, was only eight years older than R. R. Wright Jr. and had just earned his doctorate in 1902. It rankled Wright to have a man he regarded as both a racist and from a lower-class, nonintellectual background as his advisor.

R. R. Wright Jr. had grown up surrounded by literature, music, and art. The Wright home was a secular sanctuary of classical texts and modernist ideals in post-Reconstruction Georgia. His mother devoted herself to her home, church, and children, and his father read daily from the Bible printed in Latin, Hebrew, Greek, French, and German. The Wright family's study contained an extensive collection of books by Negro authors that Wright Sr. had painstakingly gathered in the United States and Europe. It was decorated with pictures of the senior Wright's heroes—Richard Allen, Toussaint L'Overture, Cetewayo Zulu, Frederick Douglass, and the radical AME bishop Henry M. Turner. Wright Jr. had met Douglass, Turner, the lecturer Frances Watkins Harper, and many other black leaders in his home during his childhood. In fact, Carl Kelsey's small town rural upbringing was not dissimilar from the first generation of American sociologists, including Albion Small, whom the historians Dorothy Ross and Robert C. Bannister have argued used the professionalization of the discipline as a means of achieving upper-middle-class status and stature as well as establishing themselves as authorities on the relationship between humanity and society.[54]

Carl Kelsey's swift rise at the University of Pennsylvania was due in part to his senior professors' recognition of his talents, the noncontroversial nature of his research findings, his willingness to teach the race courses that were becoming a part of the curriculum of most sociology departments, and the fact that he was a Christian white male.[55] Both Frances Kellor and R. R. Wright Jr., who had similar educational training and skills, were marginalized within the developing discipline of sociology because their sex and race kept them from being considered as faculty members. Kellor's major studies were funded by progressive organizations supported by wealthy white women. Wright Jr. and other early black sociologists tried with far less success to tap into many of the same philanthropic and social welfare organizations, such as the Charities Organization Society, Rosenwald Fund, and Russell Sage Foundation, that were utilized by white female social scientists for their research and social welfare projects.

The Segregated Scholars

The year 1905 had seen R. R. Wright Jr.'s full-fledged entry into graduate studies in sociology, and it was also pivotal for a black graduate student at Yale University, George Edmund Haynes. Haynes had earned a master's degree in sociology from Yale University in 1904 and had enrolled in the Yale University Divinity School with the intention of becoming a Congregational minister. He was forced to postpone a ministerial career and embarked on a course of work and study that would culminate in his becoming a focal figure in the ongoing development of black labor studies and the training of the succeeding generation of black social scientists.[56]

George Edmund Haynes was an early admirer and lifelong correspondent of W. E. B. Du Bois. When Haynes was a preparatory school student at Fisk University he helped with the arrangements when Du Bois delivered Fisk's 1898 commencement address on the tenth anniversary of his graduation.[57] Thereafter Du Bois took a personal and active interest in Haynes's educational and career choices, serving first as Haynes's mentor and informal advisor and later becoming a colleague and friend, in much the same fashion as he had done for R. R. Wright Jr. and Monroe Work.

Haynes's academic achievements at Fisk led to his admission to Yale University. Several of Haynes's professors at Fisk had ties to Yale University, and with their strong support Haynes received a scholarship and was able to enter the graduate school at Yale without first completing a second bachelor's degree there, no small feat at the time. The fellow Arkansan and future NAACP staffer William Pickens, an honors graduate of Talledega College, had enrolled in the junior class of Yale College one year before Haynes's arrival in 1903. There were then perhaps one dozen black students enrolled in undergraduate and graduate programs at Yale University. At Yale, Haynes took graduate courses in sociology and economics, including a seminar taught by William Graham Sumner, a prominent Social Darwinist and one of the most influential figures in early American sociology. Despite his often expressed belief in white superiority, William Graham Sumner apparently regarded Haynes as a good student and supplied Haynes with a letter of recommendation that stated that Haynes's participation in the seminar had been distinguished by the "zeal with which he had done the work."[58] Although Haynes subsequently attended three other institutions, he frequently referred to Sumner's influence on his development as a sociologist. Sumner's seminar had given Haynes a basic knowledge of how to employ sociological methods, and he also claimed to have gained an appreciation of Sumner's concept of folkways and mores. Sociology was not yet systematically offered as an undergraduate course when Haynes

George Edmund
Haynes.
(Photographs and
Prints Division,
Schomburg Center
for Research in
Black Culture, The
New York Public
Library, Astor,
Lenox and Tilden
Foundations)

was at Fisk University, so Sumner's seminar was probably his first exposure to disciplinary methodologies. Haynes may have derived some of his methods from Sumner, but the theories in Haynes's writings were always firmly in the anti–Social Darwinist camp. Haynes's belief in the efficacy of social work among blacks explicitly rejected Sumner's assertion that folkways were innate and could not be unlearned.[59] George Haynes's debt to Sumner is not apparent in Haynes's social studies, which are far more empirical and much more obviously inspired by his association with W. E. B. Du Bois, James Angell of the University of Chicago, and his doctoral professors at Columbia University.

Despite his success in Sumner's seminar, George Haynes did not immediately decide to become a sociologist. When he earned a master's degree in

The Segregated Scholars

sociology and economics at the end of his first year in residence, Haynes was awarded a scholarship to Yale's divinity school and spent a second year in New Haven. At this point, much like R. R. Wright Jr. a few years earlier, Haynes was equally interested in a career as a minister as he was as a sociologist or college professor. Haynes's divinity studies were interrupted, however, because his mother needed assistance with the tuition and expenses for his only sister, Birdye, who was about to enter Fisk's preparatory department. Frank Saunders, dean of the Yale University Divinity School, helped to arrange a job for Haynes as an assistant to William Alphaeus Hunton, organizer of the Colored Men's Department of the International Committee of the Young Men's Christian Association (YMCA). Hunton and Jesse Moorland were the only two black professionals on the staff of the YMCA, but the YMCA movement was strong among black college students. Haynes was offered the position of YMCA traveling secretary with primary responsibility for organizing and assisting the segregated college chapters. Haynes was already familiar with the work of the YMCA on college campuses; he had been a student leader of the YMCA at Fisk University and had undoubtedly met Hunton at YMCA activities. Haynes had attended a large and integrated YMCA conference in Toronto, Canada, as an undergraduate delegate from Fisk University and had given a report on his Canadian experiences at a segregated regional conference in Montgomery, Alabama, in late 1902 or early 1903.[60]

Even though Dean Saunders generously offered to allow George Haynes to reenter Yale's divinity school at a later date, Haynes worried that he might be making the first step in what could prove to be a momentous career decision and asked W. E. B. Du Bois to help him evaluate the YMCA job in connection with his future career options. Haynes wanted to find a career in which he could best serve the needs of his people, and he never doubted that one could become a racial leader simply by having a superior education and a commitment to racial progress, but he was in a quandary as to how to make the best career choice. In the spring of 1905 Haynes wrote to Du Bois and asked for help in deciding whether a job at a black college or in the pulpit would better prepare him to be a "religious and moral force among those who are to be the future leaders of the race." Although Du Bois admired a number of black clergy, he did not regard the ministry as necessarily the best career for talented young black men. Haynes was a Congregationalist, and Du Bois was cynical about the willingness of white church leaders to promote desegregation and improvements in black living conditions. Du Bois firmly believed that the social sciences were the best avenue for young men who were interested in becoming racial leaders. Du Bois held the YMCA's William Hunton—a frequent visitor to Atlanta University—in high personal esteem and suggested that Haynes's choice of a more secular career would be in the best interests of their race. He wrote to Haynes that the YMCA job offered "a very excellent field with greater possibilities than that open to a Congregational minister. The development of sufficient moral forces outside the churches to compel the churches to change face is the problem before us."[61]

Haynes accepted the YMCA job and moved to Atlanta, Georgia, the headquarters for the colored YMCA's operations. It was Haynes's job to visit black colleges' YMCA chapters, taking over some of the duties that Hunton had initiated a decade earlier. The YMCA job was a good compromise for Haynes because it was a position that articulated a distinctly Christian ethic of racial leadership via its campus meetings. Haynes and Hunton not only addressed the campus YMCA chapters but frequently spoke in the required chapel services and other large public events that were attended by both students and black townspeople. His first professional job placed Haynes into direct contact with much of the colored YMCA's southern student membership, most of whom were campus leaders as he had been. He was also able to develop personal contacts with black college administrators throughout the South. When he became a professor at Fisk University several years later, Haynes used these ties to promote the accreditation of black colleges and to establish popular summer school programs for teachers at several schools and colleges, including Hampton Institute. Because his job focused on colleges, normal schools, and institutes and left the city work to Hunton and Moorland, Haynes had the summers free, enabling him to attend graduate school at the University of Chicago.[62]

Like R. R. Wright Jr., George Haynes's decision in 1905 had a significant effect on the shaping of black labor studies. George Haynes remained a Congregationalist and was active in lay activities for the rest of his life, but he seemed to gradually abandon the idea of becoming a minister and decided to get a professional social work certificate at the New York School of Philanthropy. After working for the YMCA for three years, Haynes seized the opportunity to become a professional sociologist when it arose. R. R. Wright Jr. did not feel the same obligation to choose between sociological training and the ministry in 1905 because the AME organizational structure had niches that allowed Wright and others to do both, albeit at low or no salaries. Haynes did not have an independent black church structure to support him with a small congregation or an administrative posting while he studied. Haynes's decision to get a graduate certificate in social work may have been partly in response to the advice of Du Bois and to the concerns that R. R. Wright Jr. outlined in his article "Social Work and the Influence of the Negro Church." Wright had scourged black churches for failing to provide adequate services for Negro migrants and lamented the fact that no black men were training specifically for social work.[63] There were only a few black people in the United States working as professional social workers, not more than one or two in either New York City or Chicago in 1905. Charities and social service agencies were hesitant to hire untrained black people but slow to establish integrated programs that were based on the new professional standards of social work.[64] It is also possible that Haynes hoped from the start to use a certificate in social work as a way to enter the graduate program in sociology at Columbia University. Several members of Columbia's sociology department were on the faculty of the New York School of Philanthropy and were active members of the Charities Organization Society, the principal social welfare agency in New York City.[65] Haynes's success at Yale, additional courses at the University of Chicago, and his experiences with the YMCA made him an ideal, if wildly overqualified, student once again in the fall of 1908.

George Haynes resumed his letters to W. E. B. Du Bois seeking advice on graduate courses and moral support. Du Bois warmly approved of Haynes's choice of instructors and courses and sent him a letter of introduction to Mary White Ovington, an independently wealthy white progressive active in social welfare reform who was conducting research on black life. Du Bois advised Haynes to consult with Ovington before he began to study the economic conditions of blacks in New York City because "she knows more about it than anyone I know." Ovington in turn was impressed by Haynes's seriousness and maturity and helped to introduce him to other whites and blacks involved in implementing new programs to assist black workers.[66]

The year 1905 had been pivotal in both Wright's and Haynes's decisions to become social scientists. Wright would respond to Du Bois's tutelage with a stream of studies and articles that examined the experiences of black workers in the small towns and cities of the North.[67] George E. Haynes's social studies of black northern workers began to be published in 1912, about the time Wright's publications were slowing, and Haynes's work would extend to chronicle the Great Migration. Both Wright and Haynes worked closely with white reformers they met through W. E. B. Du Bois and with black community groups to create programs to assist black urban workers. George Haynes built on these connections to establish the National Urban League and to create a program in social science at Fisk University designed to train black social work professionals and identify future sociologists.

The year 1905 also marked a new coalition between black and white intellectuals based on common interests in survey research and urban reform. The October 7, 1905, special issue of *Charities* was an auspicious if belated response to Du Bois's 1898 call for joint black-white research efforts, even though the assembled articles represented parallel rather than truly collaborative efforts. Blacks and whites had worked together on political and educational projects since the abolitionist movement, but this marked the first step toward a scholarly collaboration in social science in which the methods of Du Bois, his tiny cadre of black scholars, the new insights of Franz Boas, and the support of white academic reformers would frame the parameters of a developing discourse on black workers and the study of black urban life. The most active white supporters of the research conducted by early black social scientists were reformers who were involved in the professionalization of charity to social work in northern cities, especially New York City, Chicago, Pittsburgh, and Philadelphia. Some were settlement house founders, such as Jane Addams. Others were social scientists already involved in social reform movements, such as Frances Kellor, the University of Pennsylvania sociology professor Carl Kelsey, and Columbia University's Paul U. Kellogg, who, with Edward T. Devine, edited *Charities* for the Charities Organization Society of New York.[68]

White Progressive Era social workers and academics often had their first introduction to black intellectuals and to the potential of empirical research on black life during the Atlanta University conferences held every spring, beginning in 1896. They met Du Bois, and the southern black intellectuals such as Lucy Laney and LaFayette Hershaw, who made the conference vibrant year after year. They were also introduced to the peculiar etiquette of segregation, since polite white Atlanta society would have little to do with the northern whites who participated in the unsegregated events at the university. Attending an Atlanta University Conference often sparked an interest in taking up similar studies on their return home. The settlement house worker Mary White Ovington began to study northern black life seriously after she attended the 1904 Atlanta University Conference, and she helped to found the NAACP five years later.[69]

The October 1905 special issue of *Charities*, "The Negro in the Cities of the North," was the first concerted attempt of northern and black Progressive Era social scientists to assert that their expertise gave them a claim to authority over the identification and resolution of the "Negro problem," just as they argued that their studies could be used to solve other urban ills. The special issue also began a long and fruitful association between *Charities*'s influential editors, Kellogg and Devine, and black intellectuals. After this issue black social reform became a regular topic in other social science journals, such as the *Annals of the American Academy of Political and Social Science*, and black social scientists became regular contributors to *Charities* and its successor, *The Survey*.[70]

The editors of *Charities* opened their special issue by deflecting potential charges of meddling in the domain of southern whites by disclaiming any encroachment on the "the more bitter elements of the race conflict which Mr. [Thomas Nelson] Page jealously insists is the Southerners' problem." They also disavowed any partisanship of the views of either Du Bois or Washington in the ongoing controversy over "two diverse programs for the education and advancement of the Negro with their conflicting ideals."[71] Most of the articles in the special issue assumed that social reform techniques could be applied to black city life and proceeded to discuss living conditions in particular cities with the idea that once the facts were known, improvements might be instituted. Although the Atlanta University Conference had taken this approach for over a decade, this was the first time an established social welfare organization had considered black people suitable subjects for reform. The more than twenty articles represented a range of opinion on the capabilities of black people, but nearly all the authors believed that most of their social problems could be improved by scientific application of social reform techniques and that black people could be assimilated into modern urban society.[72]

The contributors to the special issue were chosen by Paul Kellogg, managing editor of *Charities*, who solicited the advice of W. E. B. Du Bois and Celia Parker Wooley, the Chicago reformer. Du Bois promptly suggested that Kellogg seek essays from two persons whose work he knew well, his close associate and Atlanta University Conference stalwart LaFayette Hershaw and R. R. Wright Jr. Additionally, Kellogg apparently reconsidered his plan to ask T. Thomas Fortune, *New York Age* editor and Booker T. Washington supporter, to be a contributor after Du Bois argued that Fortune would be "inappropriate."[73] The majority of the black authors were progressive intellectuals and reformers whose writings on social issues had frequently appeared in black periodicals and local publications. They included Kelly Miller, William L. Bulkley, James Weldon Johnson, Wright Jr., and Hershaw. R. R. Wright Jr.'s article, "The Negro in Times of Industrial Unrest," was one of the earliest detailed analyses of black participation in labor conflicts and was based on his firsthand observation of the 1901 stockyards strike. A more conservative strain of thought toward both research and black labor's relationship to the agricultural sector was represented in the issue by Booker T. Washington, William Benson, and Thomas Jesse Jones, a white administrator who was then working at Hampton Institute. Of the ten black contributors, only two expressed the conservative notion that blacks should stay in the South; they were Booker T. Washington and Du Bois's good friend William Benson, who had begun a utopian industrial community in rural Alabama.

Fannie Barrier Williams's article, "Social Bonds in the 'Black Belt' of Chicago," demonstrated how difficult it had become for Washington to keep his northern supporters in line with his views on urban issues. Fannie Williams, a native of New York State, was a leader in local Chicago and national black women's organizations, and her husband, S. Laing Williams, was an attorney who owed some of his political appointments to Booker T. Washington. Washington considered the Williamses an important part of his Chicago base and tried to keep their support. Fannie Williams had built alliances with white reformers in Chicago and had been a strong supporter of Reverdy C. Ransom's Institutional Church. Fannie Williams's basic line of argument in her article, however, was much closer to the ideals of the Atlanta University than the Tuskegee Institute Conferences. Her article was a well-written and logical statement of northern educated black people's notions of social responsibility. In an article that echoed the findings of Wright Jr.'s unpublished study of the area around his Chicago mission, Fannie Williams stressed her view that the available evidence demonstrated that the social disorganization and moral decay visible among poorer blacks was caused by the lack of decent jobs and racial prejudice. She argued that northern migration was completely rational, while Washington, her husband's patron, called for blacks to remain in the South. Nevertheless, Fannie Barrier Williams's article was not without stereotypes of its own. When describing the neighborhood surrounding R. R. Wright Jr.'s Trinity Mission, Fannie Williams said that it was so dangerous that it was "properly called Darkest Africa" because there was "scarcely a single ray of the light of decency."[74] If before writing her article Fannie Williams had been able to read Franz Boas's article on African culture that appeared in the same issue of *Charities*, she might well have had second thoughts about the appropriateness of linking Africa to moral depravity.

While the direction of black labor studies would tilt northward under the weight and pull of the collected articles, the most influential article in the special issue was the Columbia University anthropologist Franz Boas's "The Negro and the Demands of Modern Life." This article helped to provide the scientific basis for northern whites to join Du Bois and his small cadre in the development of black labor studies and programs that offered services to black workers as well as degrees and career opportunities to black social scientists. Boas's argument was a careful refutation of claims that the African ancestry of American blacks made them biologically or culturally inferior. Boas's article tested the common assertion that the savagery of Africa was responsible for black maladaption to modern life. He rejected this premise out of hand and emphatically denied that Africans were savage: "To this question anthropology can give the decided answer that . . . Africans have a considerable degree of personal initiative, with a talent for organization, and with considerable imaginative power; with technical skill and thrift. . . . There is nothing to prove that licentiousness, shiftless laziness, lack of initiative are fundamental characteristics of the race. Everything points out these qualities are the result of social conditions rather than of hereditary traits."[75]

Professor Boas left it to his readers to determine whether they believed that blacks actually had picked up these odious traits during slavery. Boas also did not argue that there were no racial differences between whites and blacks, but he insisted that whatever the differences might be they need not handicap a black person. When given facility and opportunity, "blacks probably would be perfectly able to fill the duties of citizenship as well as his white neighbor."[76]

Franz Boas's article gave white progressives interested in black social problems the scientific basis they needed from a nonblack and presumably disinterested party to legitimate the expansion of their focus from immigrants and poor whites to include black people. The editors thought that Boas's article was worthy of special emphasis in their opening statement: "The scientific presumption is that the Negro has the capacity for progress, for civilization. It is the purpose of these studies to indicate how far and in what ways . . . he has realized these possibilities and what are the difficulties which he has still to surmount."[77] The editors also rebuked Booker T. Washington, without identifying him by name, for saying that blacks could not prosper in the North. Science and not sentiment would rule in the twentieth century, they declared.[78]

It had taken ten years from the time of W. E. B. Du Bois's first call for blacks and whites to collaborate in an investigative project on black social problems, but black scholars had now found a consistent group of white supporters within the social welfare community. Du Bois's dream of a large-scale research project funded by a large university remained unrealized, but the *Charities* special issue indicated that by 1905 white progressives had accepted the premises of empirical research studies that Du Bois and other black intellectuals had written. It was now possible to have the modernist position ably represented on scholarly panels without Du Bois. R. R. Wright Jr., Kelly Miller, Monroe Work, and William Bulkley were now regular contributors of articles on black workers and economic issues to academic journals and progressive magazines.[79]

In the spring following the appearance of the *Charities* special issue, the impact of the newly formed alliance for the study of black workers was evident as several of Du Bois's new and old comrades had a chance to present an even more detailed exposition of their research findings to a largely white audience at the May 1906 annual meeting of the American Academy of Political and Social Science (AAPSS). This annual meeting was devoted to the "Improvement of Labor Conditions in the United States," and one of its five sessions was entitled "The Industrial Condition of the Negro in the North." The five speakers were Hugh M. Browne, principal of the Institute for Colored Youth in Cheyney, Pennsylvania; William Bulkley, Syracuse Ph.D. and school principal[80]; Mary White Ovington; Kelly Miller; and R. R. Wright Jr. As might be expected at a scholarly meeting, the articles, with one exception, were written from a social scientific perspective and were based on primary and secondary research or on the author's firsthand empirical study of black workers. The empirical studies were used to directly or indirectly challenge Booker T. Washington's positions on black skilled workers and their experiences in the labor force.

Browne, a close associate of Booker T. Washington, delivered a paper that was completely consistent with the Tuskegean's formula of presenting a hypercritical view of the present-day shortcomings of blacks, replete with stereotypical references to laziness and a pessimistic vision of their future possibilities outside the agricultural sector. The paper by Hugh Browne, "The Training of the Negro Laborer in the North," illustrated the failure of the conservative accommodationist wing to adapt sociological arguments to support their views. Browne's paper was replete with adages directed at the largely white audience that bore little relationship to the title of the paper. He advised his listeners that racial development took centuries and compared blacks and whites to plants, each "bearing fruit after its own kind." Browne evidently was unaware that a worldwide metaphor for hard work was to "work like a Negro," and his address stressed the need for blacks to "work as laboriously" as whites. Browne's speech was virtually interchangeable with one of Booker T. Washington's addresses to a southern white audience.[81]

The four other AAPSS speakers framed their papers in academic terms, addressing the audience and the readers as peers, in stark contrast to Browne's homespun homilies. In many ways they were building on the models that W. E. B. Du Bois set forth in his 1901 *New York Times Magazine* series "The Black North" and followed by Wright Jr.'s monograph on Xenia, Ohio, and his Chicago studies as well as the *Charities* October 1905 special issue.[82] These papers were rich both in data and in their analyses of the characteristics of the northern black labor force at the beginning of the twentieth century. One consistent finding in the four papers was that young workers seeking apprenticeships and skilled workers faced the greatest difficulty in finding employment. Although skilled jobs were not readily open to qualified northern black workers, the authors' surveys indicated that black unskilled workers in the North earned about twice as much as skilled black workers in the South. Kelly Miller took Booker T. Washington to task for his repeated suggestion that blacks were losing skilled jobs because they lacked initiative, and Mary White Ovington criticized the National Negro Business League, one of Washington's major projects, for its indiscriminate support of black strikebreakers.[83]

William L. Bulkley's paper, "The Industrial Conditions of Negroes in New York City," concisely stated the three basic arguments concerning black workers made by this initial cadre of segregated scholars. First, blacks were not lazy but had always worked hard and well and possessed skills that were underutilized in the North. Second, it was racism, not laziness, that kept blacks out of manufacturing and trade jobs. Third, the migration to the North had important advantages for blacks, including education, equal protection under the law, more sympathetic whites, and a greater number of blacks who were determined to advance.

R. R. Wright Jr.'s paper, "The Migration of the Negro to the North," linked migration to improved wages as well as greater access to schools and better living conditions, and it was based on a survey Wright made of black migrants. He also used the idea that blacks were stratified into four classes that Du Bois had first developed in *The Philadelphia Negro*. Wright's paper included data on wages in the North and South for similar occupations that clearly demonstrated that northern wages were 50 to 100 percent higher than southern wages.

Charities and the *Annals of the American Academy of Political and Social*

Science continued to reflect the influence of Du Bois, Bulkley, and Wright Jr. long after their landmark issues on northern blacks. After 1906 each journal published fewer articles that said heredity rather than social and economic causes limited black people's industrial or intellectual capabilities. Both remained open to articles on black northern life and work by black social scientists and social workers and their allies.

The emergence of a unified and coherent methodological and analytical approach to black social and economic problems was met by a variety of responses by conservative whites and accommodationist blacks. Southern conservatives and segregationists generally ignored black challenges to their assertions of white superiority and questioned the notion that northern whites had any right to discuss the issue. If white southerners' racial views were not changed by the exposure of their methodological shortcomings, serious white northern academics that were sympathetic to the South were presented with a bit of an ethical dilemma. Should they expose the weaknesses of the southern argument or should they remain quiet and continue to support its conclusions? Influential white northern social scientists, such as the economist and statistician Walter Willcox of Cornell University and the University of Wisconsin labor economist John R. Commons, consistently let their prejudices against blacks affect their research findings. John R. Commons, one of the most influential early labor economists, openly espoused racist notions about blacks and other nonwhites. According to Commons, the democratic safeguards that were necessary to protect the rights of white immigrants need not apply to blacks or Asians. Commons argued that white men needed the protection of labor unions but blacks were too socially backward to be unionized. Commons's remarks were a justification of the discriminatory status quo in American unions.[84]

Walter Willcox, economist, statistician, dean at Cornell University, and advisor to the U.S. Bureau of the Census and other governmental agencies, was an influential figure in early American social science, serving as president of the American Economics Association (AEA), the American Statistical Association, and the International Statistical Institute. Willcox's research on black crime tended to confirm segregationists' claims that blacks were more likely to be criminals when outside of direct domination by whites. W. E. B. Du Bois and Kelly Miller took issue with the interpretation of data by Willcox and others, while Booker T. Washington initially found Willcox's views acceptable. Washington wrote to Willcox in 1899 to thank him for his writings on black crime, suggesting that although the statistics might be "disagreeable to many at first, in the end [they] do our cause lasting good." Washington held that Willcox's paper demonstrated that the "lack of permanent productive employment is at the bottom of a great deal of crime among the race." This view was not unlike R. R. Wright Sr.'s as he expressed it during the first Atlanta University Conference. But segregationists read Willcox's paper differently, and eventually the demagogic Mississippi governor James K. Vardaman began to cite Willcox as an independent northern authority whose work justified Vardaman's assertions that educated blacks were more likely to be criminals than illiterate blacks. Building on this idea, Vardaman argued that state funds for black education were wasted and should be completely eliminated. Confronted with this turn of events, Washington appealed to Willcox to disavow this use of his writings but was disappointed with the economist's tepid reply.[85]

Willcox told Du Bois that he was an "agnostic" on the issue of whether blacks had permanently inferior racial characteristics or whether their environment played some role in their present circumstances.[86] Du Bois could not have found this to be an encouraging remark, since it implied that Willcox had not been persuaded by Du Bois's scholarship, nor did it mark the economist as being particularly enthusiastic about the possibilities of reform. Willcox gave his strong personal support to those white scholars who claimed that slavery had had a wholly beneficial effect on blacks and who argued for white domination of blacks in every aspect of their lives. Willcox was also not above stretching his data, ignoring data that contradicted his views, and formulating studies in such a way that confirmed his opinions. While Willcox's opinions of blacks were not very different from the majority of late nineteenth- and early twentieth-century white social scientists, they were especially important because he was one of the few prominent social scientists to write about blacks. According to the economist Mark Aldrich, Willcox was well aware of the low quality of his scientific evidence, and he concealed his attempts to thwart the publication of Du Bois's counterarguments and data.[87]

Walter Willcox was instrumental in arranging for the publication and promotion of two of the most racist monographs issued by the American Economics Association. He had originally accepted Frederick L. Hoffman's "Race Traits and Tendencies of the American Negro" (1896) monograph for the American Statistical Association but persuaded the AEA to publish it in full, giving it a far wider and more prestigious outlet. Willcox was evidently not impressed by the modernists' counterclaims to Hoffman, despite the rebuttals of Hoffman by Kelly Miller and Du Bois, because he wrote the introduction for his student Joseph A. Tillinghast's 1902 monograph, "The Negro in Africa and America," also published by the American Economics Association. Tillinghast's monograph was, if anything, even more outrageous and objectionable than Hoffman's, because it claimed that blacks were naturally bestial and vicious and needed to be completely dominated by whites lest they destroy themselves and others as well. Tillinghast also directly disputed W. E. B. Du Bois's findings in *The Philadelphia Negro* and lauded the accommodationist strategy of Booker T. Washington.[88]

Du Bois was rarely hesitant to upbraid northern whites for making what he considered racist and nonscientific statements, but he was slow to criticize Willcox. At last he was provoked by a letter Willcox wrote to him expressing doubt on the impact of the color line on black economic conditions. Willcox argued:

> It is impossible for me to judge how far the present economic condition of the American Negro is due to persistent characteristics of the people and how far it is due to the heavy economic and social pressure upon them, resulting from drawing the color line in society, in politics and in industry. . . . I do not see that the evidence warrants one in holding either opinion with confidence. . . . Nor can I agree with the bitter condemnation of present social processes that characterizes your view of them. The gradual displacement of one social class by another can only by figure of speech be called murder.[89]

In his heated reply, Du Bois rebuked Willcox for his pamphlet on black crime and for writing Tillinghaust's introduction:

> I have my prejudices but they are backed by knowledge if not supported. How on earth any fair-minded student of the situation could have stood sponsor for a book like Tillinghast's and actually praised it is simply beyond my comprehension. If you insist on writing about and pronouncing judgment on this problem why not study it? Not from a car-window & associated press dispatches as in your pamphlet on crime but get down here and really study it at first hand. Is it sufficient answer to a problem to say the data are not sufficient when they lie all about us?[90]

The sharpness of the exchange between the two men did not openly change their relationship. And although Willcox spoke at the 1905 Atlanta University Conference, he also began to conceal his efforts to weaken Du Bois's impact within the world of social science.

The scholarly debate over how to study black life—emphasizing dubious biological or environmental factors—was not ended by the creation of the social reform coalition. And if modernist black scholars now had powerful allies, the acceptance of their research by some social scientists did not mean that other well-placed men and women were as easily won over to the socio-economic point of view. The emphasis on social and economic causation by W. E. B. Du Bois and his cadre of segregated scholars was a fundamental shift not only in the way many white academics identified the causes and possible cures for problems brought about by black subordination but in the way some black Americans thought about it as well. Therefore full acceptance of modernist theories took time even for blacks. At the meetings of white professional organizations, Booker T. Washington or a close associate might be asked to join a panel when Du Bois or one of his allies was making a presentation. Washington was frequently quoted by northern white academics such as Joseph Tillinghast, who felt obliged to deliver a scientific critique of the modernists' environmental thesis. The causes and possible cures for black social, political, and economic problems were debated throughout black America but especially at the annual Atlanta University and Hampton Institute Conferences. Some participants at the first Atlanta University and Hampton Institute meetings, for example, specifically denied that urban health problems such as poor housing conditions and higher death rates could be improved. Others took issue with Kelly Miller's formal challenge to Frederick Hoffman's racist views. Professor Eugene Harris of Fisk and Dr. F. J. Shadd, a Washington, D.C., physician, both ridiculed the notion that more sanitary living conditions might lower the black death rate. High death rates, in their view, were a warning to lower-class blacks to improve their moral condition or face complete extinction.[91] Booker T. Washington at times collaborated with white social scientists, such as Walter Willcox, who sought to weaken Du Bois's growing influence among those social scientists who studied American societal change. Conservative black leaders' analyses of the causes of black poverty, illness, and crime changed more completely than did the views of most white social scientists because southern white segregationists began to deftly use sociological articles to justify increasingly oppressive laws and customs. Eventually even Washington learned how to construct a basic progressive and modernist argument for a more objective interpretation of data.[92]

The American Sociological Association and the *American Journal of Sociology* did not play a major role in assisting the development of black labor studies, nor did it give much serious attention to black American life before World War I. American economists were interested in both race and labor, but their reactions to the labor studies of Du Bois were more complex. The

American Economics Association was not able to come to the same kind of general consensus on the significance of environmental causes for black social and economic problems as were symbolized by the *Charities* and the AAPSS session papers. By contrast the AEA had published two of the most detailed examples of scientific racism of the era in the works of Hoffman and Tillinghast, both of whom claimed to prove that social and economic disparities were the result of genetic differences between the two races. W. E. B. Du Bois, Kelly Miller, and others made presentations, wrote articles, and privately contacted the AEA editors to counter Tillinghast and Hoffman. Because of Du Bois's growing prominence he was asked to participate in a December 1905 AEA panel entitled "The Economic Position of the Negro," which featured papers by Du Bois and Alfred Holt Stone with four responders.[93]

Stone's and Du Bois's papers and the responses to them reflected the divisions among economists on the race question. Stone's paper, "The Economic Future of the Negro: The Factor of White Competition," argued that black workers had bad habits and permanent disabilities that rendered them unable to compete with whites for jobs. Stone saw segregation as beneficial to black laborers because it prevented their certain defeat in a truly open market. He argued that black workers' experiences in the North demonstrated that prejudice and discrimination existed only when blacks tried vainly to compete for jobs for which they were unqualified. In the South, by contrast, there was no color prejudice against skilled blacks, precisely because the color line kept white workers happy, an argument that contradicted Stone's point about black northern workers. Stone cautioned that if black people were not careful and did not recognize that the current economic and political arrangements were in their own best interest, the long-simmering patience that southern planters had for the many flaws of their black workers would boil over in frustration. Whites would be forced to replace their black workers with a more pliant workforce, he warned, and African Americans would become completely redundant. Then, unable to make a living in either the North or the South, the race would face sure extinction. Stone, who had experimented with Italian immigrant laborers on his Mississippi plantation, believed southern Europeans might provide a solution to southern labor shortages. His labor arrangements for his own plantation made at least part of his threat somewhat credible.

Stone's carefully constructed argument lacked the venom and personal invective of many southern white political extremists, but it still maintained that blacks must stay under the strict supervision of whites. His evidence was largely limited to the anecdotal statements of Booker T. Washington and

The Segregated Scholars

white segregationists presented in an academic format; Stone gave a statement of the problem, reviewed the evidence, and offered solutions and conclusions. While to Du Bois and other Niagara men, Stone's argument was just one piece of the crazy quilt of segregationist strategies, it was more bothersome to Booker T. Washington, as he would soon be obliged to try to separate his accomodationist rhetoric from the fabric of racist ideology.[94]

W. E. B. Du Bois's paper, "The Economic Future of the Negro," was a comprehensive presentation of the historical developments that led to the existing class structure and the future economic prospects of African Americans. This was Du Bois's first extended discussion of the notion of black economic development by means of a "group economy," a theme on which he would continue to elaborate throughout his life. Du Bois's view of black postbellum experience was that of steady progress against the formidable odds of the legacy of slavery, union hostility, economic discrimination, and political exclusion; it was in direct contrast to Stone's gloomy portrait of black inefficiency. The future prosperity of southern blacks, according to Du Bois, was dependent on their access to the protection of the law, voting rights, and the opportunity for a basic education. Sharecropping, he argued, was an inadequate economic system because it did not provide incentives to sharecroppers that would allow them to improve their situation. Denying Stone's claim that segregation was good for white workers, Du Bois argued that instead of protecting white wages, segregation lowered wages and working conditions for whites because employers could use the threat of a large black surplus labor force to quiet white demands. Whereas Alfred Holt Stone described the "Negro problem" as the failure of northern whites and all blacks to accept white southerners' presumed superior knowledge of the situation, W. E. B. Du Bois restated his contention that the "Negro problem" was an interwoven "plexus" of historical, economic, and political situations confronting black Americans.[95]

The full presentation of these opposing points of view posed somewhat of a challenge for the audience. On the one hand, Du Bois's argument was systematic and scientific. On the other hand, Stone was a white southern gentleman who was presumed to have firsthand knowledge of the local situation. A correspondent of the liberal *Nation* magazine praised all the speakers in the session as a "group of men qualified in a very unusual degree to speak"; he said this was the only AEA session that "left nothing to be desired," both in terms of "keen interest and actual substance." However, despite his enthusiasm for the session, the writer was troubled by the obvious contradictions in the two arguments: "But the contrariety of opinion—indeed the opposition of facts was so marked as to depress even the most optimistic believer in the possibility of a 'solution' to the Negro question. On the one hand, the Black was shown to be a thrifty, reasonably industrious peasant, whose standard of life rises rapidly under favorable conditions, and on the other hand he was characterized as a besotted degenerate, from whom neither progress nor even stability may be expected."[96] This was a rather plain expression of the differences between Stone and Du Bois and the dilemma these differences presented observers who were not already partisans in the larger questions of black political and economic rights.

After the *Nation's* review of the AEA session appeared, W. G. Leland of the Carnegie Institution defended Stone's contention that Italian laborers were more efficient than blacks. This defense of Stone's accuracy was also dependent on vague and nonscientific claims. Leland argued that it was A. H. Stone not W. E. B. Du Bois who was "truly the friend" of black people, because Stone did not look at their condition as "the blind optimist who judges the Negro masses by the talented 10th."[97] Leland's statement was a clear signal that the Carnegie Institution might not be sympathetic to studies using a socioeconomic approach to black social problems. The decision to support Stone, who had done no empirical research, and to rebuff Du Bois, who was backed by nearly a decade of Atlanta University studies, was one of the first signs that continued funding for Du Bois's research at Atlanta University, which was never plentiful, would be increasingly in jeopardy.

Nevertheless, Du Bois was successful in winning some converts, and the AEA became divided in its approach to black economic issues. This division, while disappointing to Du Bois, can be seen as an indication that his arguments were winning at least some converts. Du Bois might have had even more support if Walter Willcox, one of the AEA's most prominent members, had not worked to undercut him and promote Stone. In the long run, the AEA's failure to come to terms with scientific racism, coupled with the *American Journal of Sociology's* failure to publish substantive articles on black life, meant that serious research and writing about blacks moved just slightly outside the academic mainstream in both economics and sociology.[98] Without doubt this helped to push early twentieth-century black social scientists even closer to the applications-oriented social work publications and professional associations.

The attempts of Walter Willcox to thwart the efforts of W. E. B. Du Bois while promoting the dubious claims of southern segregationists are illustrative of the practical difficulties that early black social scientists encountered in gaining acceptance for their work. When the American Economics Association set up a Committee on the Economic Condition of the Negro to examine the differences in the claims of Hoffman and Tillinghast and those of Du Bois and the modernists, Willcox invited Du Bois's participation. However, when Du Bois was unwilling to sign the committee's final report because he thought that the dollar estimates of black wealth and property holding proposed by Willcox and Alfred Holt Stone were far too low, Willcox asked Booker T. Washington—who did not have a college degree—to support his figures. And with Washington's concurrence, Willcox submitted the report over Du Bois's objections.[99]

With Willcox's support, by 1907 Alfred Holt Stone had become the officially sanctioned expert on the "Negro problem," receiving major funding from the Carnegie Institution. Even after Booker T. Washington began to recognize the problem with Stone's arguments and opposed grants to him, the Carnegie Institution awarded the southern planter and amateur sociologist substantial funds to study and produce publications on the race problem.[100] Although Du Bois did not immediately realize it, much of his external funding stopped about the same time as Stone's began. When Du Bois wrote directly to Andrew Carnegie for funding to expand his Atlanta University studies to include "the history and condition of the American Negro," Carnegie did not bother to reply. But it was at approximately the same time that Andrew Carnegie made a large award to Booker T. Washington for his personal use and began underwriting two of Washington's programs—the National Negro Business League and the Committee of Twelve for the Negro Race.[101]

This was not the only instance in which Willcox succeeded in thwarting efforts by Du Bois and other blacks to obtain and publish accurate statistics. In another instance, Willcox stymied efforts by the U.S. Bureau of the Census to collect accurate data on lynching by changing the wording of the questionnaire. Ironically, Alfred H. Stone favored retaining the questions suggested by blacks that were designed to determine the alleged crime that sparked this extralegal murder. Stone believed these statistics would confirm his hypothesis that lynchings occurred in areas with the least segregation of the races. However, Willcox and the census director S. N. D. North were sensitive to the likelihood of strong southern congressional opposition to the collection of such sensitive information. Blacks, most significantly Ida B. Wells, had already published data indicating that the majority of lynchings were reprisals for economic independence or reactions to the perceived lack of deference by blacks and not for alleged sexual offenses. The possibility of collecting clarifying federal data was quashed. In this instance Willcox sacrificed objectivity for political expediency, and the national debate on lynching was forced to continue without data that were accepted by all parties as authoritative.[102]

Alfred Stone did attempt to placate Du Bois's criticisms—and to draw on his expertise—by subcontracting him for a small study on black business. With funding for the Atlanta University Conference at an all-time low, Du Bois was obliged to accept Stone's money in order to have any Atlanta University Conference in 1907—even though the topic that Stone selected forced Du Bois to change the sequence of annual conferences. Du Bois dealt with this incident with sarcasm in *Dusk of Dawn*, his first autobiography: "Why they selected him and neglected an established center like Atlanta University, I cannot imagine."[103] Having to work under Stone infuriated Du Bois and made him question the objectivity of his fellow scholars. In his last autobiography he expressed himself more frankly: "This is standard American procedure; if there is a job to be done and a Negro fit to do it, do not give the job or the responsibility to the Negro; give it to some white man and let the Negro work under him."[104]

In 1905–6 Du Bois could not imagine the degree of opposition that his research would encounter. What would become even more important and more disconcerting to Du Bois than having to accept money from Stone would be the suppression and then destruction of the last of his U.S. Bureau of Labor studies. This was the unmistakable sign that his research was now considered to have undesirable political connotations. For years Du Bois had been lobbying for funds that would enable him to make a comprehensive study of a Black Belt county. In early 1906, after Carroll Wright had left the Labor Bureau, Du Bois received approval to do a study of black social and economic conditions in Lowndes County, Alabama. He began in the summer of 1906 with R. R. Wright Jr. and Monroe Work as his chief assistants and approximately one dozen interviewers working with them. This was the most sophisticated social study that Du Bois had ever attempted, and for the first time he had full-time, professionally trained graduate assistants. Wright and Work were as enthusiastic about the project as was Du Bois. Both men dropped what they were doing for the opportunity to work under Du Bois. Wright was so anxious to participate in the research project that he temporarily halted his efforts to set up a workingmen's association in Philadelphia. Once the research was completed over the three summer months, Du Bois then wrote a narrative, corrected the statistical tables and schedules, prepared maps of land holdings, and prepared to forward the study to Washington, D.C. As he would not be paid the two thousand dollars for the study until it was completed, Du Bois had paid his assistants' and researchers' salaries as well as secured the necessary supplies with money advanced him by Atlanta University. He could not afford the costs to make copies of the study with all its attachments, so he forwarded his only handwritten copy to Washington, D.C. But the study was never published. Reportedly it was suppressed by the new commissioner of labor, who refused to return it to Du Bois. The only copy was apparently destroyed, no portion of it was ever published, and no trace of it has been found.[105]

The Department of Labor incident was Du Bois's first unequivocal indication that the political environment was hostile to his scholarship as well as troubled by his political opposition to Booker T. Washington. The pain and disillusionment of this realization was still palpable as he wrote about it six decades later: "So far as the American world of science and letters was concerned, we never 'belonged'; we remained unrecognized in learned societies and academic groups. We rated merely as Negroes studying Negroes, and after all, what had Negroes to do with America or science?"[106]

Even as Du Bois was completing the Lowndes County investigation, a heightening of racial tensions in the South also made it more difficult for him to continue as a social scientist. The Atlanta riot occurred while Du Bois was in Lowndes County, and he rushed home to protect his family. Support for the militant stance of the Niagara Movement grew sharply among black intellectuals in the wake of the riot. Du Bois was now ready to leave Atlanta University. He was nearing forty, and while he was his race's greatest and most prolific scholar, he believed he had not done enough to prevent the worsening conditions of black people. Du Bois was now faced with a dilemma. Booker T. Washington was apparently quashing his bids to leave the South, and Atlanta University was suffering from reduced donations from wealthy contributors irritated by Du Bois's presence on the faculty. Du Bois asked himself: "What with all my dreaming, studying, and teaching was I going to do in this fierce fight? . . . notwithstanding my deep desire to serve and follow and think, rather than to lead and inspire and decide, I found myself suddenly the leader of a great wing of people fighting against another and greater wing."[107] When the National Association for the Advancement of Colored People was organized in 1909, Du Bois was asked to move to New York City and become editor of their magazine, *The Crisis,* and director of research. He merged the Niagara Movement and the magazine *Horizon* into the new, integrated civil rights organization and quickly became its best-known spokesman.[108]

The first era of black social science was coming to a quiet end. Du Bois simply did not anticipate the obstacles he would face in raising research funds after he criticized Booker T. Washington in *The Souls of Black Folk*. Nor did he realize that white social scientists, government bureaucrats, and southern congressmen would join to limit studies on black social conditions. When black social scientists wanted to do southern survey research after 1906, they had to do it under the untrained Stone, through Booker T. Washington, or from their own pockets. The labor crisis of the Great Migration renewed federal interest in black workers, but, as we shall see in chapter 4, black scholars were restricted in their ability to conduct research in the South.

Du Bois was not the only black person who found himself pushed or pulled away from social science research in the decade before World War I. After spending the summer of 1906 with Du Bois and Monroe Work in Alabama, R. R. Wright Jr. went back to Philadelphia, where he conducted minor studies for Booker T. Washington's Committee of Twelve for the Negro Race and for Alfred Holt Stone. Wright then returned to his position as part-time field secretary of the Armstrong Association, named after the founder of Hampton Institute and funded by conservative white businessmen, and worked on his dissertation. His living expenses were partially underwritten by his salary from the Armstrong Association. As field secretary, Wright attempted to develop a program designed to improve black workers' income. He organized two hundred mechanics into the self-supporting Colored Mechanics Association, which assisted artisans in finding and bidding on jobs. Years earlier as an industrial student in Georgia, Wright had learned to read architectural drawings, and he used this expertise to help black construction tradesmen in Philadelphia develop competitive estimates. He had a black assistant who could pass for white and who got jobs for association members by not revealing their race. However, Wright's efforts were met with continuous opposition from the Armstrong Association's conservative white board members; after two years, he resigned his position. The idea that black and white intellectuals and social reformers could work together on an equal basis began to seem increasingly illusory to Wright. The AME Church's black-controlled administrative structure began to look more and more attractive, and in 1908 Wright accepted the editorship of the church's weekly, the *Christian Recorder*. When Wright completed his doctorate in 1911, he turned down an offer from Howard University to become an instructor in sociology and spent the next sixty-five years in the AME Church, serving as an editor of the *Christian Recorder*, as president of Wilberforce University, and, finally, as a bishop, the highest position in the church.[109]

There were probably fewer than two dozen blacks who had any graduate training in the social sciences by 1910, and only a few had published and participated in scholarship on a national level. In the space of one decade (1901–11), R. R. Wright Jr. had contributed articles to a number of journals, including the *Annals of the American Academy of Political and Social Science,* the *American Journal of Sociology, Charities,* and *Southern Workman;* conducted studies for the Pennsylvania Bureau of Industrial Statistics; contributed an article on black steelworkers to Paul Kellogg's influential *Pittsburgh Survey;* and produced a census of black Baptists in Mississippi for the U.S. Bureau of the Census. The departure from active scholarship of both W. E. B. Du Bois and R. R. Wright Jr., as well as Monroe Work's 1908 decision to move to Tuskegee and deemphasize the political content of his work, threatened to have a grave effect on black social science and labor studies. In 1910, however, George Edmund Haynes left the YMCA and began his career in sociology and social work, continuing the scholarship and institutionalizing the mentoring performed for the first cadre of black social scientists.

Institutionalizing Mentorship: The Vision of George Edmund Haynes

George Haynes was a clear beneficiary of the new interest that white reformers such as Paul U. Kellogg, Edward T. Devine, Frances Kellor, and Mary White Ovington had already shown in studies of black northern workers. Soon after Haynes entered the New York School of Philanthropy (NYSP) in 1908, his course work impressed Devine, who was then head of the school's Bureau of Social Research and a faculty member of Columbia University's sociology department. With Devine's assistance Haynes was admitted to the doctoral program in the sociology department of Columbia University while remaining an NYSP student. Haynes's tuition and most of his graduate school expenses were covered by research fellowships at the Bureau of Social Research.[110]

Haynes's first assignment for the Bureau of Social Research was to study the migration of blacks to New York City, a subject that would become his specialty. At the same time William L. Bulkley hired Haynes to interview students at his evening industrial school. Haynes's interviews with Bulkley's students would profoundly shape the conclusions in his subsequent studies of the Great Migration. The NYSP's Bureau of Social Research had begun its study with the assumption that blacks might be migrating north for different reasons than whites. Haynes's initial survey results convinced him that black and white migration had essentially the same economic and social causes but differing consequences due to the difficulty black workers had in finding skilled jobs. Haynes then began to focus his research on black migrants' efforts to find better jobs and to learn the mores of urban industrial life. His second study for the Bureau of Social Research was an investigation of employment opportunities, attitudes of workers and employers, and black business in New York City. Haynes summarized his studies for the Bureau of Social Research and his interviews for Bulkley in his doctoral thesis, "The Negro at Work in New York City." Haynes completed his dissertation on black workers in New York City in 1912, becoming the third black American to receive a doctorate in sociology.[111]

Upon his arrival in New York, George Haynes had also moved rapidly into mainstream efforts to institutionalize social welfare services for black New Yorkers. His research at William Bulkley's school placed him in regular contact with Bulkley and other members of the Committee for Improving the Industrial Conditions of Negroes in New York, which Bulkley had founded. Haynes's studies at NYSP and the Bureau of Social Research introduced him to Ruth Standish Bowles Baldwin, Frances Kellor, and other members of the National League for the Protection of Colored Women (NLPCW). Ruth Baldwin was the widow of William H. Baldwin, president of the Long Island Railroad and philanthropist, who had been a trustee of Tuskegee University. She was interested in continuing her late husband's interest in blacks and thought that the time had come to combine, coordinate, and redirect the efforts of the voluntary committees interested in specific aspects of black social welfare into a more permanent professional organization. Haynes helped Baldwin to formulate a plan that would bring together the NLPCW and the Committee for Improving the Industrial Conditions among Negroes (CIICN) in an umbrella-like structure that promised to retain each group's separate identity but provide more clearly defined national goals. The CIICN was initially cool to the plan, but through Haynes and Baldwin's persistence, a Committee on Urban Conditions among Negroes (CUCAN) was formed in the fall of 1910, absorbing both the CIICN and NLPCW. One year later CUCAN was reorganized and renamed the National League on Urban Conditions among Negroes, which was later called the National Urban League for Social Service among Negroes, and is now the National Urban League (NUL). Within two years of his arrival in New York City for graduate training, George Haynes had helped to found what would quickly become the most important national private social service agency for black workers.[112]

Although Haynes was named the National League on Urban Condition's first executive secretary, he carried out his duties at Fisk University, where he had accepted a position as professor of sociology. From 1910 to 1918 he spent the academic year in Nashville and part of each summer and winter vacation in New York City at NUL headquarters. This arrangement reflected the limited budget of the new organization and Haynes's belief that the program in New York City could be overseen by the board and directed by his assistant, while a program to train social workers could only be implemented by him and sustained at a Negro college.[113] Haynes was determined to combine teaching and social work administration, and he was convinced that dividing his time between the New York City headquarters and Fisk would enable him to select and train large numbers of black students in social work techniques who would be placed in positions with the NUL and private and public social service agencies. Haynes told the National Conference of Charities and Corrections that placing social work training programs at Negro colleges was logical because the best candidates for the new profession could most easily be found among "the large groups of select, capable, enthusiastic Negro youth . . . at these colleges . . . [and] because the city conditions among Negroes demand minds and characters which have been moulded by a broad course of education."[114]

George Haynes's activities at Fisk University brought him back to the script of sacrifice and obedience that he had written as an undergraduate. He was not interested in establishing a center for social research along the lines of what W. E. B. Du Bois had done at Atlanta University, but he wanted to offer sociology and black history to all undergraduates and to select the best students for advanced study in sociology or social work. Haynes was convinced that the expertise of all educated blacks was necessary to bring positive changes to the lives of black workers but that mere race pride was not sufficient to deal with black urban problems. Haynes argued that black leaders also needed to be acquainted with both the methodology of the social sciences and the principles of social work: "The problem of social uplift is so great that, in addition to expert social workers, all Negro ministers, doctors, lawyers, teachers and others should have the benefit of instruction in scientific methods and the new social point of view."[115]

In most areas George Haynes was an institutionalizing rather than an innovating force. At Fisk University Haynes followed the earlier attempts of Du Bois and Kelly Miller to introduce sociology and black history to the curricula of the liberal arts black colleges.[116] He set up a Department of Social Sciences at Fisk University that introduced sociology courses to Fisk and made Negro history a central part of the requirements for a concentration in social science. This was an indication of the equal weighting that black social scientists gave to black history and sociology in the curriculum. Haynes also required fieldwork for social work majors and introduced courses in general sociology and economics, research methods, and black socioeconomic problems.

Like his mentor W. E. B. Du Bois, George Edmund Haynes began his career as a sociologist with a plan for racial advancement that called for scientific research as the foundation for social change. Unlike Du Bois, Haynes attempted to combine an academic career with one in social welfare. Du Bois was never as interested in the administration or implementation of practical projects, preferring research and political commentary. Although Haynes's goals were perhaps less lofty than Du Bois's, they were no less ambitious. George Haynes wanted to direct the implementation of organizational goals for the NUL while he established a professional training program for black social workers. Haynes's plan for training black social workers had three components, each of which he hoped would be replicated by other institutions. The first part was the undergraduate training program at Fisk. The second was to build on his academic success in order to convince the New York School of Philanthropy faculty to regularly admit jointly selected black students as graduate students. This program, called the Urban League Fellows Program, quickly expanded to include fully funded graduate training at the master's level in sociology, economics, or social work at a number of universities. The Urban League Fellows Program had a fieldwork requirement that was fulfilled by working at the National Urban League in New York City or one of its branches throughout the country. This provided the NUL movement with highly skilled employees at no cost and avoided having to integrate placements. The Urban League Fellows Program became a feeder program for NUL branch executives and supplied the funding for master's level work in sociology or economics for many future black social scientists, including Abram L. Harris and Ira De A. Reid, whose careers are discussed in subsequent chapters. Finally, Haynes started what became known as the Broken Fellows Program, which was geared toward black teachers and other college graduates who completed their fieldwork in their communities and took courses giving them the certification necessary to prepare them for a mid-level career in social service.[117]

By insisting on a college education, field placement experiences, and graduate training for social workers, Haynes sought to keep black social workers from forming an inferior caste within the social work profession. Like other early black social scientists and their white allies, Haynes believed that professional training and methodological expertise were preferable to sentiment and empathy when working for racial advancement. But there were many obstacles in his way. Professional careers for blacks were limited largely to teaching and preaching, areas that did not require college degrees. Haynes's belief that black migrants had to be served by black professional social workers was jeopardized by the small number of blacks who qualified as candidates for graduate school. He attempted to establish social work as a graduate career at a time when less than 16 percent of all black teachers were college graduates. Haynes's success came because he was able to match training opportunities with black candidates eager for new career options. The opportunities Haynes and the NUL created attracted bright and ambitious black men and women who took advantage of the prestigious graduate school placements, the high salaries of NUL branch executives, and the possibility of having a significant influence on race relations. The most important replications of Haynes's model were the Atlanta School of Social Work and the Howard University School of Social Work, both of which were founded by NUL fellows.[118]

Conclusion

By the onset of the Great Migration the landscape of black social science and black labor studies had significantly changed. Booker T. Washington, who at the turn of the century had collaborated with the white social scientists who sought to weaken W. E. B. Du Bois's growing influence among those academics and reformers who studied American societal change, had become as adept at the arguments to counter scientific racism as the modernists. However, Washington was constrained by his sources of funding to use these arguments in private correspondence and not openly challenge segregationists. Some key white journals, such as *Charities* and the *Annals of the American Academy of Political and Social Science,* published fewer articles that claimed that heredity rather than social and economic causes limited black people's industrial or intellectual capabilities. But professional academic organizations such as the

American Sociological Association and the American Economics Association were more reluctant to give up one of the cardinal principles of scientific racism—biological determinism. The black men who had joined W. E. B. Du Bois as social scientists had become active in specific reform projects while they were graduate students in part as a way of financing their studies. In doing so they came to work closely with white reformers and with black community groups to create programs to assist urban black workers. It was George Edmund Haynes who successfully institutionalized this link between social science and social reform projects. From his base at Fisk University he worked to ensure the creation of the next generation of labor scholars and social workers. In his position at the National Urban League, he worked with northern white universities to provide fellowships and placements for the post–World War I social scientists such as Charles S. Johnson, E. Franklin Frazier, Abram L. Harris, and Ira De A. Reid.

As George Haynes began his endeavors, Du Bois encountered opposition to his scholarly work in the South. His funding for social surveys, which was always limited, began to evaporate. Although social research in the South was far more difficult after Du Bois's departure from Atlanta University in 1910, local social welfare efforts by blacks in cities such as Atlanta and Nashville grew steadily in the second decade of the twentieth century, partially fueled by the beneficiaries of Haynes's new training program at Fisk University. Wright Jr. and Haynes both found white scholars, philanthropists, and government officials who encouraged their research on black labor in northern cities, even as Du Bois's efforts to press forward with his economic studies of the South were being thwarted. The stage was set for both the geographical and the institutional shift in the center of black labor studies.

The experiences of Wright and Haynes as researchers and their efforts to work as professional sociologists were important early factors for black labor studies shifting its geographical location to the North despite the fact that, at the time, the majority of black workers remained in the South. But it was George Edmund Haynes who had made the decision by 1905 to forego a career in the ministry, who had—by his involvement in the YMCA—been perfectly poised upon his arrival in New York City to take advantage of the new opportunities for real collaboration between black and white social investigators and social reformers, and who would prepare the ground for the next generation of black social scientists. It was the careful survey and ethnographic methods that he developed in his doctoral studies on black workers in New York City that would set the model for the next era of black migration studies.

Haynes's research and organizational innovations characterized black social science during World War I and offered a programmatic strategy that would be extended by his successors at the National Urban League, such as Charles S. Johnson, and countered by black social scientists with more socialist theoretical approaches, such as Abram Harris.

3 Black Women, Social Science, and Social Reform from the Turn of the Century to the Great Migration

The Negro woman . . . alone has the power to uproot ignorance, break down prejudice and solve for us this great race problem. . . . She has not only to contend with the disabilities which affect the Negro race, but against the added disability of sex.

—Grace Hadnott, "The Mission of the Negro Woman"

The journalist and reformer Victoria Earle Matthews was applauded by other black clubwomen when she undertook a survey to determine "the true statistics of our people morally" in 1894, two years before the founding of the Atlanta University Conference on Urban Negro Problems. Black clubwomen fully endorsed Matthews's decision to turn to sociological methods: "The idea is bright, progressive. We co-workers appreciate her efforts, her executive ability, and shall ever give her our hearty support."[1] The commitment of black intellectuals to use social science as a vehicle for planning social reforms predated W. E. B. Du Bois's arrival in Atlanta; black women's individual and organized commitment to use social research to plan new programs and combat racial injustices functioned independently of Du Bois and his growing cadre of male scholars—albeit not always by choice. The school founder Lucy Laney was one of a half-dozen women social activists who presented their research on black communities during the Atlanta University Conference's first two years. By the end of the first decade of the twentieth century, black clubwomen could point to a number of concrete examples of their application of social science research in social reforms, such as free kindergartens, recreation centers, and other programs designed to assist working mothers and their children.

Young black female undergraduates at Atlanta and Fisk Universities were as eager as George Haynes and R. R. Wright Jr. to apply modern solutions to the race problem. W. E. B. Du Bois's female students at Atlanta University wrote sociology and economics theses on a wide range of topics and did most of the research for his 1899 Bureau of Labor study, "The Negro in the Black Belt." Haynes's Fisk University 1903 classmates Grace Hadnott and Elizabeth Ross shared his determination to use their education to solve the larger problems of the race. Ross crisply advised black people that progress was inevitable, and that failure to keep up with the demands of the modern era would result in having to "endure the dust" of others who were marching ahead on the road of life.[2] Echoing sentiments that had been expressed as early as 1892 by the educator Anna Julia Cooper, in the terminology of black sociologists, Grace Hadnott argued that racism and sexism had to be overcome so that an educated black woman could fulfill her mission to uplift all black people: "The future of the Negro race lies in the hands of its women. . . . She alone has the power to uproot ignorance, break down prejudice and solve for us this great race problem."[3]

Lacking the support and mentoring that helped Haynes and Wright become professional sociologists by 1910, Elizabeth Ross and her turn-of-the-century female classmates who had an interest in sociology and economics were funneled into careers in elementary school teaching and social work, with lower salaries, fewer promotions, and more severely limited opportunities to earn advanced degrees in the social sciences. Twenty years elapsed between Ross's graduation from Fisk and her master's degree in sociology, while her future husband, George Haynes, was able to earn a master's degree in 1905 and completed his doctorate in 1912, nine years after they graduated.

It is my contention that the desire black intellectuals and college students possessed to become social scientists or to use the social sciences to improve black people's economic and social conditions was not gendered. In the nineteenth century black clubwomen had an independent and parallel interest in the social sciences that predated the Atlanta University Conference, and turn-of-the-century black female college students studied sociology with the same excitement as male students. Black women's subsequent delay in obtaining advanced degrees, and failure to build careers as social scientists and or even work as labor specialists until the Great Migration were therefore the consequence of racial and gender discrimination rather than their lack of interest. In this chapter I argue that differences in women's undergraduate education, the lack of a network of academic mentors, and occupational dis-

crimination were the central causes for a delay in the training and employment of black women who may have wanted to become professional social
scientists at the turn of the century. Black labor studies as a profession developed as a predominately male endeavor, with the notable exception of a series
of studies undertaken during the Great Migration and discussed in chapter 5,
nearly silencing the voices but not completely stifling the aspirations of black
women.

This chapter covers roughly the same twenty-year time period, 1890–1910,
as the first two chapters, and follows the education, published writings, reforms, and careers of two generations of black women. Women in the first
group, referred to as black clubwomen, were born during the 1850s or 1860s,
and the group includes Victoria Earle Mathews, Lucy Laney, and other women
who were the colleagues of R. R. Wright Sr. and W. E. B. Du Bois. These black
women were the leaders and founders of a network of local, state, and national
women's clubs that championed social reforms and racial advancement.
Women in the second group, college students at the turn of the century, were
born in the late 1870s and early 1880s, and this group includes Elizabeth Ross
Haynes, Lugenia Burns Hope, and other women who were the age-mates and
classmates of George Haynes and R. R. Wright Jr. Unlike Haynes and Wright,
whose professional careers began shortly after the turn of the century, black
women in the second generation were not able to find paid work as professional social scientists until the Great Migration of blacks to the North was
underway.

In order to assess black women's interest in the social sciences in the nineteenth century, the chapter briefly resituates some of the writings and research of two black female journalists in the 1890s, Victoria Earle Matthews
and Ida B. Wells, and reconsiders the studies that black women presented at
the first two Atlanta University conferences. It then turns to the academic
preparation and socialization that black women had in and after college, which
effectively barred them from graduate schools and careers as social scientists
while motivating them to establish successful community programs based on
research they undertook as unpaid volunteers and underpaid social workers.
Finally, I contrast the occupational experiences of black women workers before the Great Migration with those of their would-be and future champions.

Independent Social Studies by Black Women in the Late Nineteenth Century

In May 1894, two years prior to the first meeting of the Atlanta University Conference, *The Women's Era* featured a report on the research design for a social study by Victoria Earle Matthews, who was the president of the Women's Loyal Union of New York City and Brooklyn. In her quest to find "the true statistics" for black people, Matthews had constructed a questionnaire to be administered by ministers, teachers, and other "representative men and women," such as the members of the Women's Loyal Union.[4] This is one of the earliest reports of a social survey that black Americans undertook, and it is worth underlining that the Women's Loyal Union not only helped to carry out the survey but their description of it as a "bright, progressive" idea indicates that they viewed it as a modernist response to social planning. Matthews attended the Colored Women's Congress at the 1895 Cotton States Exposition in Atlanta, and afterward she made her own investigative tour of southern cities, focusing on the condition of poor black women workers. On her return to New York City, Matthews founded the White Rose Mission, a social settlement house and home for migrant women.

Matthews's desire to use social science to better understand black people's lives was similar to that of R. R. Wright Sr. and the Atlanta University Conference founders, but Matthews and other nineteenth-century clubwomen and activists more quickly used their studies to design and implement new programs that assisted low-wage workers and tried to ameliorate unsatisfactory social conditions in black communities.

Matthews was similar in education and determination to other black women journalists at the turn of the century who had constructed careers and public lives as community and national leaders, including Ida B. Wells-Barnett, Gertrude Bustill Mossell, and Delilah Beasley. Born to enslaved Virginia parents in 1861, Matthews moved with her family to New York as a young child. She was largely self-educated, but became a well-respected journalist who wrote for white and black papers. In the late 1890s Matthews became concerned when she learned that some young, naive female migrants to New York City were forced into prostitution or placed in jobs in which they were virtually imprisoned. Historians have described how Matthews created the White Rose Mission in 1897, which sent social and travelers' aid workers to meet boats arriving in Richmond and New York City to provide black women migrants with information on housing and jobs. It has not been as clearly recognized that Matthews based the White Rose Mission on her research and observations of the social and economic conditions that confronted black women workers in the North and the South. She should be reconsidered as an equal partner in the intellectual milieu that inaugurated the study of black life, and as one of the major figures in social welfare on the East Coast. Matthews's premature death in 1907 prevented her from shaping the National Urban League, but her settlement house continued her mission.[5]

Ida B. Wells-Barnett was another progressive activist who used social research methods before Du Bois. Her examination of lynching in the United States suggested a strong causal relationship between these brutal state-sanctioned public murders and whites' perception of economic competition from black businesses. Wells's 1892 *On Lynching* and her 1895 *A Red Record* were interpretations of statistics she had carefully compiled, based on newspaper and court accounts. Wells used the evidence she gathered, largely from the white press, to refute white southern allegations that lynching and mob violence were justifiable responses to the rapes of white women by black men. Her books, pamphlets, and numerous newspaper articles exhaustively documenting the allegations that led to the public murders of black men and women dramatically demonstrated the potential power of social scientific methods to defend against racial injustices. Wells earned the sobriquet "The Princess of the Press" from admiring black audiences.[6]

Ida B. Wells was an investigative reporter and self-taught social scientist. Her social science training was much like that of LaFayette Hershaw, who often sent his studies to Du Bois to be incorporated in the Atlanta University Conference proceedings, but unlike Hershaw, Wells was not a college graduate. Like Victoria Matthews, Ida Wells was born a slave in the South in the 1860s. Wells had a normal school education in her home state of Mississippi, which she had supplemented with self-study and organized discussion groups. She used her pamphlets, books, and articles on lynching in much the same manner that educated black men such as R. R. Wright Sr. turned to the social sciences to combat the Social Darwinism of the period. But because Wells frankly discussed politically charged topics, such as consensual sex between white women and black men, she was threatened with death and forced into exile in the North. Wells was forced out of Memphis, but in her new home of Chicago she founded women's clubs, a kindergarten, and a settlement house and was an important member of local organizations dedicated to woman suffrage, racial uplift, and social welfare.[7]

Wells, Matthews, and Josephine St. Pierre Ruffin, founder of Boston's

Women's Era Club, incorporated their experience and commitment to insist that social services for black working women and children be part of the 1896 founding agenda of the National Association of Colored Women, the umbrella organization of state and local women's clubs. Even before the NACW existed, Ruffin had urged black women to examine labor issues. In an 1895 address to the National Conference of Colored Women she called on black women to come together to discuss preparing black children to enter the world of work. Ruffin argued that this was of "especial interest to us as colored women, the training of our children, openings for our boys and girls, how they can be trained for occupations and occupations may be found or opened for them." Dorothy Salem posits that Ruffin was invited to represent black women at the Cotton States Exposition in 1895 but refused to attend because of the segregation of black contributions. Matthews and black women from twenty-five states did participate in the women's congress at the exposition.[8] Educational and recreational programs for children, working mothers, and delinquents that black women's clubs sponsored were in place in Atlanta, New York City, Augusta, and other cities by the eve of the Great Migration, and all too often these were the only social services available to poor black workers and their families.

While Wells-Barnett, Ruffin, and Matthews were involved in the black women's club movement, they did not only study black women; their research was targeted at a variety of ills that beset black urban communities. Wells and Matthews were late nineteenth-century exemplars of what Elsa Barkley Brown has termed "womanist consciousness," in that their social activism was inextricably bound together in ideologies of sexual equality and racial uplift.[9] Black women's club local projects almost invariably assisted poor and working-class women as part of a community-improvement approach that also served children and men.[10] Wells and Matthews were responsible for important changes in the social reform movement's fight for black workers. They helped to disseminate the new approach of analysis and assessment of social problems affecting black workers to community-based activists. They set the standards for how black clubwomen would respond to the racist diatribes that stigmatized all African American women—with carefully assembled objective data. The Chicago-based Fannie Barrier Williams was one of the few clubwomen to have an article based on her observations published alongside the black male social scientists. Yet most of the early community surveys by black women were never published in their entirety, and few seem to have survived.[11] The best windows into the strengths and limitations of these self-taught social scientists are found in the proceedings of the Atlanta University conferences.

Black Women at the Atlanta University Conference

Black women were actively involved in the Atlanta University annual conference from its conception in 1895 until it ended twenty years later. Women presented their individual research, interviewed people, and conducted the annual surveys using questionnaires that were compiled into the yearly research reports—all the things that male conference participants did. The Atlanta University Conference also began holding a separate women's meeting at its second conference, in 1897. The women's meeting brought together black women reformers from all over the South, and it immediately became an important feature of the annual conference. The women's meeting, where women discussed local research projects and the social services that they were creating in their communities, was addressed by both men and women reformers but was largely attended by women. But separating the women from the men at the second conference led to separating women's concerns from the main conference and did not always give women's interests the same amount of critical attention by men and women that was given to the plenary sessions in subsequent conferences.

Louie D. Shivery and, more recently, Tera W. Hunter have detailed how the Atlanta University Conference women's meetings helped to launch kindergartens, day nurseries, and other programs designed to help working mothers. Women who attended the meeting learned about model programs and were given the moral support to start their own. Instituting similar community reforms became the official policy of the National Association of Colored Women. The Gate City Free Kindergarten Association was started in 1900 by women who had attended the first two conferences and an 1899 university meeting entitled the "The Welfare of the Negro Child." The Neighborhood Union of Atlanta, which was founded in 1908 and led by NACW member Lugenia Burns Hope, had perhaps the most fully implemented set of community programs. Hope had her first exposure to settlement work in her native Chicago, and like Matthews, she studied sociological methods on her own and developed community programs based on the results of her survey research.[12]

Black women's participation at the Atlanta University Conference was usually led by Lucy Laney, founder and principal of Haines Institute in Augusta, Georgia, and an 1874 graduate of Atlanta University's first normal school class.

Laney was well acquainted with the people and methods that animated the early black social sciences. She had attended the university's high school with R. R. Wright Sr., taught R. R. Wright Jr., and had taken summer courses at the University of Chicago at the turn of the century.[13] Laney's organizational skills helped to make the Atlanta University Conference one of the spring's most important events for southern social activists, who were linked in a network of state and national women's clubs, annual conferences of teachers and farmers at Tuskegee and Hampton Institutes, and gatherings of groups such as the Women's Christian Temperance Union (WCTU), the Young Woman's Christian Association (YWCA), and the National Baptist Women's Convention. The Atlanta University Conference was a space in which women began as equal scholarly partners, where they would gather to discuss practical applications of current research findings, and where their collective presence was an essential part of the meetings.

At the first Atlanta University Conference three of the six papers on the research topic of the causes of high black urban mortality rates were presented by women alumnae. The papers of Georgia Swift King, Rosa Morehead Bass, and Lucy Laney were as well informed and analytical as those of the three male presenters—two medical doctors and a college professor. All six suffered from the same tendency to draw some conclusions that represented their opinions rather than sticking only to those that flowed from their evidence. King, a WCTU leader, combined a learned review of the medical literature on alcoholism with her unsubstantiated opinion that the overwhelming majority of black and white city dwellers drank to excess. "It is in the cities that intemperance prevails. I believe that . . . ninety-nine per cent of the city population are addicted to some extent to the use of strong drink."[14] Bass offered a descriptive but more nuanced account of the effect of poverty on black death rates that contrasted the more healthy living conditions of the rural poor, in terms of their access to fresh water, garden vegetables, and invigorating farm labor, without romanticizing often unsatisfactory housing and living conditions in the countryside. She sarcastically described slavery as leaving black people only "the rich inheritance of a log cabin and a patch of turnip greens." Bass was no sentimentalist, and she over-optimistically predicted that the old slave cabins would "soon be entirely relegated to the barbarous past. Peace be to its ashes!" In calling for the eradication of rural one-room shacks, with their lack of privacy and history of sexual exploitation, Bass sounded a clarion call that would animate the black clubwomen's movement for the next decade.[15]

Despite the stated focus of the Atlanta University Conference on urban problems, Rosa Bass and other black women who presented papers refused to let their critical analyses be confined by either geography or gender. Time and again, labor issues appeared in women's discussions as they pursued the ramifications of black people's vulnerable economic status. Laney and Bass both described the dire consequences to child health and safety of poor black mothers having to leave their children without supervision while they worked. Although their analyses assumed that mothers bore the major responsibility for the care of children, neither placed a moral judgment on the difficult choices that working mothers faced, while other contemporary commentators, including Kelly Miller, claimed that poor black working women were willfully immoral and careless about their children.[16]

Lucy Laney's first Atlanta paper, "General Conditions of Mortality," offered multiple and interacting economic and social causes for high black communicable disease and death rates. Laney described how low incomes and cramped, unhealthy living quarters adversely affected the health of the working poor and the unemployed families in Augusta, Georgia. Her analysis took pains to establish separate classes or "grades of society" of black people based both on income and behavior, in much the same conflation W. E. B. Du Bois would make three years later when *The Philadelphia Negro* was published. Laney suggested low wages, long work days, and living conditions as factors in the higher death rates among black people. Laney described very poor black Augusta families, who survived by stringing together two or three days' worth of odd jobs and casual labor in a week, rarely earning more than fifty cents a day. These poorest families were hampered by their lack of knowledge of sanitary practices and were forced to rent single, dirty rooms from landlords who had not bothered to clean up after the previous tenants. Diseases and death abounded in such unhealthy conditions. Laney sardonically observed, "It is not long before hypostatic pneumonia or tuberculosis visits them, and finding the atmosphere congenial, abides with the family."[17]

Lucy Laney believed that the majority of blacks in her city were unable to avoid illness because of poverty, ignorance, and rapacious landlords. But she noted that even those persons who attempted to rise above the masses by buying their own homes could find that their economies forced them to skimp on food and rest. When these industrious souls amassed enough cash to purchase a plot of land, segregation limited their choices to swampy and unhealthy areas. Thus, Laney's observations led her to acknowledge that both the provident and the improvident succumbed to disease, which departed from both the gospel of wealth and the gospel of accommodationism. However, Laney undercut her findings by downplaying the probable effect of de facto housing segregation on high rates of black death and illness. She insisted that poor black people wanted to live close to each other and opened her paper with the stock phrase "birds of a feather flock together" to explain why "the poorest, most untidy, and most ignorant seek each other." This statement betrays Laney's class bias and the somewhat elitist assumptions that run through the papers of both women and men at the early Atlanta University conferences.[18]

The first three women's papers solidified women's participation at the Atlanta University Conference and seemed to lay the groundwork for increasingly more sophisticated approaches to social research by and about black women. These three papers expressed the earnest research efforts of black women reformers just before black clubwomen adopted an official approach to the problems of working-class black women. While Bass, King, and Laney, expressed critical views against poor housekeeping and drinking and called for a stronger work ethic, they did not emphasize the argument that poor and working-class black women needed to take on more elevated, moral, and cultivated behavior, which Evelyn Brooks Higginbotham has identified as the "politics of respectability."[19] Although the three clubwomen often described living conditions as deplorable, none of these papers enunciate the priority of black people to keep "true homes" that would soon be advocated by black women's clubs.

The resolutions of the second annual Atlanta University Conference, held in May 1897, revealed the public stance of black social activists on the relationship between black men's low wages and the large number of black working women, and the effects of both on family life. Calling the home "the great school for the molding of character," the resolutions developed by the women's meeting asked ministers to use their pulpits to address the failure of some men to properly support their families. The general resolutions passed during the second Atlanta University Conference strongly linked black people's poorer health and alleged immoral behavior in cities with the large number of working mothers, and declared that "the excessive mortality and . . . increase in immorality among the Negroes is chiefly due to neglect of home and family life, the chief cause of which is the extent to which mothers are obliged to go out to work."[20] This language contained the seeds of a politics of respectability, giving mothers the major responsibility for the moral and physical well-being of black families, but black women leaders were "doublevoiced," as Higginbotham reminds us, simultaneously calling for women to maintain orderly homes and supporting women who worked by creating child care and kindergartens.

Black women's work evoked much anxiety and comment among black intellectuals at the turn of the century. Kevin K. Gaines links this anxiety to an assertion of the need for stronger patriarchal authority by, but not limited to, the accommodationist Hampton–Tuskegee wing of the uplift movement, since Du Bois also conjoined class and morality with a husband's income and the wife's housekeeping skills in *The Philadelphia Negro*. The fact that so many black women worked was seen both as a detriment to the establishment of good homes and the proper care of children and as an indicator of black men's lack of economic progress. While Laney, Matthews, and other early black clubwomen leaders generally blamed the circumstances that forced women into disadvantageous positions rather than blaming black women who worked away from home, other men and women did not make this distinction. Kelly Miller, early twentieth-century dean and sociology professor at Howard University, blamed a variety of social ills on the numbers of unmarried black women in cities, whom he scorned as "surplus Negro women." The leaders of the NACW also found much wanting in the home life of working-class and poor black women, but they did not limit their actions to jeremiads like those of Miller. Instead, they devised a wide variety of practical programs to assist working mothers, job seekers, and poor communities.[21]

The Atlanta University conferences and Du Bois's Bureau of Labor studies gave black women some of the ammunition they needed to intervene in the largely male-centered assertion that women's place was limited to the home. Writing in Hampton Institute's *Southern Workman*, the educator Anna Julia Cooper used an 1899 Atlanta University study to sharply remind those advocating that black women stay out of the workplace that women were the sole or joint breadwinner in fully 57 percent of the Atlanta families surveyed. Showing impatience with rhetoric that was so far out of touch with the realities of everyday life and laying down a challenge to men to be better providers, Cooper pressed for recognition of the need for equal treatment for black women's labor in the workplace and as equal partners in their home. "If men can not or will not help the conditions which force women into the struggle for bread, we have a right to claim at least that she shall have fair play and all the rights of wage-earners in general."[22]

At the turn of the century, 54 percent of all black American women worked, two and a half times the percentage of white women in the labor force. Cooper, a widow, who had worked since her early teens, argued that black women actually suffered more than men from unfavorable economic conditions because they were left to support their children: "She is the one who must meet and conquer the conditions." It is worth noting that Cooper, an Oberlin graduate and past master of the Victorian essay with classical and biblical allusions, based her argument on behalf of working women on a sociological study. This was an indication of the way that educated black women were also utilizing the social sciences as tools to assert their authority in public discourse.[23]

The Atlanta City Conference was just one site of the ongoing sociological studies by black women, but we can best trace their activities outward from brief and tantalizing accounts within its published reports. Georgia Swift King, an 1874 Atlanta University normal school graduate, did not confine her interest in survey research to her frequent participation in the May Atlanta University conferences. She organized the Sociological Club of Atlanta "to study the condition of the lowly and in all possible ways improve it." This club had both men and women members and elected a male president. King also had moved quickly to establish social services based on her research findings. She and the WCTU had begun a "partially successful" day nursery for working mothers before the City Conference's second annual meeting in 1897.[24]

The focus of the second annual conference was on urban social and physical conditions. Black women had an even stronger presence than in 1896 because men and women met in parallel meetings, and the joint opening and closing sessions also featured women speakers. The papers in the separate men's session were studies of health and physical conditions, while the women's session focused largely but not exclusively on improving the social circumstances of city life. The six women presenters in the women's session read papers that called for day nurseries and kindergartens and described the efforts by new community organizations to visit poorer neighbors and hold mass meetings of mothers and parents that instructed those attending to be better prepared for urban life. In the second conference's concluding plenary session, the studies of child health of Adella Hunt Logan, of Tuskegee Institute, and of Lucy Laney accounted for two of the four featured papers. The women participants were already more closely involved than the men in establishing new programs to address needs that were identified in their sessions, while the male participants were more focused on using their research to refute theories they regarded as scientific racism.[25]

After W. E. B. Du Bois took over the Atlanta University conferences in 1898, the role of both male and female self-trained social scientists gradually became less prominent in the published reports. Women correspondents continued to be a part of those doing the field reports for the annual studies, but with Du Bois at the helm the popular women's sessions were not necessarily linked to the research topic that preoccupied the general body. This is not to say that women were excluded from the general sessions. In some years the conference opened with a plenary session that was followed by separate men's and women's meetings, in the pattern set by the second conference. At the end of these meetings all the participants reconvened for a closing session in which three sets of resolutions were presented from the men, the women, and the general body.

Participation and advocacy by black women in the Atlanta University conferences and other similar meetings did not lead to large-scale studies on black women workers to match those that Du Bois was doing on male skilled workers and professionals, perhaps because no cadre of younger women scholars was developed and nurtured in the same way that Du Bois was welcomed into the American Negro Academy and then assisted R. R. Wright Jr., Monroe Work, and George Haynes as they became young scholars who in turn, as we shall see, fostered another generation of male labor scholars who came of age in the 1920s.

Du Bois was silent on the exclusion of women from membership in the American Negro Academy, although he did mentor some women, notably Jessie Fauset and the anthropologist Irene Diggs. Du Bois and Fauset worked on literary projects together, and he does not seem to have utilized Fauset's training in the social sciences at Cornell University at the turn of the century, where she worked with the economist Walter Willcox. Fauset later attended the University of Pennsylvania, where she earned a master's degree. By contrast, Du Bois helped to guide Eugene K. Jones, another Cornell student, to a job assisting George Haynes at the fledgling National Urban League.

Nor were black women able to gain access to what Robyn Muncy has called the "female dominion," the educational and occupational networks utilized by the white women who became social scientists and reformers in the early twentieth century.[26] Black women had networks that were centered in the National Association of Colored Women, but while the NACW promoted a scientific approach to reforms and implemented important community programs, it lacked the ties to educational institutions, jobs, and academic journals necessary to produce professional social workers or social scientists. Black women sought to hire bright black female college graduates to run their kindergartens and recreation programs, but black clubwomen had little influence on the curriculum in Negro colleges, which, as we shall see, discouraged black women from seeking advanced degrees.

"You Must Keep Up or Endure the Dust": Black Female Students and Career Choices at the Turn of the Century

A major stumbling block for young black women interested in advanced degrees of any sort was that the higher educational system in place had produced by 1898 a grand total of 252 black women with college degrees. The number of women seeking bachelor's degrees increased rapidly after 1900, but the majority of women students at black colleges were enrolled in their certificate-granting normal school departments. There were also different requirements for female college students, substituting home economics courses for the courses in science, mathematics, and languages that were prerequisites for admission to graduate schools. W. E. B. Du Bois, about half of whose Fisk University classmates had been female, was one of many male writers who considered the very small number of black women who were enrolled in college courses at the turn of the century to be "natural."[27]

Most of Du Bois's attention to black women in his 1900 Atlanta University Conference study *The College-Bred Negro* was as marriage partners. The climate of acceptance of black women students on Negro college campuses varied, from hostility at Atlanta University to integration at Fisk University, but female students were no less interested in the social sciences and labor issues than clubwomen. Black women took much longer to gain advanced degrees or executive positions in professional arenas, including social work, despite the fact that female college students sought to gain expertise in the social sciences and clubwomen had established many of the settlement houses and community programs that served black southerners. The limitations on black women in the professions extended well beyond the years covered in this chapter. Rayford Logan reported that about a third of Howard's School of Social Work's graduates before 1950 were men, a fact Logan attributed to the expansion of desirable administrative and executive jobs that attracted male applicants and "from which a lingering prejudice still barred many competent women, white as well as Negro."[28]

Women students at Atlanta University played a central but understated role in supporting W. E. B. Du Bois's research during his Atlanta years. In the 1890s Atlanta University had many more men than women in its college department, but Du Bois had a number of women students in his economics, history, and sociology classes. He utilized female undergraduates to assist him with his studies for the Bureau of Labor and the annual conference. Four of the five research correspondents for his second Bureau of Labor study, "The Negro in the Black Belt," were young women. Most of the researchers studied their hometowns, but one of his female correspondents was a country schoolteacher whose job gave her the entrée needed to collect the data that Du Bois needed to complete his report.[29] Du Bois either did not assign or his women students did not choose feminine or domestic subjects as their thesis topics. The five women in his fourteen-person, two-term economics seminar chose topics like Lula Iola Mack's "The Credit System," C. E. Byrdie's "The Wages of Negroes," and Ruth Marion Harris's "The Rise and Development of the Wage System in the South."[30]

While there is no evidence that Du Bois stifled the ambitions of black female students, he did not apparently encourage his best female students at the turn of the century to become social scientists in the same manner in which he encouraged R. R. Wright Jr. and George Haynes to follow in his footsteps. Although none of Du Bois's male Atlanta University students of this era became influential social scientists, several of them, including Augustus Dill, who became Du Bois's assistant at *The Crisis* and coeditor of some of the later Atlanta University Conference reports, did enter undergraduate and graduate school at Harvard under Du Bois's recommendations. Women in his undergraduate classes were bright, contributed to the student newspaper, and wrote prizewinning papers on reforms. His female students seem to have been as accomplished and certainly won as many undergraduate awards as the male students.[31] At least two of the women in Du Bois's 1898 seminar, Ruth Marion Harris and Lula Iola Mack, were among the two or three students in each class who maintained high honors throughout their college years. In 1898, a year when the contest entries were deemed to be of "unusually high merit," Ruth M. Harris won the $35 first prize of the Quiz Club Prize Contest for her essay "The Need of More Public Schools in Atlanta." There were fifteen competitors for five cash awards on the general topic of "Some Needed Social or Economic Reform," and "only the best eight . . . were allowed to enter the final oratorical competition."[32] The oratorical contest was a prominent feature of the crowded commencement week exercises and helped to focus Atlanta students on their expected role as leaders who would provide social scientific solutions to educational and economic disparities. Harris's essay was not reprinted or described, but if the judges followed their contest rules, it was well grounded in social science methods. The contest rules asked students to choose between writing about "social reform" or an "economic reform," and the 2,500-word essays were to be judged on "their knowledge of the subject . . . skill in using facts or statistics for illustration, clearness and simplicity of statement."[33] The contest essays were reviewed by President Bumstead and then forwarded to the Quiz Club Prize Contest Committee in Boston, which also had a Harvard professor of English read and grade them. The eight highest scoring essays then were delivered by their authors in the oratory contest; the highest combined scores won. Female students' successful involvement in the Quiz Club Prize Contest is another indication of their interest in and skill at using the language of the social sciences to solve social or economic problems.

The third Atlanta University Conference was held the day after Ruth Harris won the essay prize, and if she attended she heard a range of papers—some were a continuation of the two previous conferences' concern with mortality statistics, others continued the women participants' interest in establishing kindergartens, orphanages, and nursery schools. This was Du Bois's first conference, and Harris may have even contributed to a presentation that prefigured one of the sections of *The Negro Artisan* when the recent alumnus George A. Towns read a paper that was "a review of the official statistics on the question of the occupations of Negroes as given by the census of 1890 and compiled by the class in sociology."[34]

Atlanta University had instituted a new curriculum in sociology and economics and gave black clubwomen and its female students the opportunity to undertake sociological studies after 1895, but its faculty, administration, and male students sent a decidedly mixed message about women's equality. Lucy Laney, Atlanta University's most influential alumna, was not able to enter its college program after completing the high school, to the relief of her classmate R. R. Wright Sr., who was irked at her fiercely competitive spirit and high grades. University publications praised the activities of Laney, Georgia Swift King, and other normal school alumnae from the 1870s and 1880s who were school founders or principals or leaders of organizations, but the public chronology of the university began with extensive recognition and accolades for the 1876 graduation of its all-male college class. The four women in Laney's normal school class of 1873 were actually the first Atlanta University graduates.[35] Only one woman earned a bachelor's degree from Atlanta University between 1876 and 1895. Seven women received bachelor's degrees from Atlanta University between 1895 and 1900, but even this small change caused unfavorable comments in the student and administration newspapers. The fact that a number of the women graduates won oratory and literary prizes caused editorial assertions that black men's position at the university was being unfairly superseded. When two brilliant young women graduated from Atlanta University in 1895, the official publication of the university downplayed the achievements of both by not giving their names, even though there were only four graduates that year. Rather than celebrate the second and third women to receive bachelor's degrees, the editor of the *Bulletin of Atlanta University* damned them with faint praise by insisting that their achievements should not be seen as taking away from those of the two male graduates. "On this occasion two such were graduated, and the fact that *one* of these took the first honor is no reflection upon the young men. . . . The other one of these two young women, by the matter and delivery of her oration, made so favorable an impression on ex-Governor Bullock that he passed President Bumstead a twenty-dollar bill to be presented with her diploma."[36]

These comments reflected the view held by a vocal minority in the administration perhaps, that the essence of Atlanta University was found in its predominantly male college program. The largely female student body of the normal school, which enrolled the majority of Atlanta University students, was not included in gendered definitions of Atlanta University, and differences in the curricula of the lower normal school and the high school meant that it was hard for normal school graduates to enter the college department without taking high school courses.

Young women attending Atlanta University at the turn of the century did not meekly accept subordinate status, and challenged the vision of the college department as a male bastion in essays published in the student newspaper, *The Scroll.* Lula Iola Mack wrote an uncompromising statement on gender equality in the classroom and the workplace: "The fields of labor which are now open to women require the training of every faculty which they possess . . . and must not be limited to any particular sphere." In her essay "The College Woman," Mack, a member of the Atlanta University class of 1900, did not use a racial uplift argument or claim a unique role for women as guardians of the purity of black homes. She said that educated women who entered the arena of work should prepare themselves like athletes for a race in which men had been given a head start. Mack argued that the enlargement of the "woman's sphere" from the home to the workplace required that women receive the same courses in the sciences, mathematics, and languages as male students so that they could compete for the same jobs.[37]

Du Bois's alma mater, Fisk University, in contrast to Atlanta University's ambivalent response to its women graduates, had welcomed women into its college division from its earliest days.[38] At Fisk the administration and student body did not debate whether women should be full members of the campus community. The largest and most elaborate building on campus was Jubilee Hall, the women's dormitory and home of the Ladies Department, a clear sign of the importance and dualism of women's education at Fisk. Educated women's special feminine qualities were seen as key to race advancement because "the highest interests of any race depend largely upon the intelligence, frugality, virtue and noble aspirations of their women." The example of the Jubilee Singers was central to Fisk's identity as a university and to women's identity as full citizens at Fisk. The receptivity that Fisk University had for women students was signaled in recurring advertisements from the 1880s that discussed women's education at Fisk. "Fisk University has from the first recognized the absolute necessity of the right education of the girls and young women of the race. . . . In the classroom they have equal advantages with the young men and can pursue any one of the courses of study established in the University. In addition special provision has been made in a department peculiarly their own."[39]

Fisk students before, after, and during Elizabeth Ross's time at the turn of the century wrote numerous essays on the roles of black educated men and women. There was no hint in the *Fisk Herald* or administration or alumni publications that Fisk's male students were uncomfortable with women's self-assertion and intellectual competition. Many female students did adopt the idea that racial advancement depended on their virtuous behavior and intelligence with the same eagerness and youthful bombast of male students such as W. E. B. Du Bois, George Edmund Haynes, and Charles H. Wesley. An 1880s secondary student named Maggie J. Murray argued that women's role as homemakers made their education even "more essential" than men's and that it was the duty of all black mothers to see to it that their daughters were educated. Murray, who was to become the third wife of Booker T. Washington, reported that in 1882–83 there were ninety-four girls in the student body "and we would be glad if we could have next year, as many more."[40]

Women students at Fisk wrote on a variety of topics, including race, politics, and women's rights. When Fisk women wrote about gender they were extending and redefining their roles as educated black women and race leaders, and not defending their right to a college education as was the case at other schools. Elizabeth Ross brought a no-nonsense approach to racial advancement to the pages of the *Fisk Herald*. In "You Must Keep Up or Endure the Dust," Ross's first article in the *Fisk Herald*, she sounded a rallying cry to her fellow students that utilized the language of both accommodationism and self-help nationalism.

Ross argued that black people had come a long way and should just keep going without complaining about segregation. "Sometimes we grumble because we cannot dine at fine hotels. . . . Why not have fine hotels of our own? Colored cooks . . . can cook as well for Negroes." Ross made no special mention of black women in her assertions of the inherent equality of blacks and whites, and followed standard literary practices, employing masculine terminology to indicate black people as a collectivity, arguing that "we have form, features, intellect like those of our white brothers."[41]

Male and female students at Fisk University were both inculcated with the idea that they had special duties to other black people that came as a direct result of their educational advantages. At Fisk, women students were explicitly instructed that they had two spheres, home and work, in which they were expected to lead, while male students were encouraged to link their individual achievements to the fulfillment of racial responsibilities. Grace Hadnott of Fisk's 1903 class embraced the idea of a special mission for colored women and argued that women's gender discrimination made them uniquely prepared to solve racial problems: "The future of the Negro race lies in the hands of its women. . . . The Negro woman . . . alone has the power to uproot ignorance, break down prejudice and solve for us this great race problem. . . . She has not only to contend with the disabilities that affect the Negro race, but against the added disability of sex."[42] This was the logical if solipsistic conclusion of Fisk's uplift discourse. The attainment of a successful professional career was the principal manner in which a black man could show that blacks were competent, while black college women had to not only excel in their chosen career but also had to renovate the home life of their people.

Despite Fisk University's stated commitment of equality to its women students such as Elizabeth Ross and Grace Hadnott, its curriculum undercut their ability to enter graduate school. Fisk's emphasis on a special domestic role of educated black women led to differences in the required courses for women in the college department. Fisk women students taking the classical or scientific courses leading to bachelor's degrees took Trigonometry and Domestic Science rather than Trigonometry and Surveying in the second semester of their first year, which prevented them from completing the full mathematics sequence with ease. The gendered differences in the course work at

Fisk undermined the concept of equal bachelor's degrees and left women students short of the necessary requirements for advanced degrees.

Black women who were college students at Atlanta and Fisk Universities in the 1880s and early 1890s wrote numerous articles in college newspapers that explained and expanded women's rights and responsibilities. These articles reveal that younger women were beginning to write using careful historical documentation and were experimenting with the language and methods of the social sciences at the same time as Victoria Earle Matthews and Ida B. Wells. College students used Emancipation Day and graduation orations on women's roles and progress to disseminate their increasingly womanist arguments to the large public audiences that attended these events. Mattie F. Childs evoked R. R. Wright Sr.'s signature phrase in her 1894 Emancipation Day address at Atlanta University, "The Progress of the Colored Women since 1863." Black women "can look in the face of any man and boldly say: 'We are rising.'" She argued that God had made men and women equal, and extolled a number of black women leaders. Du Bois's Fisk University classmate Mary Steward, of Oswego, New York, gave her commencement address, "Women in Public Life," at their 1888 graduation.[43]

Black female college graduates, already a distinct minority, were less likely than their male counterparts to qualify to enter graduate programs without first earning a second bachelor's degree. Fisk University's best male graduates, George Haynes and Charles Wesley among them, began to be admitted directly to graduate programs at prestigious white institutions such as Yale University at the turn of the century, while other Negro college graduates earned a second bachelor's degree and then were admitted to graduate school. But black women, who had not taken the same courses, faced an additional barrier because Harvard, Yale, and Columbia did not admit any women to their undergraduate colleges. Radcliffe and Barnard, the private women's colleges that had close formal relationships with Harvard and Columbia, could not or did not promise admission to these graduate programs upon successful completion of a second bachelor's degree. The University of Chicago and other co-ed universities such as the University of Pennsylvania and Cornell University that admitted black women students as undergraduates would have been the most logical alternative, but most were disinclined to accept black women into their graduate or professional programs when Elizabeth Ross graduated in 1903. The University of Chicago's summer programs thus had an even greater importance as a point of access for black women than for black men, but the full potential of the University of Chicago for black women social scientists and academics was not realized until decades after black men enrolled in its social science courses. The first black woman, Birdye Haynes, did not earn a University of Chicago social service certificate until after 1918, and the first University of Chicago master's degree in sociology earned by a black woman was probably Myra Hill Colson's 1927 degree, which came two decades after those of R. R. Wright Jr. and Monroe Work.[44]

Elizabeth Ross Haynes's schooling and early career illustrate the difficulties faced by young black women who wanted to work as social scientists at the turn of the century. The education, social science studies, and professional careers of black women who were interested in social research between 1890 and 1910 were dramatically different from those of the men in the first cadre of scholars. Ross Haynes's assertion in *Who's Who in Colored America* that she too was a "sociologist and author" rested on a slender curriculum vitae that was nonetheless representative of the quality of labor studies conducted by black women in the early twentieth century.[45] Elizabeth Ann Ross was in the same Fisk University 1903 graduating class as her future husband, George Edmund Haynes. They both began as talented post-Reconstruction children of slave-born parents who sacrificed to give them a secondary education then available to few black children in the rural South. In 1900 when Ross began her college studies at Fisk University, there were only 70 black public high school students in her native Alabama. There were no black students enrolled in college-level courses in the state-supported Negro colleges in Alabama or in George Haynes's home state of Arkansas, and only 103 black students were enrolled in the two states' private colleges. In 1900 there were 2.5 million school-age black children in sixteen southern states. These states enrolled just under 4,700 black students in normal schools and fewer than 1,750 black college students.[46] Ross's years at Fisk University had brought her accolades from the faculty that matched those given to George Haynes, but the divergence between their later achievements was apparent within a decade after their graduation. The philosophy professor and college pastor Cornelious Wortendyke Morrow tempered his warm congratulations on George Haynes's 1912 doctorate with the observation that his own wife regularly reminded Fisk faculty members who proudly boasted of George Haynes's accomplishments that Elizabeth Ross had been his intellectual equal, or better. "Mrs. Morrow says to them, 'Oh, but you ought to see our Elizabeth,' intimating that if they did Edmund would not be in it."[47]

When Elizabeth Ross and George Haynes graduated from Fisk University in 1903, she began five years of work as a teacher, while her college sweet-

The Segregated Scholars

heart Haynes received a scholarship to Yale University through the intervention of Yale University and its divinity school alumni on Fisk's faculty. Ross's desire for more education was manifested in her attendance at three summer sessions at the University of Chicago, 1905–8, but differences in the courses required of men and women at Fisk meant she had to take undergraduate-level courses, while George Haynes was earning his master's degree. She worked steadily during the seven years between her graduation in June 1903 until her marriage in December 1910. Both of her first two careers, school-teacher and YWCA college campus organizer, gave her unpaid summers in which she could and did take summer courses. Ross planned to take the language courses in Latin, German, and French she needed to enter a graduate degree program.[48] Her courses indicate that she was attempting to earn a second bachelor's and a master's degree from the University of Chicago through summer school and correspondence courses.[49] George Haynes, by way of contrast, was supported by graduate fellowships while he got his degrees, although he worked full-time for the Young Men's Christian Association (YMCA) for three years between his master's and doctorate. In two of these years he joined Ross in taking summer school courses in Chicago.

In 1908 Ross left classroom teaching permanently and became the national student secretary for the YWCA. This newly created job was patterned on the position at the YMCA that George Haynes had begun three years earlier. Her mentor at the YWCA was Addie Waites Hunton, wife of William Alphaeus Hunton, the YMCA official who had hired George Haynes. Addie Hunton had begun to work for the national YWCA board in 1907, and she recommended Elizabeth Ross as her assistant to work on the organization of student chapters at Negro colleges.[50]

Elizabeth Ross's newly created job for the national board of the YWCA was in a rapidly professionalizing occupation—social work. W. E. B. Du Bois, George E. Haynes, and R. R. Wright Jr. each had worked for social settlements at the beginning of their careers. But Ross's job was neither a survey like Du Bois's Philadelphia assignment nor a research fellowship combined with graduate school like Haynes's at Columbia or Wright's at the University of Pennsylvania. Social work as an occupation for black women became an end in itself, whereas many men used social work as the stepping stone to higher administrative and executive positions and academic careers.

Ross's decision to marry George Haynes in December 1910, after he had completed his doctoral course work and begun to teach at Fisk, was one factor that curtailed her ability to continue her education or to work as a social scientist; and the birth of a son in 1912 caused further delays in her professional training. Master's and doctoral programs at the University of Chicago each required at least two terms of residence, and this would have required Ross to have enough savings to live in Chicago and to delay marriage or live separately from her husband. Finances were so strained for the young couple that they raised produce in Nashville and sold cattle from Ross's mother's Alabama farm. Elizabeth Ross Haynes left her full-time job as student secretary but continued to work on YWCA assignments for a number of years, most likely out of financial need as well as commitment to her budding social work career. She finally earned a master's degree in sociology in 1923 at Columbia University, twenty years after her college graduation and one decade after her husband had finished his doctorate.[51]

While a myriad of personal choices can determine how long a given individual takes to earn a degree, not a single black woman earned a doctorate before 1920. Black men were far more successful than their wives and sisters and increased the total number of doctorates earned by blacks threefold to twenty-five by 1921. Social science fields accounted for only about a quarter of these advanced degrees up to World War II, refuting the often expressed notion that black scholars were steered toward studying black communities. Black women first earned doctorates in 1921, and their numbers grew from three in that year to a total of ten by 1933, while fifty more black men were added to the ranks. They were the leading edge of a major expansion of black women with undergraduate and graduate degrees, but in 1921 there were still three black male college students for every female student. It is telling that two of the first four black women to earn doctorates came from the generation of clubwomen and schoolteachers who were children at Emancipation, and two were born in the 1890s when Elizabeth Ross Haynes's talented post-Reconstruction generation was entering college. The younger pair, Sadie Tanner Mossell Alexander (1898–1989) and Eva Beatrice Dykes (1893–1986), had straightforward graduate school experiences that nonetheless indicated the continuing differences in curricula at black and white colleges and the impact of middle-class intellectual and financial support. Alexander and Dykes both grew up in the nurturing homes of uncles who lived and worked as professors on the campus of Howard University. Having an established breadwinner to support their extended families meant both could attend graduate school full time. Although she was obliged to enroll in the mostly female College of Education and had to make up a math requirement, Sadie Alexander avoided most of the pitfalls of poor preparation and gendered curricula that hampered the forward educational progress of most black women by attending the University of Pennsylvania for both undergraduate and graduate school, which enabled her to earn a doctorate in economics in 1921 at age twenty-three, six years after she matriculated. Alexander was the first black American with a doctorate in economics and for more than a dozen years the only black woman with a doctorate in the social sciences.[52] Although Eva Dykes—the third black woman to get a doctorate—had graduated from Howard University summa cum laude in 1914, she was required to enroll in Radcliffe College in 1916 as a junior and complete the undergraduate program before she was admitted to the graduate program in English. She used the earnings from two years of teaching school and the support of her family to complete her second undergraduate and two graduate degrees in five years. The two older women scholars, Georgiana Simpson (1866–1944) and Anna Julia Cooper (1858–1964), began their teaching careers in the mid-1880s. Both were single heads of extended families, and their degrees came after decades of summer and correspondence courses and saving to underwrite the residency requirements while on leave without pay from their jobs. Like Elizabeth Ross Haynes, these talented women completed their final degrees more than two decades after their age-mates W. E. B. Du Bois, William L. Bulkley, and Lewis Baxter Moore. Simpson held an 1885 normal school certificate and methodically undertook fifteen years of summer and correspondence courses at the University of Chicago before earning a degree in German on June 14, 1921, at age fifty-five. Anna Julia Cooper was an 1884 Oberlin College "gentlemen's course" graduate who returned to the classroom in her fifties. She also used summer and extension courses at Columbia University and in France before enrolling in the Sorbonne in 1923 and completing her dissertation in 1925.[53]

Education was only the first barrier; working as a social scientist was even more difficult for black women. George Haynes was paid for his work as a social scientist from 1905 until his retirement about 1955, and he published widely. Elizabeth Ross Haynes had a twenty-year career as a social scientist, including working for the U.S. Department of Labor, but she was paid to work as a social scientist for only about one year. Her published labor studies consisted of her master's thesis and a single article. Ross Haynes often assisted her husband's work but was unpaid because of formal and informal rules about nepotism. The contrast between the scholarly production of Elizabeth Haynes and George Haynes is important because the difference between the two was not simply the result of choices that Elizabeth Ross Haynes made to be a wife and mother, but of lost opportunities to publish and to earn a living that were denied her because she was a black married woman.

Unmarried black alumnae were better placed to obtain a graduate education, but they still did not have the same opportunities as males for professional positions because of the continuing double barriers of race and gender. Simpson and Dykes both returned to high school teaching at Dunbar High School—the new name of M Street—in the fall of 1921, although nearby Howard University did not have any black faculty members with doctorates in their fields. Sadie Alexander was able to combine marriage with a career, but she had to give up any hope of a career as a social scientist; instead, she earned a law degree and worked for her husband's firm. George Haynes arranged for Charles H. Wesley and other bright Fisk men to attend the graduate school at Yale University in 1911, but he sent their classmate, his younger sister, Birdye, to the Chicago School of Philanthropy for a certificate in social work. Wesley was subsequently hired by Howard University on the strength of his Yale master's degree in economics and history, and then he became a professional historian. Birdye Haynes became a settlement house worker.[54] Emma L. Shields Penn, another talented student of George Haynes, was hired by him and worked as a social scientist at the U.S. Department of Labor during the war labor emergency. But when this window of opportunity slammed shut at the war's end, Shields returned to the feminized professional world of the YWCA and public schools. We will consider her contributions to black labor studies as part of the important but forgotten studies of black women workers that were done by four pioneering black female social scientists after we examine the expansion of the cadre of black male social scientists during the Great Migration in chapter 4.

4

Mapping the Great Migration

Black Social Scientists, Social Research, and Social Action, 1910–1930

Modern civilization and improvements in . . . transportation favor the urban centers. . . . Migration is easier toward the city than away from it. . . . The Negro is in the Population Stream.
—George Edmund Haynes, *The Negro at Work in New York City*

The full unfolding of the Great Migration kept workers at the center of black social scientists' research and reform agendas from 1910 until 1930. The first cadre of scholars' shift of focus to northern workers after 1905, discussed in chapter 2, now seemed prescient to the businesses, government, and social service agencies who eagerly sought socioeconomic explanations for the mounting exodus. In this chapter I look at the multifold activities of black male labor analysts in the areas of research, institution building, and public policy as they sought to study, plan programs, and influence public policy for the first million black workers who left the South for the cities of the North and Midwest. An expanding number of scholars mapped the contours of the migrants and also claimed that as social scientists they had a legitimate basis of authority to represent the interests of black labor to white employers, governmental agencies, and urban reformers. Two new sets of institutional frameworks initiated by George E. Haynes and Carter G. Woodson augmented the informal training and mentoring networks, doubling the ranks of significant black labor scholars by five men, from four to nine, by the mid-1920s and helping many more younger intellectuals to become social workers, social scientists, and historians. The new generation of labor analysts, represented here by Charles H. Wesley, Charles S. Johnson, Ira De A. Reid, Abram L. Harris, and Lorenzo J. Greene, extended and complicated the scholarship on black workers with more sophisticated theoretical frameworks and methodologies.

By the late 1920s the younger scholars had begun to play important leadership roles in the organizations that had given their careers direction, such as the National Urban League and the Association for the Study of Negro Life and History, sometimes complementing but more often clashing with their mentors.

The numbers of black migrants grew steadily after Emancipation, with families initially moving westward toward agricultural lands, small towns, and cities. More black workers moved within the South before World War I, chiefly from economically depressed rural areas to rapidly growing cities such as Birmingham and Atlanta, than left the region. In light of the vastly larger numbers of whites moving to American cities, black migration to the North before 1915 was minuscule, numbering about twenty thousand black workers and their families annually, compared to the yearly influx of one million foreign-born whites and the hundreds of thousands of native-born whites who swelled U.S. cities at the turn of the century. European immigration was halted after 1914 by the outbreak of World War I, while war production and the demand for labor increased dramatically. Suddenly black migration to the North transformed from what Charles S. Johnson would term a "tiny restrained stream" to a full flood of humanity, with crests of up to sixteen thousand persons a month. Four hundred and fifty thousand black people left the South in the four years between 1916 and 1920.[1]

Public interest in analyses of black workers was no longer limited to the small group of academics and social reformers discussed in chapters 1 and 2. Articles on the Great Migration appeared in a much wider range of publications, from national magazines such as the *Nation, Current History,* and the *Atlantic Monthly* and scholarly journals such as *Industrial Psychology* to the new black monthlies *The Crisis* and *Opportunity.* The increased urbanization of black Americans also increased the circulation of race newspapers and magazines. *The Crisis*'s circulation was over fifty thousand and sold more than one hundred thousand copies in April 1919. R. R. Wright Jr.'s *Christian Recorder* was considered the largest black nationally distributed newspaper.[2]

Because their studies of black workers in the North predated the Great Migration, it is tempting to claim that Du Bois and the first cadre of black labor analysts fully anticipated the onset or the inevitability of the Great Migration and predicted its social and political consequences, but the size, scope, and rapidity of this mass movement, which began in earnest in 1916, surprised most black and white contemporary observers, excepting perhaps the migrants themselves. The philosopher and social critic Alain Locke described the migrants as being animated by "a new vision of opportunity, of social and economic freedom," and the migration process as one in which it was "the rank and file who are leading, and the leaders who are following."[3] Black social scientists were nonetheless well placed physically and methodologically to investigate migrant life and work by building on the methodological expertise and earlier research of Du Bois and the first cadre.

Black labor studies underwent additional changes in its professional geography between 1910 and 1930, leading the segregated scholars in directions that did not always parallel the mass exodus. As W. E. B. Du Bois and R. R. Wright Jr., the two most important labor analysts in the first decade of the twentieth century, moved away from social research and into social commentary, the first detailed studies of the Great Migration were written by George Haynes and Carter Woodson as the opening salvos of their careers as scholar-advocates.[4]

Haynes followed his migration studies with a three-year tenure as the director of the Division of Negro Economics for the U.S. Department of Labor, 1918–21, a precedent-making opportunity to influence public policy concerning black labor issues. Between 1910 and 1922, the first four labor scholars—Du Bois, Wright Jr., Haynes, and Woodson—successively left academic or social welfare careers they found too limiting. These moves shifted the base of operations for activist black social scientists away from segregated colleges to independent institutions, such as the NAACP, the NUL, the ASNLH, and the Federal Council of Churches. The new generation of scholars— Charles H. Wesley, Charles S. Johnson, Ira De A. Reid, Abram L. Harris, and Lorenzo J. Greene—had professional migrations that differed from their mentors' and from ordinary workers'. They were first pulled to the North and Midwest in the 1910s and 1920s for their graduate education. Then during the 1920s they emerged as public intellectuals based in Chicago, New York City, and Washington, D.C., with distinctive individual political views that often clashed with the more senior black labor scholars who had served as their teachers and mentors. But as the national economy stalled in the late 1920s, all five of the younger labor analysts took Jim Crow jobs at black colleges, while the older scholars and the one million migrants resolutely stayed put outside the academy and outside the Deep South.[5]

These five younger labor scholars were part of a wider cohort of black men with social science training after 1910 who had been able to gain admission to graduate school and find jobs with decent salaries in Negro colleges and social service agencies. By 1920 black male researchers, social workers, and administrators were employed by federal, state, and local governments. Their research findings and opinions were increasingly sought after and debated.[6] As we have seen in chapter 3, black women faced far more difficulties both in obtaining graduate degrees and in establishing professional careers as social scientists. Nevertheless, a small group of pioneering black women social scientists was able to publish significant labor studies during and just after World War I. Their short-lived research careers are considered separately in chapter 5.

Studies of African American migration and urban economic life dominated the writings of black male social scientists between 1910 and 1930. The distinguished labor and urban historian Joe William Trotter Jr. has characterized early twentieth-century studies of black migration from *The Philadelphia Negro* through the early 1930s as being dominated by a "race relations imperative" due to the authors' underlying interest in reform and problem solving.[7]

Black migration scholarship was directed toward multiple audiences: the academy, black intellectuals, white reformers, the business community, and governmental policy makers. Initially there was no national or scholarly consensus either on the causes of the mass exodus of blacks or the possible solutions to any actual or anticipated social problems. White elites in the North and in the South found the suddenness and the size of the mass movement difficult to fathom. Federal, city, and state officials, white businessmen, and black organizational leaders tended to agree only on one point: the departure of black people from the South was the most serious manifestation of the "Negro problem" in the twentieth century. By the time of the Great Migration, the term "Negro problem," and its sibling "the race question," had long been a trope of overlapping meanings that simultaneously referred to the paradox of segregation within a democracy, the ideology of white supremacy, the quest for racial advancement, and the flattened features of everyday black life under Jim Crow. Black commentators often referred to a so-called Negro problem and suggested that if blacks had selected the phrase, it would have been "their 'white problem.'"[8]

Black social scientists seized on the Great Migration as a rare instance of popular puzzlement on the race question to offer their studies, programs for social reform, and professional expertise as a means of comprehending what was clearly an unanticipated social phenomenon. Black social scientists' redefinition of the "Negro problem" as a set of measurable social and economic indicators that could be used to guide reforms was meant to provide an objective, moderate, and intellectualized basis for discussions between black and white elites. Race relations as a philosophical approach and an operational strategy was further institutionalized, but, as we shall see, it was only one of the solutions proposed by the studies of black migrants.

There were three distinct phases of migration studies before the Depression that were linked by common themes but differentiated by the methodologies and political philosophies of the individual scholars. In every phase there were detailed answers to three questions: the size, the causal factors of the migration, and the best ways to solve any social problems engendered from the mass migration. The first phase, 1912–22, was largely coincident with the first large surge of workers to the North and was dominated by the contrasting analyses by George Haynes and Carter Woodson. Both men used studies of black labor and migration to foreground divergent discussions on the roles of black professionals and the goals of racial advancement. From 1918 to 1921 Haynes had the opportunity to coordinate and document the employment of black workers in war industries as director of the Division of Negro Economics at the U.S. Department of Labor. The second phase of labor analyses, 1922–27, paralleled a second wave of migrants and was dominated by a new generation of sociologists and economists led by Charles S. Johnson. Johnson directed a number of surveys of black urban workers and published monthly analyses of the lives and labors of the migrants by rising scholars such as Ira De A. Reid and Abram L. Harris in the NUL's monthly magazine, *Opportunity*. In the third phase, 1927–31, the younger and older generations were both fully engaged. The studies of George Haynes and Charles Johnson continued to emphasize the importance of race relations as the preferred solution to black workers' economic and social problems. Woodson and the fledgling historian Lorenzo J. Greene produced a descriptive history of black workers, *The Negro Wage Earner*, that extended Woodson's emphasis on working-class racial solidarity. Two younger scholars, Charles H. Wesley and Abram L. Harris, broke methodological and ideological ranks with their mentors with fresh interpretations of black workers, subordinating migration as a process to issues of racism in the workplace. Their work would inform the studies and influence the ideology of a final group of segregated scholars, who began writing and became labor advocates in the 1930s and 1940s, the subject of chapter 6.

First Interpretations of the Migration:
George E. Haynes and Carter G. Woodson

George Edmund Haynes and Carter G. Woodson became the first major analysts of the Great Migration at the same time Du Bois and Wright Jr. began to serve more as black labor advocates than analysts in their new positions as editors of national publications. Du Bois and Wright had extensively studied black workers in the North and migration between 1898 and 1911, but having become influential editors, neither made major scholarly studies of black migrants after 1915, even though both men were involved in public discussions on black people's participation in the war, race riots, and strikebreaking. Du Bois gave the readers of *The Crisis* brief reports on the Great Migration in his "Along the Color Line" column and wrote illuminating editorials at the many flash points of controversy, such as the riots in East St. Louis in 1917 and Chicago in 1919, but his most detailed analysis of the Great Migration, "The Hosts of Black Labor," did not appear until 1924, as another one-half million black people had begun to arrive in the North.[9]

R. R. Wright Jr. used the *Christian Recorder* to enthusiastically boost Philadelphia as a terminus during the Great Migration. He viewed the newcomers as a means to increase church membership as well as provoking major social changes that required the intervention of educated churchmen and churchwomen. Robert Gregg's study of the African Methodist Episcopal (AME) Church in Philadelphia asserts that Wright's pro-migration articles and editorials in denominational publications were as effective in his readers' decision to leave the South as the much better known efforts of the *Chicago Defender,* and he suggests that Wright was "the Robert S. Abbott of the Philadelphia migration." While Wright did use his skills as a sociologist to construct surveys of new church members, he was more a publicist than a student of this exodus. Wright contended that the migration was an opportunity for black people in the North to build a solid professional class and use their numbers to gain real political and economic power, while weakening Jim Crow. "Every Negro who leaves . . . means less money in the white man's pocket." Wright took several concrete steps to increase black workers' economic independence, setting up a building and loan association at his church, Jones Tabernacle, to assist skilled workers finance business projects and buy houses. He also became a director of the Citizens and Southern Bank, founded in Philadelphia in 1920 by his redoubtable father, who had retired and joined the migrating stream up the southern seaboard.[10]

Two sets of studies of the first wave of migrants by George E. Haynes and Carter G. Woodson determined the general parameters for future inquiries by focusing the size, causal factors, and solutions to the social problems resulting from large population shifts by black workers. Haynes's analyses in *The Survey* and Woodson's *A Century of Negro Migration* used the most recent federal and state census data, Labor Department reports, estimates from large industrial plants, and social service agencies in the urban areas as a baseline from which to conservatively estimate the probable size of the migration. Both men insisted that the fivefold annual increase in black northern migration needed to be understood in a national perspective. They reminded their readers that the annual immigration of whites to the United States between 1890 and 1913 was larger than the total number of black people now living in the North. Although the public was preoccupied with blacks leaving the South, Haynes and Woodson also informed their readers that more black people had migrated to southern cities than to northern urban centers and that far more native-born whites migrated to the North than blacks did.[11]

Woodson and Haynes asserted that economic causes were at the root of the Great Migration, which was the standard conclusion of black social scientists over the next two decades. Both men argued forcefully that the overwhelming evidence suggested that economic considerations were the primary cause of the migration, with racial violence and segregation as important secondary causes. In this finding they differed from popular black newspapers such as the *Chicago Defender* that asserted that lynching and Jim Crow were the main factors that drove black people out of the South. The determination of the causal factors underlying migrants' decisions to relocate was a standard part of sociological inquiry but had rarely been a concern of the public, which accepted the notion that economic factors brought most European immigrants to the United States but had difficulty believing that black workers responded to economic stimuli. Haynes and Woodson employed the same methodologies widely used by other American social scientists to measure the social and economic "push and pull" factors affecting the flow of whites to cities, but they drew their supporting evidence from a wider range of demographic and documentary sources. Their findings also refuted the charges of some white southern officials who claimed that labor agents illegally lured reluctant black workers to the North with false promises. Each man centered his findings on the motivations of the migrants in first-person accounts, using interviews, folksongs, and content analyses of the letters sent to friends, family, and the *Chicago Defender* and other papers. Carter Woodson's migration writings emphasized his view that the Great Migration was the result of rational and autonomous decisions of working-class people.[12]

Woodson's biographer, Jacqueline Goggin, has argued that Woodson used his migration studies to demonstrate the class consciousness and resistance of the masses. Woodson published an extensive selection of the letters of migrants in 1919 in the *Journal of Negro History* as a way of underlining black agency, and he also included a section on migration that stressed economic factors in his history textbook for elementary schools.[13] In 1921 Woodson published a major study of the first phase of the migration by a young black Yale graduate student in economics named Henderson Donald, and a few years later he published Elizabeth Ross Haynes's analyses of black domestic workers.[14]

Carter G. Woodson's *A Century of Negro Migration* was the first detailed historical analysis of both migration and black workers. Woodson combined a demographic analysis of the federal and state censuses with more traditional historical methods in a straightforward manner. He also framed his historical overview of black migration movements in a provocative and highly ideological set of assertions concerning the effect of Jim Crow and black intraclass conflicts on black communities. Without stretching the data to prove his points, Woodson vividly depicted segregationists as keeping black people in a state of semislavery that defeated their ambition and sapped their manhood. But he agreed with less outspoken observers that local economic conditions and strong demand from the North, not racism and lynching, were the principal factors responsible for the unprecedented numbers of blacks who left the South after 1910. *A Century of Negro Migration* also laid out Woodson's highly critical view that black southern elites betrayed the aspirations of the masses through their cooperation with segregationists.[15] Woodson believed that the departure of well-educated and industrious blacks from the South during the late 1890s had left the masses to the untender mercies of a "sycophant, toady class" who upheld the status quo: "Southern Negroes . . . have been robbed of their due part of the talented tenth." Looking back on the 1890s, when he left his native Virginia to work in the coal mines of West Virginia, Woodson declared that "only a few intelligent Negroes . . . had reached the position of being contented in the South."[16]

Woodson's political commentary and his conclusions were more obviously ideological than were George Haynes's dispassionate presentation of similar findings. Carter Woodson did not separate his opinions from his scholarship in the same deliberate fashion as W. E. B. Du Bois did, nor did he share

Haynes's much criticized tendency to avoid apportioning any responsibility to the white employers and white workers who discriminated against black workers. Woodson was likewise far more critical of blacks who appeared to accommodate segregation than was Haynes. Woodson, like Marcus Garvey, believed that white segregationists acted out of their own self-interest and saved his scorn for black accommodationists who acted against the self-interest of their race. He used a content analysis of white newspapers' discussions of black migrations to give his readers a wider range of white than black opinion. Woodson was careful not to claim greater political or social dissatisfaction among black unskilled workers than the data seemed to reveal, but he showed no such restraint when criticizing black leadership. Woodson was a nationalist and an endless defender of his understanding of the aspirations of the masses, but his training as a social scientist made him avoid overstating his empirical findings.

In *A Century of Negro Migration* Woodson had begun to conceptualize an argument that posited an economic basis for black class and ideological stratification more than one decade prior to the publication of his 1933 jeremiad *The Miseducation of the Negro*. Woodson used highly subjective terms to characterize the views of those black leaders with whom he disagreed. In Woodson's stern analysis the black persons who remained in the South after the turn of the century—90 percent of all black people—fell in three basic categories: the uneducated and unskilled masses, an assortment of spineless Negro educators, and "numerous unscrupulous" Negro businessmen who preyed on their hapless customers. In his view almost all educated and successful black persons in the Jim Crow South were economically dependent on the patronage of racists or threatened by mob violence; their dependence left them hopelessly corrupt or completely cowed. The Great Migration, therefore, offered the long-suffering black masses an opportunity to escape from a land governed by an army of segregationists and their black lieutenants, whom Woodson derisively dubbed as "assistant oppressors."[17]

George Edmund Haynes's twin bases of operation in Nashville and New York City from 1910 to 1918 made him ideally placed to immediately assess the causes and effects of the Great Migration. Haynes sought an ideological middle ground between the class-based racial polemics of Woodson and Du Bois's faith in the talented tenth as race leaders. Based in Nashville and leading a moderate New York social agency, Haynes tended to camouflage his pro-migration stance in the details of his findings. His many articles on black migrants in the North used the same methods and drew many of the same conclusions that had characterized his 1912 book, *The Negro at Work in New York City*. Haynes had argued then that blacks migrated for the same reasons as whites, using "such facts as are available" to show that it was "ill founded" to believe that black migration was "affected by causes of a different kind from those moving other populations."[18] Haynes asserted that black migration to the city was best understood as a part of the nationwide movement away from agriculture and rural areas spurred by changes in the U.S. economy. As he quickly recounted historical patterns beginning with the end of slavery and reestablishment of one-crop agriculture, Haynes gave more or less equal weight to additional factors such as black workers' pent-up desire to move on after the Civil War (that he called "the inevitable *Wanderlust*"); terrorism from the Ku Klux Klan; the exploitative share-cropping and crop lien systems; and the labor surpluses in rural areas with the fall of crop prices. He used charts and tables to illustrate that rates of population increase in southern cities from 1880 to 1910 were similar for blacks and whites.[19]

Throughout his chapter "The City and the Negro," Haynes indicated somewhat obliquely that he was aware of Booker T. Washington's argument that the rural South was the best place for blacks. While Woodson declared flatly that this idea was wrong and that industrial education was a reasonable idea that had been irreparably subverted by segregationists, Haynes avoided directly rebutting Washington's philosophy; but, rather, Haynes insisted that there was a solid empirical basis for his view that black urbanization was a part of an inexorable process. "The efforts that are being put forth to improve rural conditions and to advance agricultural arts . . . are highly commendable and effective. The thesis of this chapter is that . . . the Negro, along with the white population, is coming to the city to stay . . . that the problems which grow out of his maladjustment to the new urban environment are solvable by methods similar to those that help other elements of the population."[20]

Haynes's argument that economic considerations were the most important to black migrants was a major aspect of his program of reforms at the National Urban League. If black workers migrated for the same rational reasons as white workers, then they were deserving of the same treatment afforded to white workers by the government, businesses, and labor unions. The NUL also wanted to make black workers more efficient industrial laborers, so some branches handed out cards to workers on the street with admonitions not to be late for work and not to question authority. One of the stated purposes of the NUL was to assist migrants in becoming "fit" to and for work.[21]

George Haynes was by no means a champion of the economic or political savvy of ordinary black people in the style of Carter Woodson. Haynes and those who followed the "race relations imperative" believed that the interests of the black masses were best communicated to policy makers through black social scientists and social workers, since the departing field hands and laborers had not "done any great reflection and philosophizing [*sic*] about the race problem." However, he did frequently base his discussions on the reasons blacks left the South on firsthand accounts, music, and popular culture. In 1918, for example, Haynes argued that the apparent silence of southern black workers did not mean that they were satisfied with their lot. He used folk sayings and songs, "a bit of doggerel from the cotton fields," to indicate what two black workers actually thought about economic life in the South. Their economic insecurity as sharecroppers and farmers was heightened by racism, crop failures, and war. One said:

De white man he got ha'f de crap [crop].
Boll-weevil too' de res'.
Ain't got no home.
Ain't got no home.

Another echoed:

Boll-weevil in de cotton,
Cut wurm in de cawn [corn]
Debil in de white man,
Wah's [war is] goin' on.[22]

Haynes used these verses as an important counter argument to paternalistic assumptions by white southerners who frequently claimed to understand the views of the masses of black people because they employed them or were the sons of slaveholders. Haynes's use of black migrants' words also was a corrective of the tendency in earlier labor scholarship, including his own, to speak for rather than to or through black workers.

George Haynes began to collect data on migrants in 1916, when it became clear to him that a much larger and different movement was underway, and he quickly visited seven southern states. By the winter of 1916–17 Haynes had sent approximately 150 people a fourteen-question survey on northern migration from the towns and rural communities of fifteen southern states. He asked his correspondents what types of labor agents had come to their communities and to provide him with names of the married and single men and the women and girls who had migrated independently of their families, the numbers of persons who had already left and those who were planning to leave, and the types of jobs and amount of wages that had been promised. For each category of migrants the canvassers were asked to "please state definitely why they left" and to answer the question, "Do any of those who left intend to make money and return?" While this full study was apparently never published, a synopsis of his findings appeared in *The Survey*. In 1917 Haynes conducted a study of migrants in Detroit, where the small black prewar population had swelled by nearly 600 percent.[23]

Haynes's various surveys all indicated that economic reasons were paramount for a black workers' decision to migrate. A disastrous summer of 1916, with floods and boll weevil damage in Alabama, Mississippi, and Georgia, was blamed for causing great unemployment. At the same time the North experienced severe labor shortages because of decreased European immigration and increased production demands for the manufacture of war materials and supplies. Haynes also found that there was "another set of fundamental causes" that underlay the immediate economic factors for black mass migration: widespread dissatisfaction with social, economic, and political realities in the Jim Crow South. Haynes cited letters from blacks that he argued "express the desire to get a better job, to have a better home, and to live a larger life."[24]

The "larger life" included good schools for their children, equal justice, and decent pay and working conditions. Haynes hoped that his analysis of the migration would encourage southern white businessmen and local officials to improve wages, upgrade the schools, and cure the gross inadequacies of the legal system if they hoped to stem the tide of black migration. At the same time Haynes hoped to assure the white northern reform-oriented readers of *The Survey* that black migrants were coming to the North for legitimate goals that were shared by all Americans.

George Haynes, by nature an optimist and a moderate, stressed the importance of a better mutual understanding between blacks and whites in order to guarantee white philanthropic and business support of specific programs to be run by black professionals. His beliefs were deftly illustrated in the seal of the National Urban League. It featured a goddess with a staff and outstretched arm standing in front of the portals of Justice, with the rising sun at her back, the buildings of the city and university to her left, and smokestacks of factories to her right. The league's motto, "Not Alms, But Opportunity," and an anchor completed the seal. Members of the NUL viewed the organization as an anchor and advocate for black migrants. The modern city with its greater possibility for equal justice represented a place where black workers could start anew. Cities were envisioned as places where the difficulties of urban life and labor could be overcome if black social workers were able to apply the scientific problem-solving techniques they had apprehended in the university. The goddess symbolized enlightened philanthropical practices that would enable the league to function as a vehicle for social reforms. The National Urban League's stationery also reflected its race relations approach in a quotation from the cofounder Mrs. William H. Baldwin that stressed a shared vision of the urban American future: "Let us not work as colored people nor as white people for the narrow benefit of any group alone, but TOGETHER, as American citizens for the common good of our common city, our common country."[25]

George Edmund Haynes believed that social scientists would provide the research findings on which to base reforms and that black social workers should serve as the principal intermediaries and interpreters between black workers and their employers and between black migrants and the city. His appointment as director of the Division of Negro Economics at the U.S. Department of Labor gave him a chance to direct research and to represent workers' interests in the public sphere.

The Division of Negro Economics: The New Negro to the Rescue

George Haynes built on his reputation as a moderate social scientist who was acceptable to white businessmen and black leaders to win a contested appointment as the director of the newly created office that focused on black labor issues at the U.S. Department of Labor during World War I. Haynes was selected after an intense campaign by interracial organizations to prevent the selection of a southern antimigration advocate. He seized this opportunity to demonstrate that his race relations approach could both serve the needs of wartime employers and promote the goals of black workers for better jobs, and he took care to make sure that research to create an empirical record of black labor force participation was carried out by the new division. His new post also allowed Haynes to gracefully bow out of the NUL, that he had cofounded, after he had been edged out as the executive director by his former assistant Eugene K. Jones.[26]

Ironically, the name and idea for the U.S. Department of Labor's Division of Negro Economics originated with a vocal opponent of the Great Migration, Giles B. Jackson, a black Richmond, Virginia, attorney. Jackson had close ties to his hometown's chamber of commerce, which had given him $1,000 to publicize the reasons blacks should not leave the South. Jackson was the co-author of a misleadingly titled accommodationist textbook that was used in many segregated classrooms, *The Industrial History of the Negro Race of the United States,* which insisted that black people's "place" was in southern agriculture, dependent and submissive to whites. The Jamestown Tercentennial Exposition of 1907 and Giles Jackson lingered in the public consciousness of black Americans some fifteen years after the event. When the young editors of the *Messenger* wanted to indicate how disreputable Marcus Garvey had become by meeting with Ku Klux Klan officials, they used Jackson as their political benchmark, declaring that no American black leader would have stooped as low as the Jamaican, *"not even Giles Jackson."*[27]

Jackson had long been a controversial figure in national black political circles, in part because of persistent allegations of fiscal irregularities surrounding his use of an appropriation of $250,000 for a Negro exhibit at the 1907 Jamestown tercentennial celebration. The content of the completed Negro exhibit and the rampant segregation at the Tercentenary had provoked a firestorm of protests from black intellectuals opposed to Jim Crow. In 1907 W. E. B. Du Bois issued a public letter that branded a suggestion that he had prepared the Jamestown exhibit as "an impudent lie" and attacked the whole affair as a "shameful and discredited enterprise."[28]

The Department of Labor initially received with some interest Giles Jackson's plan for a bureau dealing with black labor problems. Jackson's backing included Samuel Gompers, president of the American Federation of Labor (AFL), and the Virginia congressional delegation.[29] An editorial in the *New York Times* praised Jackson's efforts as "mouth piece of the Richmond Chamber of Commerce" and quoted him as having urged the Southern Commercial Council to "do everything in its power to stop this migration of the Negro."[30]

One of his sponsors frankly acknowledged Jackson's lack of experience in a letter to President Woodrow Wilson's influential personal secretary but urged he be appointed on the grounds of his time-tested loyalty to the Democratic Party and the fact that he "would be least objectionable to the white citizenry of the Southland." Giles Jackson, the letter writer assured, was "a good party adherent . . . allied with that old element of the colored people known as 'ante-bellums.'" He should be given "the first 'try-out' . . . and in the event of failure then the new Negro [should] be called to the rescue."[31]

When news of Jackson's candidacy to be the head of a federal bureau became public, the leaders of black and interracial organizations mounted a furious letter-writing campaign to block his appointment. Shortly after the appearance of the *New York Times* editorial, the DOL began to receive letters from prominent blacks and whites that attacked Jackson and argued that the selection be based on educational qualifications. The African Methodist Episcopal Zion bishop George C. Clement wrote President Wilson to explain that Jackson's "appointment to any responsible place in government would be regarded by many self-respecting Negro leaders as a calamity."[32]

W. E. B. Du Bois's strenuous private condemnation of Jackson as "one of the most disreputable scoundrels that the Negro race has produced. . . . If he has not a jail record, it is not because he has not deserved it" caused Assistant Secretary of Labor Louis F. Post to express his wonder that Jackson could be so strongly supported by his congressional delegation and so castigated by black leaders.[33] The *Bee,* a widely read black Washington, D.C., newspaper reported that rumors were circulating that Jackson had the backing of the AFL, the cabinet, and the president. The *Bee* editorialized against both a "jim crow labor bureau" and Jackson's appointment in the strongest terms. "Giles Jackson has about as much to recommend him for . . . any position save as dog catcher, as the devil has to recommend himself for a position on the right side of the Lord in Heaven. The very suggestion of Giles Jackson for such an important position—one requiring brains, honest and unselfish devotion to the masses—is absolutely repugnant."[34]

Secretary of Labor William B. Wilson was sent a joint letter signed by four white and six black heads of organizations, including the NAACP, the NUL, Tuskegee Institute, and the Anna T. Jeanes and John F. Slater Funds, that insisted the war emergency warranted a departure from the "accustomed practice" of making a purely political appointment and urging that a "Negro expert on labor problems" be appointed to lead the proposed bureau.[35]

The three top administrators at the Labor Department—Secretary of Labor William B. Wilson, former head of the United Mine Workers Union; Assistant Secretary of Labor Louis F. Post; and War Labor Administrator Felix Frankfurter—were progressives who were more interested in professional solutions to black labor supply problems than to political fixes. All three were sympathetic to the goals of the NUL and the NAACP. The acute labor shortages after the United States entered World War I allowed Post and Wilson to recast black migration as a patriotic response to a national emergency and to cast the position of director of the Division of Negro Economics as requiring a technocrat who would follow up on their earlier attempts to study the migration and race riots involving black and white workers.[36]

Although there were a few other candidates, George E. Haynes quickly emerged as the person with the broadest range of supporters who was acceptable to the senior administrators of Department of Labor. John R. Shillady of the NAACP, James H. Dillard of the Jeanes and the Slater Funds, and L. Hollingsworth Wood of the NUL board were among the influential white race relations activists who pushed for Haynes. Haynes also received strong letters of recommendation from the Commercial Club and the Civic Association of Nashville and other white southern businessmen that counterbalanced Jackson's similar backing in Richmond. The Commercial Club boosted Haynes as being "gifted with executive ability far above average." The letters opposing Jackson had the effect of changing the expectations for the Negro labor advisor in such a way that only a social scientist could be appointed. Giles B. Jackson thus became ineligible for the job he had created.[37]

George Edmund Haynes was named the director of the Division of Negro Economics (DNE) in the spring of 1918, reporting directly to Assistant Secretary Louis Post, and became the first black administrator at the DOL. The early press releases describing the Division of Negro Economics stressed the fact that Haynes was a southerner endorsed by white southern businessmen, along with his expert qualifications.[38]

The white southern businessmen who supported Haynes's candidacy believed that improvements that could be made in the quality of black life on and off the job, resulting in a more stable local workforce without changing the fundamentals of segregation. Haynes's black supporters understood that as a former NUL official he would be committed to having a black staff, opposed to governmental intervention to halt the migration, and in support of black industrial employment. His black detractors were divided into three groups: Jackson supporters and opponents of the Great Migration; integrationists, such as Butler R. Wilson—Boston attorney, NAACP leader, and Atlanta University Conference founder—who were opposed to having black advisors on the grounds that they reinforced segregationist practices; and socialists, who objected to Haynes's failure to more sharply critique the business sector and push labor solidarity. Butler Wilson feared that if the DNE was made permanent, the precedent of a segregated unit would be set.[39]

The program Haynes sought to implement in the Division of Negro Economics had four major emphases, three of which focused on the monitoring and managing of the supply of black workers to meet the demands of employers and one which attempted to map the progress of black labor. His program emphases were: the establishment of Negro Workers Advisory Councils on the state and local levels to advise employers and counsel workers; the hiring and direction of black professional staffers in field offices and at headquarters; the publication of major research studies of black workers that were designed to be used by the government and businesses when planning postwar reconversion labor policies; and the implementation of an interagency advisory service on matters concerning black labor.[40]

George Haynes's two longest-serving field agents were Charles Hall and William B. Jennifer, who were supervisors in Ohio and Michigan, respectively. Both men were U.S. Bureau of the Census employees who were on loan from the Department of Commerce. Hall later returned to the Census Bureau, where he was the chief specialist on black population matters for many years. Hall had already written a number of Census Bureau reports on blacks, and in 1917 he and Jennifer had been loaned to the DOL to do a report on black migration that was used to justify creating the Division of Negro Economics. Haynes attempted to do two major studies while at the DNE, but he was able to publish only one, *The Negro at Work in World War and Reconstruction*. Haynes and his assistant Karl Phillips fought to make this report comparable to other DOL statistical publications, even insisting that their statistical charts have values to the third decimal. Phillips vowed he would "give the last ounce of blood to this Negro cause" of completing the publication, despite the fact that departmental funds were limited and Haynes was not a full-time employee after the spring of 1920.[41]

Haynes's most concrete accomplishment at the DNE was the establishment of the Negro Workers Advisory Councils. By 1920 Negro Workers Advisory Councils had been established in 225 counties and cities, and there were eleven state committees with an estimated one thousand active members.[42] The composition of these councils was carefully and deliberately set by Haynes to maximize their acceptance in the white business community. Haynes chose the black advisory council members and always selected a prominent local white businessman or government official to serve as the state or local council's chair. This practice was doubtless designed to undercut the inevitable charges by segregationists of "Negro domination" and also to exclude radicals of any stripe from the councils. Haynes thought black workers should be allowed to join unions but preferred to try to use his influence with employers rather than direct labor organizing because he believed that the American Federation of Labor was opposed to black workers entering skilled occupations.[43]

In the South the statewide DNE programs were launched at war rallies by the governor so as to get the maximum political cover. These rallies stressed black workers' patriotism and desire to assist their states and nation in a cooperative effort. After only two months on the job Haynes had gotten the enthusiastic support of the governors of North Carolina, Florida, Kentucky, and Ohio. Governor Bickett of North Carolina was "particularly pleased with Dr. Haynes's attitude" at the state's organizing meeting, and he privately congratulated the DOL for hiring "such a clear headed colored man." Publicly Bickett was quoted as finding the meeting "one of the most patriotic he has attended recently."[44]

Although George Haynes was sometimes charged by black socialists with being hostile to unions, he believed that black workers should be able to unionize and, accordingly, attempted to persuade white unions to enroll blacks. Significantly, in an uproar over blacks joining the militant International Workers of the World (IWW) union in Florida, Haynes refused to take an antiunion stance, and as a result, he lost his entire southern field staff.[45]

Florida's Governor Sidney Catts had initially warmly welcomed the DNE, but powerful timber interests were opposed to Florida's Supervisor of Negro Economics William Armwood, a local civil rights activist. Armwood and the white U.S. Employment Service (USES) state director both refused to yield to the timber industry's demand that they prevent the IWW from organizing black turpentine workers and insisted that they were legally obligated to remain neutral in labor disputes. Governor Catts bowed to the passions of the moment and demanded that Armwood be fired outright and that the USES head be replaced by a "real cracker." When George Haynes arrived with other DOL officials to mediate the dispute, Florida's state officials walked out of the meeting rather than recognize that a black man was their equal. After Haynes subsequently refused to order Armwood to make antiunion statements, Florida newspapers accused the DOL of trying to force "Negro domination" on their fair state. As a result of this controversy, the Department of Labor pulled all of the black DNE field staff from the South, despite Assistant Louis Post's personal feeling of disgust at the behavior of the Florida officials.[46]

Haynes's black staff of state supervisors of the Division of Negro Economics gave one dozen black men an unprecedented professional opportunity to work together on a collective task within the federal government, and many became executives in social work agencies after the war. Haynes borrowed

The Segregated Scholars

some of his staff from other government agencies and also drew on his contacts at the National Urban League, the YMCA, and Negro colleges. Haynes's supervisors of Negro Economics were not always able to give black workers the same assistance that the DOL offered white workers because of Jim Crow practices in the USES. Haynes was able to open the USES job and housing registries in many cities and to ensure that housing for black workers was inspected and met departmental regulations. Each supervisor of Negro Economics was assigned to a state and reported to the state USES supervisor and to Haynes in Washington, D.C., and many of the U.S. Employment Service supervisors did not like the dual reporting. His state supervisors of Negro Economics sent Haynes monthly reports surveying the number of black migrants, the types of housing, and the jobs openings. Haynes sent summaries of their reports to the secretary of labor and used them in his publications.

If not for the Florida episode, the DNE might have become a permanent division of the DOL. The Women's Bureau and the USES were the only two of more than thirty special wartime agencies that became permanent bureaus. The Division of Negro Economics failed by one vote in the U.S. Congress to achieve the same status.[47]

Whether or not a permanent DNE would have helped black workers is another question. Haynes's assistant Karl Phillips, an attorney and civil service–rated secretary, remained at the DOL and prepared an annual report on migration for many years. Although he responded to inquiries about black workers, he had no executive authority. Given Haynes's approach to social problems, the DNE would have probably functioned much like the Women's Bureau, had it been given permanent status. Under the leadership of Mary Van Kleeck and Mary Anderson, the Women's Bureau became a pioneer in systematic research on women workers and was a focal point for the airing of the Progressive Era point of view on the amelioration of the problems of women. Still, having a Women's Bureau did not prevent women workers from unequal treatment in the labor force. And while having federal bureau status may have given a select few black social scientists and social workers an opportunity to press forward with moderate reforms, the DNE would not have provided a panacea for the most serious ills of black workers.

In fact, Haynes's experience at the Division of Negro Economics points to a major flaw in a strategy that stressed publication, agitation, and publicity as ways of addressing racial discrimination in the workplace. Haynes's patriotic speeches and press releases for his division extolled the hard work of black war workers. He focused on the model workers at model plants to bolster his view that when black workers were well paid and had decent working conditions they were less likely to leave the South.

Officials at the NAACP and the NUL also used this strategy during World War I and the Depression. Annual meetings of black leaders with organized labor became almost ritualized affairs of standard complaints about black exclusion from unions and repeated, but less than sincere, promises of new organizing efforts. Black workers with major grievances against their employers found some sympathy but little concrete relief from Haynes at the DNE, or the NAACP and NUL. Poignant letters arrived in the offices of the three organizations from black railroad firemen and engineers protesting their sometimes violent exclusion from long-held railroad jobs, but little was done on their behalf.[48]

As the director of the Division of Negro Economics, George Haynes was under constant fire from black socialists who opposed his reform-oriented, pro-business philosophy. The sharpest criticism came from the *Messenger*, a new radical magazine edited by two young black socialists, A. Philip Randolph and Chandler Owen, who attacked the politics and the masculinity of all "Old Crowd Negroes." From the perspective of Randolph and Owen, there were few meaningful differences in the views of black leaders over the age of thirty-five. George Haynes had reached the ripe old age of forty in 1920, and the *Messenger*'s young editors and writers believed that the founders of the NAACP, the NUL, and the growing numbers of interracial organizations were too satisfied with their own high status, manipulated by powerful white capitalists, and set too much stock in irrelevant studies and meaningless social programs while the political and economic status of the black working-class deteriorated. The editors called for new leadership with "manly courage" to work for decent wages, protest segregated army units, and fight against lynching and disfranchisement.[49]

A. Philip Randolph and Chandler Owen iconoclastically appropriated for themselves the same term, "the New Negro," that W. E. B. Du Bois and George Haynes had used to describe themselves two decades earlier and that was about to come into common usage. By 1925 "the New Negro" would be used to stand for the entire generation that came of age during the Great Migration. Haynes and Du Bois were bluntly asked "to make way for the new radicalism of new Negroes." While the old guard did not exit as demanded, the younger men began to stake out their positions vis-à-vis black workers. The newest "new Negroes" sounded the first notes in a cacophony of internal criticism that would characterize the 1920s among black intellectuals. Du Bois and other early social scientists were given little respect in the early years of the *Messenger*. Haynes's and Du Bois's scholarship was seen as far too literary and not very scientific. "Sometimes Dr. Du Bois has been termed a sociologist. The alleged Negro historian, Benjamin Brawley, makes this inexcusable error. . . . Dr. Du Bois has often written upon sociological titles, but the sociology is not to be found as we understand it. His 'Suppression of the African Slave Trade' is a purely descriptive, quasi-historical work. His 'Philadelphia Negro' is a heavily padded work, filled with superfluous matter, very much like a similar work by Dr. George E. Haynes, entitled 'The Negro at Work in New York City.'"[50]

George Haynes was even more regularly abused by the *Messenger* than was Du Bois. The *Messenger* grudgingly gave Du Bois some credit for having founded the Niagara Movement, terming him a bridge and a "good transition from Booker Washington's compromise methods to the era of the new Negro."[51] Haynes was depicted as indistinguishable from "that extremely conservative wing of Negroes, who can qualify to the satisfaction of Tillman, Blease and Vardaman," such as Robert Russa Moton, Booker T. Washington's successor at Tuskegee, who was acceptable to the most racist politicians.[52] The Division of Negro Economics was lampooned, and Haynes's publications were ridiculed. One *Messenger* headline trumpeted the charge that "George Haynes Compromises the Case of the Negro Again," while another article depicted Haynes as belaboring the obvious in needless studies and as "pouring over figures to find out whether Negroes are actually laboring in the United States."[53] Randolph and Owen began to moderate their rhetoric and personal attacks about 1923, when the *Messenger* joined the NAACP and the NUL in an anti-Garvey campaign. Having finally found some common ground on which to meet, when Randolph founded the Brotherhood of Sleeping Car Porters both Du Bois and Haynes supported the union's efforts to organize.

Haynes and Woodson Institutionalize Training and Scholarship

The five new men who became major labor analysts in the 1920s accessed the informal networks that had helped the first cadre but were among the first beneficiaries of more permanent mechanisms for obtaining graduate degrees and getting published. They were a new generation, born between 1891 and 1901 to pious, working-class parents or in the genteel poverty of a minister's family. They were at least a dozen years younger than the first cadre of Haynes,

Wright Jr., or Woodson and more than twenty years younger than Du Bois. Despite being two generations removed from slavery, it was still no simple matter for a black person to get a high school education between the turn of the century and World War I. Lorenzo J. Greene and Abram L. Harris were able to stay in their hometowns but Charles H. Wesley, Charles S. Johnson, and Ira De A. Reid each had to leave home as teenagers in order to attend preparatory school before they could be admitted to college.[54] These five are representative of the first sizable number—about two dozen—of black social scientists and historians who earned doctorates between 1920 and World War II. The younger social scientists reaped the benefits of the new institutional frameworks created by George E. Haynes and Carter G. Woodson in terms of fellowships, jobs, and publishing opportunities. The education, early careers, and first labor studies of these five men best illustrate how the combination of informal mentoring and new institutional mechanisms helped to nurture and develop the next generation of scholars.

At the beginning of their careers and at great personal cost, George Haynes and Carter Woodson gave building the formal structures that would help to develop another generation of black social scientists a priority equal to their analyses of black workers. Haynes and Woodson often diverted their own funding sources to ensure positions for their students and younger colleagues. Financial security did not seem to play a major role in either man's career decisions, since both would have earned higher salaries as college administrators or even as public school principals. George Haynes supplemented his inadequate salaries from Fisk University and the NUL by teaching in summer programs, raising vegetables, and selling hogs and cattle. He only earned his posted Department of Labor salary for about one year and was then forced to work on a daily rate, while keeping his staff employed full time. Carter Woodson's spending habits made frugal people seem like spendthrifts. He poured his salary, speaking fees, and book profits into the *Journal of Negro History* and the Association for the Study of Negro Life and History. Both eagerly identified talented young men and tried to mold them into professionals who shared their zeal for racial uplift. All five members of the rising generation of black labor scholars utilized a combination of the institutional resources of Haynes or Woodson to obtain graduate fellowships, employment, and publishing outlets and benefited from the informal network of recommendations, advice, and collaboration that had characterized the first decade of the twentieth century.[55]

The Segregated Scholars

Carter G. Woodson.
(Courtesy of the
Moorland-Spingarn
Research Center,
Howard University
Archives)

George Edmund Haynes and Carter G. Woodson spent the decade between 1908 and 1918 earning their doctorates, launching their careers as social scientists, and institution building. Both men completed their dissertations in 1912 and moved quickly to institutionalize the production of black scholars. Haynes was focused on the formal training and placement of social workers and social scientists, while Woodson sought to create a corps of professional historians and the operational capacity to document black life and history and to disseminate their scholarship to diverse audiences.

Carter Woodson left the University of Chicago in the fall of 1908 with a master's degree in history and immediately entered the doctoral program in history at Harvard University. He could only afford to stay in residence for the required year, so in the fall of 1909 Woodson moved to Washington, D.C., and taught in its segregated public high schools for the next decade, at the same time he was establishing the building blocks to professionalize the study of African American history.[56]

George Haynes's idée fixe was to have black professionals research, assist, and manage the labor and urban problems of black workers. To accomplish this goal he cofounded the National Urban League in 1910 and created the social science department at Fisk University, where he taught its first courses in sociology, economics, and Negro history. He developed a sequential social science curriculum for undergraduates, graduate, and professional students and placed his students in jobs that assisted workers and migrants. His initiatives placed far more emphasis on producing and placing black social workers than on finding jobs for working-class urban migrants. Haynes's undergraduate program trained social workers, and he helped his most talented male students get into graduate school using the informal network of sympathetic white faculty and administrators at Yale and Columbia Universities that Haynes found so essential as a graduate student. The formalized structure of the NUL Urban Fellows Program that Haynes established extended the number of universities that admitted black graduate students and supported them through placements at league branches.[57] Four of the five new labor analysts—Charles H. Wesley, Charles S. Johnson, Abram L. Harris, and Ira De A. Reid—used one or both of Haynes's networks.[58]

Carter G. Woodson's singular assumption of black history as "the cause" was no less ambitious than Haynes's mission, and he imbued his crusade with the zeal of a prophet. He soon established a professional association, a scholarly journal, and a publishing house that would undertake the comprehensive study of African American culture, began to win disciples who would spread the gospel of Negro history, and used innovative means to disseminate materials about the storied past of peoples of African descent. In 1915 Woodson established the Association for the Study of Negro Life and History with friends and associates from his student days at the University of Chicago. George Haynes was a founding member of the new organization. The ASALH was a forum for black scholars, intellectuals, teachers, and Negro history buffs. Woodson used research grants from foundations to pay his younger assistants and to underwrite the graduate school tuition for promising black students. The *Journal of Negro History*, which Woodson founded in 1916, was the first scholarly journal devoted to African American history, while his Associated Publishers ensured the publication of book-length historical studies, textbooks, and socioeconomic studies. As a dean at Howard University from 1918 to 1921, Woodson reorganized the curriculum, began a master's degree program in history, and taught the university's first black history courses. But by 1922 Woodson had left the academy for good to devote all his time and energy to "the cause," the promotion and dissemination of black history.[59]

Woodson also had a measurable impact on the development of black labor scholars. Woodson published several manuscripts as well as many articles in the *Journal of Negro History* by emerging scholars on labor, professionals, business development, and women workers, including the research of two pioneering black women social scientists, Myra Colson Callis and Elizabeth Ross Haynes. Woodson used research grants to fund studies of black workers and to support younger historians, such as A. A. Taylor's graduate studies in economic history at Harvard University. Carter Woodson's most extensive relationship with younger labor analysts was in his long and complicated association with the historians Charles H. Wesley and Lorenzo J. Greene, but black sociologists and economists were also active members of the ASNLH throughout the thirty-five years that Woodson was its director. The economists Abram Harris and Robert C. Weaver were among the labor experts who regularly delivered conference papers at ASNLH meetings.[60]

The historian Charles H. Wesley was influenced by both George Haynes and Carter Woodson. Wesley's early professional development illustrates the interaction of individual aptitude, mentoring via informal networks of black intellectuals, and the new formal structures. Wesley was one of George Haynes's first undergraduate students and later became one of Carter Woodson's most effective associates. Charles Wesley was born in Louisville, Kentucky, in 1891, the oldest of his generation of scholars. He was a nineteen-year-old college senior excelling in vocal music, theater, and football when he fell under the influence of the young new social science professor George Haynes.[61]

Haynes quickly developed a personal mentoring relationship with Wesley that was much like the one he had enjoyed with Du Bois, and he urged Wesley to become a sociologist like himself. Haynes scolded his student after Wesley confessed that he did not like the social work aspect of sociology and was more inclined toward history, even though Haynes had taught the Negro history and economics courses that had made Wesley interested in these subjects. Despite his initial disappointment at his pupil's rejection of sociology, Haynes helped Wesley to win a fellowship to attend Yale University in

Lewis Baxter Moore.
(Courtesy of the
Moorland-Spingarn
Research Center,
Howard University
Archives)

1911. At Yale, Wesley developed a reputation as an "independent type of colored man" for speaking his mind in his classes in economics, history, and education.[62]

Charles Wesley's first job teaching also came via the informal network of well-placed Fisk alumni. In the summer of 1912, while Wesley was singing in a quartet to earn money for graduate school, he met Lewis Baxter Moore, the innovative dean of Howard University's Teachers College. Moore, a Fisk graduate and one of the eight black men who had earned doctorates in the nineteenth century, promised to hire Wesley in the fall of 1913 after he earned his master's degree. In 1915 Haynes wrote to R. R. Wright Jr.'s old nemesis, the sociology professor Carl Kelsey at the University of Pennsylvania, in an attempt to secure a fellowship for Wesley so that he could begin work on a doctorate.[63]

Over time Charles Wesley made a successful transition from Haynes's student and protégé to a modernizing colleague. Wesley initially taught foreign languages and pedagogy as well as history courses at Howard University. The university's trustees had long rebuffed faculty attempts to offer courses in Negro or African history, but with Moore's approval Wesley added lectures on

The Segregated Scholars

black history to his American history classes. When Carter Woodson became dean at Howard five years later, Wesley benefited from the reorganization of the history courses at Howard into a single department. As the history department chair and dean of the school of liberal arts and the graduate school, Wesley further expanded departmental offerings. Wesley thus began his thirty-year career at Howard University assisted by the types of informal academic relationships that had characterized the building of the first cadre of social scientists. As his career developed, Wesley was helped by and in turn helped to build the scholarly institutions that Carter Woodson controlled.

An academic career was only one aspect of Charles Wesley's professional life. Wesley, like Haynes and Wright before him, was drawn to the ministry, and he eventually became an ordained AME minister.[64] He rose rapidly in

Charles H. Wesley. (Courtesy of the Moorland-Spingarn Research Center, Howard University Archives)

the church's hierarchy with the backing of Reverdy C. Ransom, one of R. R. Wright's early patrons and now a powerful bishop and protector of young intellectuals. Perhaps because he became a minister after he had established his academic career, social science and the church did not exert the contradictory pulls on Wesley that had caused Haynes to abandon divinity school in 1905 and Wright to turn down an offer to teach at Howard University in 1911. Rather than choose a single career Charles Wesley, simultaneously maintained two extremely busy lives: one in the academy, where he was a historian and an administrator, and one in the black public sphere, where he was a presiding elder of the AME church, fraternal leader, and champion of "the cause."[65]

Charles Wesley first encountered Carter Woodson in 1916, the year Woodson founded the *Journal of Negro History*, and he had immediately joined the ASNLH and soon began publishing in the *Journal of Negro History*. Wesley's involvement in both new enterprises proved to be providential for the development of Negro history as a scholarly discipline. When Woodson published a series of articles based on research papers that Wesley had begun at Yale in the early volumes of the *Journal of Negro History*, that helped to solidify the publication's reputation for careful scholarship. Wesley quickly became one of Woodson's most gifted contributors, whose earliest articles offered fresh insights on the Civil War and extended the periodical's purview to the Caribbean and Africa. Wesley was also handsome and an accomplished public speaker and choir director who quickly became one of the ASNLH's most popular organizers. The relationship between the two men was often stormy, however, because Woodson thought Wesley should concentrate his full energies on an agenda of research, publications, and public outreach. Wesley ignored Woodson's sarcasm, forgave his lengthy periods of not speaking, and disregarded the times Woodson fired him from projects. His ability to rise above his mentor's pettiness set the pattern for younger black historians in their interactions with Woodson. Woodson's habit of scornfully dismissing his young colleague for weeks or months and then resuming the relationship without apology, as if nothing had happened, did in fact hurt and infuriate Wesley. Charles Wesley was only willing to put up with Carter Woodson's obsessive personality because of the older man's devotion to black history. "The cause is greater than the man," was the terse explanation Wesley used to explain his lifelong loyalty to the irascible Woodson. When Wesley's former student Lorenzo J. Greene became Woodson's research assistant and book agent

Lorenzo J. Greene. (Library of Congress, with permission of Lorenzo T. Greene)

at the end of the 1920s, this explanation served as a steadying mantra for Greene as well.[66]

Carter Woodson's research support and dedication was a major influence on Lorenzo J. Greene's career as a social historian. Greene was born in 1899, and unlike the other labor analysts of his generation, he attended integrated public schools in his hometown of Ansonia, Connecticut. He came to Howard University as a premedical student but decided not to become a physician after taking history courses under Wesley, Walter Dyson, and the Africanist Leo Hansberry. Despite his change of majors, Greene was not very interested in black history until after he worked closely with Woodson for a few years. Charles Wesley's interest in black labor history developed independently of Woodson, having begun with his studies under George Haynes and intensified at Yale, but Greene undertook his first two studies of black workers at Woodson's behest.

Lorenzo Greene's first work for Woodson proved to be a baptism by fire, when he was a research assistant in 1928 on a study of the black church and Woodson peremptorily fired Charles Wesley, the study's director. This study helped to confirm Greene's agnosticism, and he became a severe critic of the black church. When Greene's public condemnation of the alleged greed and ignorance of selected ministers was reported in the black press, R. R. Wright Jr. felt obliged to reject the messenger and the ASALH. Wright sent out his own editorial countering Greene's findings and boycotted the 1931 ASNLH meeting. Greene was sternly rebuked by Woodson, whose views were virtually identical, but who depended on good relations with ministers to hold ASNLH meetings at their churches, to host speakers on black history, and to sell the books of the Associated Publishers. Greene said later that his experience with Woodson taught him how to "preach the gospel of Negro History." By 1930 he had also become "one of the most knowledgeable scholars about economic conditions at the advent of the Great Depression."[67] The first research on black workers done by Greene resulted in *The Negro Wage Earner*, which began as a year-long assignment from Woodson from 1928 to 1929.

The Depression and his fierce independence drastically cut into Woodson's outside funding for research projects. He used his steadily dwindling funds to support Greene's research on black workers and to fund his graduate studies at Columbia University, where Greene's principal advisor was the moderate white southern historian Evarts B. Greene. During the academic year 1931–32, Woodson supported Greene with a $1,200 fellowship, sending him $900 during one period while Woodson himself lived on $750. Greene's diary of the period records how Woodson bombarded him with advice on his courses and exams and with demands for assistance in proofreading various new books for Associated Publishers. Although the job market for historians was tight, Woodson rewarded his young assistant with a strong recommendation for a position at Lincoln University in Jefferson City, Missouri, which Greene accepted in 1933. Woodson's efforts to develop black historians first flowered in the 1930s and 1940s, when Lorenzo Greene and A. A. Taylor and other men he had supported earned doctorates and master's degrees. Before 1930 only three men—Du Bois (1895), Woodson (1912), and Charles Wesley (1925)—had earned doctorates in history, compared to the eight men and one woman with doctorates in sociology and economics.[68] Without Woodson's financial support, sponsored research, and publishing opportunities, and the

The Segregated Scholars

collegial support that the ASNLH offered, the steady growth in the number of professional historians after 1930 would have been much smaller.

The sociologists Charles S. Johnson and Ira De A. Reid and the economist Abram L. Harris utilized the well-established programs of graduate funding and executive placements that grew out of the institutional relationships between the NUL branches and university social work, sociology, and economics departments that George Haynes had set up one decade earlier.[69] First they became social work executives and later these relationships facilitated their evolution to social scientists. The formal and informal fellowship programs earmarked black graduate student placements for NUL branches, augmenting their staffs and at the same time avoiding a direct confrontation with discriminatory practices at the public and private social service agencies where white students were placed. Charles S. Johnson, for example, learned that his funding in the sociology department at the University of Chicago was tied to his assignment at the Urban League's Chicago branch, but he used this experience to secure a succession of research positions in which he examined black workers. The University of Pittsburgh was one of an expanding number of graduate schools who supported the NUL Fellows Program by providing tuition and a stipend for fellows chosen in a national competition to complete their master's degrees. As fellows at the university, Ira De A. Reid and Abram L. Harris conducted detailed studies of black industrial workers and worked for the Pittsburgh Urban League.[70] All three men were later hired as branch or national league executives, and their experiences deeply colored their methods and their maturation as social scientists.

Charles S. Johnson was born in 1893 in Bristol, Virginia, a small town near the southeastern tip of Tennessee. His father was a minister and bibliophile who sent him to Richmond as a young teenager to attend preparatory school and Virginia Union, a Baptist college. After his graduation in 1916, Charles S. Johnson enrolled in the Department of Sociology at the University of Chicago. Johnson's initial decision was to attend a school with a strong religious affiliation and can be linked to the same impulse that had drawn R. R. Wright Jr. and Monroe Work to Chicago fifteen years earlier, but the department was no longer dominated by ministers. Johnson soon met Robert Park, who had recently joined the faculty after serving as Booker T. Washington's ghostwriter. Park was also the president of the Chicago Urban League, and within one year of his arrival Johnson became director of research and records at the busy branch office, bringing his work to the attention of white social reformers in the city. Johnson's postgraduate studies did not proceed as smoothly. Because

Virginia Union did not have as strong a curriculum as Fisk or Atlanta Universities, Johnson was obliged to earn a second bachelor's degree, a Ph.B., as a prerequisite for admission to the graduate program in sociology. Then his plans to complete the program were interrupted when Johnson was called to active duty in World War I. After returning from France his graduate studies were permanently interrupted by the 1919 Chicago race riot. Much as witnessing the 1902 stockyards race riot had helped to push R. R. Wright Jr. toward his decision to become a sociologist, Charles Johnson seems to have been galvanized by his narrow escape from injury during the melee, and he left graduate school to work in the field of race relations. Johnson spent the next decade trying to link social research on black urban workers to social policies that would improve their living and working conditions.[71]

The Chicago race riot also gave the twenty-six-year-old Johnson his first opportunity to demonstrate his skills as a researcher, writer, and race relations expert to a broader audience. He was appointed associate executive director of the Commission on Race Relations, and he did most of the research and writing for its well-received 1921 report detailing the underlying causes of the riot and making recommendations for the future. Johnson was then named director of the Department of Research and Investigation, a new program of the NUL in New York, by Executive Director Eugene K. Jones, a fellow Virginia Union graduate. Johnson's appointment began the organization's systematic research program, finally fulfilling the last of George Haynes's original objectives. Charles Johnson was now in a position to make a real difference in black labor studies through the community studies he commissioned and his editorship of *Opportunity* magazine.[72]

The institutionalization of admission for outstanding black students to major university graduate programs and the placements helped Charles S. Johnson gain the empirical skills he needed for his new position, but the informal networks of black college alumni and white social reformers also played a role in his rapid rise.[73] Although he was not yet thirty and did not hold any advanced degrees, Charles Johnson's position at the NUL placed him at the center of research on black workers, with the ability to shape both scholars and scholarship. Johnson's new position in New York had a direct effect on the early careers of Abram Harris and Ira Reid.

By the time Abram L. Harris and Ira De A. Reid became Urban League Fellows at the University of Pittsburgh in the mid-1920s, the personal link to George Haynes was nearly erased within the NUL. Each man's early career was funded by league fellowships and employment, and Harris and Reid each began to write about black workers in the 1920s as a result of their association with Johnson. Both men did their doctoral studies at Columbia University, where the academic success of Haynes and the first decade of fellows at Columbia University had helped to make the social science faculty as receptive to black graduate students as was the University of Chicago. Reid and Harris found ample support for the theoretical and methodological innovations in labor studies they carried out in their doctoral studies, avoiding Charles Wesley's difficulties with his advisors at Harvard. Both men continued to study black workers after leaving the league to teach at Negro colleges, and each long admired and became close associates of W. E. B. Du Bois during the 1930s. Despite these similarities, the two men developed political philosophies that were distinct and were reflected in their mature studies of black workers and economic development.[74] The similarities in the career trajectories of Reid and Harris demonstrate that George Haynes's vision of creating educational and career opportunities that would produce black social workers and social scientists had been fully institutionalized.

Ira De Augustine Reid was born in 1901 in Clifton Forge, Virginia. He was the youngest of the five new labor scholars. Reid, like Charles S. Johnson, was the son of a Baptist minister and left home to attend high school. When the Reids moved to Savannah, Georgia, there were no public high schools for black children, so Reid's father contacted John Hope and arranged for his son to attend Morehouse Academy. He was drafted and served in World War I but completed Morehouse College in 1922. In his dogged pursuit of an education and immense intellectual curiosity, Ira Reid began to follow the distinctive route of the segregated scholar while a student at Morehouse. In 1923, between brief stints as a high school teacher in Texas and West Virginia, Reid attended summer school at the University of Chicago. Rather than next doing studies for a university settlement as had Du Bois, Wright, and Haynes, however, Reid, like Johnson, worked for the National Urban League as he continued his graduate study. In 1924 Reid won a NUL fellowship to the University of Pittsburgh, where he wrote a master's thesis entitled "The Negro in the Major Industries and the Building Trades of Pittsburgh."[75] Reid's success at developing programs during his placement at the Pittsburgh Urban League led to a full-time position as industrial secretary for the NUL's New York City branch, and he began doctoral studies in sociology at Columbia University. Charles S. Johnson quickly put Reid's considerable survey research skills to work on projects at the national office, giving him commissions to undertake community studies, asking him to assist on larger projects for the Research

Ira De A. Reid and W. E. B. Du Bois. (Atlanta University Photographs, Robert W. Woodruff Library of the Atlanta University Center; Photographer, Griffith J. Davis)

Division, and making him a regular contributor to *Opportunity*. Four years later, when Charles S. Johnson left the NUL to become chair of the Department of Social Science at Fisk University in 1928, Ira Reid became the research director of the NUL.

In 1934, when he was named professor of sociology at Atlanta University, Ira Reid became the last of the 1920s generation of black labor analysts to join a college faculty. As an already experienced researcher with his own distinctive voice, the thirty-three-year-old Reid became more a colleague than a protégé of W. E. B. Du Bois, whose return to Atlanta University coincided with Reid's arrival. The two men worked closely together to reenergize the social science curriculum and faculty. Reid would later succeed Du Bois as chair of the Department of Sociology and editor of *Phylon*, much as he had succeeded Charles S. Johnson fifteen years earlier.[76]

Abram L. Harris Jr. was born in 1899 in Richmond, Virginia, to working-class parents. He attended Virginia Union in his hometown, and after his graduation in 1922, Harris went to New York City and began taking courses at the New York School of Social Work and New York University. Two doors

Abram L. Harris.
(Courtesy of the
Moorland-Spingarn
Research Center,
Howard University
Archives)

were always open to the newly arrived Union man in New York City—at the
moderately conservative NUL and at the radical news magazine the *Messenger*. Abram Harris used both the NUL and the *Messenger* as bases when he
arrived in New York City. He made good use of the contacts he made through
his fellow alumni Eugene Jones and Charles S. Johnson at the NUL to fund
his further graduate studies and to secure his first full-time employment. The
Messenger staff introduced Harris to New York's leading black and white
socialists and radicals and helped to launch him as a social critic. The *Messenger*'s coeditor Chandler Owen was a Union alumnus who had been one of the
NUL's first fellows, but Owen and most NUL staffers were by then at such
political loggerheads that his name was frequently omitted from lists of former fellows.[77]

Harris's first professional job in New York City was as Charles S. Johnson's
assistant in the NUL's newly created Department of Research and Investigation. He helped Johnson get *Opportunity* magazine started and was soon
chosen to be an Urban League Fellow, where he earned a master's degree in
economics at the University of Pittsburgh. This placement was critical in the

---

development of Harris's economic ideas because it gave him greater insights into the role of blacks in basic industries than he might have received had he remained in New York City at the New York School of Social Work. After receiving his master's degree in 1924, Harris taught briefly at West Virginia Collegiate Institute, where he made some pioneering studies of blacks in the coal-mining industry, and then he became the executive secretary of the Minneapolis Urban League. Up to this point, Harris seemed outwardly to be proceeding along the path toward racial leadership that George Haynes had paved and Johnson and Reid had followed. Harris had an advanced degree and training in social work, and he was directing an agency dedicated toward social reform. But Harris had already denounced George Haynes in print as a throwback to Booker T. Washington and was moving steadily away from the NUL's philosophical orbit to become one its most vociferous critics.[78]

Black Labor Studies during the Migration's Second Wave, 1921–1927

A second phase of migration and labor analyses was centered in the NUL community studies and publications that were directed by the young sociologist Charles S. Johnson. This phase, from about 1921 to 1927, roughly paralleled the second wave of migrants, which brought another half million black folk to the North over the period between 1922 and 1925. A core of the younger group of social scientists who were connected to the National Urban League—Johnson, Reid, and Harris—had the clear edge in the quantity of the descriptive studies if not always the quality of their prescriptive analyses, but all three generations of black labor analysts were engaged in research or public debates. Documenting the causes for the migration continued to occupy black social scientists, but social studies of employment and living conditions of black workers in cities such as Minneapolis and Baltimore began to appear along with examinations of specific occupations, such as domestic service and coal mining. This period of labor studies was marked by continued similarities in the methods of black social scientists and a general concurrence on the causes for the migration, but growing differences in their conclusions that were based on competing philosophies of racial uplift. Joe William Trotter Jr. has argued that while scholarship during the Great Migration "placed black migration within a larger historical context," this often came at the expense of examining in depth the processes of black migration over time.[79]

In the mid-1920s George Haynes, R. R. Wright Jr., Carter G. Woodson, and

W. E. B. Du Bois were deeply involved in the overall debate concerning the success of the migration and of black northern workers but did few new empirical research projects on these topics. George Haynes's detailed study of black workers in war industries, *The Negro at Work in World War and Reconstruction,* helped to mark the transition between the first and second phases of black migration studies. In 1922 Haynes became the director of the Department of Race Relations at the Federal Council of Churches, but he did not end his academic interest in black workers and frequently served on panels as a labor expert.[80]

W. E. B. Du Bois continued to discuss migration and labor, in *The Crisis* and in "The Hosts of Black Labor," his most extended commentary. He was concerned about the impact that the migration was having on black people already living in the North, a theme underlined in the 1921 research on family budgets of Sadie Tanner Mossell, the first black person to earn a doctorate in economics.[81] The 1920s were a highly productive period for Woodson, who continued to write on economic themes in the same vein as in *A Century of Negro Migration,* and he published two comprehensive analyses on the migrants and domestic workers in the *Journal of Negro History* by the Yale graduate student Henderson Donald and Elizabeth Ross Haynes, respectively.

R. R. Wright Jr.'s ongoing editorship of the *Christian Recorder* kept him from launching new labor research projects, but he filled the "Pulpit and the Pew" section of the paper with advice for northern congregations to do more for migrants and was a leader in the Colored Protective Association, which was organized after the race riots in Philadelphia in 1918.[82] He also served as the secretary for Philadelphia's Interdenominational Ministerial Alliance, which tried to find jobs and housing for new arrivals. Wright introduced black labor studies to his thousands of weekly readers via a "Book Week," featuring black social scientists such as W. E. B. Du Bois, Kelly Miller, Carter G. Woodson, and Monroe Work, who spoke on topical issues at local churches.[83]

The NUL's Department of Research and Investigations and its *Opportunity* magazine accounted for much of the survey research and published data on black workers in the 1920s. The new department was initiated by an $8,000 three-year grant from the Carnegie Corporation that allowed the NUL to make the detailed community studies it had long insisted were a necessary component to planning and social reforms. As the first director, Charles S. Johnson's initial salary was $3,600, quite a bit more than most social scientists earned at the time.[84]

Charles S. Johnson fully embraced the optimistic race relations policy of the NUL that permitted him to mildly critique but not upset the status quo. The new department's case studies enabled the NUL to help its branches base their programs and their financial appeals on detailed descriptions of local black employment patterns, housing and recreational needs, and other social indicators. Johnson conducted many studies personally, among them a community study of Baltimore and a large research project in which the racial practices of labor unions were investigated. The community studies followed a similar format. First meetings were held with white and black community leaders and league officials. Then questionnaires designed or approved by Johnson were administered to workers and employers by local league staff and volunteers.[85]

Johnson increased his ability to direct survey research with a small staff by making efficient use of branch managers who were professional social workers and NUL fellows who were required to do their fieldwork at local league branches. League Fellows Ira Reid and Abram Harris's master's degree theses on black industrial workers were designed so that they could be used to plan the Pittsburgh branch's programs. When Abram Harris became a branch director in Minneapolis he undertook local studies under Johnson's direction.[86]

Under Charles S. Johnson, packaging objective survey research became an art form in which data were collected that clearly demonstrated the blatant discrimination black workers faced in hiring, salaries, access to skilled work, union membership, housing, health care, and almost anything that could be measured. Few conclusions, however, were drawn using this data; most of the blame that was apportioned fell squarely on the shoulders of the already overburdened black workers. The black executives and white board members of the NUL believed that emphasizing political and legal injustices would antagonize powerful business interests that would eventually be persuaded to hire, train, and promote black workers by research publications and publicity campaigns. Recommendations, not surprisingly, were heavily weighted toward establishing or reinforcing league programs. National Urban League community studies always resulted in noncontroversial recommendations to be taken up by the local branch in conjunction with business and labor officials. Although the historian Nancy J. Weiss states in her history of the NUL that the Department of Research surveys were "never prescriptive," it was more the case that the mild prescriptions that they contained were unlikely to cure much more than the most minor headaches of black workers and never attacked the cancer of racism.[87]

Trotter has suggested that the emphasis on reform in most migration studies before the 1930s overemphasized the "pathological" aspects of the migrants' behavior and social conditions. While the reformist tendency of black social scientists is seen most clearly in the work of those associated with the NUL, the same impulse that led writers to overstress the negative behavioral characteristics that southern blacks allegedly brought with them caused Johnson to oversell the minor successes of individuals in the workplace as great racial accomplishments. Weiss has detailed how Charles S. Johnson and his successors carried articles featuring black workers' rise in new occupations, while most of the placements of the league and most of the experiences of the majority of black workers were in the traditional low-wage areas of domestic work and unskilled labor.[88]

Simultaneously with the conduct of research studies, Charles S. Johnson began *Opportunity* magazine in January 1923 and opened its pages to the new generation of black social scientists and social workers. He called the magazine a "new effort" with "the desire to approach . . . new problems with an increased technique for dealing with them."[89] *Opportunity* was a national publication whose peak circulation was less than a tenth of the 100,000 who read *The Crisis* in 1918, but it reached a well-educated audience of black professionals and younger artists and wealthy white NUL supporters. Johnson also published the poems, short stories, photographs, and illustrations of artists of the Harlem Renaissance. The historian David Levering Lewis has argued that Charles S. Johnson had a "vast influence" on the Harlem Renaissance by working behind the scenes and through the *Opportunity* awards that helped some younger artists attract publishers and patrons.[90] One difference between the New Negro literature and the labor studies in *Opportunity* was that while the literary artists represented the most talented of the younger New Negro writers and artists, its labor studies were a continuation of the descriptive, moderate-to-conservative, nonpolemical studies that had characterized the work of George Edmund Haynes and writing that reflected the philosophy of the NUL. Nevertheless, *Opportunity* was even more influential in the development of black labor studies in the 1920s than it was for black literature, in part because black workers and migration were its major concern. The editorials in the first issue deftly emphasized that problems such as black migration, race riots, and better jobs could be resolved through the careful aggregation of data by specialists, cooperation among representative Negroes and white industrial and political leaders, and social work. *Opportunity's* readers were given a clear signal that the National Urban League was not a militant organization. Statements on migration, employment, and scientific research from speeches about racial problems by the conservatives President Warren Harding, Henry Ford, and Abbott Lowell, president of Harvard, helped to reinforce that impression. Henry Ford suggested that jobs were more important to black workers than any feelings of antipathy from their white coworkers. "He needs a job, he needs the sense of INDUSTRIAL BELONGING which it ought to be the desire of our industrial engineers to provide."[91] Black workers at Henry Ford's auto plants had the sense that "industrial belonging" came at a price: Ford was the last to unionize; and black workers had the worst jobs and were barred from living in Dearborn, Michigan, a town he had built for white Ford workers.

Charles Johnson believed that "facts carry their own light." He approved of Lowell's statement that black people had been given sympathy out of northern whites' sense that they owed black people justice. But what whites really owed the Negro, according to Lowell and Johnson, was "their thought . . . to investigate his needs, his capacities, and therefore the opportunities that can be opened up to him."[92] W. E. B. Du Bois's consistent insistence that survey research could be used to plan for progressive social change and full equality was redefined by the NUL as research that provided for "racial adjustment," "interracial cooperation," and "opportunity." *Opportunity's* goal was to promote interracial cooperation and to "present objectively, the facts of Negro life" to blacks and whites as "a dependable guide to understanding." The ambiguity of the NUL magazine's ultimate purpose was deliberate so that it could appeal both to black intellectuals and to its white, more conservative supporters.[93]

Johnson's first articles in *Opportunity* consisted of summaries of league research department reports, articles on black workers by industrial social workers, black and white social scientists, and white businessmen. Charles S. Johnson's personal style was different from George Haynes's; he was young, a patron of the black arts, and most of the younger intellectuals such as Abram Harris, who agreed with the *Messenger* that Haynes was a hopeless mossback, believed they saw a different type of black man in Johnson.

Comprehensive annual reports on black labor and a regular column on labor began to appear in *Opportunity* after 1925, when the National Urban League established a separate Department of Industrial Relations, headed by the former Chicago Urban League executive director T. Arnold Hill, another Virginia Union graduate.[94] Hill's labor column reflected the tendency of *Opportunity* not to draw conclusions from its data that challenged the NUL's relationships with its partners in the business community or its friends in social welfare agencies. But his columns clearly depicted the worsening economic situation for blacks in the late 1920s, and they provide the best contemporary data on the growth of black unemployment before the Depression. Hill's data showed unequivocally that the economic situation for blacks in the South in the late 1920s was disastrous and that the position of black workers in the North became increasingly vulnerable in the slowdown in the economy that occurred at least one year before the stock market crash.[95]

Johnson's *Opportunity* studies provided close analyses of the Great Migration, offering a raison d'être for the expansion of the NUL branches and giving them the authority to provide social service programs to black workers.[96] He wanted black migrants to be seen by whites as coming to cities and factories to work hard and not as refugees. Johnson argued that knowing the reasons that blacks migrated was necessary for planning effective social service programs. "Knowing just why Negroes left the South and what they were looking for will carry one further toward making their adjustment easier." Ironically, he felt unable to argue another, perhaps even more fundamental reason that many black workers were motivated to leave the South: lynchings and racism. Johnson appears to have assumed that northern whites would find the latter reason unacceptable as a motivation for blacks to migrate: "The thought of flight from persecution excites little sympathy either from the practical employer or the northern white population among whom these Negroes will hereafter live. Every man who runs is not a good worker."[97] After Johnson left the NUL in 1928, *Opportunity* carried fewer literary contributions and its articles were more focused on the labor and work issues that confronted local branches, but his descriptive imprint on *Opportunity* was long lasting.

While Ira Reid worked for the NUL in its New York City branch as the industrial secretary from 1924 to 1928, and after he succeeded Charles S. Johnson as the director of the Department of Research and Investigations of the NUL, his official writings on black workers followed the lines of the deeply descriptive and mildly prescriptive literature that had become the league's specialty, with a significant variation. Reid's writings frequently revealed a nuanced appreciation of black folklife and working-class culture and were written with a sense of humor and a graceful style that were rarely matched by many of his contemporaries.

An early example of Ira Reid's sensitivity to black working-class culture can be found in his 1927 short story "Mrs. Bailey Pays the Rent." Reid uses a pseudoscholarly frame to trace the southern origins of the rent party and its northern manifestations during the Great Migration. The rent party as cultural practice is revealed to be a lively adaptation to financial distress. The short story purports to explain the social consequences of the actions depicted in the popular song "Won't You Come Home Bill Bailey." Reid's role as a character within this story is similar to the role of the narrators in Claude McKay's *Home to Harlem* and *Banjo*, and it anticipates Langston Hughes's "Simple Stories." All three feature a college-educated man serving as a witness to the trials and triumphs of urban folk culture, which is both richer and more complex than black middle-class life. Instead of having educated blacks act as interpreters of white culture to the poor, or as the "talented tenth" bent on creating their own high culture, Reid depicts working-class black folk as fashioning their own inventive strategies for coping with urban life, even finding it necessary to explain "the facts of life" to their more educated but politically naive brothers.[98]

Ira De A. Reid's NUL reports were supposed to follow its explicitly noncontroversial formula, but he occasionally found ways to subvert their studied absence of critical opinion. In one instance he used the frontispiece of the league's completely descriptive study of black workers and organized labor to more vividly detail how various labor union's practices were used to exclude and marginalize black workers. The same information was dryly itemized in the text of the league's study. Reid counterpoised the statements of two characters in Claude McKay's *Home to Harlem* as if they were in dialogue in order to capture the starkly contrasting views of black workers toward organized labor. Zeddy, the strikebreaking worker, militantly defended his right to a decent job by declaring, "I'll scab through hell to make my living." His friend Jake, the novel's protagonist, refused to scab but was pessimistic in his assessment of the realities of black-white, working-class unity. "Nope, I won't scab, but I ain't a joiner kind of fellah. . . I ain't no white folk's nigger, and I ain't no poor white's fool. When I longshore in Philly I was a good union man. But when I made New York I done finds out that they gives the colored mens the worser piers and holds the best o' them job for the Irishmen. No, parder keep you card. . . . But I tell you, things ain't at all lovely between white and black in this heah gawd's own country."[99]

In his selective use of McKay, Reid placed himself firmly along the side of those in the New Negro movement who sought to celebrate the joys and woes of working-class black life. Reid offered a view of a black man whose working-class consciousness is firm but not doctrinaire. Jake fully understood the dilemma of black workers who attempted to hold to the ideals of labor solidarity in the face of racism. In response he had fashioned a personal solution that allowed him to maintain his sense of integrity. Reid's use of this passage was all the more subversive because NUL branches were sometimes accused of using their job registries to place strikebreakers.

Like Reid, Abram Harris began writing on labor issues under the influence of Charles Johnson and the National Urban League. He produced his first work for the league in 1923, after taking classes at the New York School of Social Work and while working as Charles S. Johnson's assistant in the Department of Research. He was the business manager for the first five issues of *Opportunity,* contributing book reviews as well as articles during the magazine's early years. Between 1923 and 1926 Harris earned a master's degree from the University of Pittsburgh, taught at West Virginia Collegiate Institute, and served as the executive secretary of the Minneapolis Urban League. He also helped with the *Messenger* and began to publish articles on migration, coal miners, and black intellectuals in mainstream journals such as *Current History* and *Social Forces.*

Harris's first labor writings on the migration itself and about black coal miners were well within the league's framework, even though he departed slightly from Johnson's "consciously optimistic" formula for presentation of data on black workers. Harris's articles on coal miners contained more detailed accounts of socialist politics in the South, of direct Ku Klux Klan activity, and of union organizing than were usually found in *Opportunity.* Still, Harris's criticism of white socialists in one article and his failure to provide a solution to black coal miners' "plight" in another show that at crucial points Harris stayed just inside Johnson's carefully drawn ideological boundaries.

One of Abram L. Harris's earliest national publications was his analysis of contemporary black intellectuals' ideologies, "The Negro Problem as Viewed by Negro Leaders," published in *Current History.* In the article, Harris develops his own point of view. His conclusions were more complex than the reflexive condemnations delivered by the *Messenger* essayists when writing about older black public figures. Harris placed black leaders along a spectrum from conservative to radical, with the most conservative leaders portrayed as closely allied with southern segregationist business interests. Robert Russa Moton, Booker T. Washington's successor at Tuskegee, was considered by Harris and other self-consciously New Negro writers to be the most conservative and the most worthy of scorn. Harris considered George Haynes to be far more conservative than Charles Johnson or Eugene Jones, terming Haynes a "direct adjunct of the Tuskegee philosophy." Initially Harris treated the NUL as an organization that advocated racial advancement in a generally positive fashion. By the late 1920s, however, he would begin to find unacceptable Johnson's unwillingness to draw political conclusions from his data. Abram Harris was drawn to the scientific aspects of Du Bois's early work and to his role as founder of the Niagara Movement. Harris did not agree with the *Messenger*'s condemnation of Du Bois's scholarship. He believed that Du Bois's "scathing yet admittedly brilliant and scholarly" writings were crucial to black people's ability to gain their self-respect. This perception of Du Bois as a radical helped to enable Harris to imagine himself as a radical scholar in his own right and to ultimately reject the philosophy of the NUL. Harris and Du Bois began to be serious correspondents in 1924 and had a warm personal relationship for the next decade.[100]

Old and New Approaches, 1927–1931

At the end of the 1920s five major studies of black workers were published by black social scientists that made this short period as critical to the future direction of black labor studies as 1905 had been for earlier developments in the field. This literature no longer moved in a unified direction, however, because theoretical and methodological differences between black labor scholars now served as proxies for wider political debates on class and race consciousness that were taking place. New books by Charles S. Johnson, Ira De A. Reid, Abram L. Harris, Charles H. Wesley, Lorenzo J. Greene, and Carter G. Woodson were each a part of the redirection in black labor studies. Their movement away from studies of migrants and their experiences, and toward broader examinations of black men and women in the workplace, was important in part because the studies helped to locate competing assumptions concerning racial consciousness and class formation that were at the heart of public discourse on the roles and visions of black intellectuals during the Depression and New Deal, a topic we will discuss in full in chapter 6. More immediately, these books were significant because when taken together they illustrated four methodological, theoretical approaches that marked the maturation of the discipline of black labor studies into a field that offered powerful insights on work, race, and class in America. The black labor scholars who wrote these texts went on to play a crucial role in the development of the social sciences at black colleges in the 1930s. Charles S. Johnson, Charles H. Wesley, Abram L. Harris, and Ira De A. Reid helped to establish major social science programs at Fisk, Howard, and Atlanta Universities and led younger black social scientists back to the academy.

Three of the five new books used approaches that had characterized black labor studies for more than a decade, but Abram Harris and Charles Wesley made significant departures from the past models of black labor scholarship. The work Ira Reid contributed to the NUL's *Negro Membership in American Labor Unions* (1930) and Charles Johnson's *The Negro in American Civilization* (1930) illustrated a methodological approach that deliberately presented reams of almost raw data with little interpretation. *The Negro in American Civilization* explicitly synthesized contemporary research findings, as if all but the most egregiously racist studies had the same theoretical point of view. The NUL and its allies thought that this method let the facts speak for themselves.[101]

Lorenzo J. Greene and Carter G. Woodson's *The Negro Wage Earner* was almost as empirical as the Johnson and Reid studies but continued Woodson's much more interpretive analyses and his sardonic criticism of the interracial cooperation philosophy of Johnson and Haynes. The absence of theory in Carter Woodson's historical writings was not as unusual in his discipline. Woodson would likely have successfully counterclaimed that his decision to make black people historical subjects was in itself a theoretical breakthrough. American historians were not yet as interested in theory as were sociologists or economists in the late 1920s. Empiricism almost completely unsullied by theories of sociology or history was the order of the day in these three studies.

Charles S. Johnson solidified his position as the research embodiment of the NUL's moderate race relations or interracial cooperation philosophy in *Negro Membership in American Labor Unions* and *The Negro in American Civilization,* studies that he began in the mid-1920s when he served as director of research at the NUL. His studies are important today because their empiricism helped to secure Johnson's place as the primary beneficiary of the funding allocated to support research on black social and economic life from the late 1920s through the 1940s.

Although one of Johnson's major projects, *Negro Membership in American Labor Unions* was researched and largely written by Ira Reid. It was a hallmark of NUL survey research, an empirical document that contained little interpretive analysis aside from Reid's attempt to introduce the voices of black workers in the frontispiece. It presented the total number of black trade unionists, with breakdowns for occupations and unions, and it listed the unions that prevented blacks from becoming members. The NUL plainly hoped that a comprehensive collection of data would help them pressure the AFL to increase the number of blacks in member unions, despite the fact that the trade union's leadership had been making hollow promises to the league about organizing black workers for at least fifteen years. The black sociologist E. Franklin Frazier was damning *Negro Membership in American Labor Unions* with faint praise when he described it as an "excellent companion" to Abram L. Harris and Sterling D. Spero's much more "interpretive and synthetic study," *The Black Worker.*[102]

The Negro in American Civilization, subtitled *A Study of Negro Life and Race Relations in the Light of Social Research,* demonstrated the central role of black labor studies and the moderate interracial relations formula in Charles S. Johnson's ability to gain the full confidence of white educational foundations. The groundwork for this study was laid by George Haynes, who had organized a conference on race relations in March 1925 that concluded with a resolution calling for a comprehensive examination of the survey research on black economic and social life. The National Interracial Conference was made up of sixteen national religious and social welfare organizations whose sole purpose was to oversee a research team, cosponsor a 1928 conference, and produce a final publication that reviewed and summarized contemporary scholarship on African Americans. This body's tasks echoed somewhat the format of the Atlanta University conferences that had ceased a dozen years earlier. The Russell Sage Foundation executive director Mary Van Kleeck served as chair of the executive committee, and George Haynes was named executive secretary; his office at the Federal Council of Churches became the administrative headquarters. Charles S. Johnson was appointed the research secretary and given the task of synthesizing the reports of selected black and white social scientists and directing a small group of researchers from his office at the NUL. The Social Science Research Council granted $5,000 to hire research assistants. Johnson assembled a 244-page data book that was given to participants at a December 1928 conference that was held at Howard University. This was in a sense the sort of joint black and white social study that Du Bois had called for as a young man in "The Study of the Negro Problems," some thirty years earlier, and he was present at the research conference to deliver a paper on citizenship. The research of black social scientists would get an official legitimation that was long overdue. The involvement of the Russell Sage Foundation and the Social Science Research Council brought scholarship on black working people into the mainstream. The labor studies of the conference attendees Du Bois, Woodson, Lorenzo Greene, Charles Wesley, and Ira Reid were liberally cited, as were the works of the conference organizers Johnson and Haynes. In the words of Van Kleeck, "this recognition by the Social Science Research Council of the significance of the task" was "more important even than financial support."[103]

Black workers and black labor studies were at the heart of both the investigation and the conference that produced *The Negro in American Civilization*. The book began with nine chapters on black workers, from the role of black labor in the establishment of the Americas to migration, organized labor, and women and children in industry. Mary Van Kleeck, of the Russell Sage Foundation, defined the good society in Socratic terms as "the power of each individual in the state to do his own work." This view placed finding remedies for black people's restricted economic opportunities at the center of the study of black Americans. The volume's final findings were praised because they "revealed a sound basis for planning programs of improvement" and allowed readers to authoritatively reject allegations of black people's genetic inferiority or inherent criminality as "a case not proved." Alain Locke, a philosophy professor at Howard University, believed that the conference was unique because it recognized the value of social research. He argued that "never before had the entire gamut of social thought and programs connected with the race problem been spanned in an effective conference."[104] *The Negro in American Civilization* was supposed to represent in a single volume "a reasonably faithful contemporary picture of Negro life and relationships with the white race in the United States." The radical journalist Benjamin Stolberg differed sharply with the mainstream's approval of Johnson's methods, particularly his lack of interpretation. His review in the *Herald Tribune* called the compilation "the most competent example of a very bad book," asserting that its dearth of critical analysis meant that readers would learn no more from the book about black life "than you know about American society after you have read the Almanac." Stolberg, who was a close friend of Abram Harris, overstated the descriptive nature of the text, but his essential point was nonetheless correct.[105]

Abram L. Harris, who was a member of the economics department at Howard at the time of the National Interracial Conference, was notably absent from the long list of attendees. One wonders if he was deliberately excluded from the conference. His biographer, William Darity Jr., has detailed how Harris had the opportunity at the 1930 Interracial Seminar at Washington's elegant black-owned Whitelaw Hotel to make an extensive public criticism of the consequences of the NUL and Federal Council of Churches' approach to the problems of workers. Harris made an incendiary luncheon speech entitled "The Black Man and This Economic World," and he boasted privately that his verbal battle with George Haynes was praised by Howard University president Mordecai Johnson and the philosopher Alain Locke. "When I finished with Haynes I had him proving that the Negro Church and leaders like himself had been the employers' greatest friend and the Negro workers' worst enemy." Characteristically, Harris did not publicly take on his friend Charles S. Johnson at the luncheon but told him privately that he thought little of the methods used in *The Negro in American Civilization* and insinuated that Johnson was an opportunist. "When I told him that the foundations paid liberally for his stuff because he refused to draw conclusions and refused to finance my work because I do draw conclusions he said that I had a persecution complex."[106] The two men would not agree, but Harris's description of their disagreement lies at the heart of the differences in their views toward research methods.

While most of the black labor scholars, with the exception of Charles Wesley, were outside of the academy from 1910 to 1930, Charles S. Johnson helped to lead the way back to black colleges. Johnson became the head of the Department of Social Science and the director of the Social Science Institute at Fisk University and moved to Nashville in the summer of 1928. Social sciences instruction had languished after George Haynes left the university in 1918, but Johnson had been assured of the university's renewed interest and their new commitment to research and graduate programs. Johnson was able to use his success at the NUL and with the National Interracial Council to draw significant foundation support for a large-scale social research program. Charles Johnson assured the president of Fisk that he was not planning to continue to do northern community studies as he had at the NUL: "My research interest is definitely committed to the South." He intended to turn his attention to designing a series of socioeconomic studies of black life in the South, a research focus that had been seriously neglected in the fifteen-plus years since Du Bois had left Atlanta University for the NAACP. Johnson assembled an outstanding group of social scientists at Fisk University over the next two and a half decades, including E. Franklin Frazier, Preston Valien, Robert Park, and Oliver Cox.[107]

While George Haynes's and Charles S. Johnson's close ties with foundations and moderate views were lightning rods for the criticism by Abram Harris and the more radical black social scientists, Carter Woodson's studies of black workers did not elicit the same fury. Woodson and Harris clashed over Woodson's support for black business, but their differences were grounded in theory rather than disagreements over racial consciousness. Woodson's exacting standards of obligation to the race, his constant criticisms of black professionals, and his fierce independence from and criticism of white foundations protected him from the personal attacks that were openly directed at George Haynes and whispered about Charles S. Johnson by Harris and the younger radicals. The younger black labor scholars did not reject Woodson's methods so much as they attempted to supersede them with more synthetic treatments, and in the case of Charles H. Wesley, a more clearly defined theoretical framework.

The mixed reaction to *The Negro Wage Earner*, Carter Woodson's second monograph on black workers during the Great Migration, was a measure of the much greater expectation for theoretical and methodological sophistication that had been raised by the work of Charles Wesley and Abram Harris. *The Negro Wage Earner* was begun in 1928 by Woodson's then full-time research assistant Lorenzo J. Greene. Greene did most of the research and writing of this study of the major occupations of black men and women. Lorenzo Greene was last of the five younger scholars who began to study black workers, largely because he did not become interested in black history until after he started working for Woodson in 1927 as a research assistant, traveling book salesman, and jack-of-all-trades. He had met Charles S. Johnson about 1924 at the beginning of his graduate studies in history at Columbia University, but Greene resisted Johnson's and the NUL head Eugene K. Jones's joint efforts to persuade him to apply for an Urban League fellowship.[108] In his own account, Greene received only a minimum of direction from Woodson, who provided his young protégé with a chronological format and instructions to collect data that would "show the various occupations in which Negroes have been employed and to determine whether or not they have increased or decreased." Greene maintained that Woodson contributed little to the work, but when the book was ready for publication, Greene was stunned to discover that Woodson was listed as his coauthor and miffed that Woodson would condescendingly claim that he had "reduced the work to literary form."[109]

Greene's diaries and *The Negro Wage Earner* itself reveal a slightly more complicated story. Woodson closely directed Greene on the study, taking him to the Library of Congress, writing letters of introduction to archivists, overseeing his selection of source materials, and regularly reviewing his notes. While Greene was shortchanged in terms of sole authorship, Woodson's heavy hand was all too evident in *The Negro Wage Earner*. Woodson also commissioned Greene and the sociologist Myra Colson Callis to undertake a shorter descriptive study on black employment in Washington, D.C. Over time Lorenzo Greene became increasingly aware of the limitations of *The Negro Wage Earner* as an analytical history, as opposed to an interpretive demography, although he was no less embittered about the coauthorship. Greene's mature style, as seen in his pathbreaking *The Negro in Colonial New England,* bears little resemblance to Woodson's, except for his continuing interest in black workers' economic position. Woodson and Greene fell somewhat short of their aim of providing the interpretation of the data that would allow them to make good their claim that *The Negro Wage Earner* was an "interpretative . . . economic history of the Negro in the United States since emancipation." Woodson's description more aptly fit Charles Wesley's *Negro Labor in the United States* than it fit his own monograph.[110]

Contemporary reviewers had rather faint praise for *The Negro Wage Earner,* indicating that a more theoretical approach was desired. Lorenzo Greene confided to his diary that he was not surprised at the harsh reviews. "In fact I even rejoice because Woodson's name is there. He felt he was injuring me." Many journals reviewed Greene and Woodson's *The Negro Wage Earner* and Abram Harris and Sterling Spero's *The Black Worker* together; the latter was seen as more interpretive, insightful, and analytical. While Greene held that *The Black Worker* was "well written" and recognized that Harris's approach was "concerned with theory," the poor reviews did not sit at all well with Woodson, and the *Journal of Negro History* responded with a rather peevish review of the Harris and Spero book. When Abram Harris published his critique of black businesses, *The Negro as a Capitalist,* a few years later, the *Journal of Negro History* responded as if it had been personally attacked.[111]

In contrast with the fact-laden descriptive studies of Johnson, Reid, Woodson, and Greene, Abram Harris and Sterling Spero's *The Black Worker* and Charles H. Wesley's *Negro Labor in the United States* offered fresh and brilliant uses of theory with new levels of methodological sophistication that made them the two best studies of black workers in the first three-quarters of the twentieth century. Charles Wesley's and Abram Harris's comprehensive narratives both began as dissertations but were departures from the labor studies that preceded them. Both men had returned to graduate school after establishing flourishing professional careers and publishing a number of articles in their fields. Each man was drawn to the intellectual challenges of graduate school and took advantage of this opportunity to sharpen their already impressive methodological techniques. Wesley and Harris also possessed the desire and ability to step beyond both the methodological and theoretical approaches of their disciplines and the older generation of black social scientists—Haynes, Woodson, Johnson, and Du Bois. Harris's writings had an independent, non-doctrinaire, radical socialist viewpoint from the early 1920s. Wesley had not planned to do his dissertation on black workers, but once he chose the topic his earlier course work at Yale gave his writing a part of its unique breadth. The shape, if not the content, of their important books derived from their graduate experiences while working on their doctorates. Wesley had an un-happy experience with his advisors at Harvard that determined the types of arguments he made in his study, but he extended and deepened his friend-ships with other black intellectuals who were in residence at the same time. Harris by contrast had a positive experience with his advisors at Columbia, and his book began as a joint dissertation project with a white graduate stu-dent named Sterling D. Spero.

Charles H. Wesley's innovative methods and crisp analysis in *Negro Labor in the United States* grew out of the combination of his training in economics at Yale, his work with George Haynes and other black labor scholars, and a dispute with his graduate advisors at Harvard. August Meier and Elliott Rud-wick's study of black historians called Wesley's study "avant-garde and pio-neering." It was important new work in American history as well as black labor studies because it marked a major methodological and theoretical step from the traditions of black labor analysts and predated the new social history and new labor history by more than fifty years. Wesley's skillful blending of histor-ical analysis with economic interpretations won the immediate admiration of his colleagues. Charles S. Johnson hailed *Negro Labor* as "the most immedi-ately valuable contribution in recent years to the history of the Negro." Look-ing back, over thirty years later, the noted sociologist E. Franklin Frazier described the publication of *Negro Labor* as marking the moment when "sci-entific social research began at Howard."[112]

Wesley's decision to get a doctorate in history can be traced to his rejection of social work as a career in 1911 during his senior year in college, and his graduate work in history and economics at Yale from 1913 to 1915. Wesley's classes in history, sociology, and economics at Fisk and Yale and his seven years of college teaching and writing made him better prepared and more resolved than most other graduate students to write a pathbreaking dissertation. While he taught French, American constitutional history, and European history between 1913 and 1920, Wesley attended Howard University Law School for one year and studied French, music, language, and history in Paris. His first articles were on teaching methods in history, a subject that would engage him throughout his life. The confidence that he gained as a teacher and author would serve him well when he had a series of disagreements with his advisors over his proposed first thesis topic on the Confederacy and on his final topic on black labor.[113]

George Haynes and Carter Woodson both had encouraged Wesley to get a doctorate in history, but Wesley had married while he was at Howard University and was also supporting his widowed mother. He had a low salary even for Howard, and both of his protectors in the administration, Dean Moore and Carter Woodson, had left the university in 1920, making it difficult for Wesley to arrange a leave of absence in order to fulfill graduate program residency requirements. In the end, the Harvard historian Albert Bushnell Hart arranged for Wesley to be awarded the same Austin Scholar Graduate Fellowship that Du Bois had won at Harvard thirty years earlier. More important, as a Howard University trustee, Hart helped Wesley get a leave of absence in 1920. Because Hart was on leave that academic year, Wesley's advisor was Edward Channing, the author of an extensive multivolume history of the United States that was referred to as "the great work." Wesley did well in his course work and on his exams despite commuting to Washington, D.C., every other Sunday to preach so that his family might live in a church parsonage. He took his comprehensive examination under Channing, Frederick Jackson Turner, Arthur Schlesinger Sr., and Frederick Merk, all outstanding historians of their era. Merle Curti, distinguished American historian, was a fellow student in the Channing seminar and told Wesley what Arthur Schlesinger had said about his examination: "Schlesinger . . . said your special was one of the very best, if not the best he had ever listened to. . . . I am glad to have my own view of your ability borne out by someone else."[114]

Wesley had initially proposed a dissertation on his novel idea—at the time—that the Civil War had been lost due to a loss or collapse of popular support in the South for the Confederacy. Wesley's seminar paper entitled "The Collapse of the Confederacy" had won the only A awarded in the class. Channing found Wesley's thesis compelling and sent his dissertation proposal to Albert Bushnell Hart, an authority on the Civil War. Hart objected to the proposal in the strongest terms because it challenged his own thesis that the South had been militarily defeated, and he flatly forbade Wesley to continue. This was a time of great administrative turmoil at Howard University, so Wesley chose not to defy Hart, a powerful figure at both Harvard and Howard. Instead, Wesley picked another subject that had interested him since the beginning of the Great Migration: black workers. "I saw no reason to confront Professor Hart.

I told Channing that I would take a subject on 'Negro Labor' and he agreed. . . . Nevertheless, I continued to research and write on the Collapse of the Confederacy." Unfortunately, by the time Wesley's *Collapse of the Confederacy* appeared (1937), other scholars, including Channing, had "borrowed" his terminology and his argument, and Wesley's once seminal work was deemed derivative.[115]

The methods that Wesley used were developed and elaborated in response to Hart's challenge of his first idea and Channing's racist views concerning black workers. Wesley introduced far more statistical studies, census data, and other social studies than historians had previously used. But, unlike Charles S. Johnson, Wesley did not trust the facts to speak for themselves. So he provided a closely argued analysis of his materials. Channing was Wesley's thesis advisor, and he mistakenly believed that Wesley wanted to prove that mulatto workers were more capable than "purer blooded Negroes." Accordingly, Channing wrote Wesley a letter approving what he thought was the new topic of the thesis: "I had . . . the general idea that Negro labor is inefficient compared to white, except where the gang system can be employed." Channing's words repeated those of antebellum slavery apologists and contemporary segregationists who purported to believe that black people had to be compelled to work satisfactorily.[116] Channing bombarded Wesley with letters that revealed his beliefs that black people were inferior. Channing and Arthur Schlesinger Sr. both thought Wesley was using far too many statistics, and Wesley's study was unusual for its time in this aspect, but Wesley refused to omit this aspect of his work and pressed on. Wesley's replies indicated that he was determined to use statistical methods to support his interpretation and analysis: "I was determined that in the presentation of this study, it should be so documented and so dependent on the material . . . that no one should be able to doubt that my interpretation had sound historical bases."[117]

In the introduction to his book Wesley said that he wrote *Negro Labor in the United States* to combat unscientific treatments of black workers and ill-informed public views of black labor and to substitute facts for "personal opinion, unsupported assertions and public discussion." In his book Wesley defended black workers from negative opinions concerning their job worthiness. He chose a broad range of source materials and organized an impressive array of statistics to support his arguments. The chapter on Reconstruction, "Will the Negro Work?—The Problem of Reconstruction," challenged the public belief shared by Channing that black people needed the lash in order to be productive. In a chapter on industrial work at the turn of the century, "The Group Movement Toward Skilled Labor," Wesley condemned scholars who uncritically repeated racist rationales for job segregation, such as the notion that factory work was too dangerous for black people because the machinery's noise would cause them to fall asleep. He regarded these statements as "dogmatic generalizations that are not only unscholarly but untrue." Wesley used the surveys of employer attitudes that Du Bois had used in his Atlanta studies and accounts of black workers in cotton mills and iron works to argue that assertions that blacks were physically incapable of industrial employment were counterfactual.[118]

Wesley avoided the more anecdotal style of Woodson, but he shared Woodson's critical attitudes toward the historical role of black middle-class leaders and Woodson's tendency to blame black elites and white trade unionists for many of black workers' problems. Wesley pictured black politicians of the nineteenth century as helping to sabotage efforts to build black unions because they were more interested in patronage jobs than they were in furthering the progress of black workers. Wesley presented a strong case that all major changes in the fortunes of black workers came as a result of a combination of their own efforts and changes in the economy, rather than from race leaders. This argument foreshadowed the political arguments that black labor scholars would have in the 1930s because it called into question both the interracial relations approach favored by Haynes and Johnson and the notion of Du Bois's that the race as a whole would be lifted by its educated black leadership.

Abram L. Harris's coauthored study *The Black Worker: The Negro and the Labor Movement* was another theoretical departure from earlier black labor studies. Like Charles Wesley's *Negro Labor*, Spero and Harris's *Black Worker* would eventually be recognized as a major contribution and departure in the way American workers were studied. Published to excellent reviews in 1931, its greatest impact was on left-of-center black labor scholars, radical social scientists, and students at Negro colleges. Despite its full title the book was not really a simple study of blacks and organized labor because it viewed its subject through a socialist lens, calling for a multiracial labor movement. As Herbert Gutman observed, "its greatest value is that it is a corrective to the dominant scholarship in American labor history."[119] Gutman was referring to the institutional studies of trade unions churned out by the Wisconsin school of labor economists, starting with John Commons and continuing with his many students—most notably Selig Perlman and Philip Taft. The lasting importance of Abram Harris's writings on black workers lies in his emphasis on the importance of industrial jobs to black economic stability.

Abram Harris began his doctoral studies in economics at Columbia University in 1926 after resigning his position as head of the Minneapolis Urban League branch. He probably had come into contact with some of the faculty in 1922 when he attended the New York School of Social Work, which shared several faculty members from Columbia's economics and sociology departments. Harris was a forceful man, and his Marxist leanings were well known; he also was well regarded by the Columbia faculty. At Columbia, Harris worked with Henry R. Seager and studied economic history under Wesley Clair Mitchell. He worked on a banking study and was the anthropologist Melville Herskovits's research assistant. The economist William Darity has argued that Harris was his former professor's "principal tutor on economics when Herskovits wrote the first major text in economic anthropology." Harris regularly commuted between Howard, where he started teaching economics in 1927, and New York to meet with his professors. Like Wesley, Harris easily passed his doctoral examination. Herbert Seligmann, economics department chair and longtime NUL supporter, remembered Harris's exam as "one of the most brilliant in the history of the department."[120]

In *The Black Worker* Harris relied on statistics and logically constructed arguments to prove his points, but he was always keenly aware of the difference between economic or social theory and actual conditions in the workplace or union hiring hall. Harris was not an orthodox Marxist. He acknowledged that racism on the part of white workers, in particular, prevented the Socialist and Communist Parties and progressive unions from turning their ideals into concrete actions that could benefit black workers. Harris did not minimize the problem of poor housing and schools, but he consistently insisted that the central problem that black workers faced was not simply race but economic discrimination based on race and class.

Charles S. Johnson's collaborative books with moderate southern academics in the 1930s would represent a conscious effort to demonstrate that blacks and whites could cooperate to improve race relations without ending segregation or challenging capitalism. The Harris and Spero collaboration was an effort to build a case for working-class unity. W. E. B. Du Bois attempted to mesh socialism and racial consciousness or nationalism, but Abram Harris emphatically rejected the validity of racial consciousness as a programmatic strategy because he believed that it vitiated the possibility of black and white working-class alliances. He supported the *Messenger* columnist George Schuyler's position that black culture was not more worthy of solidarity than class interests. While he rejected the notion that blacks were culturally different from whites, Abram Harris did believe that an educated black person had a special obligation to bring about some improvement in working-class blacks' political, social, and economic condition.

While Harris did not publicly condemn Charles S. Johnson, he did make a clean break with the National Urban League, and his writing became more critical of the league's economic practices. Harris believed that NUL branches readily engaged in supplying black strikebreakers and that this behavior reflected the skewed values of the black middle class. When these charges were detailed in *The Black Worker*, they infuriated the Chicago Urban League. The executive in Chicago demanded that the NUL make Harris retract his accusation that the Chicago league staff placed scab labor. The NUL chose not to support the Chicago branch in its campaign against Harris, although the director of industrial relations, T. Arnold Hill, and Charles S. Johnson both had worked in Chicago during the periods covered by Harris's charges. Despite the fact that NUL officials privately agreed with Harris's claims of NUL support of strikebreaking, Harris joined Chandler Owen as persona non grata at the league.

Both Charles Wesley and Abram Harris concluded that black workers had to control their own destiny, but their arguments were distinct. Charles Wesley tended to explain the dynamics of black labor problems more in terms of antagonism between black and white workers or black and white politicians rather than as a manifestation of the capitalist economic structure as Harris did. Wesley tended to be more sympathetic to the political problems that black workers faced in the nineteenth century than was Harris. Abram L. Harris argued that blacks had failed to understand their own interests when they did not explore coalitions with the greenback National Labor Party or the Democratic Party. Wesley believed that black laborers understood their weak position in the labor force all too well and made the best of a bad situation. Wesley was not overly sympathetic to capitalism, however. He did not share George Haynes's view that with industrial social workers and fair hiring practices modern welfare capitalism was good for black workers. Wesley described capitalism as "human bondage, a debasing wage slavery" in which black workers must "struggle not only against the usual obstacles of the average American working man but also against the special handicaps of race and color."[121]

By the end of the 1920s the Great Migration had become a chapter or two in the larger attempts at economic histories of black workers by black social scientists, rather than their research focus. Their attempts to determine the motives of migrants gave way to more searching inquiries of the motives of members of their own class as representatives of racial uplift or working-class unity. For the first time in the 1920s, black labor analysts and black social scientists were not synonymous, as other gifted scholars such as the psychologist Francis Sumner and the sociologist E. Franklin Frazier began to extensively publish other topics. The Depression decade bore the fruits of an overall expansion in the number of black social scientists, and major departments of social science were developed in three black colleges—Howard, Fisk, and Atlanta Universities. Carter G. Woodson was well on his way to becoming a School in himself; only Charles S. Johnson could later claim to have supported more black social scientists than the Association for the Study of Negro Life and History, Associated Publishers, and Woodson's foundation grants. Wesley and Greene were two of seven historians who are seen as his first generation of associates. Many others gave their first papers at ASNLH meetings or were first published in the *Journal of Negro History.* The meetings of the ASNLH continued to be one of the places that all black social scientists gathered to exchange ideas. Du Bois and Reid reestablished a philosophically independent group interested in voting rights and workers' education in Atlanta, where they would be joined by Rayford Logan, Hugh Smythe, and other young men. Charles Johnson's research shop in Nashville was regarded as either a timid group of fact collectors or an impressive research enterprise, depending on the assessor's political views. And in reality it was both. Although Howard University had not been a major force in shaping the studies of Charles Wesley or Abram Harris, they became a part of a nucleus of towering intellects and much-loved teachers that gathered at the university after 1925 when Mordecai Johnson became president. The group of social scientists often called the Howard radicals included E. Franklin Frazier, Ralph J. Bunche, Emmett E. Dorsey, and Charles H. Thompson.[122]

Howard University president Mordecai Johnson had a sometimes stormy relationship with his faculty, but he zealously protected the radicals, who students irreverently dubbed "the drinkers and the thinkers," from charges that they were communists. Chapter 6 details how methodological and theoretical differences between black social scientists helped to form the basis of a robust discourse on what should be done to assist black workers during the Depression. Du Bois, Woodson, Harris, and a new young economist, Robert C. Weaver—the final segregated scholar—played major roles.

Black women who aspired to be social scientists during the Great Migration had very different experiences from the five male labor scholars who each had their education and writing supported during the 1920s, had a significant study published by the beginning of the Depression, and had secured influential positions on the faculties of the best black colleges. As this chapter has detailed, at the First World War's end Abram Harris and Ira Reid had finished college and were beginning graduate programs, fellowships, and jobs in social work that served as apprenticeships as they became the influential and contentious third generation of black male social scientists. The five black women social scientists discussed in chapter 5 had far more experience as survey researchers and more formal training at the beginning of the twenties than Harris or Reid, but they were unable to establish careers in the field.[123] Sadie Tanner Mossell Alexander did not get any offers to teach or work as an economist at the National Urban League or a Negro college after she earned her doctorate from the University of Pennsylvania in 1921—a year before Abram Harris finished his undergraduate work at Virginia Union and while Charles S. Johnson was at work on the report of the Chicago race riot.[124] A few black women did finally get the opportunity to demonstrate that they were capable social scientists during and just after World War I, but when the war labor shortages were over, so were these opportunities. More troubling, however, than the absence of black women with doctorates, was the fact that after Sadie Alexander had become an economist and other black women had demonstrated their aptitude and skill as social researchers between 1918 and 1922, the prospects for black women who wanted to work as sociologists were only marginally greater in 1923 or 1933 than they had been in 1903 when George Edmund Haynes and Elizabeth Ross graduated from Fisk University.[125]

Chapter 5 examines the brief opening of a window of opportunity for a forgotten generation of black women social scientists to better understand how gender and race shaped the development of black labor studies.

5

"A New Day for the Colored Woman Worker"?

Recovering the Labor Studies of Black Female Social Scientists during the Great Migration

> Underneath the movement of Negro women toward industry there is nothing antagonistic to the common interests of the laboring classes. . . . But they are a hitherto unplumbed source of native labor that may be developed into a valuable economic asset to the nation. *The industrial problem is fundamental.*
> —Helen Brooks Irvin, "Conditions in Industry as They Affect Negro Women"

Black female social scientists were as much a "hitherto unplumbed source of native labor" as the industrial and domestic workers they studied during the Great Migration, but four black women—Gertrude Elise Johnson McDougald, Helen Brooks Irvin, Emma L. Shields Penn, and Elizabeth Ross Haynes— took full advantage of their brief opportunities to earn a living as survey researchers. A fifth black female social scientist, Sadie Tanner Mossell Alexander, was completing her doctorate in economics as the other, older women were completing their research projects, but her 1921 doctorate from the University of Pennsylvania's Wharton School did not help her find work as a social scientist. Unlike the others, she never earned a living as a social scientist. Sadie T. Mossell Alexander, generally regarded as the first black American to earn a doctorate in economics, fell victim to a social environment that seemed to say to talented black women, "One study and you're out."

Major studies of black female workers began in 1918 after war-related labor shortages drew black women into industry in larger numbers and female analysts embarked on studies of this underexamined group. These societal changes in the demand for labor did not, however, resolve the problems that black women social scientists faced. For example, Elizabeth Ross Haynes had to wait fifteen years from her first nonteaching job in 1908 to 1923, when she published her first major labor study. While Ross Haynes's career as a social scientist was stalled, she and other black clubwomen stuck to an ambitious agenda of local social reform projects that were based on the best practices of social work and community surveys. Black clubwomen's initiatives were an indication of the continued importance of social science methods to their implementation of programmatic reforms. In 1908 as Elizabeth Ross was making a transition from teaching school to organizing work with the Young Women's Christian Association (YWCA), black clubwomen in Atlanta and other cities were founding community service agencies such as Atlanta's Neighborhood Union. These agencies were based on social scientific methods and theories gained through women's participation at the Atlanta University conferences, directives of the National Association of Colored Women (NACW), and their own self-study. Over the next decade a slowly growing number of black women gained jobs as social workers, often working in community projects or in city jobs, with their salaries paid for by black women's associations, church groups, or community chests.

In this chapter I closely review the experiences of four black female social scientists and recover their most important research from its undeserved obscurity. This chapter opens with a brief account of the use of social science methods by black clubwomen after the first Atlanta University Conference through World War I and closes with the ironic experience of Sadie T. M. Alexander. Although Alexander was one of fewer than one dozen black social scientists with doctorates, and her dissertation was published in a solid academic journal, she was nevertheless unable to find a permanent job as an economist. In the 1920s, after all five women had proven their ability as researchers, employment for black women as social scientists was like the new occupations temporarily gained by their sisters in the factories—short-lived, lacking advancement possibilities, and abruptly terminated after World War I.

The studies of black women labor analysts shed considerable light on the experiences of black women workers during the Great Migration that were not captured by the U.S. Bureau of the Census or in the studies of black male and white female social scientists. The restoration of black women to the ranks of the segregated scholars continues the examination of the impact of racism and gender discrimination on black women who were interested in the social sciences, as we have seen in chapter 3, and parallels the work of their black male classmates, teachers, colleagues, and husbands. The five black women social scientists under study in this chapter were twice silenced as social scientists—once by their society, which limited their careers but not their activism, and again by the historical record, which has all but erased them.

Black women did not receive the same levels of institutional support as their black male counterparts did for their labor and community studies, nor the same level of attention once their work was published. One of the major reasons that important studies of black women workers have not been recognized as the work of black female social scientists is because they were commissioned by social welfare organizations or the federal government and were often published with the sponsoring group as the author. These studies were frequently their author's single major research study, and as historians have become interested in the development of social research on black Americans and black social scientists, they have tended to first examine those persons who left an identifiable body of work or those persons whose college teaching influenced later scholars. Early black women social scientists were employed outside of the academy and published in less prestigious journals. The five women discussed in this chapter were a part of a not insubstantial number of black women with some training in social science methods. The research-oriented social welfare activities of black women's clubs continued to implement community programs. By 1920 there were more than seven hundred black women employed as social workers who had some training in the social sciences and understood survey research methods and goals.[1]

The same racial and gender discriminatory practices that had prevented black women from gaining jobs as social scientists before the Great Migration now facilitated their conditional and temporary entry into such jobs because federal agencies and social welfare organizations urgently wanted data-based studies, and it was now deemed desirable to have investigators of the same race and sex as those being interviewed. Black professional women were employed to interview black working-class women in factories and in their homes; some were contracted to analyze and interpret the results of studies done by others for other purposes. A few black women carried out ambitious social studies of their own design. Unlike their black male counterparts, the double burden of gender and racial discrimination meant that the first black female social scientists were unable to work consistently as social scientists, and thus these women formed more of a cohort of individuals than a well-defined, self-conscious cadre of scholars.

Black female social scientists apparently did not have the same close personal relationships with each other as did black male social scientists. But it is not possible to recover fully the detailed records and personal histories of black female social scientists because they rarely left complete records of their correspondence. Nevertheless, we can recover and reconstruct the general outlines of their professional activities, as well as recapture snapshots of the finely grained lives of some of the most important researchers. It is the purpose of this chapter to recover the lives of four key black female social scientists and restore them to greater visibility than has so far been the case. But these four may be just the tip of the iceberg, since there were many other black women participating in the world of social science. In the collection of black social scientists that I call the segregated scholars, we can begin to restore more balance by including the signal contributions of women as well as men.

The Women of the Neighborhood Union: Social Scientists without Portfolio

Important examples abound of black women working to establish programs based on objective analyses of community conditions. However, the women who led these efforts have not always received the serious consideration they deserve. Historians Jacqueline Rouse and Tera W. Hunter have begun to give one such person—Lugenia Burns Hope and her unpaid social welfare work—a more complete examination. Hope had worked as a paraprofessional in white social welfare agencies in Chicago before her 1898 marriage to John Hope. When they moved to Atlanta and John Hope became first a professor and later the president of Morehouse College, Lugenia Burns Hope began constructing her largely unpaid career as a reformer by participating in the Atlanta University conferences. She also conducted a careful self-study of sociological methods. More than anyone else, Lugenia Hope should be credited for fully extending the substance as well as the spirit of the Atlanta University conferences into the social welfare work of black women. Hope was the guiding light of the Neighborhood Union, an Atlanta community-based social service organization founded in 1908, whose initial leaders were drawn across class lines and represented all areas of the city. Hunter argues persuasively that the Neighborhood Union's "distinctive infrastructure enabled and required the participation of many working-class women." Hope used social surveys and community studies to plan and to defend the goals of the Neighborhood Union. She was one of many black clubwomen around the country who helped build on the NACW's national priorities for establishing day nurseries, kindergartens, and other programs through a wide range of community programs. Hope's influence was felt nationally because of her leadership roles in the NACW and in the YWCA, and locally through survey research–based projects of the Neighborhood Union. She also played a key role in establishing the Atlanta School of Social Work.[2]

Lugenia Burns Hope and the women of the Neighborhood Union used community studies to document for Atlanta city authorities the material needs of its black residents. The publication of their studies led to the hiring of teachers and recreation workers and physical improvements at schools and in black neighborhoods. At first the women did their own studies. As they grew more sophisticated, they worked with faculty members from Morehouse College, Atlanta University, and the Atlanta School of Social Work to custom design more ambitious surveys. The Neighborhood Union began a summer social service institute at Morehouse College in 1918 to train men and women for social work careers, and the Atlanta School of Social Work grew out of this institute. The Atlanta School of Social Work was initially an independent institution whose director was a faculty member on loan from Morehouse College. Lugenia Hope was a member of its first faculty, teaching courses on community development, but black and white men occupied all the executive positions. The Neighborhood Union surveys provided black social scientists with opportunities to refine their methods and gain experience. The two surveys undertaken by the second Atlanta School of Social Work director E. Franklin Frazier were among the first community studies he made as a young professional and may have helped him when he designed his doctoral study of black families in Chicago.[3]

During the First World War, Lugenia Burns Hope and many of the women of the Neighborhood Union and other National Association of Colored Women members worked to assist black workers and soldiers through national organizations such as the YWCA and through new black-run organizations such as the Circle for Negro War Relief, which sought to counter discriminatory practices in the Red Cross and other voluntary agencies. Burns Hope helped direct the staffing and training of black women who served as hostesses in the segregated recreational facilities for black soldiers. She also continued to press the YWCA national board to address the concerns of black women in the segregated city chapters. The NACW members Addie Waits Hunton and Kathryn Johnson directed the efforts of black social workers who assisted the black troops stationed in Europe.[4]

The YWCA was a bridge between the social reform activities of black clubwomen and black women who had some formal training in survey methods but were only sporadically employed as social scientists. The experiences of these black women, who if they had been male or white would have had steady employment, call for further examination and reinterpretation. For example, on the eve of the Great Migration, Mary E. Jackson was one of the few black women who worked as a social scientist for state and local agencies. At the beginning of the First World War, Jackson was appointed as a "special worker for colored girls" on the YWCA's War Work Council, and she used her social science training directly in her attempts to analyze trends and suggest programs. In her influencial history of southern clubwomen, Cynthia Neverdon-Morton cites a 1918 survey of industrial opportunities for black women that was "prepared and disseminated" by Jackson in her discussion of the over one hundred black women, many of whom were trained social workers, who staffed the YWCA's eight hostess houses and forty-five industrial and recreational centers during World War I.[5] It is not possible to fully identify all of these black women who were training and interested in working as social scientists but were instead employed as teachers or YWCA secretaries or underemployed as hostesses at camps for black soldiers. But articles on black women workers that began to appear in the press suggest that black women's interest in labor matters was not significantly different from black men's.

Black women social scientists' primary research appeared at the same time that the writers Alice Dunbar Nelson, Helen Sayre, and Mary Louise Williams offered socioeconomic analyses of secondary sources. These women wrote insightful articles about the jobs that black women filled during the First World War, which displayed their author's familiarity with census data, scholarly literature, and contemporary political debates. Well-known clubwomen such as Mary Church Terrell and Georgia Douglas Johnson worked as employment assistants and aides for the U.S. Department of Labor (DOL) but were apparently not involved in survey research. If the sudden demand for studies of black women workers came from anxious public and private agencies, the supply of well-prepared black professional women who were now able to qualify for paid jobs assisting wartime workers and carrying out survey research can be linked to the lasting commitment of black clubwomen and college graduates to use social science to respond to community needs.[6]

Four Pioneering Black Women Social Scientists during the Great Migration

Important studies of black women workers during and just after the war were done by such nonacademic agencies as the U.S. Department of Labor and local service organizations. These studies offer the most detailed surveys of local and national economic realities for a range of black women workers during the Great Migration. They also gave black women their first opportunities to serve as principal investigators, writers, and authors. The Consumers League for the City of New York was among the first to publish studies of black women's entrance into industrial jobs. Soon after its study, with Gertrude McDougald as the coauthor, was underway, the U.S. Department of Labor authorized Helen Irvin and Emma Shields to undertake investigations of black women workers' experiences during and just after World War I. Elizabeth Ross Haynes had her long-deferred opportunity to have her sociological work published in 1923, when the *Journal of Negro History* featured her monograph on black domestic workers that she began while working at the U.S. Department of Labor. A full understanding of these four studies and the other labor writings of their authors is necessary to assess the intellectual contribution of this lost generation of black women social scientists.

The Consumers League investigated citywide hiring practices and on-the-job experiences of black women in New York City. The New York study, which was overoptimistically entitled *A New Day for the Colored Woman Worker,* was codirected and coauthored by Gertrude McDougald, a veteran school-teacher who was then in her early thirties. Her research on black women industrial workers in New York was a part of her decades-long involvement with labor and industrial issues in Harlem. The research studies of Gertrude McDougald form a bridge between the unpaid social investigations of black club and social workers and the DOL's studies by black female social scientists in the early 1920s. McDougald was not a college graduate, and like Lugenia Burns Hope, she grew up in the North and had studied business in high school. Unlike Hope, who did not have a high school degree and had attended trade and art schools, McDougald had graduated from high school before enrolling in the New York Training School for Teachers. She took courses at the College of the City of New York, Hunter College, New York University, and Columbia University.[7]

A New Day for the Colored Woman Worker was published in 1919, but it described the labor market conditions between July and November 1918, just

---

before the Armistice. The importance of the issue of black women working in industry to the social welfare community in New York is found in the study's sponsorship by a joint committee made up of representatives of labor, social work, and black organizations, including the Consumers League for the City of New York, the New York Urban League, the Division of Industrial Studies of the Russell Sage Foundation, the Committee on Colored Workers of the Manhattan Trade School, the Women's Trade Union League, and the YWCA. The joint committee directed the study with assistance from the YWCA. The sponsoring committee intended to portray black women's delayed entrance into industrial jobs in New York as a way of giving voice and statistical credibility to women who were "voiceless and defenseless."[8]

Gertrude McDougald obtained the names of 400 black female industrial workers after a wide-ranging effort to cull some of the names of the 2,185 black women who were working in 242 factories surveyed in Manhattan and Brooklyn. She was able to carry out in-depth interviews of 175 female factory workers, 8 percent of the total. Jessie Clark, the white coinvestigator, interviewed 300 employers. It is possible that the division of labor between Clark and McDougald indicated that the Consumers League believed that white employers would feel more comfortable with a white interviewer. Using a survey instrument that was more sophisticated than those later used by the U.S. Department of Labor, McDougald gathered detailed data on black women's previous work history and wages, education, family, and housing costs. The factory schedule examined workfloor conditions and hours and compared wages paid to men and women by race. Black women were found to have replaced both men and boys and white women in some industrial jobs, but these were inevitably jobs that were dirty, arduous, and low paying. Black women's wages were much lower than white women's in the same jobs, but the majority of black women in New York were in jobs that white women were able to either escape or avoid because of the labor shortage. Only a third of black female workers earned wages that equaled those of white women in the same factories doing the same jobs. Sixty-five percent of black women workers reported weekly wages of $11 or less, compared to 69 percent of white women who earned at least $12 a week. The vast majority of black women interviewed, 68 percent, were young single women under twenty-six years old living with families as lodgers. Black women factory workers were more educated than their white counterparts. Thirteen percent of the black women but only 4 percent of the white women workers had attended at least two years of high school. The higher education of black women factory workers was a reflection of their exclusion from clerical and many teaching jobs. In New York City black women factory workers had jobs that before the war went to white, poorly educated, largely immigrant women.[9] Few of the black women McDougald interviewed had previous experience in industry or had attended trade schools, but those who did have training or experience rarely found jobs that matched their skills. *A New Day for the Colored Woman Worker* condemned racial prejudice for consigning black teachers and stenographers to menial industrial jobs, "unskilled, monotonous work—their spirits broken and hopes blasted because they had been obliged to forfeit their training on account of race prejudice." The employer interviews that Jessie Clark conducted were used to make the case that black women's inexperience in industry rather than racial traits was the real basis for tensions between employers and employees. However, the interviews found that most employers believed that black women had performed well.[10]

The New York study's argument for employing black women as factory workers rested on three premises: an examination of the common stereotypes against black workers, a declaration of the need for universal application of democratic values, and the productive allocation of resources. The study reminded the reader that black women workers had responded to a national emergency by proving themselves to be as capable as any other women and they now deserved democratic treatment in the postwar period, to do any less risked wasting productive assets. The report concluded that black women industrial workers had been mistreated during the war despite their faithful service. "The American people will have to go very far in its treatment of the colored industrial woman to square itself with that democratic ideal of which it made so much during the war."[11] The three final recommendations of *A New Day for the Colored Woman Worker* were not particularly consistent with its findings. Two of the recommendations emphasized what black women workers should do to be better accepted in the workplace, advising them to become better educated, attend trade schools, and try to join labor unions. But the overwhelming evidence within the report was that black women workers were already better educated than their white counterparts and that racial discrimination in hiring meant that skills were only rarely a factor in black women's hiring. The committee's third recommendation called for "an appreciation and acceptance of the Colored Woman in industry by the American Employer and the public at large," which better reflected the research findings but lacked any implementation strategies such as fair employment laws or nondiscriminatory practices by unions.[12] The recommendation thus was unlikely to result in increased hiring or better pay for black women in factories in the postwar period.

Although Gertrude McDougald's name is not recognized today as a social scientist, her involvement in later studies, especially of women and children, went well beyond the publication of *A New Day for the Colored Woman Worker.* McDougald began her professional life in 1905 as a teacher in the public school system of New York City. After her marriage in 1911 she took an eight-year leave of absence, ostensibly to raise her two children, but during the latter half of her leave she was employed as a specialist on labor and employment issues by local social welfare organizations and government agencies. McDougald became the assistant industrial secretary for the New York Urban League in 1915; she served on the staff of the Henry Street Settlement, where she helped find jobs for the black women and children of Harlem; and she worked at the Manhattan Trade School and in the New York office of the U.S. Employment Service during World War I. She returned to the city school system after the war as a vocational guidance supervisor for the Harlem public schools and was able to use her extensive knowledge of the city's labor market to place black students in jobs. Gertrude McDougald also sought funds for a variety of studies of black employment opportunities in New York.

McDougald was involved with a most intriguing 1921 study that polled four thousand employers of black workers, black parents, and school principals in New York City. The aim of the study was to determine the vocational opportunities available for black students. It also proposed changes in course offerings in public schools. This survey was proposed by McDougald on behalf of a black citizens group that she had organized through the Henry Street Settlement: the North Harlem Vocational Guidance Committee. It was cosponsored by the New York Board of Education and the U.S. Department of Labor. The survey as planned by McDougald was delayed because the DOL withdrew the official who had been loaned to supervise the project. She protested to the U.S. Congress and eventually the study was completed. McDougald and the citizens committee used the results of the survey to pressure the schools to improve educational practices and to open all courses in the public school system's Manhattan Trade School to black students.[13]

The clearest indication that McDougald's expertise as a social scientist was respected throughout the 1920s by other social scientists was her appointment as the only woman and one of only three black social scientists to serve on the thirteen-person research committee that guided Charles S. Johnson's structuring of *The Negro in American Civilization.* The black YWCA administrator Eva Bowles and the white anthropologist Margaret Mead were on the executive committee, although they were given only such modest tasks as taking charge of the ushers for the research conference that preceded the publication.[14]

McDougald's knowledge of black women workers in New York City was also called upon when she was selected to contribute to the famous Harlem issue of *Survey Graphic* in 1925 and the subsequent *The New Negro*. McDougald received her largest audience in these publications.[15] Her resulting essays explored the interplay of racial discrimination in the workplace and sexual oppression in the home. McDougald contrasted the experiences of women in a variety of occupations in New York and other cities. She identified four primary categories of black women based on their occupations or marital status. She was most sympathetic to the struggles of the fourth and largest group: the domestic and casual workers whose drudgery gave other women leisure time often at the expense of their own families. In the first group were the wives and daughters of professionals and businessmen, a "very small leisure group . . . picked for outward beauty by Negro men." These women did not work and were "touched only faintly by their race's hardships."[16] The second and third groups of women were those in the professions, business, trade, and industry, and their lives were characterized by "a spirit of stress and struggles." McDougald lamented the old customs that barred black women from more than menial positions in "the great commercial life of New York City," and she decried the more recent city civil service policies that instituted personal interviews of those who were the highest ranked on civil service tests. Black women who passed written exams were disqualified after these interviews, when their racial identity was determined. The outlook for black women in business and the professions was more hopeful than in the trades but was still problematic. Black professional women's best opportunities came in jobs that were controlled by or serving other black people. In New York City teaching and nursing offered the largest number of these jobs and even had a few women in higher administrative positions. Social work was also a field with a demand for college-educated women, but McDougald found that "even in work among Negroes, the better paying positions are reserved for whites." For black women in social work, low wages were the rule, job advancement rare, and they were in the field out of a desire to improve the lives of other black people. "The Negro college woman is doing her bit at a sacrifice . . . as probation officers, investigators and police women in the correction department, . . . attached to the Children's Court . . . for relief organizations, missions and churches . . .

Gertrude Elise Johnson McDougald (Ayer); sketch by the artist Winold Reiss for *The Survey Graphic*, March 1925, accompanying her article (authored under the name Elise Johnson McDougald). (Photographs and Prints Division, Schomburg Center for Research in Black Culture, The New York Public Library, Astor, Lenox and Tilden Foundations)

and as . . . welfare workers in recreation and industry."[17] In the mid-1920s Gertrude McDougald became active in labor and socialist causes. She worked with A. Philip Randolph and the Brotherhood of Sleeping Car Porters and was vice-chair and appointed to the executive board of the Trade Union Committee for Organizing Negro Workers, which she had helped establish. She also attempted to organize laundry workers with the Women's Trade Union League. In her essay in *The New Negro*, McDougald is describing herself when she discusses an anonymous unpaid labor organizer whose attempts to keep black women from strikebreaking had led her to become "convinced that the problem lay as much in the short-sighted . . . policy of the labor unions themselves, as in the alienated or unintelligent . . . Negro worker."[18]

Gertrude McDougald's memoir reveals that she was not fully satisfied in her work as a schoolteacher and administrator despite nearly fifty years of employment. Her involvement in the labor movement and continued interest in social research indicate that she might have preferred paid work as a social scientist. Although she did like working with children, McDougald soon discovered that she was exhausted by the demands of the classroom and became "determined to get into the more rewarding work of vocational guidance and administration." After winning a competitive examination, she became an assistant principal of Public School 89 in Harlem in 1924. And then after a decade as an assistant principal, she was appointed principal of P.S. 24 in Harlem, where upon her remarriage she served under the name Gertrude Elise Ayer from 1934 until her retirement in 1954 at age seventy.[19] McDougald Ayer was the second black person and the first black woman to be a principal in the New York City school system (the first having been William L. Bulkley, whose establishment of an evening school for black workers, writings, and involvement with George Haynes and the founding of the National Urban League are discussed in chapter 2). McDougald's emphasis as a public school administrator on vocational training, adult education, trade unionism, and advocacy followed and updated the model that Bulkley had set at the turn of the century.

However, their tangible successes did not materially increase the numbers of black principals in the New York City schools. In the mid-1960s, a decade after her retirement and in her eighties, McDougald Ayer remained an outspoken advocate for the children of Harlem and sharply criticized a superintendent of schools for disparaging the abilities of black children and their parents. McDougald Ayer's example of competence and confidence inspired several generations of black students, including the writer James Baldwin, to succeed in a variety of occupations.[20] Carleton Mabee's history of black education in New York locates McDougald among the light-skinned, "well educated, upper-class black women" who taught at the de facto segregated schools of New York City.[21]

McDougald's life was far more complicated, of course, and she had much more in common with working-class black women than it appeared on the surface, although she hinted as much in her writings about racism and sexism. McDougald urged her readers to avoid stereotypes of color and class and to understand that black women did not have a single persona but were "a colorful pageant of individuals. . . . From grace to strength they vary in infinite degree, with traces of the race's history left in physical and mental outlines on each. With a discerning mind, one catches the multiform charm, beauty and character of Negro women; and grasps the fact that their problems cannot be thought of in mass."[22]

Gertrude McDougald's unhappy personal experiences as a daughter and wife clearly suffused her sharp analysis of black women's "double task" to achieve sexual and racial emancipation. She expressed privately her deep regret that the misogyny of her father, a physician, and the misanthropy of her first husband, a lawyer, had required her to work her entire adult life rather than being allowed to stay at home with her children, even after her relatively happy second marriage. McDougald was speaking from her heart as much as her research when she discussed the absence of sexual equality between black men and women despite women's economic and domestic contributions. She argued that employed working-class black women might actually experience fewer problems on the home front. McDougald believed that black women's growing economic independence "caused her to rebel against the cruder working-class Negro man" and his efforts to be domineering at home to compensate for his relegation to menial jobs in the workplace. While black women's work might promote more equality between husbands and wives, McDougald worried that a mother's absence from the home contributed to black men's lack of respect for black women. Drawing on but not citing her own painful experiences, McDougald argued that even boys who grew up to be professionals did not learn to respect women if their fathers were frustrated or absent and their mothers were working. According to McDougald, black women's efforts to raise respectful sons were often trumped by the hard realities of the workplace. Black fathers' "baffled and suppressed desires to determine their economic life are manifested in over-bearing domination at home. Working mothers are unable to instill different ideals in their sons." She found hope in her observation that some better-educated younger men were less sexist in their interactions with women. "Trained in modern schools of thought, they begin to show a wholesome attitude of fellowship and freedom for their women." McDougald challenged black feminists of the time to cooperate with these men and to work for sexual as well as racial equality and not subordinate the former to the latter.[23]

Gertrude E. J. McDougald Ayer became invisible as a black woman social scientist, for historiographical and personal reasons that affected women much more than men, despite her prominence in New York City black progressive circles during the Great Migration. Her one published survey appeared as a publication of the Consumers League for the City of New York;

her other surveys were never published. Much of the evidence of McDougald's work as a social scientist and labor organizer is contained in unpublished letters and brief references in historical accounts. During her lifetime, McDougald used two different first and last names, and later historians have separated her life as if she were three different people. Gertrude E. McDougald was the name given to the social scientist, vocational guidance specialist, and labor activist. Elise Johnson McDougald was the name she used in her articles on black women's need for racial and sexual emancipation. When McDougald remarried sometime in the late 1920s, she became Gertrude McDougald Ayer or Gertrude Elise Ayer. Most of the discussions of her role in the school system call her Gertrude Ayer because she used this name in the 1930s when she became a school principal. The scholars who have studied her previously have not connected Elise Johnson McDougald with Gertrude E. Ayer, and none of the literary collections with Elise J. McDougald's articles discuss Gertrude McDougald's life as a social scientist.[24]

Three Black Women Social Scientists and the Department of Labor, 1918–29

As we saw in chapter 4, the U.S. Department of Labor renewed its interest in black studies that W. E. B. Du Bois had begun at the turn of the century by creating the Division of Negro Economics (DNE) to monitor, manage, and analyze black war workers. The DOL also created a Women's Bureau to analyze and respond to the needs of women in the workforce. It is my contention that the study of black female workers fell between the interests of these two bureaus and thus did not receive the attention that it deserved, given black women workers' importance as a segment of working women and as black workers. In this section we examine the activities of three black women social scientists who conducted studies for the DOL—Helen Brooks Irvin, Emma L. Shields Penn, and Elizabeth Ross Haynes.

It was after intensive lobbying by interest groups that the U.S. Department of Labor created distinct offices for both black and women workers among its burgeoning wartime bureaucracies. Contradictory complaints from unions, employers, black organizations, and southern government officials concerning the growing numbers of black migrants who moved out of the South to better jobs during the two years before the U.S. entry into World War I revitalized the DOL's formal interest in studies of black workers that had been abandoned after the suppression of W. E. B. Du Bois's Lowndes

County study in 1906. In the spring of 1918 George Edmund Haynes was appointed the director of the Department of Labor's new Division of Negro Economics after he emerged as a consensus candidate of interracial organizations, national black organizations, and New South businessmen. Mary Van Kleeck, a white administrator and social researcher at the Russell Sage Foundation, was appointed to head the newly formed Women in Industry Service (WIIS), which became a permanent agency—the Women's Bureau—after the war's end.[25] Black women's interests as workers were distinctly secondary in both of these offices because neither consistently viewed black women as an important part of their constituency, staff, or purview.

Black female social scientists, including George Haynes's wife, Elizabeth Ross Haynes, were marginalized by both the DNE and the Women's Bureau. Black women professionals were given only token positions of limited duration in either agency. The marginalization of black female social scientists hampered their ability to obtain long-term jobs, limited the number of investigations they were able to undertake, and gave them fewer chances to write effectively about the experiences of black women workers. Black women social scientists were less able to use their experience effectively as the basis for their future careers in the social sciences. During the four years the DNE was in operation, George Haynes employed an all-male staff of state directors. Van Kleeck had to be pressed to hire any black women at all, and she and her successors failed to hire a single permanent black employee other than janitors after the war.

Most of George Haynes's young male staff built careers in social service after the war or returned to civil service jobs in the government, two areas that allowed them to continue to analyze black economic and population trends.[26] Two of the three black women who worked as social scientists at the U.S. Department of Labor, Elizabeth Ross Haynes and Emma L. Shields Penn, continued to be involved with issues concerning black women workers through the YWCA, but they did not continue to publish widely or build on their promising beginnings as social scientists.

Helen Brooks Irvin and Emma L. Shields carried out studies of black women in industry that were published by the Women's Bureau. Both Irvin and Shields were contract employees of the Women's Bureau. Elizabeth Ross Haynes had moved with her husband to Washington, D.C., and because of a federal ban on both spouses being employed by the government, she served as a dollar-a-year advisor to her husband's agency and to the Women's Bureau for most of the war. Ross Haynes attempted to emulate the type of volunteer service and leadership that white businessmen were giving to the war effort but did not have clear functional duties at either the Division of Negro Economics or the Women's Bureau. Ross Haynes did not publish a study on black workers until she left Washington. She used materials that she gathered on domestic workers while living in Washington in her sociology master's thesis, which was later published by Carter G. Woodson in the *Journal of Negro History*.[27] The Women's Bureau of the U.S. Department of Labor was designed and supported by a broad coalition of white women's clubs, trade unions, consumers leagues, and social welfare organizations that were primarily concerned with working conditions and protection for white women in industry and that insisted on a research bureau run by females that was separate from the staff of the Bureau of Labor Standards. According to one of the founding documents of the bureau, the first principle guiding the establishment of twelve proposed working committees was that membership should be as representative as possible. This principle was clearly violated in the case of the committee on colored women, which was chaired by the Chicago philanthropist Sophisonia Breckinridge.[28] The fact that black women's organizations were not perceived by the directors to be a part of the constituency of the Women's Bureau from its inception, as well as prejudice and acceptance of segregation on the part of its staff, complicated and limited the bureau's willingness to materially assist black women workers. We have seen that black female workers were one of the chief constituencies of black clubwomen since the turn of the century, so that the virtual omission of black women from advisory roles in the Women's Bureau should be read as deliberate.

Black women workers initially came to the attention of the WIIS staff due to pressures within the DOL from the office of Secretary of Labor William B. Wilson and from George Haynes's DNE. Black organizations and intellectuals viewed the war work of black women differently than did the white women and men in the Department of Labor. Black organizations generally saw the black women's employment in industry as both a positive racial advance and as clear evidence that black women were patriotic and deserved democratic treatment in return. Black women's increasing share in the industrial workforce was viewed by the DOL and the Women's Bureau as "a problem," necessitated by the war labor shortage, rather than seeing black women as an important segment of women workers. Wilson called for the WIIS and George Haynes as director of the DNE to cooperate and "undertake some active work" to combine their efforts "on the whole problem of the employment of Negro women."[29]

The first conflicts between black labor advocates and white women's goals came over staffing at the Women's Bureau. Director Van Kleeck, whose salary was $5,000, wanted to pay no more than $1,800 for a black staff member and allocated another $1,200 for expenses and per diem factory investigators. George Haynes insisted that the cost for properly assisting black women workers was at least $1,500 higher.[30] While the Women's Bureau was a bastion of employment for white female social scientists and enjoyed a staff of fourteen to twenty professionals in Washington during the 1920s, it avoided hiring black women professionals. After the first director, Mary Van Kleeck, returned to the Russell Sage Foundation, the Women's Bureau employed black women who were hired for short-term assignments or paid by other agencies. Van Kleeck, a 1904 Smith College graduate, had worked briefly as a social worker before receiving a fellowship from the College Settlement Association to investigate the status of factory girls, which she followed with a study of child labor in New York City tenements and employment bureau practices. Van Kleeck had been involved with the National League for the Protection of Colored Women and the National Urban League and had much better working relationships with black men and women than did her successor, Mary Anderson, a former secretary of the Chicago Boot and Shoe Workers Union. Anderson did not share Van Kleeck's reputation as a friend of the race and rarely began investigations of black workers without pressure from outside. Under Anderson's long administration, black working women received a comprehensive study only about once a decade, despite the fact that black women were disproportionately represented in the female workforce.[31]

Women's Bureau officials were generally anxious to design studies that met the needs of their perceived constituencies, but toward the end of the 1920s its staff rebuffed several requests from the YWCA's national board to undertake a national study of black women. The Women's Bureau staff insisted that its study of laundry workers was sufficient for understanding all black women workers. The Woman's Bureau also did not respond to a request from the National Association of Colored Women to appoint a permanent black staffperson and to provide more services to black female workers.[32]

The lack of research on their occupations was not likely to have been as pressing an issue for black female industrial workers as was the failure of the Women's Bureau to oppose the segregation in employment and housing services offered by the U.S. Employment Service (USES). Services to black women workers were sorely lacking during and after the war, and the Women's Bureau seemed indifferent to their problems in finding adequate and safe housing, dealing with dangerous working conditions, and facing racial discrimination by coworkers, foremen, and employers. While Van Kleeck headed the Women's Bureau, she and her assistant Mary Anderson were more concerned about complaints they received about black women working for lower wages or more hours at men's jobs on the railroads and in cafeterias. They steadfastly advocated equal pay for the same work and limited hours for women workers, despite the reality that black women could be dismissed in favor of white women, boys, or men in such situations.[33] While white men and women could use the housing and job registries of USES, this employment agency only assisted black men and women after the DNE, as a matter of priority, assigned a dozen men to serve as state directors of Negro Economics for greater coordination with USES. A few black women, including Elizabeth Ross Haynes, were eventually hired by USES to maintain registries of domestic workers, but they did not have the authority of the DNE state directors to work directly with employers, housing officials, and community groups.

Despite the fact that the Women's Bureau needed to be prodded to investigate on behalf of black women workers, it completed three important studies of black women workers during the 1920s and many other examinations of states and occupations in which black women workers were significant. The scope and design of these studies reflected some internal dissension within the bureau as to which black women should be studied, by whom, and why. In the view of black social scientists, who uniformly believed that well-conducted studies of workers would aid in the acceptance of black women and men in new occupations, the stakes were high. Black female social scientists along with black social and political activists hoped at a minimum to use data on black women's industrial experiences during and after World War I as a permanent wedge in the factory shop door. Reports of the U.S. Department of Labor and the Census Bureau were deemed particularly important because they became a part of the official federal record. The Women's Bureau also recognized the importance of its reports as public records, but was only mildly interested in studies of occupations that black women dominated, such as domestic workers, and the construction of its other studies, by state or industry, often did not allow for a coherent national portrait of black female workers.

The Women's Bureau research reports on black women workers that the black investigators Helen Brooks Irvin and Emma L. Shields conducted in the 1920s each show their attempts to contextualize black women workers' specific situation within the national occupational hierarchy of race and gender stratification. Each of their reports focuses on working conditions, answers allegations of black women's unfitness for industrial work, probes their lack of job advancement, documents racial discrimination, and proposes solutions. The studies that white Department of Labor analysts conducted tended to uncritically repeat charges that black women were unsuited for skilled jobs and downplayed racial discrimination. They were likely to view the status quo as reflective of an optimum situation for black women. In 1929 a dry Women's Bureau report on black women was grudgingly compiled only after repeated requests from the YWCA. Its dated statistical materials, limited conclusions, and lack of qualitative analysis were in stark contrast to the vivid language in the immediate postwar surveys of Helen B. Irvin and Emma L. Shields. At the end of the 1920s, the quality and quantity of data available concerning black women workers had narrowed rather than expanded because of the Women's Bureau's indifferent stance.[34]

Helen Brooks Irvin: The Industrial Problem Is Fundamental

Helen Brooks Irvin was the first black woman that the Women in Industry Service hired to collect data and report on black female industrial workers. Details about Helen Brooks Irvin's life before and after her study of black women workers are sketchy, and the extant correspondence with Irvin during her employment at the U.S. Department of Labor is limited. What is known is that Irvin was an instructor in domestic science at Howard University from 1906 to 1914, and she was also a 1914 graduate of the Teacher's College at Howard. The Teacher's College, under Dean Lewis Baxter Moore, offered most of Howard's social science courses, so it is possible that Helen Irvin had some familiarity with social scientific research and methods prior to her service in the DOL. Irvin was among the first to earn a master's degree, in 1919, under the reorganization of the graduate department that was led by Carter G. Woodson. At the time, master's degrees required at least one year of course work in residence. Certainly her eight years of teaching home economics at Howard University would have given her both professional and personal insights into black women's occupational training. Domestic science courses at Howard University were not college-level courses and were taught in the high school and in the normal school program. Irvin was not single, but Howard University's general policy of not hiring married women in faculty positions may have meant that she was widowed or divorced.[35]

Irvin began her work at the WIIS in November 1918 with the approval of

George Haynes and the Division of Negro Economics, while Van Kleeck hired the rest of her staff. Irvin must have been highly thought of by George Haynes because he usually had a strong preference for Fisk University graduates who had completed his training courses or the Urban League Fellows program. Mary Van Kleeck also indicated her regard for Helen Irvin by sending her out as an advisor to the Consumers League for the City of New York, and as a speaker at professional conferences and to women's groups. Van Kleeck advised the secretary of labor that it was "highly important" to her bureau to extend Irvin's contract so she could write her report because they wanted to use its findings to make programmatic recommendations.[36] Helen Brooks Irvin's title was industrial secretary; she was the only black professional and one of two industrial secretaries among the fourteen women who staffed the WIIS. Irvin's salary at the WIIS was recorded as $2,000 per year, the fifth highest salary, but earlier bureau correspondence indicates that Irvin may have been shared between the WIIS and the DNE, and that she was paid a per diem and not a regular salary, as were the white women on the staff. During her assignment at the WIIS, Irvin visited 152 plants in six states that employed more than 21,000 black women. Unlike the segregated research teams deployed in Consumers League studies, Irvin interviewed both black women and their white employers.[37]

Helen Brooks Irvin spent the end of 1918 and much of 1919 investigating working conditions, housing, and employment services for black women. This is the only period for which there is direct information about Irvin's work as a social scientist, but the glimpses that are available of Irvin in her job in 1919 indicate that she was a capable researcher and writer and an effective spokeswoman for black women workers. Director Van Kleeck suggested that Irvin could meet with the Consumers League of Philadelphia's field workers as they planned their study. In addition to her research and writing, Irvin's job included public speaking engagements to explain the programs of the Women's Bureau and the Department of Labor to black women's organizations and to describe the situation of black women workers to the social service community and public at large. One condescending reporter was surprised by Irvin's attractive attire and her professional demeanor: "She had the charm of not appearing to possess consciousness of her race. Her talk of Negro working women is as dispassionate as it would be if she were speaking instead of white women."[38] When the DOL held an Informal Conference on the Problems of Negro Labor in the winter of 1919, Helen Irvin, Mary Van Kleeck, and the YWCA industrial secretary Mary E. Jackson, a black national board staff member, were featured on a panel entitled "Special Problems of Women in Industry."[39] Despite this high-powered female panel, the conference resolutions did not give much attention to the needs of black women workers, as the historian Cynthia Neverdon-Morton has observed.[40] Mary Talbert, president of the National Association of Colored Women, also spoke on a panel concerning governmental cooperation with private organizations. Hearing Mary Talbert speak at the conference may have prompted the WIIS director Mary Van Kleeck to authorize expenses for Irvin to speak to a meeting of colored women's clubs in New Jersey as well as lecture at two Negro colleges in North Carolina, because Van Kleeck thought "it is very important and desirable . . . that the colored people of the South know what our Department is doing." Favorable publicity would have been desirable because the Women's Bureau was not yet permanent and the Department of Labor was receiving complaints from the National Association for the Advancement of Colored People and other organizations about coercive "work or fight laws" in a few southern states that were aimed at preventing black women from migrating or having a choice in their employment.[41] Black northern voters were already highly suspicious of Woodrow Wilson's administration, which had instituted segregation in the civil service and federal buildings in Washington, D.C.

Helen Brooks Irvin's 1919 address before the National Conference of Social Work provides more direct indications of her analytical ability, views on labor matters, and strategy for advocating fair treatment of black women workers. Irvin placed her agency's concern for American women workers in an international context of increasing and stabilizing democracy, citing the rise of the Labor Party in Great Britain and the inclusion of labor standards at the Peace Congress in Paris. She emphasized that black women were a part of the native-born American workforce of women workers who had proven their value to industry during the war. The Women in Industry Service's purpose was to guarantee that standards of working conditions in terms of wages, hours, health, and safety were used to protect women. Irvin argued that democracy at home should apply to all working women. "These standards must be applied with absolute impartiality to all groups of working women. Most urgently are they needed where workers are apt to be exploited, as is often the case among Negro women." Repeating the mantra of black social scientists from W. E. B. Du Bois through George Edmund Haynes, Irvin reasoned that evaluations of the worthiness of black women workers should be based on objective research. "This almost untried group has become the target for much adverse criticism and for such wide speculation that the unbiased facts concerning their defects and assets must be frankly faced before we can arrive at any decision concerning their value to the world of industry."[42]

After her general plea for open-mindedness, Irvin turned to anecdotal summaries of a half-dozen or so cases of achievements of black women from her fieldwork, constructing a circumstantial case that the alleged defects of black women workers were applicable to any workers in a new field, regardless of race. Irvin described without criticizing the ongoing process by which black women factory workers who had worked satisfactorily were being displaced from their jobs not only by returning soldiers but also by white women. While Helen Brooks Irvin seemed to accept the fact that women factory workers would be replaced by men and that black women would lose their jobs to white women, she was adamant in her condemnation of domestic service. Irvin welcomed a possible extension of wage and hour standards for domestic workers but scornfully charged that white housewives were attempting to force "the emancipated Negro housemaid and laundress out of her new industrial position and back to the dissatisfaction of the other woman's kitchen." Irvin concluded her address to the assembled social workers by warning organized labor that its failure to organize black women could lead to their working as scabs, and pleaded for a greater acceptance of black women in industrial jobs. "We know that the true situation . . . It is vital to the entire field of labor that we face this situation frankly and intelligently . . . and that we make public recognition of the fact that underneath the movement of Negro women toward industry there is nothing antagonistic to the common interests of the laboring classes. . . . But they are a hitherto unplumbed source of native labor that may be developed into a valuable economic asset to the nation. *The industrial problem is fundamental.*"[43]

Helen Irvin's specific findings and assessments of the experiences of black women as a result of her eight-month survey of black female workers and their employers were published as a chapter in George Haynes's *The Negro at Work in World War and Reconstruction,* his major research effort while the head of the DNE.[44] Haynes had initially hoped to produce a separate volume on all aspects of black women's work after his study of black male workers, but by the summer of 1920, with the DNE reduced to one assistant and one clerk, it was clear that he would not have the funds or the time to undertake the study of women as he had wished. Instead, Haynes decided to include Irvin's work in his larger study. Irvin's documentation of employer attitudes toward black women workers showed that those who hired black women were generally satisfied with their performance. She also discussed the persistence of discriminatory practices, dangerous working conditions, and black women's placement in the least desirable jobs. Irvin argued that racial discrimination created unmotivated workers, whereas employing black supervisors and providing equal pay improved productivity.

After Haynes agreed to utilize Irvin's materials in the study he was about to publish, he was able to convince the officials of the Women's Bureau to hire another young black woman, Emma L. Shields, to make an additional three-month study and produce a report that would reflect black women's experiences in the immediate postwar period. In contrast to Irvin, whose later activities remain unknown, more biographical information is available about Shields.[45] After fewer than eighteen months, Irvin left the newly named Women's Bureau and the historical record. A new study of black women workers was assigned in the fall of 1920 to Shields, a wartime employee of the Children's Bureau and a Fisk University graduate.

Emma L. Shields Penn: New Negro Social Scientist

Emma L. Shields, the second of our trio of U.S. Department of Labor social scientists, was a former student of George Haynes's who was teaching high school English, Latin, advanced algebra, and music in Wheeling, West Virginia, at the beginning of the Great Migration. Shields had internalized and operationalized Fisk University's expectation that its graduates work for racial advancement. She and several other high school teachers began a night school for working adults and held entertainment programs for children; and she also ran a Saturday afternoon story hour. Shields credited her courses in social science at Fisk for enabling her to introduce social service programs for the black townspeople. She explained to Haynes, "I do not feel that I should have been able to cope with any situations . . . had I not taken the social science courses which I had under your direction at Fisk." Her interest in research on black workers was also evident before the establishment of the Division of Negro Economics or the Women's Bureau. In 1916 Shields volunteered to assist Haynes in an early study he was undertaking of the migration and offered to interview and photograph black industrial workers in West Virginia.[46] Still, while supportive, this relationship was not the same close mentoring relationship as Haynes had with some of his male students, such as Charles H. Wesley.

As was the case of Gertrude McDougald, Elizabeth Ross Haynes, and Sadie T. M. Alexander, teaching did not completely fulfill Emma Shields's career ambitions. Notwithstanding the obvious need for black teachers and community services where she was, Shields expressed a longing to be employed as a social worker in a "real social center."[47] By 1920 Shields was in Washington, D.C., working at the DOL as a special agent in the Children's Bureau and she was transferred to the DNE and Women's Bureau in late summer or early fall. Her new assignment to undertake a study of black women workers for the DNE and the Women's Bureau must have been exactly the type of work she desired.

Emma Shields's three-month survey in the fall of 1920 yielded a comprehensive Women's Bureau report that was based on a large sample of black women in occupations that were newly open to them and at tasks to which they had been consigned since Emancipation. George Haynes most likely helped Shields construct the questionnaires because he was somewhat dissatisfied with the instrument that Irvin had used in her study. Shields's study contained data from interviews with the managers of sixty-three plants, a characteristic feature of Haynes's studies that he had adapted from W. E. B. Du Bois's *The Negro Artisan,* and it was used in most of the wartime studies of black female workers to demonstrate their capability to work in factories. White women's labor studies more rarely used this type of interview.[48] Emma Shields's study encompassed 11,812 black women workers in 150 plants in nine states. The black women studied were in industrial occupations in which they had been traditionally concentrated, such as tobacco farming, and in the newer areas of industry from which they had been effectively barred, such as the metal trades. Shields's survey examined a significant percentage of the black women who were industrial workers in the 1920 U.S. census, by which time many factory workers had already been dismissed from their new positions. Shields not only complied and presented black women's varied occupational categories, salaries, working hours, and employer satisfaction, but she also presented a detailed analysis of the often adverse working conditions and discriminatory practices that black women faced. She was particularly detailed in her depiction of unsanitary and dangerous working conditions in some plants and the consequences in terms of health and safety, employee turnover, and productivity. The *Monthly Labor Review* digest of Shields's report detailed her most politically potent finding: that racial prejudice was responsible for black women's relegation to the most undesirable jobs. The *MLR* quoted approvingly from Shields's report, citing her descriptions of black women working under "especially unsatisfactory" conditions in terms of seating, ventilation, and sanitation, and it highlighted her arguments that employing black nurses and forewomen made for a much more productive workforce. The conclusion that the *MLR* drew was exactly what Shields and George Haynes must have wanted: "The impression is left that negro [*sic*] women have encountered many obstacles in their new activities that might, advantageously to both sides, be avoided; and while they have not yet acquired a permanent position in industry they have made a beginning, that they respond quickly to fair treatment and to opportunities for trade training and industrial self-improvement; and that in them there is a potential labor supply of much value which has hitherto been largely neglected."[49]

The description of Shields's report by the Women's Bureau was much more neutral. It accurately described Shields's main findings but omitted her charges of racist practices, substituting the idea that "great unrest" might occur between black and white women if black women continued to have lower pay, less desirable jobs, and worse working conditions in the same plants. The bureau suggested that the report "will provide a basis for definite recommendations of the wisest employment methods and industrial uses for Negro women." Research that would lead to social change was a goal of black social scientists such as Shields, but the Women's Bureau did not make such recommendations with enough force to change working conditions or increase black women's access to cleaner, safer, or more skilled jobs. Another goal of black social scientists was to review and if possible rebut charges of black inferiority. These included white workers' charges that blacks were genetically unqualified for skilled work, and were lazy, inattentive workers with high turnover rates and little work ethic. Shields found managers willing to admit that black women could and often did make cigars and cigarettes as well as white women, albeit never at the same wages. Allegations about high turnover and poor work ethic were more complicated, but Shields, like Irvin, argued forcefully that when black women were treated with respect and had healthy shops and unbiased forewomen, they had low levels of turnover and absenteeism. Both women suggested that any worker, regardless of race or nativity, who was in a low-wage job with no prospect of advancement had little incentive to be productive.[50]

Shields's DOL study and two subsequent articles took an in-depth look at black women in the tobacco industry. More than half of the black women in industries that Shields examined were tobacco rehandlers, an occupational niche that had been reserved for black women since slavery. Because the number of black women in the tobacco industry was so large, Shields made a special additional survey of the three largest tobacco-growing areas of Virginia, examining the awful conditions not only in the plants but also visiting eighty-five homes of tobacco workers. She was appalled by the unhealthy conditions under which black women were forced to work, the casual racism, and the occasional sadism of plant managers, and Shields was alternatively depressed and inspired by the attitudes of the women she interviewed. Black and white women in the tobacco plants were physically separated, with white women making cigars and cigarettes under much better, although not ideal, working conditions and wage levels than black women. The legacy of slavery in the Virginia plants was almost as thick as the tobacco dust and stench of poor sanitation that pervaded the workrooms. Diseases were passed via the common cup and bucket of water passed to women, with no eating or washing facilities. Tobacco managers readily told Emma Shields that they thought of the older black women as their personal property. The majority of black female tobacco workers worked more than fifty-five hours a week and were paid less than $12 a week, a figure so far below the minimum wage of $16.50 a week then being established that even the Women's Bureau director Mary Anderson commented on its inadequacy.

Emma Shields called herself a New Negro woman and rejected the submissive demeanor expected of southern blacks by whites. In her two published articles on female tobacco workers, Shields analyzed her complicated reaction to the seemingly childlike loyalty of old women in the plant to the paternalistic plant managers. Their mournful singing of songs such as "By and by I'm going to set down this heavy load" seemed to her to be "both beautiful and pathetic." Shields thought that her off-site interviews had detected a few women who shared her New Negro spirit and also yearned for "a new industrial emancipation." She warned her readers in *Life and Labor* that labor organizers were not likely to quickly change the situation.[51] Curiously, Shields's article in the conservative *Southern Workman* ended on a more militant note. "A half-century of toil has evolved a new Negro woman worker in the tobacco industry, one who is seriously opposed to the subservience and subjection to which many of the previous workers were inured. . . . She is deeply cognizant of the modern standards of employment and is desirous of those safeguards, incentives, and rewards in industry. . . . It is with this 'Americanized' Negro woman, who has imbibed the national spirit of opportunity and freedom, that the future tobacco industry in the South must reckon."[52]

Like Gertrude McDougald Ayer, Emma L. Shields Penn remained active and involved in assisting black women workers after her first survey research project. But even though she remained actively engaged in research, she did not publish another major study. Shields moved to New York City in the early

1920s and became the full-time director of the Harlem YWCA's Trade School in 1922 or 1923. As Emma Shields Penn, she built the Trade School from 240 students to more than 2,000 by 1937 and implemented "an integrated program of counseling, training and placement." She continued her research interest in black female workers in her New York University master's thesis, which was entitled "Vocational Adjustment Problems of Negro Women in New York City." In this neglected thesis Shields Penn examines the job placements of 3,400 black women in New York City between 1927 and 1931, offering a detailed portrait of the job market in the two years before and two years after the stock market crash. This study complemented and extended her Women's Bureau report of a decade earlier. In 1937, after fifteen years as director, Shields Penn left the YWCA Trade School for a position as a vocational and educational counselor in the New York City public schools.[53]

Elizabeth Ross Haynes: A Dollar-a-Year Social Scientist

Elizabeth Ross Haynes was also employed as a social scientist at the Department of Labor between 1918 and 1921. Her study of black domestic workers was the best-known study completed by a black woman social scientist at the time, and it was the most frequently cited by contemporary scholars after its publication. In the 1970s and 1980s, when interest in black workers' history revived, this study was generally considered to be one of the most important. Ross Haynes's study of black domestic workers was begun in 1918 or 1919 but was not published until 1923, making her a transitional figure between generations. She, like McDougald and Irvin, stood in between the generation of clubwomen and the generation of Shields. Shields's generation worked first as teachers, then briefly as social scientists, and finally as teachers, guidance counselors, or social workers. A new generation of slightly younger women, such as Sadie Tanner Mossell Alexander and Myra Hill Colson, had begun to emerge as well. They tried to begin their careers as social scientists in the 1920s and 1930s and studied migrants and women workers. Elizabeth Ross Haynes brought to the Women's Bureau and the Division of Negro Economics a vast amount of experience from her decade of YWCA work with young black women workers, but as the wife of the director of the DNE, she was unable to legally earn a salary until George Haynes was no longer on the payroll. Ross Haynes seems to have attempted to become an unpaid manager rather than a part-time volunteer, following the example set by the white male corporate executives who led numerous federal wartime agencies as dollar-a-year workers. Ross Haynes did advise both the Women's Bureau and the DNE on matters concerning black women workers and at times served as a volunteer industrial secretary, visiting plants and work sites. She contributed to Helen Brooks Irvin's report by visiting factories, but the completion and publication of her own study of black domestic workers was postponed until after she left Washington. Elizabeth Ross Haynes's decade of work for the YWCA and black women's organizations and her interest in social research should have made her a more valuable asset to both the Women's Bureau and the DNE, but her expertise seems to have been underutilized during the war.

Although she subsequently described herself as working for both agencies, there is little in the records to indicate that Ross Haynes was considered by either agency to be anything more than a rather important volunteer. Her correspondence with the Women's Bureau suggests that Ross Haynes and bureau officials were frequently out of sync in their interpretations of the meaning of the wartime service of black women workers.

Elizabeth Ross Haynes personifies a number of themes emphasized in this book—including the different attitudes of blacks and whites and men and women toward black labor force participation, especially black women's participation. For example, Elizabeth Haynes attempted to promote the image of black women as hardworking and efficient to counter widespread negative views about black women workers. She had to work within the limits of her role as an unpaid assistant to her husband, whereas Irvin and Shields could explicitly examine allegations about black women's competence in their reports. Both Elizabeth Haynes and George Haynes believed that patriotism could be demonstrated by working harder, faster, and longer hours than other workers, views that were diametrically opposed to the mission of the Women's Bureau, which wanted more restrictive hours for women. In one instance, Ross Haynes sent a Women's Bureau official a glowing description of the long hours worked by a black woman at the U.S. Bureau of Engraving. The Division of Negro Economics regularly had press releases with accounts of black people working overtime or exceeding their production quotas, which were designed to demonstrate their competence and patriotism. In the view of the DNE, the war offered black male and female workers an opportunity to prove their abilities in semiskilled and skilled jobs and occupational categories from which they had been barred. The views of the DNE differed from those of the many white male trade union officials who saw black women's lower wages and longer hours as a threat to white male and female workers. Trade union officials regularly complained to the DNE and the Women in Industry Ser-

Elizabeth Ross Haynes. (Franklin Library Special Collections, Fisk University)

vice that black women were illegally taking the jobs of white men at lower wage levels or were working longer hours than women were legally allowed. The policy of the Women's Bureau was to enforce limits to the hours and type of work that were available to women, and Women's Bureau officials were generally not sympathetic to arguments that stressed the role racism played in constricting black women's choice of jobs.[54]

Differences in their attitudes about how black women workers could demonstrate their abilities to perform the wider range of jobs that had now opened to them may have undercut the ability of the DNE and the Women's Bureau to work together effectively to improve the status and working conditions for black female workers. In one instance, Elizabeth Ross Haynes sent the Women's Bureau assistant director Mary Anderson a brief account of a visitor's experiences at the U.S. Bureau of Engraving that described a group of black women and showcased the wife of a soldier stationed in France. Mrs. Anna R. Grant, "a Negro expert currency examiner," worked twenty-eight hours at a stretch, doing the work of three people in "an example of rare efficiency and fine spirit."[55] The account of black women at the Bureau of Engraving moved from Mrs. Grant to the other black women at the Bureau of Engraving and economically countered several myths about black women workers. "The Negro girls as a whole . . . are very satisfactory. They complain less. . . . There is less subordination among them. . . . They are just as neat and tidy and healthy . . . but as a large group they are not as well educated."[56] In her reply Anderson agreed that the "girls" were competent but strongly objected to their overtime work, despite the fact that their regular wages were low, on the grounds of the "bad effect that the overtime would have upon the [other] workers in general."[57] This conflict between the two agencies over basic goals and the meanings of the work of black women, as well as Ross Haynes's somewhat nebulous position as a dollar-a-day worker, has left only a faint impression of Ross Haynes's activities in the records of the Women's Bureau and those of her husband's Division of Negro Economics. Her own accounts suggest that she may have played a larger role than can be reconstructed from the available materials. Ross Haynes's master's thesis and an article she wrote on black women workers indicate that she was assembling her data and crafting her own study while working at the Department of Labor.

Much like her husband and other black social scientists of the New Negro period, Elizabeth Ross Haynes's primary interest was in documenting northern workers outside of agriculture. Her master's thesis lacked detailed descriptions of black domestic workers in the South. Ross Haynes's 1922 *Southern Workman* article "Two Million Negro Women at Work" did not give equal time to the one million black women still at work in agriculture in 1920; instead, it described the impact of the postwar economic slowdown on black women in domestic service and manufacturing jobs. Ross Haynes adopted the neutral analytical tone of the social scientist and her personal opinions are less evident in her writings about women and domestic workers than in her other published works.

Her study, coming on the heels of her work experiences in wartime Washington, also helped to change Elizabeth Haynes's self-definition. After the publication of "Negroes in Domestic Service in the United States," Ross Haynes described herself in biographical sketches as a "sociologist and author."[58] The studies of McDougald, Irvin, and Shields emphasized black women who were industrial workers, whereas Ross Haynes's study offered the first extensive examination of the domestic service occupations such as maids, cooks, cleaners, and housekeepers, fields in which more than three-quarters of black women were employed. In "Negroes in Domestic Service,"

Ross Haynes's methodology joined a descriptive analysis of black women's—and men's—labor force participation based on the 1900–20 U.S. occupational censuses with data she gathered in Washington, D.C., New York City, and at least ten other cities between 1918 and 1923. To extend the cities for which she had data on domestic work, Ross Haynes used survey questionnaires that volunteer correspondents completed in distant cities, a method first used by W. E. B. Du Bois to study black workers in 1902 in *The Negro Artisan,* and that black sociologists continued to use, even in government studies, throughout the 1920s.[59] Elizabeth Ross Haynes's experiences at the DOL had shown her that the broad occupational categories of the federal census did not always reveal the swift changes in black employment patterns that had occurred during the Great Migration. She used data from registration cards filled out by job seekers when she was an employment secretary at the U.S. Employment Service in order to more carefully characterize these changing patterns of employment. Ross Haynes was also interested in analyzing employers' assessments of their domestic workers. She was more sensitive to the notion that workers and employers often had far different perspectives on the same behavior than were most black male and white female social scientists who had used similar techniques. She gave equal attention to employees' dissatisfaction with working conditions, particularly in household work. She argued that domestic workers' dissatisfaction, not incompetence, resulted in high labor turnover and a growing disinclination by black women to accept live-in positions. Ross Haynes also briefly sketched the education, training, health, labor organizations, and social life of domestic workers.[60] "Negroes in Domestic Service" attempted to provide a balanced portrait of both male and female domestics, but offered more varied information on women's employment, in part because Ross Haynes had greater access to contemporary employment data on female household workers. Ross Haynes's detailed employment records of 9,976 persons employed in Washington, D.C., during 1920–22 included only 202 males. Her data on wage differentials of black domestic workers in a number of cities was extensive, but the possibility of incomparability of the data made Elizabeth Haynes shrink from making many comparisons of wages paid in different cities. Ross Haynes documented the influence of wages on black domestic employment, and on the frequent substitution of white workers for black workers when wages rose. Her most critical comments decried the displacement of black female domestics by white workers after the passage of minimum wage legislation in Washington, D.C. Ross Haynes and her husband had fought the passage of this law behind the scenes at the Department of Labor. Ross Haynes also condemned private employment agencies for overcharging employers and employees. She believed her research proved that these agencies were all too frequently associated with vice and crime and that they exploited unsophisticated migrants.[61] This finding indicated that these problems were not much different from those that Victoria Earle Matthews uncovered twenty years earlier.

Ross Haynes also documented the continuing scarcity of adequate day-care services for black women with young children, despite two decades of efforts by black women in the National Association of Colored Women to establish nursery schools and kindergartens. Most of the cities she surveyed had neither public nor private nursery schools that accepted black children. Domestics who lived in, and many who lived out but worked twelve or more hours a day and did not have family members to care for their children, were forced to find other places for their children to live. A large number of the women interviewed in Elizabeth Clark-Lewis's study of black women domestic workers in Washington, D.C., first came to the city to care for the children of older siblings who were working in. Boarding children in Washington, D.C., cost $6 a week, while the average weekly wage for domestic workers was $9.58.[62]

The five studies of black women workers during the Great Migration discussed in this chapter did not examine with equal intensity the working lives of all black women. The one million black women who were farm workers in 1910 and 1920 were not given much critical attention from social scientists, aside from Emma Shields's analysis of tobacco workers and Women's Bureau statistical compilations of rural industries, such as oyster and clam processing in the Chesapeake, and nut packing in Missouri, which employed large numbers of black rural women. Elizabeth Ross Haynes's study was significant because it dealt with the occupation of the majority of black women workers, and because scholarly studies of domestic work were dated by the 1920s, having been done principally at the turn of the century. Except for Ross Haynes's contemporary research, nearly all of the commentary concerning black domestic workers during the migration was based on anecdotal sources and stereotypes. Unfortunately, there were few other published nongovernmental studies of either black women workers or domestic service for forty years after Ross Haynes's study.[63] The four years Elizabeth Ross Haynes spent in Washington, D.C., at the Department of Labor were critical to her self-perception as a sociologist and an author, as well as to the resumption of her public voice after almost a decade of marriage. Ross Haynes's first book, *Unsung Heroes,* biographical stories for black children, was published in 1921 by W. E. B. Du Bois and Augustus Granville Dill's short-lived publishing company. She most likely wrote this book while she lived in Washington.[64]

Elizabeth Ross Haynes spoke out publicly on behalf of black women workers as an individual rather than as a governmental social scientist. When the white American trade union women who organized the First International Congress of Working Women in 1919 failed to include black women as delegates or have their concerns directly addressed at the congress, Ross Haynes was one of a dozen black women who signed a memorial petition on behalf of black working women that was presented in one of its final sessions. In this petition her occupation was listed as "working woman," and Ross Haynes was designated as the contact person for communications on issues concerning black women workers.[65]

When her husband's agency, the DNE, was drastically downsized in 1920, Elizabeth Haynes took a salaried job overseeing the placement of domestic workers in the Washington, D.C., office of the U.S. Employment Service, until George Haynes found a full-time position in 1922 with the Federal Council of Churches in New York. Both Hayneses later constructed their public biographies so that this two-year period of financial and personal difficulties was not easily detected. George Haynes's biography hid his underemployment, and Elizabeth Ross Haynes's concealed the fact that her salary was necessary to the family by suggesting that she did not work for a salary after her marriage. Her position at USES was Ross Haynes's first full-time job since her marriage ten years earlier. Her need to enter the workforce, and George Haynes's inability to find full-time work despite his doctorate, decade of service to the NUL and Fisk University, and his federal service, must have brought home to her with special force the economic vulnerability of black families and the limited types of jobs then available for black women, regardless of educational levels. Ross Haynes and her family moved to New York City permanently in 1922, where she used most of the data she had collected while working in Washington as part of the findings in her master's thesis in sociology from Columbia University.[66]

Elizabeth Ross Haynes's activities after she left Washington reveal a rarer type of transition, from a paid job with the Labor Department to unpaid positions on the national YWCA board and assisting her husband at the Federal Council of Churches. Most black women professionals, including married women such as McDougald and Shields Penn, worked well into their fifties and sixties in paid positions. Elizabeth Ross Haynes instead became a professional volunteer and community activist while continuing her interest in scholarship.

When she moved to Harlem in 1922, Ross Haynes was in her early forties, with an adolescent son and a husband who was by now a race relations executive. She took the initiative to complete her master's degree in sociology at Columbia University. We are fortunate she did, since her master's thesis and a few articles are all that remain on the public record of her many decades of study on behalf of black workers. With this educational accomplishment, she then looked at opportunities for work. Teaching school was a possibility, but it offered limited choices since there were few positions in high schools or in the two or three elementary schools based in Harlem. Alternatively, she could have tried for a paid position as a social worker, but this too posed problems. With her age, education, and experience she would have warranted one of the handful of administrative positions available for black women in city or state social welfare administration. Or she might have found a position in a private welfare organization. However, all these positions were highly contested and she failed to get a paid position. Ultimately, during this period, her search for paid employment was fruitless. Elizabeth Ross Haynes did not retire from public life, but neither did she hold a salaried job for at least two more decades.

Instead, she became involved in political activities in her own right. First she worked for the GOP; later, she was among the first blacks to switch to the Democrats. Then she was rewarded by becoming coleader of Harlem's Democrats. In 1924, after a decade of demands for a black woman board member, led by Lugenia Burns Hope and other activists, Elizabeth Ross Haynes was elected to the national board of the YWCA. She also used ad hoc committees to champion the employment of black nurses and social workers in Harlem. Not only did she engage in these political affairs but once again Ross Haynes assisted her husband, this time in his new job at the Federal Council of Churches.

Although her social science study was central to the scholarly understanding of black women workers, Elizabeth Ross Haynes was apparently never called on to do further studies of black workers. Her expertise as a labor analyst was desired during the Depression, when Governor Herbert Lehman appointed Ross Haynes to the Temporary Commission on the Status of the Urban Colored Population. She was the first woman appointed to the commission. Ross Haynes and her fellow commissioners held statewide hearings on the impact of the Depression on black people and proposed wide-ranging legislation to ban discrimination.

Ross Haynes's study of black domestics was published by Carter G. Woodson in the *Journal of Negro History* in 1923, giving it greater visibility to later generations of scholars than the studies of the other black women social scientists. Woodson was interested in black women domestic workers; he wrote about them, used Ross Haynes's data in his study of black workers, and commissioned a study of domestic workers in Washington, D.C., a decade after he published Ross Haynes's study.

But Ross Haynes was not the only black woman to gain some visibility in this period. In the early 1930s Woodson selected Myra Hill Colson Callis, a young black woman with a master's degree in sociology from the University of Chicago who had done a study of black women in homework industries in Chicago, to analyze the results of a survey on domestic workers in Washington. Woodson published this work as part of Lorenzo J. Greene's study of black employment in the nation's capital. Colson Callis taught the first social work courses at Howard University as a part-time instructor, even though her master's degree and publications more than qualified her to be an assistant professor.[67] Shields Penn also remained in the public eye; during the 1920s her Women's Bureau study was probably the most widely circulated study by a black male or female social scientist because it "ran through three editions, with a total of 21,000 copies."[68] In Harlem it is also probable that more working-class black women knew of Gertrude McDougald Ayer or Emma Shields Penn than the other black female social scientists because of their involvement in local schools, trade unions, and the YWCA.

Many black men who worked as labor analysts and social scientists during World War I went on to academic careers or became well-paid executives in social service agencies. None of the black women had such experiences. It is clear, however, that most of them wanted and sought rewarding jobs that would more fully utilize their skills as researchers. Gertrude McDougald Ayer spent more than a decade as a vocational counselor in New York City public schools, all the while trying to undertake a variety of studies of black economic life. The studies of McDougald Ayer, Ross Haynes, Shields Penn, and Irvin were widely cited in black and white social welfare circles as proof of the need for better treatment for black women workers, but these same communities seemed to ignore the employment needs of black women social scientists.[69]

The Segregated Scholars

A New Day Deferred for the First Black Women with Doctorates in Social Science

Nothing more vividly demonstrates that the work experiences of black women social scientists during and immediately after World War I directly paralleled the fortunes of the women they were hired to study than the case of Sadie Tanner Mossell Alexander. Her case illustrates that the barriers to black women in employment could not simply be overcome by having the right mix of skills, training, age, or marital status. In 1921 Sadie Mossell was a young, unmarried social scientist with a doctorate in economics and outstanding recommendations. However, she could not get a job as an economist.

Sadie Mossell was just graduating from the University of Pennsylvania in 1918 at the time of the first demands for studies on black female migrants. It had taken her just three years to complete her degree in the School of Education, the school in which most female students at the University of Pennsylvania were obliged to enroll until the early 1960s. She received financial support from her socially prominent but not wealthy family. Mossell's outstanding undergraduate academic record earned her fellowships to the University of Pennsylvania's graduate school, where she began in history and shifted to economics, earning a masters' degree, and doctorate in 1921. No other black social scientist had completed a residential doctoral program so quickly, and few would do so subsequently. Although she was interested in black women's economic issues, when Mossell entered the doctoral program at Penn she decided to write a dissertation that analyzed the household budgets of one hundred migrant families in Philadelphia.[70]

Her education and obvious ability should have placed Sadie Mossell in a favorable position in the job market. At the time, she was the only black American to have earned a doctorate in economics, and the only social scientist among the three black women in 1921 who were the first to earn doctorates. The economics faculty fully supported her scholarship and recommended that her thesis be published in the *Annals of the Academy of Political and Social Science.*[71] Sadie Mossell Alexander's pride in her accomplishment soon vanished; she found she could not get a job commensurate with her education. There were no positions as an economist in the Northeast or Midwest for Sadie Mossell, despite the fact that her advisors at Penn apparently had gone to great lengths to entreat white insurance firms to hire her. As she later ruefully recalled, "All the glory of that occasion faded, however, quickly when I tried to get a position."[72]

Sadie Tanner Mossell (Alexander); photograph by Gilbert and Bacon Studios, Philadelphia. (From the Collections of the University of Pennsylvania Archives)

The evidence of gender discrimination against black women could not be clearer than in the case of Mossell Alexander and her two sister scholars of the same period. Like Alexander, the other two black women who earned doctorates in June 1921, Eva B. Dykes and Georgiana Simpson, were also not immediately materially improved by their accomplishments. After receiving their degrees, Dykes and Simpson went back to teaching their classes at Dunbar High School in Washington, D.C., because Howard University and most other black colleges rarely hired black women outside of the home economics department and the normal school. Gender discrimination stunted the careers of these women in ways that race discrimination alone did not for their male colleagues. Carter G. Woodson congratulated Eva Dykes "on having made such thorough preparation to serve efficiently," but he cautioned her to "leave Washington as soon as possible that you may have an opportunity for development."[73] After Howard reorganized in the late 1920s, under President Mordecai Johnson, both Dykes and Simpson were appointed to faculty positions.

Georgiana Simpson was sixty-five years old when she joined Howard's faculty. She had never married, and like so many less-educated black women, she may have worked well into her older years because she needed to support herself. Eva Dykes was also single and not very well paid; she sometimes worked as a waitress at private homes even after she was a Howard University professor of English, a condition few of her male counterparts were likely to face.[74]

Opportunities for academic work, like the ones provided by Johnson at Howard University, should have been even more widely available for female social scientists than for humanities scholars. If Sadie Mossell Alexander had been a man, she would have been able to work as an executive director for a National Urban League or YMCA branch, one of the better salaried jobs in the country for a black person. In the case of the NUL, this was also a position that involved directing research. The majority of black men who held these jobs had only bachelor's or master's degrees; indeed, many black men, such as Charles S. Johnson and Forrester B. Washington, used NUL positions as stepping-stones to appointments as heads of college departments and schools of social science and social work. Virtually all of George Haynes's male staff from the DNE or the NUL went on to receive good jobs in social welfare agencies, where they continued to do survey research and receive better and better positions. Younger black men, such as E. Franklin Frazier, Abram L. Harris, and Ira De A. Reid, who were Sadie Alexander's contemporaries as undergraduates, delayed their graduate studies during the war but used Urban League fellowships and jobs as stepping-stones to academic careers. When Frazier became head of the Atlanta School of Social Work in 1923 he was not much older than Mossell and had only a master's degree. Sadie Mossell Alexander and many other black women knew Du Bois, Haynes, and the other male mentors as classmates, friends, and teachers, but these personal acquaintanceships were not enough to lead to long-term gainful employment.

Sadie Mossell Alexander, though, was not without connections among the black elite, and as a single woman she should have been able to get a college teaching position. Her grandfather, Bishop B. T. Tanner, had been the president of Wilberforce University and had served on the board of trustees of Howard University; her uncle by marriage, Lewis Baxter Moore, had been the dean of Howard's Teacher's College for twenty years. As Mossell was becoming more and more desperate about ever securing a job, North Carolina Mutual Insurance Company president C. C. Spaulding came to her rescue and hired her as an "assistant actuary." Despite her distinguished doctorate from a leading university, Sadie Mossell did not ever work full-time as a professional economist. Her career as a social scientist was modest—a single study of black tuberculosis rates in Philadelphia that the Phipps Institute commissioned her to do while she was waiting to get a regular job in 1921, and then two years in Durham in a position that did not require or utilize her expertise.[75]

When Sadie T. Mossell, a fifth-generation descendant of free northern blacks on both sides of her family, and perhaps an overly proud "Old Philadelphian," reached the South, she immediately detested it. Two years later, after her college sweetheart, Raymond Pace Alexander, graduated from Harvard Law School and set up a law practice, Mossell promptly resigned her job to marry him and return to Philadelphia. After her marriage, Mossell Alexander still wanted a career rather than a job, and she was unwilling to have children before she found a desirable vocation. Again facing a job market in Philadelphia in which black women were only hired at the elementary school level, Sadie Mossell Alexander enrolled in the University of Pennsylvania's Law School, where she overcame the hostility of its dean, who permanently barred her from membership in the women's law society and blocked her from the law review staff for one year. Upon her graduation Alexander worked in her husband's firm. Other black women lawyers in the 1930s also began at family firms. Alexander's work as a law associate provided steady employment but did not completely shield her from the sexism of Raymond Alexander's male associates or the experience of receiving job assignments that the men in the firm declined to take.[76]

Alexander practiced law for fifty-five years but maintained an interest in economics, often giving carefully researched speeches on economic conditions. Regrettably, she has remained largely invisible in the published discourse on black workers.[77] Black women did not begin to get regular positions in social work schools until the early 1930s, and they did not join social science departments until the late 1930s, too late for most of the women who were pioneering investigators and analysts during the Great Migration. The next major study of black women workers did not come until the late 1930s, when the Women's Bureau again turned to a too-little-known black woman social scientist, Jean Collier Brown, to conduct the study.[78]

Conclusion

The employment and professional conditions for the segregated scholars were difficult for all its members, but they were especially severe for those among

The Segregated Scholars

them who carried the double stigma of gender and racial discrimination. It is impossible to calculate today how scholarly views of the Great Migration would have been enriched by more attention to the issues of gender and work that black women social scientists tried, against the odds, to present. We would have had a more complete picture of the conditions under which the poorest of the poor were forced to work, as we saw in the tobacco industry. The consequences for scholarship of gender discrimination were double edged. On the one hand, gender discrimination in education, training, and employment meant that young black women were less likely to go to graduate school and more likely to earn professional degrees and enter the feminized professions such as social work, teaching, library science, or nursing. While the law and medicine were overwhelmingly male, black women in these fields were better able to establish practices, albeit usually with their fathers or husbands, than black women with doctorates were able to succeed in the academy. On the other hand, we have seen that even when their research and writing were successfully completed, black women social scientists were more likely to be ignored and overlooked. The forced marginalization of black women social scientists also reveals the stratified and unequal nature of the American labor market for educated social scientists.

It is certainly clear that our understanding of the complexity and difficulties of black scholarship in the 1920s and 1930s and beyond has been stunted because the initiatives, successes, and challenges of black women scholars have been unrecognized. Still, in the face of racial and gender discrimination, the research and social commentary on black migrants by Sadie Tanner Mossell Alexander, Elizabeth Ross Haynes, Gertrude McDougald Ayer, Helen Brooks Irvin, and other women still awaiting reclamation served to create and keep alive a tradition of black women's social science that began at the turn of the century. As the Depression began, the black women whose labor writings had begun the 1920s were involved in other, often underpaid, projects to improve their communities' economic standing. Black women social scientists would finally be accepted in small numbers in the academy beginning in the late 1930s, but they now more rarely studied women workers or labor issues.[79] As black labor scholars' ideological rifts widened considerably over solutions to problems of unemployment and poverty during the 1930s and 1940s, there was not a body of scholarship that considered black women workers' situation, although their economic contribution to their families and communities was far greater than their white counterparts'. Charles H. Wesley was the only one of the five male social scientists who at the end of World

War I had published more than had the women we have discussed in this chapter. While Abram L. Harris, Ira De A. Reid, and Charles S. Johnson had begun the 1920s with far less research and publishing experience than the five women detailed in this chapter, it was the ongoing studies, debates, and economic plans of younger and older male social scientists that shaped black labor studies and advocacy in the 1930s and 1940s.

6

"A Corporal's Guard" for Negro Workers

Black Labor Scholars during the New Deal and the Second World War, 1930–1950

I plan to work on something in the field of Negro Labor. Indeed I cannot see how a person interested in the economic life of the black American could hope to escape treating of the Negro worker.
—Robert C. Weaver to W. E. B. Du Bois, Jan. 29, 1931

The Negro is dedicated to fight for the right to work. The danger ahead is that his fight . . . may occur in a society with not enough jobs to go around and result in racial conflict. . . . In the United States, it's work or fight on the color line.
—Robert C. Weaver, *Negro Labor: A National Problem*

In this chapter I consider the conflicts and the collaborations of the black labor scholars across a widening ideological spectrum. During the Depression and New Deal, a time of great labor and economic crisis for black workers, black social scientists clashed over master plans, but they also found ways to work effectively together on important challenges to government inaction and discrimination. The two decades from 1930 to 1950 are particularly interesting because all three generations of segregated scholars were actively debating the role of black intellectuals, working together in intergenerational coalitions to put forward new economic analyses and prodding black organizations to better attend to the problems of black workers. The chapter begins by examining the fiery critiques and plans of Carter G. Woodson and W. E. B. Du Bois that were designed to solve the economic crisis and to better assist workers, and then this chapter moves to the more pragmatic efforts of Abram L. Harris and Robert C. Weaver to alter the ways in which uplift groups represented the interests of black workers. Next, Weaver's experiences as the Roosevelt administration's principal black labor advisor are closely examined. The writings of Weaver, Harris, Du Bois, and Woodson illustrate the general boundaries of the discourse among black social scientists in the 1930s and the 1940s, but Charles H. Wesley, George E. Haynes, Ira De A. Reid, and Charles S. Johnson also made important interventions. Black workers continued to engage black social scientists across disciplines, and, accordingly, academic labor studies increased as a number of African Americans with new doctorates began to write about black labor.[1] As the figurative last segregated labor scholar, Robert Weaver's combination of scholarship and government service and his connections with both older and younger scholars made him the pivotal figure in what would be their final decades of influence. Weaver's prophetic postwar study, *Negro Labor: A National Problem,* became the culmination of three generations of black labor studies and the last major work that fully reflected the ethos of the segregated scholars.

The steady deterioration of the economic situation for black workers after the October 1929 stock market collapse should not have been a surprise to black social scientists or the labor experts in the National Urban League (NUL) and National Association for the Advancement of Colored People (NAACP) because black workers' already serious economic difficulties had been covered in their own writings and in *The Crisis, Opportunity,* and the popular press in the 1920s. What was remarkable, in retrospect, was the long period of indecision and hesitation before the development of comprehensive programs by the established race relations organizations, such as the NUL and the NAACP. For at least four years the NAACP and the National Urban League operated in much the same fashion as they had before the Depression. They relied on conference resolutions, ineffectual negotiations with unions, the government, employers, and publicity campaigns that produced little in the way of either more jobs or increased relief payments for needy black families. Not surprisingly, both the NAACP and the NUL suffered a decline in their revenues and in subscriptions to *Opportunity* and *The Crisis.* The NAACP's individual memberships also fell off sharply as black people had less disposable income. Both organizations' constituencies dropped, and their influence waned.[2]

Black workers' dependence on relief and federal emergency employment was staggering; over a quarter of the total population of black people in large urban areas was on relief. On the local levels the numbers of ad hoc responses to unemployment, evictions, and the racial disparities in the distribution of relief payments by black community groups mushroomed. There were Don't

Buy Where You Can't Work campaigns in Washington, D.C., New York City, and other cities to secure jobs in local department and retail stores. The Washington "Don't Buy" campaign was led by a young black political scientist named John A. Davis. Southern moderate educators called for black people to go "back to the farm," and black businessmen tried to get consumers to support a cooperative venture of black grocery stores. Black workers joined the Congress of Industrial Organizations (CIO) drives and helped the Communist Party in Alabama. The criticism of black intellectuals, race organizations, and their economic strategies by the elders Carter Woodson and W. E. B. Du Bois suddenly had more resonance because of the silence and inaction of the traditional racial uplift groups.[3]

Starting with its origins under George Haynes, the National Urban League had asserted that it offered social science–based programs to help workers adjust to urban life and work, but the league had a particularly tepid response to the Depression. Ira Reid was the NUL director of research from 1928 to 1934, and he continued to do the descriptive urban case studies of black employment that Charles S. Johnson had originated. The league's only new initiative was a vocational opportunity campaign launched with great fanfare in a few cities. It offered general information about occupations but not actual jobs or training. Without new programs to increase job placements, the NUL continued to make private appeals to business executives to hire black workers. As the Depression deepened, the NUL's existing placement programs were reduced to listings of an ever-decreasing number of unskilled low wage jobs for domestics and laborers.[4] In 1930, as the effect of the stock market collapse on black employment became painfully clear, the former Chicago Urban League executive director T. Arnold Hill was candid in his description of the limited way that the league was helping unemployed workers: "Perhaps the greatest service we have rendered . . . was to stimulate Negroes to think on problems touching their work relationships and to encourage self help and training as a means of combating influences that are retarding the development of Negroes in occupations."[5]

The reality was that the one-third of black American workers who were unemployed did not need the NUL's stimulation to think about the problems they had finding rewarding jobs. The solutions that the NUL proposed—self-help and training—had proven to be inadequate in a normal job market. These strategies begged the questions of how self-help could prepare a person for an industrial job and how black workers were supposed to obtain training when the NUL's studies showed that most union apprenticeship programs barred black trainees. The historian Nancy J. Weiss's study of the league argues that its activities in the Depression were predicated by much earlier decisions to emphasize publicity about black workers and the training of social workers over and against direct services.[6] In this vacuum the initiative was seized by labor scholars and other intellectuals with competing strategies for achieving black economic recovery.

Woodson and Du Bois: Lions in Winter

As what were already hard times for black workers in the late 1920s deepened into the Great Depression, W. E. B. Du Bois and Carter G. Woodson wasted no time in offering detailed explanations of what was wrong with black class and labor relations. In 1930 Du Bois was sixty-two and Woodson was fifty-five, and they were drastically altering the optimistic scenarios of racial advancement they had sketched during the Great Migration. Now their analyses mixed one part economic theory with three parts jeremiad. Both men were surrounded by more younger scholars and intellectuals than ever, but they were deeply hurt that the entire "talented tenth" did not share their selfless devotion to race work. Ironically, however, although Du Bois and Woodson claimed to be concerned with the problems of the masses, in the final analysis neither man offered a critical perspective that placed black workers at the center; instead, both focused on the lack of proper leadership in the black middle class and the need for racial consciousness and economic self-help strategies.

As hard economic times struck black America, Carter Woodson joined local efforts to force white businesses to hire black employees; published a series of descriptive historical studies of black workers, farmers, business, and professions; used the *Journal of Negro History* and the Association for the Study of Negro Life and History (ASNLH) as forums for economic analysis; and tirelessly denounced well-educated black folk as "the seat of the problem."[7] Woodson's stocktaking of the talented tenth began in 1931 with a series of lectures and articles that were published as *The Miseducation of the Negro.*[8] Like his good friend Nannie Helen Burroughs, Woodson's reputation for honesty and plain speaking made him a regular and popular columnist, speaker, and fund-raiser in churches, schools, and clubs all over black America.[9] Much of his credibility with his audiences came from the fact that he had demonstrated his abilities as an entrepreneur and organizer and did not depend solely on white funding. Woodson's chief targets were the leaders whom he considered to be "racial toadies" because they impeded group progress.[10] Woodson articulated a basic vocabulary of black self-determination. He stressed the virtues of mental toughness, a positive self-image, and hard work, all of which he argued had sustained black people during slavery and after Emancipation, yet were now in short supply among the educated. As the self-made son of slave parents, Woodson was a consistent champion of the freed people and the hard-working masses, and he now railed at the betrayal of their sacrifices and hard-won gains by an educated elite filled with pompous posers with "darkter's 'grees."[11]

Woodson also used *The Miseducation of the Negro* to make a thinly veiled attack on the social and economic philosophies of moderate race relations advocates such as George E. Haynes and Charles S. Johnson, school administrators, and ministers. He used satire, which delighted his working- and lower-middle-class audiences, to identify three types of self-appointed race leaders that were especially odious: "racial racketeers"—race relations professionals who turned the suffering of black people into lucrative careers; "hirelings in the place of public servants"—black school officials and politicians whom he believed helped to reinforce the ideology of white supremacy; and the Negro church's "exploiters, grafters, and libertines"—hypocritical ministers who looted the earnings of their hardworking congregants.[12] Woodson claimed that most organizations that touted "interracial cooperation" were really established to maintain white privilege. Some of his readers would have understood this as a pointed reference to the National Urban League, George Haynes's department at the Federal Council of Churches, and Charles S. Johnson's participation in the work of the Commission on Interracial Cooperation. Woodson said that his independence made him a truer exemplar of black and white cooperation, and he made the well-respected Haynes and Johnson objects of a contemptuous joke that was apparently making the rounds:

> Cooperation implies equality . . . but the whites . . . work out their plans behind closed doors, have them approved by a few Negroes serving nominally on a board, and then employ a white or mixed staff. . . . This is not interracial co-operation. . . . To express it in post-classic language . . . "The Negroes do the 'coing' and the whites the 'operating.'"[13]

Carter Woodson's economic analysis in *The Miseducation of the Negro* and *The Negro Wage Earner* did not fully integrate the important changes that had occurred in the general American economy or for black workers since the turn of the century. The most problematic aspect of Woodson's analysis of black workers was his neoclassic economic assertion that earning lower wages for the same work was beneficial to black workers. Carter Woodson argued that the dual wage system—which paid black workers lower hourly wages than white workers—could be used as a weapon against white workers' hegemony in the marketplace. Woodson and others who supported different pay scales for blacks and whites reasoned that low wages were black workers' chief bargaining chip, and if they demanded equal wages they would be replaced by white workers. However, if the dual wage theory actually was an economic law, then black workers should not have lost their edge in southern skilled trades since their wages had remained lower than white workers' wages. When Carter Woodson boasted that the wages of black skilled workers controlled the wages of white skilled workers in the South, he was speaking as a propagandist and wishful thinker rather than as a social scientist. Low black wages kept white wages low, to be sure, but this was because white employers controlled many of the decisions about wages, using black labor as a reserve against white labor militancy, and not from a collective effort of black workers to ward off racist white workers. Most other black labor scholars were opposed to making the unofficial reality of dual wages for black and white labor federal or state policy, but their opposition had no practical effect until Robert Weaver and George Haynes began to argue against having dual wages set in the codes of the National Recovery Administration in the period from 1933 until 1935. As we shall see, they argued that a separate wage scale would prevent any sort of labor unity in the future and that a separate minimum wage would quickly become the maximum wage for blacks.[14]

Woodson's views on the structure of the black labor force were not informed by the writings of one of his associates at the ASNLH, Charles H. Wesley. In *Negro Labor in the United States* Wesley was veering closer to a radical critique of labor market forces in the late 1920s, but Woodson's explanations were more simplistic.[15] Woodson believed that the opposition to black skilled workers was centered in the racism of the white working class and merely sanctioned by white employers. The belief that the racist behavior of the white working class was the principal factor that kept blacks from getting skilled jobs led Woodson to oppose communism and socialism because he believed white workers would never drop their resistance to black workers having good jobs. Racial prejudice was a far more important determinant of white behavior than class interests, and while Woodson's beliefs flew in the face of contemporary economic theory and Marxism, they did appear to conform closely with the experience of black workers in the labor force. His observations were not particularly inaccurate so much as they were incomplete, since they ignored the role of white employers in hiring practices and failed to foresee the economic self-interest that characterized the organization of black industrial workers into the CIO. Nevertheless, as long as trade unions blocked black workers' entry in to their skilled and semi-skilled ranks, solutions such as Woodson's that called for racial unity and black business development would resonate throughout the black community. The harsh appraisal of middle-class political irresponsibility in *The Miseducation of the Negro* would be repeated twenty-five years later by E. Franklin Frazier in his bitter book *Black Bourgeoisie*. Woodson's charge of black self-hatred would be elaborated as a rejection of black culture by Harold Cruse in his 1967 influential polemic *The Crisis of the Negro Intellectual*.[16]

Woodson was active in local efforts to aid black workers from the early 1930s and used the *Journal of Negro History* and the Association for the Study of Negro Life and History's annual meetings to bring together the economic analysts he favored. In 1930 Woodson was a cofounder of the Committee for Improving the Industrial Conditions among Negroes in the District of Columbia and served as its spokesperson, using his columns and speeches to argue for black economic solidarity to "use segregation to kill segregation." He supported the New Negro Alliance's boycott of stores in Washington that did not hire black workers.[17] In 1928, one year before the stock market crash, Woodson began a series of monographs designed to provide a "portraiture of the social and economic conditions of the Negroes."[18] The theme of the 1928 ASNLH annual meeting was devoted to the "Economic Condition of the Negro."[19] Most black social scientists were ASNLH members and regular participants in its meetings even after 1936, when they formed their own organization, the Association of Social Science Teachers in Negro Colleges.[20] Woodson controlled the selection of presenters at the ASNLH meetings and rebuffed the twenty-five-year-old Robert Weaver's desire to give a paper on black labor problems in 1933, airily claiming that studies of current problems were not welcomed, "except so far as they show an historical connection deeply rooted in the past."[21] This was far from an accurate statement of the ASNLH's interests, and seventeen years later Weaver would give a prophetic ASNLH keynote address on the contemporary status of black workers.[22]

Younger black radical social scientists were more vociferous critics of Woodson's economic analyses than his much maligned contemporaries. In 1936 the *Journal of Negro Education* carried a review by Horace Mann Bond that the historians August Meier and Elliott Rudwick considered a "devastating analysis" of Woodson's *The Miseducation of the Negro*. Bond was a young researcher at Fisk University with close ties to the Rosenwald Fund.[23] Although much of Woodson's critique was aimed at George Haynes and Charles S. Johnson and race relations executives, they ignored him. But his economic views were most strongly attacked by the economist Abram Harris. By the end of the 1920s Harris had concluded that in an era of monopoly capitalism any theory of black capitalism was at best a misguided strategy for racial progress. Between 1927 and 1936 Harris had published a series of critiques of black business that culminated in his book *The Negro as a Capitalist*. At the time, Abram Harris stood virtually alone among black social scientists and intellectuals when he criticized the widespread belief that a prosperous black business class could provide a means to overcome black poverty and racial discrimination. Harris linked "racial consciousness" ideologies with Garveyism, and he considered any emphasis on black business development backward and conservative. In his view black intellectuals needed to guide their people to a better understanding of capitalism, not toward racial isolation. "If the Negro's ever-increasing self-assertion is not guided by Negro intellectuals possessed of catholic vision, it will build within the present order a self-illuminating black world oblivious to things white."[24]

Harris was particularly critical of the small businesses and banks that the black middle class seemed to view as financial panaceas. He insisted that these two areas were hopelessly at odds with contemporary trends in the national economy and could not add many new jobs. In Harris's opinion it was far too late in the cycle of capitalism for the development of a true black bourgeoisie, and since black capitalism was not going to be based on the production of capital goods, it was unlikely to be able to produce the financial resources necessary for the economic development of black communities. Abram Harris's position, however correct, won few supporters among black labor scholars. Although W. E. B. Du Bois was a self-described socialist, he, like Woodson, was also a strong supporter of black business development as an answer to black economic problems. Du Bois's economic suggestions called for even greater reliance on black financial institutions than Woodson's less precise calls for support of black businesses.[25]

When Harris published *The Negro as a Capitalist* in 1936, the *Journal of Negro History*, which was under Woodson's firm editorial control, responded as if it had been personally attacked.[26] Although Abram Harris and Carter Woodson both rejected interracial cooperation strategies because they appeased white employers at the expense of black workers, their differences with regard to black business made them more personally estranged from each other than either was from Haynes and Johnson. Woodson and Haynes continued to be friends; and although Harris and Haynes sometimes clashed in public meetings, they worked together on the Joint Committee on Economic Recovery (JCER), discussed later in this chapter. Black radicals who were critical of Woodson's strong endorsement of black business development often failed to acknowledge their shared antipathy for black middle-class consumerism. Woodson held that the black businessperson was more important to racial progress than professionals who exploited their working-class clients to support lavish lifestyles manifested in the "gew-gaws and toys of life" purchased from "the exploiting oppressors of the race."[27] Neither Woodson, Du Bois, nor Harris were invited to the annual meetings of white and black race experts that Charles S. Johnson held in Nashville in the 1940s.[28] Woodson and Du Bois differed in that Woodson identified black middle-class self-hatred as the main cause of their massive failure to provide leadership for the working class. Woodson believed that "the seat of the trouble" was educated black people's "attitude of contempt toward their own people."[29] In his view segregation had alienated educated people from the masses and at the same time made them feel inferior to whites. Woodson argued that only those blacks who were not well educated or who had institutional bases that were independent of white support—such as the Negro church—were likely to have positive self-images. Woodson called on black people to take control of their education unless they wanted to be permanently oppressed. Woodson also maintained that blacks could not afford the luxury of behaving like white consumers when they were discriminated against socially, economically, and politically.[30]

W. E. B. Du Bois concluded that black people's lack of collective economic action was a more fundamental problem than self-hatred and insisted that his program would be directed by black experts, advising his readers that "we must lend every effort to establish an economic general staff."[31] His audacious call for a "segregated economy" helped to provoke an even wider-ranging debate than Woodson's attack on the system of black education. Du Bois first set forth many of the points that he would later use to justify his economic plan in a 1930 speech entitled "Education and Work" that he gave at Howard University. He asserted that Negro colleges failed to understand the modern era or the role of blacks in society and had moved too far away from business development. Du Bois indicted black campuses as anti-intellectual strongholds of vulgarity. "Our college man today is . . . untouched by real culture . . . affecting to despise scholarship and the hard grind of study and research. The greatest meetings of the Negro college year . . . have become vulgar exhibitions of liquor, extravagance, and fur coats."[32] Du Bois called for a rededication to the selfless ideals of poverty, work, knowledge, sacrifice, and beauty. His views strongly paralleled Woodson's argument in *The Miseducation of the Negro*, but neither man would ever acknowledge the coincidence of their arguments.[33]

In his editorials in *The Crisis* in the early 1930s Du Bois stressed the need for black self-reliance and extolled the potential virtues of a black consumer and cooperative movement. Over time his economic ideas and his criticism of black college students combined in his call for a segregated economy. In a 1931 editorial, "The Negro's Industrial Plight," Du Bois suggested a "group effort to retain present employment, enter new fields of industrial technique, expand retail business, and live within our incomes." Now was the time for a black consumer movement targeted at stores without black employees, which would "make a religion of our determination to spend our meager income . . . in such ways as will bring us employment."[34] By 1932 Du Bois had begun to suggest that segregation and Jim Crow were unbreachable barriers and argued that the only hope of blacks was to build their own economic institutions in the form of nonprofit economic cooperatives under the guidance of black academics. "It [the racial economy] not only is possible but it is already beginning and it only needs scientific guidance and technical skill to make it spread."[35] His increasingly querulous calls for a segregated economy continued through 1933 to 1934. Du Bois's "nation within a nation" plan called for blacks to voluntarily withdraw from much of white economic life and set up farm, consumer, and manufacturing cooperatives. He reasoned that if black income could be kept from flowing outside the boundaries of their separate economy, black economic woes could be solved. "It is the race-conscious black men cooperating together in his own institutions and movements who will eventually emancipate the colored race, and the great step ahead today is for the American Negro to accomplish his economic emancipation through voluntary determined cooperative effort."[36]

The Du Bois plan's implementation and final structure was to be developed by teams of black experts who would see to it that the new system was both racially segregated and governed by socialist nonprofit institutions rather than capitalist market forces. The plan explicitly rejected the idea of black and white labor solidarity, a startling reversal of his long union advocacy.[37]

One important flaw in Du Bois's nation within a nation schema was that it did not include industrial workers except as consumers, yet the plan was based largely on the assumption of the full cooperation of the black working class. One did not have to be a professional economist to question the viability or utility of a closed economic system that depended on wages earned from outside the system, whose principal businesses were retail stores, and that did not have the funds to promote economic development or to create new jobs. The segregated economy's chief source of revenue was to be the wages of black blue-collar and domestic workers rather than reinvested profits from capital-producing industries. Du Bois believed that racial self-interest should prevail to make such a system work, but he never fully answered the question of why black workers should pay higher prices for goods and services when the proposed system could not guarantee their wages, except by insisting that it was good for the race as a whole.[38]

The debate over Du Bois's call for voluntary segregation as a solution to the national economic crisis helped younger radical academics to come together in opposition to his program from the left and gave his opponents within the NAACP a long-sought rationale for forcing his resignation. The sociologist E. Franklin Frazier led the chorus of black and white leftist scholars and intellectuals who attacked Du Bois's plan. By uncharitably characterizing Du Bois as a hopelessly romantic mulatto who had probably outlived his usefulness as a social critic, Frazier slipped into the type of color-coded insults that had demeaned Du Bois's dispute with Marcus Garvey. He scathingly attacked Du Bois's antimaterialistic call to "embrace the ideal of poverty" as a "share our poverty program."[39] Frazier and other Howard radicals—Ralph J. Bunche, Sterling A. Brown, and Emmett E. Dorsey—wrote an open letter in support of Benjamin Stolberg, a white socialist who had attacked the Du Bois plan on the grounds of racial chauvinism. They described the Depression as a worldwide economic calamity that placed particular stress on blacks because of their historically disadvantaged position in the labor force. Racism redoubled black workers' vulnerability by preventing government relief and employment programs from being distributed equitably.[40] Frazier, Bunche, and Brown still admired Du Bois as a scholar and racial leader, but their letter served as a declaration of intellectual independence. Du Bois had invited most of the younger radicals to the 1933 Amenia Conference, cosponsored by the NAACP president Joel E. Spingarn, and he continued to ask both Frazier and Brown for comments on his works in progress.[41]

The economist Abram Harris should have been the loudest critic of Du Bois's plan, given his opposition to Woodson's promotion of black businesses and his place of pride among the Howard radicals, but he pulled his punches publicly with Du Bois because he was trying to change the NAACP into an organization that better served black workers' concerns and he hoped to keep Du Bois on as the editor of *The Crisis*. Harris did not publicly break with Du Bois, but the idea of a separate economy program was an anathema to Harris. Accordingly, he wrote to Du Bois to explain privately and gently that he could not support his program.[42] When *Black Reconstruction* appeared in 1935, after Du Bois had left the NAACP, however, Harris was unmerciful in his criticism of the book's economic analysis.[43]

W. E. B. Du Bois's program had its most critical reception from the NAACP national board, which had employed him since its founding in 1910. The circulation and income of *The Crisis* dropped sharply, and Du Bois's editorial independence and expenses were long-standing organizational concerns. The NAACP board was now infuriated by Du Bois's editorials on segregation in *The Crisis*, their official publication, and moved to curb his autonomy and provoke his departure.[44] In the summer of 1934 W. E. B. Du Bois relinquished his positions at the NAACP as the director of publications and research and editor of *The Crisis*. At the time of his resignation Du Bois was living in Atlanta, completing a long-delayed study of Reconstruction. He now formally rejoined the faculty at Atlanta University as professor and chair of the sociology department.

In his public letter of resignation Du Bois referred to "deeper reasons" than disagreements over his economic plan that motivated his departure. Du Bois had in a sense become a prisoner of his own rhetoric in the case of the segregated economy. He had hoped to stir up controversy, but it was never clear that Du Bois wanted to direct this new economic policy, and the mechanics of his proposal were vague. He never seemed to have given much thought as to how the general public might react and never framed his argument in terms that were positive. By insisting that voluntary segregation was imperative and by not choosing to use less charged terminology, Du Bois forced the NAACP, an organization founded to promote the integration of blacks into American society, to publicly repudiate his plan. His public indictment that the NAACP "finds itself at this time of crisis, without a program, without effective organization, without executive officers who have either the ability or disposition to guide it . . . in the right direction" was lost in the debate over voluntary segregation and his resignation.[45] The task of changing the NAACP to better address the growing economic distress among black people was left to Abram Harris. In the final analysis neither Carter Woodson nor W. E. B. Du Bois was able to mobilize the intelligentsia in the 1930s to follow their plans for eco-

W. E. B. Du Bois addresses 1944 Annual Spring Forum at Howard University.
Professor Herman Branson is on the right. (Courtesy of the Moorland-Spingarn
Research Center, Howard University Archives)

nomic salvation, but their failure as labor savants was followed by fifteen years
of scholarly productivity in other areas. Woodson continued to run the ASNLH,
edited the *Journal of Negro History*, introduced the *Negro History Bulletin*
for schoolteachers, wrote popular histories of Africa, and commissioned an
economic study of Washington, D.C. Du Bois completed the pathbreaking
Black Reconstruction; founded a fine new journal, *Phylon,* with the able assistance of Ira Reid, who had joined the Atlanta University faculty; and continued his extensive scholarship and commentary at a pace that was unmatched
among American intellectuals.

The Harris Plan

The Depression also spurred Abram Harris in 1934 and 1935 to spearhead an
attempt to reorganize the NAACP and make it more broadly reflective of the
economic needs of its branches and individual members. As a member of the
NAACP board of directors, Harris failed to avert Du Bois's resignation, but

he was plunged into the forefront of those who wanted major organizational changes after his friend and mentor left. The NAACP head Walter White named Harris the chair of the Committee on the Plan and Program of the Association and Future of *The Crisis*. This committee had only one other member who was firmly in the Du Bois camp, the Howard University English professor Sterling Brown, but Harris outmaneuvered its more conservative members by appointing his political allies to special advisory sub-committees that prepared the final report.[46] One of Harris's earliest suggestions would have both carried forward the younger radical's economic program and continued Du Bois's association with *The Crisis* magazine by forming a new five-member editorial board, including Du Bois, E. Franklin Frazier, and Executive Director Walter White. Each board member was to contribute a monthly feature article, but Walter White was determined that Du Bois not retain any relationship with *The Crisis,* so this proposal was quashed. Harris and his allies inside the organization, including William Pickens, an NAACP long-time staff member who was critical of some of its policies, and the legal counsels William Hastie and Charles H. Houston, persevered with their plans to force changes in the NAACP that would make it more appealing to the "man on the street."[47]

The Harris committee unveiled its proposals at the 1935 annual meeting of the NAACP in St. Louis. This meeting must have alarmed the moderates on the board because the Howard radicals were in full control of the program, which emphasized new economic initiatives, support of industrial unions, and workers' education. Moreover, conference delegates were receptive to the calls for societal change that came from the speaker's platform. They enthusiastically reacted to the speech by Howard Kester, a white socialist organizer from the Southern Farm Tenants Union. John P. Davis, director of the Joint Committee on Economic Recovery, gave the main address, a fiery and rousing call to arms that was widely publicized and reprinted in the Negro press. This gave Davis the national audience on which he would build as he created the National Negro Congress.[48]

The main provisions of the Harris report called for a reorientation in the NAACP's programmatic focus from civil liberties toward specific activities in the economic arena, the most important of which was to be the inauguration of workers' education courses in the NAACP branches. Believing that its elitist structure hampered the NAACP's ability to respond to community needs, Harris's plan called for local branches to have more control over the choice of national board members. The Harris report was formally accepted by the NAACP but never implemented because the national board rightly saw it as an attempt to reduce its power. Executive Secretary Walter White was able to deflect the growing internal pressure for radical changes by appearing to accept the plan and then ignoring its most sweeping recommendations. Harris may also have been too optimistic about the branches' desire to begin workers' education programs or to fully support the Congress of Industrial Organizations' organizing drives. Nevertheless, several changes were forthcoming. Some labor education courses were given, the national office became more involved in economic issues than ever before, and the local branches did eventually gain more say in determining the makeup of the national NAACP board of directors.[49] Abram L. Harris consistently courted the approval and sought the advice and assistance of W. E. B. Du Bois as he evolved from disciple to associate. In 1934, as the controversy over Du Bois's statements in *The Crisis* was heating up, Harris asked Du Bois to join an effort to create a lecture bureau composed of progressive black intellectuals. A decade earlier, in 1925, Harris had attempted to get Du Bois interested in a "Newer Spirit College" for black students, designed along the lines of the New School of Social Research. Harris and the psychologist Francis Sumner had privately concluded that the contemporary system of Negro education was harmful to black people, but unlike Carter Woodson, they eschewed the racial alternative, opting for liberalism. Harris outlined the rationale for such a school to Du Bois and the purpose for writing to him. "The cultural development of the Negro people is bound up inextricably with the life or death of liberalism in the various universities and colleges. . . . The best way to convey liberalism to the Negro is not by going into the present institutions. . . . A new college . . . must be founded. . . . We think the idea . . . is worth your consideration . . . since you may rightly be called the Father of the Negro intelligentsia."[50]

Du Bois expressed his interest in the concept but was pessimistic about such young men's ability to obtain funds for the venture.[51] Harris's lecture bureau would provide speakers who could shake the complacency out of black college students. The exchanges between Du Bois and Harris, who was thirty years younger, provide interesting clues into their perceptions of other scholars' racial commitment and progressive orientation. They also reveal that Du Bois wanted to use the bureau to promote his economic plan of collective "action toward economic salvation."[52] But Harris's intent was even more basic. "No program of economic welfare . . . for the Negro is going to succeed until his so-called intelligentsia is emancipated so that it can furnish guidance. We can't wait for minds and scholars to spring up out of the earth. We have got to develop them ourselves."[53]

Neither Harris nor Du Bois questioned their ability or right to mold young minds, but who else was up to the task? Both men easily agreed that any progressive speakers bureau should include E. Franklin Frazier, the anthropologist W. Allison Davis, Sterling Brown, and the historians Charles Wesley and Rayford W. Logan. Du Bois asked Harris to add Robert C. Weaver, then a young economist working at the Department of the Interior, because "an evening's conversation with him has impressed me greatly." Du Bois was somewhat "leery" about including the philosopher Alain Locke and Charles S. Johnson, and he could not make a decision on either the political scientist Ralph Bunche or the Howard Law professor William Hastie. The lecture bureau was never established, but Harris and the Howard radicals were soon joined by a core of progressives around Du Bois at Atlanta University, including Ira Reid and Rayford Logan, who made their voices heard during the Depression.[54]

Abram Harris's efforts to change the NAACP and reorient college students overlapped with a more direct challenge to New Deal policies begun by the young man who had so impressed Du Bois, Robert Weaver. Weaver's efforts are important because they helped to sidestep the bureaucratic inaction that was stifling change in both the NAACP and the NUL and because he became one of the first black scholars to move outside the segregated colleges and race relations associations, albeit as a federal Negro expert.

Robert C. Weaver: From Race Scholarship to the Black Cabinet

Robert C. Weaver's career as an economist marked the end of black social scientists' collective scholarly contribution to labor studies and the beginning of the gradual incorporation of black scholars in positions in the federal government, philanthropy, and the white academy. Although his early career was focused on black economic issues, Weaver never established a career at a Negro college, and his high-ranking government posts during the New Deal and postwar university and foundation positions were among new opportunities offered to a small vanguard of black social scientists. Weaver's activities between 1933 and 1946 also demonstrate that younger black social scientists continued to see W. E. B. Du Bois as their intellectual avatar and carried forward his sense of obligation to engender social change.

Robert C. Weaver was born in 1907, making him the youngest segregated scholar. He was forty years younger than Du Bois and only the second labor studies theorist to be born in the twentieth century. His closest contemporaries in age, Abram Harris and Ira Reid, had been writing for a decade when Weaver began his career. Weaver, the younger of two sons, grew up in a close-knit, lower-middle-class family in Washington, D.C., that placed an equal emphasis on educational achievements and obtaining a skilled trade. Weaver's mother, Florence, was a normal school graduate whose father, Robert Freeman, had graduated from Harvard Dental School. Weaver's father, Mortimer, was a skilled tradesman who worked as a postal clerk. Robert Weaver's parents made financial sacrifices to pay his Harvard College and graduate school tuition, allowing him to complete his doctorate much more quickly than Harris, Reid, or Lorenzo J. Greene. Weaver was also required to learn a trade, and he became an electrician while he was still in high school. His family background may have given Weaver an early interest in black skilled workers, and he always felt a kinship with working men.[55]

Weaver's family and his schoolteachers helped him to avoid internalizing the personal sense of inferiority that Carter Woodson claimed pervaded the segregated educational system. His parents refused to patronize openly segregated movies, theaters, or restaurants or even to discuss segregation in an effort to limit the children's direct exposure to Jim Crow. They may have reasoned that their two sons could develop a healthy self-image before they discovered the limitations placed on black people in the world beyond the family, church, and school.[56] Weaver attended the two best schools for black students in Washington, D.C., traveling far across the city to Lucretia Mott Elementary School, which was just across the street from Howard University. Mott served as a feeder for Dunbar High School, Washington's black college preparatory high school. Dunbar's teaching staff was regarded as the most educated in all of Afro-America. When Weaver attended Dunbar, his teachers had earned as many doctorates as nearby Howard University's black faculty.[57]

Weaver's early education reinforced a positive sense of racial identity and intellectual curiosity that other black social scientists shared. Teachers at Mott and Dunbar told their students that they were as capable as any white person and that they would prove this when they attended the best colleges in the country. The economist Sadie T. M. Alexander (class of 1915) recalled that her teachers "put in us a determination that no one would beat us."[58] Students were told of the academic successes of alumni such as Alexander, William Hastie, and Charles Houston. *The Crisis* carried pictures of Dunbar's

Robert C. Weaver, 1961. (Photographs and Prints Division, Schomburg Center for Research in Black Culture, The New York Public Library, Astor, Lenox and Tilden Foundations)

valedictorians. Dunbar alumni and classmates became a crucial part of the network of mentors, friends, and associates on which Weaver would draw in college and when he began efforts to give black workers better opportunities under the New Deal.[59] Thanks to his family and his schooling, Robert Weaver was able to enter Harvard College in 1925 with a greater sense of entitlement and financial comfort than most of the other black labor scholars had had as undergraduates. His sense of self-confidence helped Weaver to transform a personal tragedy into the life-changing decision to become a labor economist.

The heroes of the black men at Harvard in the mid-1920s, according to Weaver, were W. E. B. Du Bois and the New Negro writers. Weaver considered Du Bois to have been "a titan . . . an inspiration to many social scientists of my generation."[60] There were many differences between the undergraduate experiences of W. E. B. Du Bois and Robert Weaver at Harvard College. Both men spent most of their time and many extracurricular energies with other black people, but Robert Weaver did so more by choice and to save money. Although small in number, there was a critical mass of black students

The Segregated Scholars

at Harvard while Weaver was there, 1925–33, and most lived near one another in off-campus boarding houses run by black families. They had frequent discussions about their future roles as race leaders. These sessions included the Dunbar alumni William Hastie and John P. Davis, who were at Harvard Law School, and the graduate students Rayford Logan and Ralph Bunche, with whom Weaver would work closely during the New Deal. Weaver graduated cum laude from Harvard College, and he worked well with all but one professor while he was in graduate school.[61] Professor Frank W. Taussig was opposed to admitting black students to the economics department, and his insulting demeanor made Weaver even more determined to complete his doctorate. Taussig was openly hostile and informed Weaver that he did not believe that black people had the mental ability to do doctoral work in economics. Weaver told Alma Williams and the author that the only B he ever received in economics was from Taussig. Weaver had already experienced one memorable incident of racial bias during his undergraduate years. The Harvard University president Abbott Lowell had barred him from attending an intercollegiate debate at Princeton, even though he had won the Harvard College's Boylston Prize and Pasteur Medal in debating.[62]

Robert Weaver, like Charles Wesley and Lorenzo Greene, decided to become a social scientist when he was a senior in college. At the time, 1928, two of the dozen black men and women with doctorates in the social sciences were in economics.[63] Robert Weaver did not initially choose economics as a field of study out of a desire to use it to advance his race as had Wesley and Haynes. Despite all the careful preparation by his parents and teachers and the reinforcement of determined black students around him, Weaver was not a serious student at first. He was content to rest on the considerable laurels of his older brother and best friend, Mortimer, and he changed his major from engineering to economics in order to have a fuller social life. When Mortimer Weaver died unexpectedly, Robert felt that he had to devote himself to race advancement in order to make up for his loss. Since his undergraduate grades in economics were excellent, he decided to get a doctorate in the field. Weaver's parents arranged a financially risky mortgage of their house during the Depression to help him finance his graduate training.[64]

After Weaver decided that he would use his education to help the race, his next step was to do what Haynes, Wright, Woodson, and other race-conscious black students had done: he wrote to W. E. B. DuBois seeking his advice. Confidently expressing the belief that his "future work will compensate you for any inconvenience," Weaver served notice that he intended to make his own mark as a scholar.[65] In the letter to Du Bois, Robert Weaver revealed his decision to make labor and race his life work. His belief that black workers were at the heart of any economic study of black Americans echoes the theme of earlier letters from George Haynes and Abram Harris to W. E. B. Du Bois. "Since my particular interest is in Labor Problems, and since I am a Negro (and most of my future work will concern Negroes), I plan to work on something in the field of Negro Labor. Indeed I cannot see how a person interested in the economic life of the black American could hope to escape treating of the Negro worker. . . . I would like you to express your opinion of the value and the possibilities of the project. . . . I would appreciate any further suggestions . . . that your vast experience . . . may prompt."[66]

Du Bois responded to Weaver's letter by saying that he thought his topic was "of very great interest." He sketched out the three or four questions the doctoral student should address, and he suggested a format that was much like the one Du Bois had used himself to examine industrial education in *The Negro Artisan* (1902). He also included a copy of his somber 1930 speech "Education and Work" and recommended that Weaver read *The Black Worker* by Sterling D. Spero and Abram L. Harris.[67]

In the end, Robert Weaver did not write his dissertation on a topic that was explicitly racial, but his topic did inform his later political activities. His dissertation, entitled "The High Wage Theory of Prosperity," helped to create the economic basis for Weaver's opposition to lower wage scales for black labor as well as his subsequent conviction that black workers needed government intervention in order to enter the skilled labor force. Robert Weaver completed his course work in economics by the late spring of 1933. He went back home to Washington with the outlines of a plan to try to make the New Deal a better deal for black workers.[68]

Robert Weaver had watched the Depression unfold and was alarmed at what he considered an inadequate response from the NAACP and National Urban League. He decided to launch a campaign that was specifically targeted at making the Roosevelt administration more responsive to black workers' need for higher wages. In their Harvard bull sessions Weaver and John P. Davis had formulated the concept of an organization that would use economic research and legal briefs to make their case to the federal government. Their idea was simple and direct. They would found an umbrella group of black associations that would fund research and prepare data on the status of black workers in various industries. Their findings would then be used to apply pressure to legislators, federal administrators, and industrialists to address and

The Segregated Scholars

improve the often dire situation of black workers.[69] His firm belief that scholarship and activism would result in racial progress linked Robert Weaver to the earlier black labor scholars and helps to explain his sense of urgency during the early days of the New Deal.

The fact that two unemployed men who were twenty-five and twenty-seven years old could take a general idea and turn it into a program of decisive action on important New Deal legislation when the major race relations groups seemed paralyzed was a measure of the resolve of both Weaver and Davis. Neither Weaver nor Davis had jobs during the summer of 1933, so their quick rise to prominent positions just two years later in 1935 indicated the fluidity of black leadership during the Depression. That same summer of 1933 another important movement was launched in Washington, D.C., by a young man named John A. Davis, a recent Williams College graduate who later became a political scientist. The New Negro Alliance was inspired in part by the work of Abram Harris and influenced by his critique of racial chauvinism in the Don't Buy Where You Can't Work movements. The New Negro Alliance was typical of local organizations of working-class black people and intellectuals that were formed to address local economic issues. Its short-lived, but lasting importance is that a legal suit brought against the alliance established the precedent that black consumers had the right to wage economic boycotts.[70]

In the summer of 1933 there were hearings on the Code of Fair Competition under the National Recovery Act (NRA) to set wage scales for industries and occupations. Presentations by organized labor and employer groups dominated these hearings, and black organizations were not involved. Weaver and Davis became convinced that without expert testimony on their wages and working conditions, black workers, particularly those in the South, would be placed at a tremendous disadvantage. As Davis recalled later, "There seemed to be no Negro organization ready to represent the interest of the race in these new economic arrangements."[71]

Weaver and Davis decided to put their ideas into effect immediately by setting up a paper organization called the Negro Industrial League (NIL), and they began research on the occupations to be covered by the NRA. The NIL operated out of a small office at 717 Florida Avenue near Howard University, which was provided to them at little cost by a black retired government employee. Robert Weaver was the NIL's director of research. Using U.S. census data and other statistics, he began with an economic analysis of the effects on black workers' incomes of the proposed wage and hour codes for the cotton textile industry. John P. Davis, NIL executive secretary, detailed their findings in legal briefs and often testified. They started work in July 1933, and by August they had testified at four hearings on proposed wages and hours for the textiles, coal, lumber, and timber industries.[72] Working nonstop and virtually alone, Weaver and Davis demonstrated that it was possible to make compelling statistical arguments that most of the proposed codes would have an adverse effect on black industrial workers.

Robert C. Weaver and John P. Davis demonstrated an impressive familiarity with contemporary labor conditions in a number of industries. Their NIL briefs were straightforward, factual, and unadorned by partisan rhetoric. In the cotton textile hearings Davis displayed Weaver's tables and text describing the changing fortunes of 14,000 black skilled workers, operatives, and laborers in 1930. Weaver's argument against setting wage minimums by job classifications rested on his assertion that black workers would be classified in the lowest wage categories but would be expected to do other types of jobs. "If a picker-tender were to be classified as within the pale of the minimum wage and maximum hour regulations, the employers would classify him as a sweeper or a cleaner and thus evade these provisions." Weaver and Davis's NIL cotton textile statement pointed out that the code proposed to exclude the majority of black workers from its wage and hour provisions and argued that this seemed to be contrary to the professed social policies of the New Deal—that by rights should offer the workers with the lowest wages more protection. They also argued that limiting black wages decreased the buying power of black consumers, thereby also harming regional economic growth. They claimed that in 1929 black consumers in large urban areas had spent $100,000,000—more than the value of U.S. exports to Mexico and Central America. Therefore, the reduced income of black textile workers ultimately hurt the cotton textile industry and southern businesses as a whole.[73]

Weaver's and Davis's presentations were covered by the white and black press, which affirmed the importance of these hearings. Both men were considered experts on Negro labor by the end of the summer, and they could claim a few concrete accomplishments as well. Wages were not set in black workers' benefit in the textile industry because so many of their job classifications were exempted from government protection, but the NIL claimed partial credit for President Franklin D. Roosevelt's conditional approval of the code with the provision that exempted occupations be included by January 1934. Robert Weaver made the NIL's presentation for the timber industry codes, which had a huge differential in the wages of blacks and whites. He argued against setting regional differences in wages and hours. The timber industry proposed paying the mostly black southern timber workers twenty-two and a half cents an hour for a forty-eight-hour workweek, while white workers in the West were to have their wages set at forty cents an hour for a forty-hour workweek. The NIL "furnished data in vigorous opposition" to these tremendous differentials in the wages and hours. Their testimony helped to bring about a forty-hour week for southern timber workers, but the southern minimum was raised only one and a half cents, to twenty-three cents an hour. Weaver and Davis believed that even these "very unsatisfactory" changes demonstrated that their work was worthwhile, as well as possibly meaning that "15,000 additional Negroes" would be hired as a result, at an "added weekly income of about $125,000."[74]

The initial actions of Weaver and Davis led to the formation of an umbrella association, the Joint Committee on Economic Recovery, in the late summer and early fall of 1933. Several older labor scholars moved quickly to secure funds and sponsors, but the Negro Industrial League's earliest institutional sponsors were the heads of black denominations and fraternities, not civil rights or race relations organizations. The existing records on the formation of the JCER are sketchy, but Nannie Helen Burroughs and George Edmund Haynes were the most important early church and social science supporters. Burroughs was perhaps the first nationally prominent person to aid the NIL. She provided the first public signal that the NIL might become a "united front" of black organizations when she helped Weaver make a dramatic presentation at the soft coal hearing. Burroughs obtained a telegram from Robert Russa Moton, head of Tuskegee Institute, which gave the conservative educator's support for equal pay scales. When Weaver used the telegram in his testimony, he effectively prevented the southern coal industry from claiming that they had the support of major southern black leaders for the pitifully low wages they proposed. Organized labor now began to support the NIL, too. A newspaper report of the hearing proclaimed, "Moton's telegram creates sensation" and said that when Weaver read it, labor leaders such as "John L. Lewis, white, head of the United Mine Workers" pledged the NIL "their support in the fight being waged for equal treatment of Negro labor."[75] John P. Davis thanked Burroughs profusely for "the impetus which your name and your effort have lent to our fight for Negro labor" and begged her to become the treasurer of the new coalition. "It is most essential to the success of our program that every dollar collected and spent be handled with scrupulous honesty. That is why we cannot afford to have any one but you as treasurer of the organization. . . . In short we need "Caesar's wife . . . and hence you are chosen."[76]

Nannie Helen Burroughs agreed to become the JCER's treasurer, and her involvement lent the two-man operation an aura of credibility as well as the support of the National Baptist Convention. Several older black labor scholars also played key roles in getting the initial organizations to lend their names and to pledge their financial support. George Haynes made personal appeals to the AME bishop Reverdy C. Ranson and the AMEZ bishop E. W. D. Jones to endorse the NIL's testimony at the soft coal hearing that allowed Weaver to claim that the Negro Industrial League represented over one million black people.[77]

Abram Harris probably was one of several people behind the NAACP's decision to send Roy Wilkins down to Washington in early August to listen to Weaver's and Davis's plans. The NAACP's participation allowed the NIL and JCER to become involved in labor issues in a way that answered some of the ongoing criticisms from their own branches and Du Bois. Charles Wesley may have also been a key behind-the-scenes player in getting both the AME church and the Alpha Phi Alpha fraternity to become sponsoring organizations of first the NIL and then the JCER. R. R. Wright Jr. was then the president of Wilberforce College; he joined the JCER as an individual member and worked to insure that AME churches fulfilled their financial obligations.[78]

Myra Colson Callis, an as yet unsung female social scientist whose research was on home industries and domestic service, helped to convince the national Young Woman's Christian Association (YWCA) to become a sponsor of the JCER. George Haynes spent part of August 1933 "busily working up new contacts" for the NIL. His involvement brought in interracial groups such as his Federal Council of Churches and the Catholic Interracial Council; he also helped to arrange for the endorsement of Weaver's research by well-respected white social scientists such as Mary Van Kleeck of the Russell Sage Foundation. Davis and Weaver made presentations that summer at the annual meetings of the Elks and the National Negro Business League, which solidified these groups' vocal support of the NIL and made them among the first to join the JCER. The enthusiastic support of the NIL and JCER by black denominations and fraternal groups is significant because black labor scholars and other intellectuals so often charged these groups with placing conspicuous consumption above their obligation to provide leadership for the masses. The JCER could rightly claim to represent millions of black people through its member organizations—something neither the NAACP nor the NUL could do.[79]

Despite many entreaties, the National Urban League refused to join the Joint Committee on Economic Recovery during its more than two-year existence. The NUL claimed that the JCER's programs overlapped with or duplicated league programs, but it also may not have wanted to challenge some of its corporate benefactors who were involved in setting the codes. Years later Robert Weaver speculated that George Edmund Haynes agreed to become the chair of the JCER board "out of spite" when the league refused to join, but his high profile involvement may have kept the NUL from ever becoming a part of the JCER.[80] Haynes's prominence on the JCER lent the politically inexperienced team of Weaver and Davis the prestige of a race relations expert and the expertise of a senior social scientist. Haynes began helping the NIL with its testimony in July 1933. His Federal Council of Churches office soon was issuing detailed reports praising Weaver and Davis for having been "zealously active in presenting evidence" at the early code hearings, which he sent to white and black denominations and to the press.[81]

George Haynes's press releases contained quite a bit of information about the testimony presented at the code hearings, but he could not resist using them to obliquely criticize the inactivity of his former associates at the NUL. Haynes opened his report on the iron and steel codes with the remark that the "Negroes present to care for the interest of the thousands of Negro workers . . . were conspicuous by their scarcity."[82] Haynes's careful accounting made it clear who was not there. He listed the time of arrival of each of the five black people present among the throng of five to six hundred whites attending the late July hearing that would determine the wages of a hundred thousand black workers. The only black people present were Haynes; Weaver; Davis, who gave a presentation; Robert W. Brooks, a black Baptist minister; and "one Negro worker from one of the steel districts." Secretary of Labor Frances Perkins also spoke on behalf of black workers. When there were seven black people present among one thousand at the soft coal hearings and the NIL was the only group that made a presentation, Haynes told his correspondents that once "again . . . Negro workers were represent[ed] only by a corporal's guard."[83] The jibes must have increased the defensiveness of league executives, but as a result of their intellectual prowess, Weaver and Davis were cast in roles that they both coveted, as racial heroes.

The main purpose of the Joint Committee on Economic Recovery was to support and fund the research and testimony of Weaver and Davis at the code hearings and to offer critiques of other New Deal programs that affected black workers. By 1934 the JCER board was composed of twenty-four organizations: black denominations, fraternal organizations such as the Elks, and interracial groups, such as the colored YWCA and the NAACP. The presence of so many mainstream black and interracial organizations on the committee was a clear indication that they all rejected Woodson's analysis of the dual wage theory as being beneficial to black workers. Having Haynes as chair of the board and Nannie Helen Burroughs, president of the Women's Auxiliary of the National Baptist Convention, as the treasurer gave the JCER instant political legitimacy, which the NIL alone did not have.[84] Elizabeth Ross Haynes was a member of the national YWCA board and may have also played a role in getting the YWCA to get a five-hundred-dollar anonymous donation for the JCER that was presented by Elizabeth Eastman, a wealthy white YWCA board member. Frances Williams, a young black employee of the YWCA in New York City, found that she could get the YWCA national board to sign on because they would "be impressed with the fact that being on the joint committee does involve our relationship with important organizations in Negro life."[85] The National Negro Business League, a traditionally conservative group, joined the Joint Committee on Economic Recovery in part because the NIL had targeted some of its testimony in support of black businesses but also because the proposed low-wage scales would hurt their customers' ability to use their services. The member organizations were supposed to exert political pressure; accordingly, the National Negro Business League, the Elks, and the Baptist women sent state and federal officials resolutions that incorporated Weaver's statistical analyses even before the Joint Committee on Economic Recovery was completely organized.

Member organization support for the new JCER plans was solid, but the funding base was problematic, which led to the NAACP playing a larger financial role once the JCER was organized. The NAACP secured a special grant that partly covered John Davis's tiny salary of $50 to $75 a month, monies for some part-time researchers, and limited clerical support. Most of the sponsoring organizations were slow in coming up with their financial pledges, making the JCER dependent on the NAACP for its funds. Robert Weaver wanted to stay in Washington, and he had support among the JCER board members, but the available funds would not pay for two full-time staff people. He had to leave Washington by the end of September "to earn his bread and butter."[86] The JCER's inability to pay Robert Weaver helped to set the stage for his accepting a federal government position in late 1933, in which he sometimes clashed with his former associates.

In the fall of 1933 Robert Weaver reluctantly began teaching at North Carolina Agricultural and Technical College in Greensboro, North Carolina, and took the title of technical advisor to the Joint Committee on Economic Recovery. In the space of three months in the summer he had provided the research and made many of the presentations on black workers for the code hearings and deliberations for the cotton textiles, timber and lumber, shipbuilding, iron and steel, bituminous coal, structural clay products, and fertilizer industries. He and Myra Callis also made a statistical study of black domestics because the 1.4 million black workers who fell into that category were not covered by any of the proposed wage and hour laws.[87] Weaver maintained a long-distance relationship with the Joint Committee on Economic Recovery. His work for the NIL and the JCER brought him to the attention of C. C. Spaulding, a wealthy black insurance company owner in Durham, North Carolina. Spaulding augmented Weaver's small teaching salary with research monies for Weaver to prepare the evidence necessary for a full presentation on black tobacco workers for the tobacco industry code hearings. The source of funding was kept secret so that Spaulding's assistance would not be suspected by the tobacco companies. Spaulding's willingness to support the preparation of testimony was another indication that Weaver and Davis had been correct when they said they could find broad-based support among black leaders to fight the imposition of lower wage codes for black workers.[88] Weaver settled down to a teaching schedule, but an opportunity to return to Washington came more quickly than he could have anticipated.

One of the first actions of the Joint Committee on Economic Recovery was to ask the Roosevelt administration to appoint black advisors with technical expertise in what would soon be called Negro affairs for key New Deal agencies. Having black "experts" became a major issue for black organizations during the New Deal. The JCER wanted the government to stop making political appointments in areas that required a social science, legal, or technical background. They used arguments similar to those used to secure George Haynes's appointment at the Department of Labor fifteen years earlier: black advisors were more desirable than equally qualified whites because blacks had firsthand knowledge of black culture and because having qualified blacks at high levels in any one area would also help to break down the resistance of white federal officials to the hiring of blacks in other areas. In September 1933 the JCER specifically asked the Department of Labor secretary, Frances

Perkins, to place a black person, namely the economist Abram Harris or union president A. Philip Randolph, on the Labor Advisory Board of the National Recovery Administration. When Randolph decided that he did not want to be considered, George Haynes asked the member organizations, then numbering eleven, to send telegrams to Perkins urging Harris's appointment. Despite the JCER's efforts, Harris did not receive this unpaid appointment.[89] Perkins's later choice of a rather weak political appointee as her Negro advisor meant that progressive black organizations had little leverage at the Labor Department during the New Deal.

Carter Woodson's contemporaneous criticism of interracial cooperation had centered on the tendency of some whites who worked in interracial organizations to claim that whites were better advisors on black issues than black people. This was counter to the arguments that had secured Haynes's World War I position, and the majority of black organizations were opposed to having whites being named Negro advisors. This issue soon surfaced in a dispute between the JCER and Weaver. Edwin Embree, of the Rosenwald Foundation, and Will Alexander, of the Commission on Interracial Cooperation, agreed that the New Deal needed advisors on Negro affairs, but they argued that a white person would be a more effective spokesman in the face of Jim Crow restrictions and white prejudice. Many black social scientists and intellectuals agreed wholeheartedly with Woodson, who suggested that this attitude on the part of their erstwhile supporters was hypocritical, self-serving, and demonstrated less than complete confidence in the ability of educated blacks to represent their own interests.[90] Robert Weaver became entangled in the struggle between black leaders and white liberals over having advisors on black affairs.

The 1933 appointment of Clark Foreman as Negro advisor at the Department of the Interior illustrated the differences and distrust between black activists and white race relations executives. The Roosevelt administration preferred that any advisors on black people also bring in black votes, so outside funding had to be sought to secure the appointment of a labor expert. Two of the most influential white race relations executives, Edwin Embree and Will Alexander, arranged the funding and appointment of a young white southerner, Clark Foreman, as the advisor on Negro Affairs in the Department of the Interior. Foreman's salary was paid by the Rosenwald Fund. The black press reacted angrily to Foreman's appointment, and in an obvious effort to make peace with black leaders, Robert Weaver was appointed as Foreman's assistant. This situation did not satisfy everybody. Some black people mis-

The Segregated Scholars

trusted the motives of Embree and Alexander, others questioned Foreman's competence. Weaver's colleagues at the JCER questioned his racial loyalty because they had been unsuccessful in securing the position at the Labor Department for Abram Harris and believed Weaver's acceptance of the job undercut their efforts. John P. Davis's angry reaction to Weaver's appointment caused a break in the two men's long friendship that took some time to heal. Weaver wrote Davis that he did not plan to change his philosophical position, saying, "My attitudes on the problems as they present themselves in my new position will be guided by my former points of view."[91] Davis was not persuaded and wrote to Interior Secretary Harold Ickes and others to protest Foreman's and Weaver's appointments, alleging that Foreman was a segregationist and intimating that Weaver was not the choice of black leaders.[92] The futile protests in the black press and the JCER's inability to persuade the Roosevelt administration to change its mind were a sign of the relative weakness of black organizations to affect policy. Robert Weaver became Foreman's assistant, and, despite his rocky start, it did not take long for him to become the co-leader of the Black Cabinet, with Mary McLeod Bethune. The "Black Cabinet" was an informal working group of the principal black advisors in the Roosevelt administration. They often met in Mrs. Bethune's Vermont Avenue home, headquarters of the National Council of Negro Women. At the meetings they continued the kind of conversations on how to improve race relations and living conditions that Weaver and his college friends had at Harvard. They considered themselves to be a black parallel to Roosevelt's famous Brain Trust of intellectuals, and they excluded from their meetings those black appointees who they felt were strictly political appointees or those with whom they had philosophical differences.[93]

There were three important aspects to Robert Weaver's governmental service during the Roosevelt administration. First, Weaver was the first black New Deal official whose hiring was officially designated to have been the result of his competence and not his race or political connections. His service, therefore, demonstrated publicly that black social scientists could carry out technical and administrative functions. Of course, Robert Weaver was hired in part to quiet complaints from blacks about Clark Foreman, but he did not bring potential votes to the job as did other black appointees such as Robert Vann, editor of the *Pittsburgh Courier*. Weaver was the first of a series of black specialists—social scientists, social work executives, and lawyers—in high-profile governmental positions during the New Deal. He helped to create a model of decorum and technical competence in office. Second, and more important, Weaver developed and administered the first federal affirmative action employment program. Third, Weaver used his influence to assemble a large number of black professionals for a major research study on black workers on the eve of the postwar era. Thus, like other black labor scholars, Robert Weaver created a professional life that combined scholarship and social action.

Robert Weaver spent the first decade of his career, 1933 to 1944, as a federal administrator assigned to employment and working-class housing programs. As such, he tried to demonstrate that black social scientists were better able to design programs for black workers than black political appointees without expertise in labor problems. Weaver also demonstrated his commitment to academic labor studies by publishing in scholarly as well as topical journals. In fact, Weaver was one of the most prolific of the black social scientists in the 1930s and 1940s, publishing two books and more than twenty-five articles on black workers, segregation, and economic issues related to housing.[94]

Weaver's writing style was clear, accessible, and analytical. He tended to knock the federal government's inadequacies as often as he pushed its promising programs. It is clear from his own recollections, as well as his labor writings and the policies he implemented during the New Deal, that Weaver was consciously picking up Du Bois's mantle of activist scholarship. His decision to use the opportunity to be the Roosevelt administration's expert on black labor was modeled on the example set by George Haynes's work at the Division of Negro Economics. Weaver held that his own efforts were more important to black workers than Haynes's Division of Negro Economics, but he admired George Haynes's labor studies. Weaver characterized *The Negro at Work in New York City* as "path-finding."[95] Haynes's technical and political assistance to the Joint Committee on Economic Recovery also gave Weaver some insight into his scholarly competence and contacts. He found Haynes more substantive than Urban League director Eugene K. Jones or its industrial secretary T. Arnold Hill. In contrast, fellow economist Abram Harris had long emphasized his own antipathy of Haynes's close ties to religious and interracial organizations.[96]

Robert Weaver directed a research project in 1935 on black workers that gave him the opportunity to do two things he believed were crucial to his effectiveness as an administrator: obtain more empirical data to use to force long-term federal policy changes, and force the Works Progress Administration (WPA) to change its hiring policies in the short-term. The WPA had not

The Segregated Scholars

hired many black applicants in their Professional Relief Program, so Weaver's research project was purposely designed to employ a large number of black academics. He hired the sociologist Ira De A. Reid to create the research design and direct the survey, while Charles S. Johnson supervised the tabulation. Reid and Johnson employed many of their underemployed colleagues at black colleges and hired as many black graduate students in the social sciences as they could.

Unfortunately, the resulting two-volume study, with *Statistics by Regions* appearing as the first volume and *Male Negro Skilled Workers in the United States, 1930–1936* as the second, was much in the style of the massive data presentations that Reid and Johnson had done at the National Urban League, and its analysis was perfunctory. This was the hallmark of Johnson's style, not Weaver's subsequent labor studies. Ira Reid was moving away from this sort of empiricism in his research on black immigrants, young black southerners, and sharecroppers.[97] The decision by Johnson, Weaver, and Reid to use occupational categories that departed from the standard census categories further limited the study's comparability. This was ironic because Weaver would later criticize George Haynes's World War I study *The Negro at Work during World War and during Reconstruction* for making similar changes. Neither Weaver nor Reid had the time to give the masses of data that were collected the amount of analysis that would have made the study truly valuable.[98]

Robert Weaver's evolving duties tell us a lot about the changes in the attitudes of and opportunities for black social scientists as they continued their attempts to help black workers during the New Deal. Weaver was in the Interior Department in several different jobs from late 1933 to 1938. After one year as Foreman's assistant, Weaver succeeded him as the advisor on Negro affairs, then was named an assistant in the Housing Division of the Public Works Administration (PWA). When the housing programs of the PWA were transferred to the newly organized United States Housing Authority (USHA), Weaver became special assistant in charge of race relations to Nathan Straus, administrator of the USHA. His relationship with Straus was as good as the one he continued to enjoy with Interior Secretary Harold Ickes. During America's defense buildup before World War II, Weaver, by now somewhat a fixture in the government, became the administrative assistant to the Labor Division under Sidney Hillman, national defense advisor. He spent his last four government years in the Roosevelt administration, coping specifically with black employment problems for various wartime agencies. Controversies over Weaver's job titles were at times more pointed than the criticism of his policies. His appointment as chief of the Negro Employment and Training Branch of the Office of Price Management in 1940 was criticized by the NAACP as a Jim Crow job, but they later approved of him doing pretty much the same things with the title of administrative assistant to the executive assistant.[99]

Although not to the extent he had hoped, Weaver was effective when he was working directly in the area of his greatest interest—the employment and training of black workers. He was able to make specific interventions in selected programs, but he could not alter the widespread discrimination against black workers throughout New Deal agencies. The key to successful implementation of programs for blacks in the New Deal was the willingness of the secretaries of federal departments and administrators of agencies to override opposition to changes in the status quo for black workers. Robert Weaver had a good record while at the Department of the Interior, in terms of ensuring that Interior programs were open to black participation, but many of the New Deal programs were segregated. Weaver's rapport with Ickes and Straus and their personal commitment to racial justice led to meaningful improvements in Interior and PWA projects.[100]

The fact that segregation was legal gave Weaver a number of moral dilemmas that opened him to criticism that he was upholding the status quo and not helping black people advance, which had been his own criticism of other black advisors before he joined the administration. Weaver and other black administrators were frequently placed in the position of overseeing segregated projects or foregoing black participation in these areas. When Weaver began to work as a housing specialist, he worked within the system and did not fight for integrated housing except in border states and areas in which he and Secretary Ickes and Administrator Straus believed they could build a few integrated federal housing projects. The three men rationalized that they were keeping the principle of integrated housing alive within contemporary political realities. Weaver insisted that federal housing for blacks met the same standards as white projects, and he concentrated on getting black architects, construction workers, and trained housing managers for the black projects that were built.[101]

In 1934 when Weaver went to the PWA, it had embarked on an ambitious program of public housing projects. He helped to set up the first affirmative action program for black workers. For black Americans the issue was not just whether to accept segregated housing projects—an issue over which they had little choice—but whether there would be black housing projects at all, who would build them, and what methods would be used to displace residents of the decaying neighborhoods that these projects were designed to replace. Robert Weaver hoped to establish new guidelines and requirements for black employment on all government-funded housing projects. Weaver got William Hastie's assistance in creating a program that would require that contractors hire a specific number of skilled black workers. The program benefited from the legal reasoning that Hastie and Charles Houston were using to develop the NAACP's employment and desegregation cases. Secretary Ickes gave Weaver's and Hastie's ideas an objective hearing and overrode the objections of organized labor to their plan, which was apparently the first use of mandatory quotas for hiring black workers.[102]

The Weaver and Hastie plan created requirements for contractors who worked on projects related to blacks; black workers were guaranteed a specific percentage of the payroll. The percentage of workers to be hired was based on the numbers of black skilled and unskilled workers in the 1930 occupational census for each city. Weaver called this "prima facie evidence criteria," and contractors were required to demonstrate that they were in compliance with the regulations. The quotas were set at significantly lower levels than the census figures in order to facilitate compliance and lower resistance from white unions. For example, in Atlanta black skilled workers were 24 percent of the construction force, but contractors were only required to set aside 12 percent of the skilled payroll for blacks. Weaver attempted to prevent the temporary hiring of blacks by making weekly payrolls rather than the overall percentage of black employees the basis for contractor compliance. Weaver considered this project his most significant accomplishment up to the time he became the first black to become a cabinet secretary, thirty years later. He claimed that by 1940 the housing program was worth $2,000,200 in salaries for black skilled workers and that 5.8 percent of the skilled payroll in PWA projects was black. White unions prevented greater participation by black workers in the construction industry as a whole by refusing to admit them to their unions and by giving them work permits that were good only for jobs on housing projects. Thus, while the Weaver and Hastie plan helped only a fraction of the black skilled construction workers who needed employment, there is no doubt that it provided a rare source of skilled jobs during the Depression.[103] Robert Weaver was realistic about the limitations of the quota system. He did not view it as opening new areas so much as an attempt to "regain past occupational advances of blacks in a period of extreme slack labor demand."[104] Unlike George Haynes's efforts during World War I, Weaver was able to do more than get jobs for black professional and unskilled workers. Robert

Weaver demonstrated again that a segregated scholar could maintain his credibility as an objective analyst and still develop and implement policies that would materially benefit black labor. These benefits, however, were frustratingly small and incremental when compared to the needs and hopes of black workers.

Robert Weaver held moderate political views during the New Deal; this was manifested in the approbation of his writing and his activities by most black labor scholars. He had easy relations with W. E. B. Du Bois and Charles S. Johnson and was a great admirer of the work of Abram Harris. Robert Weaver did not alter his early observation that "the economic problem of the Negro is almost exclusively a labor problem," but he eventually won over Carter Woodson.[105] In 1949, at the last meeting of the ASNLH during Woodson's lifetime, Weaver was a featured speaker. Woodson said Weaver's paper "Negro Labor since 1929" was "a most scholarly address."[106] Although Weaver's labor writings never went as far to the left as Abram Harris's, he did not place as much reliance on black business as a solution to labor problems as did Du Bois and Woodson. Weaver held that Abram Harris was the first to understand the role of black workers as a labor reserve, and some of Weaver's first articles attempted to elaborate the disastrous implications of structural unemployment for black progress. Weaver was the first of the segregated scholars to place equal weight on labor unions, management, and the federal government for black workers' inability to gain their proper occupational distribution in the marketplace. He joined Charles H. Wesley in articulating an appreciation for the importance of pressure group politics in terms of voting and direct action campaigns in gaining black skilled jobs.[107]

Robert Weaver tried to use the labor shortages during World War II to press for greater black employment, much as George Haynes had attempted during World War I. Weaver's argument to whites was that job discrimination was wasteful and unpatriotic, but at the same time he warned black workers to demand skilled jobs now or never hope to get them. Weaver foresaw that ongoing structural changes in the American economy would eliminate many unskilled occupations, and he feared that this would create a large segment of the black population that would be permanently unemployed. Weaver placed little hope in black people staving off the effect of what he saw as inevitable economic changes simply by taking vocational courses, as the NUL had proposed. Instead, he called for government intervention to bring about the employment of blacks in skilled occupations, saying that blacks could not raise themselves by their bootstraps because their feet were "set in concrete" by racial discrimination.[108] Weaver wanted workers to use their growing political importance to agitate for a federal commitment to full postwar employment. He understood that his own government positions had come about as a result of an attempt by the Roosevelt administration to address growing black political strength. Weaver did not overestimate his effectiveness, and he was the first to admit that the Black Cabinet's combined achievements were not as important as the two victories extracted from President Roosevelt at the threat of the March on Washington orchestrated by the black labor leader A. Philip Randolph. These were Executive Order 8802, banning discrimination in the defense industry and in its enforcement agency, the Federal Employment Practices Commission.[109]

Robert Weaver's analysis of black labor problems turned away from the idea that black intellectuals were the sole group who would advance the race, without the harsh criticism of the intelligentsia of Woodson. Weaver's principal concern was that black workers might not benefit in the postwar period without a federal commitment to full employment. This was the subject of *Negro Labor: A National Problem,* his most important book on black workers. In this work and in his 1949 ASNLH address, Weaver used statistics to demonstrate the failure of the CIO and the black direct action movements of the 1930s and 1940s to fully achieve their goals, especially when it came to increasing the number of blacks who were employed or who had skilled jobs. These laudable efforts had failed, in Weaver's opinion, because of racial discrimination on the part of unions and management and the failure of important government agencies to insist on equal employment opportunities for black workers. Weaver's desire to combine heightened black political participation with government intervention foreshadowed the shape of events in the civil rights movement of the 1950s.[110]

Conclusion

In 1946 there was no indication that Robert Weaver's *Negro Labor: A National Problem* would be the last important labor study by a black person for three decades, or that black labor studies would adopt approaches that characterized white labor studies by focusing on organized labor and institutional studies of industries. Black labor studies was carried forward in the 1950s and 1960s largely by three young white academics, the radical labor and social historian Philip Foner, the centrist economist F. Ray Marshall, and an institutional economist, Herbert R. Northrup.[111] Although legal segregation and economic discrimination persisted for two more decades, a fourth generation of black labor scholars did not join Du Bois, Haynes, Harris, and Weaver. A number of factors combined to quietly mark the end of regenerating cohorts of black intellectuals who championed the rights and studied the plight of workers.

In 1950 the oldest of the segregated scholars were still writing, but they were nearing the end of their careers. W. E. B. Du Bois was eighty-two, George Haynes and R. R. Wright Jr. were seventy and seventy-two, respectively, although still active through the decade. Carter Woodson died at age seventy-five in the spring of 1950, leaving the Association of the Study of Negro Life and History, the *Journal of Negro History*, and the *Negro History Bulletin* in the hands of black historians. Greene, Wesley, and Logan continued the work of the ASNLH, *Journal of Negro History*, and Associated Publishers for thirty years after Woodson's death. In the late 1940s Charles S. Johnson and Charles Wesley became the presidents of Fisk and Wilberforce, respectively, with large responsibilities that allowed them to do little new research, but they continued to be productive. Charles S. Johnson died in 1956, having become somewhat frustrated that his white colleagues who had supported his race relations strategy did not support school integration.

Charles H. Wesley's radicalism prevented him from becoming the president of Fisk instead of Johnson and caused an uproar when he was fired from Wilberforce and then became president of Central State College. During the civil rights movement Wesley welcomed students whose activism had gotten them expelled from other black colleges. By the end of World War II some of the middle-aged and well-established black labor scholars began to shift their locations and their academic focus. Abram Harris and Ira Reid helped to break down racial barriers when they both left black colleges for faculty positions at the University of Chicago and Haverford College, respectively, and Robert Weaver broke the long-standing pattern of black social scientists by never establishing his career at a black college.

Although more black men and women became social scientists than ever before in the 1940s and 1950s, studies on black workers declined dramatically. Fifty years of black social science research, collective action, and increasingly contentious programs on black workers drew to an end in Robert Weaver's study *Negro Labor: A National Problem.* He offered its pessimistic forecast of a permanently underemployed group or underclass of black workers in the postwar economy unless the government committed to economic programs that promoted full employment.[112] In the 1950s the youngest of segregated scholars—Abram Harris, Ira Reid, Lorenzo Greene, and Robert Weaver—became middle-aged but continued to be professionally active. The black social scientists who should have succeeded them after writing dissertations on black workers in the 1940s did not maintain the level of publications in labor studies that was attained by the three earlier generations. Many, such as Mabel Smythe, Brailsford Brazeal, and Preston Valien, were fine scholars in their own right and were concerned with the role of black social scientists in the postwar world and their obligations to students.[113] After the war some of these younger scholars turned to other areas of research, others had trouble finding the funding necessary for large-scale research projects, and still others became so involved in college administration that their publishing was sharply curtailed. A plan by W. E. B. Du Bois and E. Franklin Frazier to coordinate a major research initiative involving black land-grant colleges that would have drawn in many of these men and women who were in their late twenties and early thirties never got completely funded.[114]

Robert Weaver had a difficult time finding a suitable job after he left the government in the late 1940s. He wanted to teach at Howard University, but the salary offered was too low after his government service. Weaver had a series of foundation-funded teaching and administrative positions and finally became active in housing administration, an area in which he had gained considerable expertise during the New Deal. In the 1950s Weaver wrote extensively on housing and other urban problems and began to feel that he was becoming more of a sociologist than an economist.[115] He became the first black American cabinet member when President Lyndon B. Johnson appointed him the first secretary of the Department of Housing and Urban Development. The civil rights movement of the 1950s did not have the galvanizing effect on the segregated scholars that one might have expected, but this was because nearly all of them had been active in political and economic campaigns since at least the mid-thirties. Lorenzo Greene, who spent most of his career at Lincoln University in Jefferson City, Missouri, was active in voter registration drives and political action campaigns in the 1940s, as was another ASNLH stalwart, Luther Porter Jackson. Ira Reid, Rayford Logan, and other faculty members at Atlanta University were involved in similar activities. Rayford Logan was a young Harvard-trained historian who had worked closely with both Du Bois at Atlanta University and Woodson through the ASNLH. Sadie T. M. Alexander spent the 1930s and 1940s working as a lawyer, and she was appointed to President Harry Truman's Civil Rights Committee and worked to establish international legal standards for women's rights within the United Nations. She spent two decades trying to get the United States to approve the UN Convention against genocide.[116]

For more than fifty years, individual black labor scholars were joined to one another by their self-confidence as intellectuals and collective sense of obligation to their people. Their work was imbedded with the same four strong threads of intentionality that had drawn Du Bois to the social sciences: Truth, Duty, Glory, and Purpose. The personal glory that Du Bois had sought as a twenty-five-year-old was not financial, but richly repaid in the shared purpose of succeeding generations of black social scientists who, like Robert Weaver, viewed him as "a titan" and who continued to believe that guiding certainties could be found in their investigations.

Why didn't a new generation of black labor historians emerge after 1950? The number of blacks who earned doctorates increased. There were openings for talented black scholars for the first time at white colleges and universities, not many, to be sure, but openings nonetheless. This question cannot be fully answered, of course, but there seem to have been individual and external factors that helped to diffuse the concerns of black social scientists. First of all, many people in the generation of scholars who had come of age in the forties resented the idea that they should study African Americans simply because they were black. An expansion in enrollments at black colleges in the 1940s led, on the one hand, to onerous teaching demands that prevented many black scholars from publishing, and, on the other hand, it provided secure jobs to those who preferred teaching to scholarship. Many of the most talented black graduate students in the late forties and fifties followed the example of Ralph Bunche and studied Africa. Since the nineteenth century, Africa had been of interest to black scholars, including the segregated scholars. As African independence became a reality, the federal government poured funds into universities to build African Studies research and language centers, and an interdisciplinary group of younger scholars benefited from these new resources.[117] A handful of white scholars, in contrast, who were shaped by either the Holocaust of World War II or their interest in interracial movements, had a new readiness to reevaluate the standard treatment of blacks in their disciplines.

I suspect that the illusion of black economic progress after the war was also a contributing factor in the drop-off of black intellectuals' interest in labor problems. The segregated scholars' strategy of using scholarship to promote racial progress resulted in fine scholarship, but it had had limited results in terms of racial progress. Therefore the success of direct action boycotts and the legal campaigns of the civil rights movement may have suggested to some black intellectuals that social science scholarship had a smaller role to play in achieving racial progress, and the success of black lawyers doubtless led many brilliant younger black men and women to careers in the law rather than the social sciences.[118]

These factors—the lack of research facilities and failure to emphasize research at black colleges, the influence of the civil rights movement, a resistance among some black graduate students to study black people, and the movement by others to study Africa—combined to bring about a general decline in major works on black Americans by new black social scientists that lasted from the early fifties to the late sixties. Paradoxically, World War II and the civil rights movement helped to bring white scholars to black studies in greater numbers. Thus, when African American history, sociology, and economics became more legitimate subjects of study by American social scientists, black scholars did not dominate the discourse. The entry of whites into fields that had been in a state of de facto segregation only served to confirm the success of the segregated scholars and other black social scientists in establishing criteria for the objective study of black people. The legacy of the segregated scholars is twofold. They developed a solid, objective body of research on black workers and black life, creating studies that have become the standards by which others measure their own efforts. They also left a model of black scholars as activists and reformers committed to creating a society that has racial justice and economic equity. The full integration of black scholarship and black scholars into American intellectual life will occur only when the dual legacy of the segregated scholars has been fully realized.

Notes

Abbreviations

AME	African Methodist Episcopal Church
AMEZ	African Methodist Episcopal Zion Church
ASNLH	Association for the Study of Negro Life and History
DNE	Division of Negro Economics
DOL	Department of Labor
GEH	George Edmund Haynes
JCER	Joint Committee for Economic Recovery
LOC	Library of Congress
NAACP	National Association for the Advancement of Colored People
NHB	Nannie Helen Burroughs
NARA	National Archives and Records Administration
NNC	National Negro Congress
NUL	National Urban League
NYPLSC	New York Public Library, Schomburg Center
RG	Record Group
STMA	Sadie Tanner Mossell Alexander
USES	United States Employment Service
WIIS	Women in Industry Service

Introduction

1. Irvin, "Conditions in Industry as They Affect Negro Women," 524, original emphasis; Robert C. Weaver to W. E. B. Du Bois, Jan. 29, 1931, in Du Bois, *Correspondence*, 1:434–35.

2. Traditionally, black intellectuals have been studied either in broad terms during a particular era or as individuals. A classic example of this that is representative of the binary approach to black thought is Meier, *Negro Thought in America, 1880–1915*. Other important examinations of studies of black thought during an era are Moses, *Golden Age of Black Nationalism, 1850–1925*; Stuckey, *Ideological Origins of Black Nationalism*; Stuckey, *Slave Culture*; and Toll, *Resurgence of Race*. Recent studies that have examined black intellectuals include Banks, *Black Intellectuals*; Dennis, *Research in Race and Ethnic Relations*; Gaines, *Uplifting the Race*; James, *Transcending the Talented Tenth*; Watts, *Heroism and the Black Intellectual*; and W. D. Wright, *Black Intellectuals, Black Cognition, and a Black Aesthetic*. John

Wright's essay "Intellectual Life" is a comprehensive introduction to major themes and trends in black intellectual life.

3. Du Bois's studies for the U.S. Department of Labor include "Negroes of Farmville, Virginia." For recent studies of *The Philadelphia Negro*, see Katz and Sugrue, *W. E. B. Du Bois, Race, and the City*.

4. Deegan, *Jane Addams and the Men of the Chicago School, 1892–1918*; Fitzpatrick, *Endless Crusade*; Muncy, *Creating a Female Dominion in American Reform, 1890–1935*. Although each of these studies pays some attention to race in the work of their subjects, there are no studies of white female social scientists that ask why black women are not a part of this cohort. For examples that do examine black women's roles in professions, see Shaw, *What a Women Ought to Be and to Do*; Harley, "Reclaiming Public Voice and the Study of Black Women's Work"; Hine, *Hine Sight*; E. B. Brown, "Introduction"; Wells-Barnett, *Memphis Diary of Ida B. Wells*; and Neverdon-Morton, *Afro-American Women of the South and the Advancement of the Race, 1895–1925*.

5. Recent interpretative biographies or collections of papers of individual black social scientists include D. L. Lewis, *W. E. B. Du Bois, 1868–1919*; D. L. Lewis, *W. E. B. Du Bois, 1919–1963*; Harris, *Race, Radicalism, and Reform*; Darity, "Soundings and Silences on Race and Social Change"; Holloway, *Confronting the Veil*; G. E. Harris, "Life and Work of E. Franklin Frazier," 231–34; Griffler, *What Price Alliance?*; Horne, *Black and Red*; Goggin, *Carter G. Woodson*; J. H. Franklin, *George Washington Williams*; J. H. Franklin, *Race and History*; Urban, *Black Scholar*; Urquhart, *Ralph Bunche*; Janken, *Rayford W. Logan and the Dilemma of the African-American Intellectual*; and Platt, *E. Franklin Frazier Reconsidered*. Studies of individual disciplines include Bond, *Black American Scholars*; Blackwell and Janowitz, *Black Sociologists*; Boston, *Different Vision*; Carlton-LaNey and Burwell, *African American Community Practice Models*; J. H. Franklin, *Race and History*; Guthrie, *Even the Rat Was White*; Meier and Rudwick, *Black History and the Historical Profession, 1915–1980*; E. L. Ross, *Black Heritage in Social Welfare, 1860–1930*; Thorpe, *Central Theme of Black History*; Thorpe, *Black Historians*; and Wood, "'I Did the Best I Could for My Day.'"

6. Boston, *Different Vision*; Meier and Rudwick, *Black History and the Historical Profession, 1915–1980*, 5–6.

7. Robert C. Weaver to W. E. B. Du Bois, Jan. 29, 1931, in Du Bois, *Correspondence*, 1:434–35.

8. Robert Weaver represents a generation of black labor economists and sociologists who came of age in the thirties and forties, leading to important works, including M. M. Smythe, "Tipping Occupations as a Problem in the Administration of Protective Labor Legislation"; M. M. Smythe, "Economics Teacher in the Post-War Period"; Cayton and Mitchell, *Black Workers and the New Unions*; P. Valien, "Southern Negro Internal Migration between 1935 and 1940"; P. Valien, "Social and Economic Implications of Migration for the Negro in the Present Social Order"; Brazeal, *Brotherhood of Sleeping Car Porters*; Warren, "Negro in the American Labor Market"; Warren, "Partial Background for the Study of the Development of

Negro Labor"; C. L. Franklin, *Negro Labor Unionist of New York*; C. L. Franklin, "Characteristics and Taxable Wages of Negro Workers, 13 Selected Southern States, 1938"; F. G. Davis, "War Economics and Negro Labor"; and F. G. Davis, "War Economics and Negro Labor."

9. Michael R. Winston brought my attention to this remark by E. Franklin Frazier, who was arguably the major sociologist of his time, from a 1940 Charter Day Address at Howard University. See Winston, *Howard University Department of History, 1913–1973*, 31; Wesley, *Negro Labor in the United States, 1850–1925*; F. R. Wilson, "Racial Consciousness and Black Scholarship"; C. S. Johnson, "History of Negro Labor"; Meier and Rudwick, *Black History and the Historical Profession, 1915–1980*, 7, 75–93; Thorpe, *Black Historians*, 135.

10. Du Bois and Dill, *Negro American Artisan*, 5.

11. Wood, "'I Did the Best I Could for My Day'"; V. P. Franklin, "Black Social Scientists and the Mental Testing Movement, 1920–1940." Michael R. Winston and John Hope Franklin also wrote important accounts of black scholars that guided my first efforts. See Winston, "Through the Back Door"; J. H. Franklin, "Dilemma of the American Negro Scholar." For more recent examinations, see J. H. Franklin, *Race and History*. Lorenzo J. Greene taught my parents at Lincoln University in Jefferson City, Missouri, in the 1940s. He and Robert C. Weaver were particularly generous with their time and advice to me at the beginning of my research. St. Clair Drake, Martin Kilson, Michael Winston, and many other students of the segregated scholars were also interviewed in the course of this project. I was not able to interview Sadie T. M. Alexander.

12. There have been a number of good studies that have examined how white social scientists have treated black Americans. Some examples include V. J. Williams, *From a Caste to a Minority*; V. J. Williams, *Rethinking Race*; W. A. Jackson, *Gunnar Myrdal and America's Conscience*; Lyman, *Black American in Sociological Thought*; Pettigrew, *Sociology of Race Relations*; and D. M. Scott, *Contempt and Pity*.

1. "To Make a Name in Science . . . and Thus to Raise My Race"

1. W. E. B. Du Bois, Diary, Feb. 23, 1893, H. Aptheker, *Documentary History* 1:753; Du Bois, *Autobiography*, 170–71.

2. Du Bois and Dill, *Negro American Artisan*, 5.

3. Painter, *Exodusters*, 14–16; Higginbotham, "African-American Women's History and the Metalanguage of Race"; V. P. Franklin, *Black Self-Determination*.

4. Moss, *American Negro Academy*, 11–12, 15–24, 121–27; Wesley, "Racial Historical Societies and the American Heritage"; Moynihan, "History as a Weapon for Social Advancement," 8–27; Wells-Barnett, *Red Record*; Wells-Barnett, *On Lynchings*.

5. Du Bois, *Philadelphia Negro*; Du Bois, "Negroes of Farmville, Virginia"; Du Bois, "Negro in the Black Belt"; Du Bois, "Negro Landholder of Georgia"; Du Bois, *Some Efforts of American Negroes For Their Own Social Betterment*; Du Bois, *Negro*

in *Business*; Du Bois, *College-Bred Negro*; Du Bois, *Negro Common School*; Du Bois, *Negro Artisan*.

6. Richardson, *History of Fisk University, 1865–1946*; Du Bois, *College-Bred Negro*, 40; Du Bois, *Autobiography*, 105–12, 123–27, 132–37; Du Bois, *Dusk of Dawn*, 34–38; Du Bois, *College-Bred Negro*, 22–26; Synott, *Half-Opened Door*, 21–23, 80–83; Rampersad, *Art and Imagination of W. E. B. Du Bois*, 20–24.

7. On James, see Stern, "William James and the New Psychology"; Myers, *William James*. On Hart, Francis Peabody, and the development of sociological studies at Harvard, respectively, see Baird, "Albert Bushnell Hart"; Potts, "Social Ethics at Harvard, 1881–1931"; Buck, "Introduction"; and Church, "Economists Study Society."

8. Du Bois, *Autobiography*, 132–53; Du Bois, *Dusk of Dawn*, 30–45; D. L. Lewis, *W. E. B. Du Bois, 1868–1919*, 79–127, 198, 218; Furner, *Advocacy and Objectivity*, 295.

9. Du Bois, *Dusk of Dawn*, 46–48; Du Bois, *Autobiography*, 162–71; Max Weber to W. E. B. Du Bois, Mar. 30, 1905, in Du Bois, *Correspondence*, 1:106–7; Broderick, "German Influence on the Scholarship of W. E. B. Du Bois"; Rampersad, *Art and Imagination of W. E. B. Du Bois*, 42–46; Rudwick, "W. E. B. Du Bois as a Sociologist," 27; D. L. Lewis, *W. E. B. Du Bois, 1868–1919*, 130–32, 136, 141–44. Du Bois and Weber became long-term correspondents after the 1903 publication of *The Souls of Black Folk*. On Schmoller, see P. R. Anderson, "Gustav von Schmoller, 1828–1917."

10. W. E. B. Du Bois to President [D. C.] Gilman, Mar. 29, Mar. 31, 1894, and D. C. Gilman to W. E. B. Du Bois, Apr. 13, 1894, in Du Bois, *Correspondence*, 1:26–29; Du Bois, *Autobiography*, 175, 183; D. L. Lewis, *W. E. B. Du Bois, 1868–1919*, 144–46.

11. Du Bois, *Autobiography*, 183–93; Du Bois, *Dusk of Dawn*, 56–58; Du Bois, *Darkwater*, 17–20, quotation on 19.

12. W. E. B. Du Bois to President [D. C.] Gilman, July 28, 1895, in Du Bois, *Correspondence*, 1:38–39; Du Bois, *Suppression of the African Slave-Trade to the United States of America, 1638–1870*; Rampersad, *Art and Imagination of W. E. B. Du Bois*, 49–50; D. L. Lewis, *W. E. B. Du Bois, 1868–1919*, 154–55, 158–59. For Du Bois's 1954 reevaluation of his study, see his "Apologia" in Du Bois, *Suppression of the African Slave-Trade to the United States of America, 1638–1870*, 327–28.

13. Du Bois, *Darkwater*, 18.

14. Ibid., 18–20; Du Bois, *Autobiography*, 185, 188, 192–93; Du Bois, *Dusk of Dawn*, 56–57; Du Bois, *The Souls of Black Folk*, 176–77. Wilberforce was several decades away from offering courses in sociology or black history.

15. Du Bois, *Darkwater*, 19–20; Du Bois, *Autobiography*, 192–93; D. L. Lewis, *W. E. B. Du Bois, 1868–1919*, 178.

16. C. C. Harrison, "To Whom It May Concern," letter of introduction for W. E. B. Du Bois, Aug. 15, 1896, in Du Bois, *Correspondence*, 1:41; Du Bois, *Autobiography*, 194–97; Du Bois, *Dusk of Dawn*, 58–59; D. L. Lewis, *W. E. B. Du Bois, 1868–1919*, 179–89; Baltzell, "Introduction," xvi–xix. On Wharton and the Phila-

delphia College Settlement, see Katz and Sugrue, "Introduction," 4–17. Harrison was a wealthy retired businessman and heir to his family's sugar fortune.

17. Du Bois, *Autobiography*, 194–95; Baltzell, "Introduction," xviii–xx; Eaton, "Special Report on Negro Domestic Service in the Seventh Ward, Philadelphia." Michael B. Katz and Thomas J. Sugrue suggest that Jane Addams had recommended Isabel Eaton for the job. See Katz and Sugrue, "Introduction," 16. David L. Lewis acknowledges Eaton's contribution to *The Philadelphia Negro*, which Du Bois characteristically downplayed. See D. L. Lewis, *W. E. B. Du Bois, 1868–1919*, 188–92, 207. Broderick, "W. E. B. Du Bois," 19; Rudwick, "W. E. B. Du Bois as a Sociologist," 25–26. Eaton did work closely with Du Bois and submitted her own comprehensive report on domestic service that was published with *The Philadelphia Negro*.

18. Du Bois, *Dusk of Dawn*, 51; D. L. Lewis, *W. E. B. Du Bois, 1868–1919*, 184, 190; Booth, *Life and Labour of the People in London*. For a recent assessment of the influence of Booth's and Schmoller's work on Du Bois's study, see Bay, "'The World Was Thinking Wrong About Race,'" 49–51.

19. Residents of Hull-House, *Hull-House Maps and Papers*; Du Bois, *Philadelphia Negro*, chap. 5.

20. Du Bois, *Philadelphia Negro*, 97, 309–10.

21. Ibid., 98.

22. Ibid., 309–10, 97.

23. Du Bois, *Autobiography*, 198; Wright Jr., preface to *Negro in Pennsylvania*; G. E. Haynes, *Negro at Work in New York City*, 8. For a summary of various contemporary scholars' assessments of *The Philadelphia Negro*, see D. L. Lewis, *W. E. B. Du Bois, 1868–1919*, 624n31.

24. Du Bois, *Philadelphia Negro*, 310–11, chaps. 9, 15, passim.

25. Du Bois, *Autobiography*, 186–87; Moss, *American Negro Academy*, 11–14, 47–51, 121–27, 264–65; Wesley, "Racial Historical Societies," 11–35. See the letter from Edward Alexander Clarke, president of the Bethel Literary and Historical Association, to Booker T. Washington, Oct. 31, 1895, which outlines the association's fall program, in *Washington Papers*, 4:666–67.

26. Moss, *American Negro Academy*, 16–46.

27. Perhaps equally significant is the fact that the American Negro Academy membership remained entirely male throughout its thirty-one-year history. Despite a discussion of women's admission at the initial meeting and a number of women with the intellectual credentials the organizers required, no woman was ever invited into membership. Only one woman, Marchita Lyons of New York, was ever invited to present a paper before the group. As we shall see, the differential opportunities for scholarly mentoring and networking significantly affected the course of black women's development as social scientists. On the American Negro Academy and the woman question, see Cooper, "American Negro Academy," 35–36; and Moss, *American Negro Academy*, 38, 40–42, 59, 78, 134. On the development of black women social scientists, see chapters 3 and 5 in this study.

28. Hoffman, "Race Traits and Tendencies of the American Negro"; Miller,

"Review of Hoffman's 'Race Traits and Tendencies of the American Negro'";
Crummell, "Attitude of the American Mind Toward the Negro Intellect."

29. Winston, "Miller, Kelly." Miller was born to a free black Virginia family in 1863, just five years before Du Bois, but he is often viewed as belonging to a different generation.

30. E. R. Haynes, *Black Boy of Atlanta*, 84, 111–13, 122–23; F. R. Wilson, "Introduction," xxxi; R. R. Wright Sr. to W. E. B. Du Bois, Feb. 20, 1936, in Du Bois, *Correspondence*, 2:130.

31. E. R. Haynes, *Black Boy of Atlanta*, 89–93; Minutes of the Board of Trustees of the Atlanta University, July 1, 1895, Memorial Hall, Hartford, Connecticut, Board of Trustee Minutes, Box 1, Folder 2, Woodruff Library Archives, Atlanta University Center (hereafter cited Atlanta University); Means, "Review of the Atlanta University Conferences and Social Studies," 9–10. For his late nineteenth-century historical studies, see, for example, Wright Sr., *Brief Historical Sketch of Negro Education in Georgia*; and Wright Sr., "Negro as an Inventor." See also the Wright Sr. testimony "Colored Farm Laborers and Farmers of Georgia," given Augusta, Georgia, Nov. 23, 1883. His most influential historical study was "Negro Companions of the Spanish Explorers." See also Patton, "Major Richard Robert Wright, Sr. and Black Higher Education in Georgia, 1880–1920."

32. The U.S. Bureau of Labor was established in 1884 under the Department of the Interior and made an independent department without cabinet rank but reporting directly to the president in 1888. From 1903 to 1913 it had the title of department but was a bureau in the Department of Commerce and Labor. The current cabinet-level Department of Labor was created in 1913. See J. Grossman, "Origin of the U.S. Department of Labor"; J. Grossman, "Black Studies in the Department of Labor, 1897–1907."

33. "Conditions of the Negro in Various Cities"; J. Grossman, "Black Studies in the Department of Labor, 1897–1907"; *Scroll* (May 1897): 7.

34. The records of Carroll D. Wright's appointments and letters for this period are incomplete, and thus it is not possible to fully corroborate a meeting between R. R. Wright Sr. and Carroll Wright. My supposition that the two men were likely to have met in Washington, D.C., during R. R. Wright Sr.'s trip is based on the detailed evidence in the available records that Carroll Wright's normal operational style included face-to-face meetings whenever possible.

35. The precise name of the conference varied, being called the Atlanta University Conference and the City Conference, among other variations. George Bradford resigned as corresponding secretary after the second Atlanta University Conference, having assembled most of the first two reports but having been unable to attend either conference. See *Scroll* (May 1896); *Social and Physical Condition of Negroes in Cities*, 31.

36. J. Grossman, "Origin of the U.S. Department of Labor"; C. D. Wright, "Growth and Purposes of Bureaus of Statistics of Labor," qtd. in J. Grossman, "Black Studies in the Department of Labor, 1897–1907," 19; U.S. Department of Labor, *Anvil and the Plow*, 275–79; Leiby, *Carroll Wright and Labor Reform*, 4, 29;

M. J. Anderson, *American Census History*, 104–10; Folbre, "'Sphere of Women' in Early-Twentieth-Century Economics."

37. J. Grossman, "Origin of the U.S. Department of Labor"; J. Grossman, "Black Studies in the Department of Labor, 1897–1907"; D. L. Lewis, *W. E. B. Du Bois, 1868–1919*, 194–95; E. R. Haynes, *Black Boy of Atlanta*, 112–13.

38. W. E. B. Du Bois to Carroll Wright, Esq., Feb. 18, 1897; Samuel McCune Lindsay to Carroll D. Wright, Feb. 24, 1897; Testimonials of W. E. B. Du Bois, Assistant in Sociology in the University of Pennsylvania, 1896–97 [handwritten heading and footing in Du Bois's hand], n.p., n.d.; "To Help the Negroes," *Philadelphia Public Ledger*, Feb. 15, 189[7]; Schedules 1–6, Condition of the Negroes of Philadelphia, Ward Seven, University of Pennsylvania; all in Records of the Bureau of Labor Statistics, Department of Commerce and Labor, Job Applications 1885–1901, entry 20, Box 2, File 1072, RG 257, NARA. Commissioner Wright's first letter to Du Bois, written Feb. 16, 1897, is lost, nor could I locate Du Bois's earlier query to him asking about "Negro statistics," to which Du Bois refers in the first paragraph of his letter of Feb. 18, 1897. Du Bois's letter seems to indicate that the two have not yet met, but the *Public Ledger* article and Du Bois suggest that the Bureau of Labor had been involved in selecting the questions for the schedules, so this was most likely done through Isabel Eaton and Samuel McCune Lindsay. Quotation of Wright's Feb. 16, 1897, letter is on the first page of Du Bois's Feb. 18 letter; Du Bois's words are on pages 2–3. Carroll Wright closely scrutinized all reports commissioned by his bureau before their publication. See also Letters Sent, RG 257, NARA. Du Bois and Carroll Wright were probably brought together by Professor Samuel McCune Lindsay, Du Bois's putative overseer at the University of Philadelphia and a contributor to Wright's labor publication series.

39. W. E. B. Du Bois to Carroll Wright, Esq., Feb. 18, 1897, in Records of the Bureau of Labor Statistics, Department of Commerce and Labor, Job Applications, 1885–1901, entry 20, Box 1, File 1072, R6 257, NARA. Du Bois's lateness to the evening session of the March 5 meeting and the subsequent reorganization of the program is detailed in Moss, *American Negro Academy*, 46.

40. W. E. B. Du Bois to Carroll Wright, May 5, June 14, 1897, Records of the Bureau of Labor Statistics, Department of Commerce and Labor, Job Applications, 1885–1901, RG 257, NARA; Du Bois, "Study of the Negro Problems"; Du Bois, "Negroes of Farmville, Virginia"; Du Bois, "Negro in the Black Belt"; Du Bois, "Negro Landholder of Georgia"; Du Bois, *Autobiography*, 202–4; Broderick, "W. E. B. Du Bois," 19; Rudwick, "W. E. B. Du Bois as a Sociologist," 40–41.

41. Du Bois, "Study of the Negro Problems."

42. Haskell, *Emergence of Professional Social Science*, 215; Moss, *American Negro Academy*, 15–16. See the special issues of the *Annals of the American Academy of Political and Social Science*'s "The Negro's Progress in Fifty Years" and "The American Negro." Chapter 2 discusses the American Academy of Political and Social Science's 1906 session entitled "The Industrial Condition of the Negro in the North."

43. Du Bois, "Study of the Negro Problems," 72–73, 71, 78.

44. Ibid., 79–84; Du Bois, *Autobiography*, 199–202, 214–15; Deegan, *Jane*

Addams and the Men of the Chicago School, 1892–1918, 13, 29n41; Deegan, "W. E. B. Du Bois and the Women of Hull-House, 1895–1899." Copies of the correspondence from Carroll Wright to Du Bois between 1901 and 1906 are in "Letters Sent, 1889–1906," Records of the Bureau of Labor Statistics, Department of Commerce and Labor, RG 257, NARA. The ledgers for 1895–1900 appear to be missing. References to the ledger volumes for 1896 are found in the materials in Du Bois's employment file, noted earlier.

45. *Mortality among Negroes in Cities*, 48–49.

46. Minutes of the Board of Trustees of the Atlanta University, July 1, 1895; *Mortality among Negroes in Cities*, quotation on 3; "City Problem Studies"; "Conference of City Problems"; *Scroll* (Nov. 1896): 4–11; *Scroll* (May 1897): quotation on 7; M. W. Adams, *History of Atlanta University*, 35, 92–94. Myron W. Adams, who was a professor of Greek and dean of the faculty, produced a history of the university that has numerous inaccuracies. For Wilson's and Hershaw's research, see Bradford, "Report from the City of Washington"; B. R. Wilson, "General Summary"; and Hershaw, "Social and Physical Progress."

47. *Mortality among Negroes in Cities*, 49.

48. E. Harris, "Physical Condition of the Race."

49. Women made up one-third of the forty-five researchers listed by name for the second Atlanta University study, the findings of which were published by the Bureau of Labor. See *Social and Physical Condition of Negroes in Cities*, app. A. Also see King, "Intemperance as a Cause of Mortality"; Bass, "Poverty as a Cause of Mortality"; Laney, "General Conditions of Mortality"; "Resolutions Adopted by the Conference"; A. H. Logan, "Prenatal and Hereditary Influences"; Butler, "Need of Day Nurseries"; Bass, "Need of Kindergartens." Laney was founder of the Haines Normal and Industrial Institute in Augusta, Georgia; Logan had served as the "Lady Principal" of Tuskegee Institute. See Patton, s.v. "Laney, Lucy Craft"; A. L. Alexander, s.v. "Logan, Adella Hunt." For the programs of the general Atlanta University Conference and the Mothers Meetings, see Du Bois, *Negro in Business*, 47–49; Du Bois, *College-Bred Negro*, 115; and Du Bois, *Negro Common School*, i–ii. For a full discussion of black women's participation in the Atlanta University conferences, see chapter 3.

Du Bois's statement that he took over the Atlanta University conferences before the second conference is incorrect. He was hired during the summer of 1897 and arrived in late December, five months before the third conference. See D. L. Lewis, *W. E. B. Du Bois, 1868–1919*, 198–99, 213–17; Du Bois, *Autobiography*, 214–15; Means, "Review of the Atlanta University Conferences and Social Studies," 9–11.

50. In early editions of Whittier's poetry the black boy is quoted as saying, "Massa, Tell 'em we're rising!" but after Wright wrote to Whittier saying that he never used the term "Massa" after Emancipation, it was changed to "General." Compare Whittier, "Howard at Atlanta," in *Complete Poetical Works of John Greenleaf Whittier*, 353, to the poem as it appears in *The Complete Writings of John Greenleaf Whittier*, 264–66. See also E. R. Haynes, *Black Boy of Atlanta*, 13–15; F. R. Wilson, "Introduction," xxviii–xxix; F. R. Wilson, s.v. "Wright Sr., R. R."; Pat-

ton, "Major Richard Robert Wright, Sr. and Black Higher Education in Georgia, 1880–1920."

51. E. R. Haynes, *Black Boy of Atlanta*, 84; Du Bois, *Autobiography*, 214; Spady, s.v. "Wright Sr., Richard Robert"; R. R. Wright Sr. to W. E. B. Du Bois, Feb. 20, 1936, in Du Bois, *Correspondence*, 2:130; *Atlanta University Bulletin* (June 1895): Bumstead qtd. on 7.

52. Du Bois, *Darkwater*, 20.

53. Du Bois to Carroll Wright, Feb. 18, May 5, June 14, 1897; Du Bois, *Autobiography*, 202–4, 213–19; Du Bois, *Darkwater*, 82.

54. Du Bois, *Dusk of Dawn*, 63–66; Du Bois, *Autobiography*, 209–10, 214–15.

55. Scruggs, s.v. "Crummell, Alexander"; Du Bois, *Souls of Black Folk*, chap. 12; Du Bois, *Dusk of Dawn*, 108; D. L. Lewis, *W. E. B. Du Bois, 1868–1919*, 44, 161–70; Crummell, *Destiny and Race*, 3–19, 90–91, 258–302; [W.] A. Davis, *Leadership, Love and Aggression*, 106–13.

56. Du Bois, *Souls of Black Folk*, 177, chap. 3.

57. Crummell, *Destiny and Race*, 37, 274, 293–95.

58. Crummell, "Attitude of the American Mind Toward the Negro Intellect," 13, 14. See also "Letter from Mr. R. R. Wright, President of Georgia State Industrial College"; "Address of President R. R. Wright"; Patton, "Major Richard Robert Wright, Sr. and Black Higher Education in Georgia, 1880–1920," 405–7, 430–33.

59. Crummell, "Attitude of the American Mind Toward the Negro Intellect," 13–14.

60. Du Bois, "Conservation of Races," 5.

61. Ibid., 5, 15.

62. Crummell, "No. 2 Character."

63. Miller, "Radicals and Conservatives," 15–17, 27–29, quotation on 15; Winston, s.v. "Miller, Kelly," 436; Meier, *Negro Thought in America, 1880–1915*, 214–17.

64. Du Bois, *Darkwater*, 20–21.

65. Rudwick, "W. E. B. Du Bois as a Sociologist," 45–47; Du Bois, "Negroes of Farmville, Virginia"; Du Bois, "Negro in the Black Belt"; Du Bois, "Negro Landholder of Georgia"; Du Bois, *Negro in Business*; Du Bois, *College-Bred Negro*; Du Bois, *Negro Common School*. Du Bois's study of black farmers would be published as "The Negro Farmer," in 1904, and reprinted in 1906.

66. Du Bois, *Negro Artisan*, 96, original emphasis.

67. "Proceedings of the Triennial Reunion of the Hampton Alumni Association," in *Washington Papers*, 3:322–47. The title of the discussion at the alumni session was "Is the Negro Holding His Own in Skilled Labor?" (see *Washington Papers*, 3:336–39). See also B. T. Washington, "Signs of Progress among the Negroes"; and "Speech Delivered before the New England Women's Club, Boston, Jan. 27 (1890)," in *Washington Papers*, 3:25–32.

68. Du Bois, *Negro Artisan*, 153–78. For studies that describe black trade unionists along the lines set in *The Negro Artisan*, see, for example, National Urban League, *Negro Membership in American Labor Unions*, compiled by the NUL's

Department of Research and Investigations; and C. S. Johnson, *Economic Status of Negroes*, 8–13, 16, 46–47.

69. S. M. Sexton to W. E. B. Du Bois, Feb. 22, 1903, in Du Bois, *Correspondence*, 1:50.

70. James A. Cable to W. E. B. Du Bois, Feb. 26, 1903, and reply, n.d., in Du Bois, *Correspondence*, 1:51–52.

71. Du Bois, *Negro Artisan*, 179, 188.

72. See, for example, New Jersey Bureau of Statistics of Labor and Industries, "Negro in Manufacturing and Mechanical Industries."

73. Du Bois, *Negro Artisan*, 14–15.

74. Ibid., 21–23.

75. Ibid., 78–79, 62–63. Du Bois did find two new approaches worthy of praise, a postgraduate trade school recently begun at Hampton Institute and the industrial settlement that his friend Henry Benson established at Kolgia, Alabama.

76. Du Bois, *Negro Artisan*, 78–82. From the mid-1890s through World War I, Atlanta University received support in the amount of $1,000 to $2,000 per year from the John F. Slater Fund to offer industrial courses. The Atlanta University conferences were run on limited budgets and at a level of financial support that was lower than that allocated to the University Quartet. The industrial program received more than twice as much funding from the John F. Slater Fund as did the Atlanta University conferences. See Financial Statements of Atlanta University, 1895/1896, 1920/1921, Atlanta University.

77. Those of his essays that would be reworked into *The Souls of Black Folk* include Du Bois, "Strivings of the Negro People"; Du Bois, "Negro Schoolmaster in the New South"; Du Bois, "Religion of the American Negro"; Du Bois, "Freedmen's Bureau"; Du Bois, "Negro as He Really Is"; Du Bois, "Relation of the Negro to the Whites in the South"; Du Bois, "Evolution of Negro Leadership"; and Du Bois, "Of the Training of Black Men."

78. *American Journal of Sociology* 8 (Mar. 1903): 854; *Nation* (Mar. 5, 1903): 186–87; *Outlook* (Mar. 7, 1903); *South Atlantic Quarterly* (Apr. 1903); *Boston Herald*, Feb. 24, 1903, microfilm, W. E. B. Du Bois Papers (hereafter cited Du Bois Papers), University of Massachusetts, Amherst.

79. Commons, *Trade Unionism and Labor Problems*, 349–70; New Jersey Bureau of Labor Statistics, "Negro in Manufacturing and Mechanical Industries"; John R. Commons to W. E. B. Du Bois, Feb. 27, 1905, and reply, n.d., Du Bois Papers, University of Massachusetts, Amherst.

80. The first five years of the conference cost $1,266, or an average of $253 yearly. From 1901 to 1910, $12,564 was expended on the Atlanta University Conference studies, a cost that was partially offset by $4,000 in grants from the John F. Slater Fund and much smaller amounts in sales of the studies. Financial Statements of Atlanta University, 1896–1921, Atlanta University. See also Du Bois, "Atlanta Conferences"; Du Bois, *Autobiography*, 199, 222–25, 228.

2. Creating a Cadre of Segregated Scholars

1. G. E. Haynes, "Lamp of Sacrifice," 8–10, 12–13, quotation on 13.

2. Wright Jr., preface to *Eighty-Seven Years*; Bond, *Black American Scholars*, 53.

3. Wright Jr., *Eighty-seven Years*, 37, 32; Bond, *Black American Scholars*, 53–54.

4. Du Bois, *Dusk of Dawn*, 37.

5. Wright Jr., "The Negro in Chicago," 553.

6. Most historical accounts of the development of black sociology at the University of Chicago begin two decades after Wright Jr., Work, and Haynes were students. See, for example, Bulmer, *Chicago School of Sociology*; B. A. Jones, "Tradition of Sociology Teaching in Black Colleges," 135–36; Lyman, *Black American in Sociological Thought*, 27–70. Two scholars who briefly discuss R. R. Wright Jr. are J. R. Grossman, *Land of Hope*, 1–3, and Christopher R. Reed, *"All the World Is Here": The Black Presence at White City*, 67, 82–83, 97.

7. See "Student Life at Chicago," an article that might have been written by John Hope, a new professor of English at Atlanta Baptist College who, like the anonymous author, had attended the University of Chicago in the summer quarter of 1898. Other mentions of students at the University of Chicago include "Baptist College," and "Hampton Incidents," the latter noting a visit by Chicago university students to Hampton. See also Goodspeed, *History of the University of Chicago*; Storr, *Harper's University*.

8. Goodspeed, *History of the University of Chicago*, 193; Bullock, *History of Negro Education in the South*, 97–100. Robyn Muncy contrasts the effect on women graduate students of the examination systems of the University of Chicago and Harvard. Harvard only allowed women to take their exam in three cities. See Muncy, *Creating a Female Dominion in American Reform, 1890–1935*, 8.

9. Maxine Hunsinger Sullivan, registrar of the University of Chicago, correspondence to the author, Dec. 8, 1995, Feb. 12, 1996, including Elizabeth A. Ross's application for the Graduate School of the University of Chicago, June 22, 1905, in the Office of the University Registrar; Goggin, *Carter G. Woodson*, 13, 19–20. Another Woodson biographer, Patricia W. Romero, states that Woodson also attended the University of Chicago in the summer term of 1903. See Romero, "Carter G. Woodson," 32–33, 53–54. Woodson's class background was more similar to Monroe Work's than to R.R. Wright Jr.'s. Both were free-born younger siblings of freed parents whose high school education did not begin until young adulthood.

10. W. L. Cash, "Study of Sociology," 3–5.

11. R. W. Logan, s.v. "Laney, Lucy Craft"; Bannister, *Sociology and Scientism*, 32–41; D. Ross, *Origins of American Social Science*, 224–29; Kuklick, "Organization of Social Sciences in the United States."

12. Tollman, "Study of Sociology in Institutions of Learning in the United States, II," includes a listing of all colleges and universities offering sociology courses. No southern white colleges are listed, but Fisk and Atlanta are. See also "Sociology in

Southern Colleges"; "Announcement of Summer School at Fisk"; Rouse, *Lugenia Burns Hope*, 14–17, 23–29.

13. Spear, *Black Chicago*, 48.

14. Roberts, "George Edmund Haynes," 98–99; Wright Jr., *Eighty-Seven Years*, 37–38, 56; McMurry, *Recorder of the Black Experience*, 17.

15. Wright Jr. was living in Divinity Hall in the summer of 1904. See microfilm, Reel 2, F-0218, Du Bois Papers, University of Massachusetts, Amherst. Wright Jr., *Eighty-seven Years*, 132–34; Romero, "Carter G. Woodson," 64; Fitzpatrick, *Endless Crusade*, 182, 173–90; Sophonisba Breckinridge to Edith Abbott, June 28, 1907, Breckinridge Family Papers, LOC. At the time she was excluded from the University of Chicago dormitory, Georgiana Simpson was forty-one years old (see Johnson, s.v. "Simpson, Georgiana"). Muncy, *Creating a Female Dominion in American Reform, 1890–1935*, 68–74; John Hope to Frank J. Miller, May 24, 1911, and reply June 2, 1911, microfilm, John and Lugenia Burns Hope Papers, Atlanta University; W. E. B. Du Bois to Sophonisba Breckinridge, Aug. 6, Aug. 14, 1914, Du Bois Papers, University of Massachusetts, Amherst; Sophonisba Breckinridge to Du Bois, Aug. 14, Aug. 19, 1914, Breckinridge Family Papers, LOC. The historian John W. Davis became the president of West Virginia Collegiate Institute (later West Virginia State College for Negroes). In this capacity he hired Carter G. Woodson, Abram L. Harris, A. A. Taylor, Francis Sumner, and other black social scientists and historians to develop the college department. On Davis, see Meier and Rudwick, *Black History and the Historical Profession, 1915–1980*, 27; Goggin, *Carter G. Woodson*, 53–55. Mordecai Johnson became the president of Howard University, the first black person to hold that post. See R. W. Logan, *Howard University*, 248–251. See also R. W. Logan, s.v. "Hope, John."

16. Wright Jr., "Industrial Condition of Negroes in Chicago"; Spear, *Black Chicago*, 11–49; Drake and Cayton, *Black Metropolis*, vol. 1; Philpot, *Slum and the Ghetto*, 116–35.

17. Willcox, "Negro Population."

18. Drake and Cayton, *Black Metropolis* 2:399; Spear, *Black Chicago*, 58–71, 95–96, 101–106; J. R. Grossman, *Land of Hope*, 140–43; "Fisk Club of Chicago."

19. Wright Jr., *Eighty-seven Years*, 38, 40–41; McMurry, *Recorder of the Black Experience*, 22–23. Until 1911 the summer sessions were the most heavily enrolled sessions at the University of Chicago, attracting about twice as many students as the fall and winter sessions. Goodspeed, *History of the University of Chicago*, 392–95.

20. Wright Jr. *Eighty-seven Years*, 30, 32, 53, 186, 200–201; McMurry, *Recorder of the Black Experience*, 8–17, 21–24.

21. Handwritten record of James R. L. Diggs, Special Collections Illinois Wesleyan University Library; Aug. 25, 1997, letter to the author from Robert L. Mowery, Archivist and Special Collections Librarian, Illinois Wesleyan University. See also Allan, "History of the Non-residential Degree Program at Illinois Wesleyan University, 1873–1910."

22. Handwritten record of James R. L. Diggs. Illinois Wesleyan University was one of forty-five universities in the United States at the turn of the century that

offered more than three courses in sociology according to Tollman, "Study of Sociology". Illinois Wesleyan's nonresidence program was chiefly for the clergy and had outside examiners, reading lists, and a required defense. The Fisk University graduate A. O. Coffin received a doctorate in biology in this program in 1889. Allan, "History of the Non-residential Degree Program at Illinois Wesleyan University, 1873–1910."

23. A copy of J. R. L. Diggs's dissertation has not been located, telephone conversation of author with Dr. Robert Mowery, archivist, Illinois Wesleyan University, Aug. 19, 1997; Burkett, *Black Redemption*, 99–102.

24. Taylor qtd. in McMurry, *Recorder of the Black Experience*, 18–19; Work, "Crime among the Negroes of Chicago." Work regarded this as the first article by a black scholar published in the *American Journal of Sociology*.

25. McMurry, *Recorder of the Black Experience*, 21, 24–29.

26. McMurry, *Recorder of the Black Experience*, 23; Wright Jr., *Eighty-seven Years*, 67, 94–95; Spear, *Black Chicago*, 63, 95–96; Wills, "Reverdy C. Ransom"; Lasch-Quinn, *Black Neighbors*, 68; Morris, "Black Advocates of the Social Gospel"; Morris, "Richard R. Wright Jr.," 24; Lindley, "Neglected Voices and Praxis in the Social Gospel"; Philpot, *Slum and the Ghetto*, 318.

27. Wright Jr., *Eighty-seven Years*, 94, 148, 180, 122.

28. Wright Jr., *Eighty-seven Years*, 94–96, 148; Invitation to Inter-Collegiate Banquet and Reception at the Institutional Church, 3825 Dearborn Street, Chicago, n.d., microfilm, Reel 2, F-0218, Du Bois Papers, University of Massachusetts, Amherst.

29. Work and the Editor, "Middle West, Illinois"; McMurry, *Recorder of the Black Experience*, 40–41; Wright Jr., *Eighty-seven Years*, 96, 204.

30. Work, "Negro Real Estate Owners of Chicago"; McMurry, *Recorder of the Black Experience*, 29–30, 37–46. The University of Chicago required three years of residence for the Ph.D. but most likely would have counted some of Work's five years of residence. He would have had to take some additional courses, however, for the doctorate, as well as write a dissertation, and McMurry says that he was anxious to have full time employment. See Work, "Negroes of Warsaw, Georgia"; Work, "Negro Church and the Community."

31. In addition to his conference presentation "Crime in Savannah as compared with Chicago, Illinois," Work had two studies published in the 1904 Atlanta University study. See Work, "Ninth Atlanta Conference"; Work, "Crime in Cities"; Proctor and Work, "Atlanta and Savannah," 18–32. His contribution to the 1906 study was a critique of the brain size studies that purported to prove the inherent mental differences between Negro and white brains. See Du Bois, *Health and Physique of the Negro American*, 24–27.

32. Work was among the first U.S. social scientists to take seriously the study of Africa and of African American folk culture. For his studies of Africa and African American folk culture. See Work, "African Family as an Institution"; Work, "African Medicine Man"; Work, "African System of Writing"; Work, "African Agriculture"; Work, "Some Geechee Folklore"; Work, "Folk Tales from Students in the Georgia

State College"; Work, "Folk Tales from Students in Tuskegee Institute, Alabama"; Work, "Some Parallelisms in the Development of Africans and Other Races"; McMurry, *Recorder of the Black Experience*, 90–96; *Tuskegee Messenger,* Mar. 9, 1929, qtd. in McMurry, *Recorder of the Black Experience,* 7; Guzman, "Monroe Nathan Work and His Contributions," 436–39, 449–51; McMurry, *Recorder of the Black Experience,* 7, 48–55, 71–76, 118–32. Nine editions of *The Negro Year Book and Annual Encyclopedia of the Negro* were published under Work's editorship between 1913 and 1938. See Work, *Bibliography of the Negro in Africa and America.*

33. Work, "Negro's Industrial Problem"; Work, "Secret Societies as Factors in the Social and Economic Life of the Negro"; Work, "Sociology in the Common Schools"; E. J. Scott, *Negro Migration during the War*; Work, "Effects of the War on Southern Labor"; Work, "Negro Migration in 1916–1917"; Work, "South's Labor Problem"; Work, "Negro Migration Changes in Rural Organization and Population of the Cotton Belt"; Work, "Racial Factors and Economic Forces in Land Tenure in the South, 1860–1930"; Work, "Problems of Adjustment of Race and Class in the South"; Guzman, "Monroe Nathan Work," 439–40, 442–49, 454–57; McMurry, *Recorder of the Black Experience,* 74–77, 78–84. See also Work, "Some Negro Members of Reconstruction Conventions and Legislatures and of Congress"; Work, "Additional Information and Corrections in Reconstruction Records"; Work, "Negro in Business and the Professions."

34. Wright Jr. *Eighty-seven Years,* 42–43. These courses may have been Hebrew Philosophy and Ethics, taught by Harper in the autumn quarter of 1899 and the summer of 1900 and open only to those who could read Hebrew fluently, or Prophecy and the History of Prophecy, which Harper taught in the winter quarter of 1899 and the summer of 1899. See *Annual Register of the University of Chicago, 1897–1898, 1898–1899.*

35. Wright, *Eighty-seven Years,* 42–43, 88–90, 149; *The Annual Register of the University of Chicago 1898–1899,* 342, 337–45, 210–20, quotation on 342; *Annual Register of the University of Chicago 1897–1898,* 335, 210; Bannister, *Sociology and Scientism,* 38; Wright Jr., "Industrial Condition of Negroes in Chicago."

36. Wright Jr., *Eighty-seven Years,* 90–91, 149.

37. Ibid., 30–31, quotation on 27; Bond, *Black American Scholars,* 53.

38. Wright Jr., *Eighty-seven Years,* 31–32, 43–45, 98–99, 130, quotation on 105; Carroll D. Wright to R. R. Wright Jr., Dec. 12, Dec. 20, 1901, Jan. 13, Nov. 11, 1902, and Carroll D. Wright to C. R. Henderson, Dec. 12, 1901, Records of the Bureau of Labor Statistics, Records of the Department of Commerce and Labor, Copies of Letters Sent, 1889–1906, Box 2, RG 257, NARA.

39. Wright Jr., *Eighty-seven Years,* 99, quotation on 115.

40. In his autobiography Wright Jr. identifies his 1904 University of Chicago master's thesis as "The Historicity of the Acts of the Apostles," 310. However, a Feb. 12, 1996, letter to the author from Maxine Sullivan, registrar of the University of Chicago, states that the title was "An Introduction to the Acts of the Apostles."

41. Wright Jr., *Eighty-seven Years,* 47–48, 99, 114–15.

42. Wright Jr., *Eighty-seven Years,* 100–15, 96, 108, quotations on 104, 105, 115; Spear, *Black Chicago,* 106; J. R. Grossman, *Land of Hope,* 230. In his autobiography R. R. Wright Jr. claimed that his survey, which has apparently not survived, was the direct inspiration for Mary White Ovington's study of blacks in New York, *Half a Man.* See Wright Jr., *Eighty-seven Years,* 47.

43. Wright Jr., *Eighty-seven Years,* 106–8, 111, 115.

44. *Charities* 15 (Oct. 7, 1905).

45. Paul U. Kellogg to Du Bois, May 8, May 15, 1905, and reply, n.d., microfilm, Reel 1, F-541–50, Du Bois Papers, University of Massachusetts, Amherst; Wright Jr., "Negro in Times of Industrial Unrest."

46. Frances Kellor, Inter-Municipal Committee on Household Research, to W. E. B. Du Bois, Feb. 10, 1905, and reply, n.d., microfilm, Reel 2, F-222–223, Du Bois Papers, University of Massachusetts, Amherst; Wright, Jr. *Eighty-seven Years,* 47–48. It is not possible to determine if Kellor and Wright Jr. took any classes together. After leaving the University of Chicago in 1901 without a degree, Kellor studied at the New York School of Philanthropy and Civics and later received fellowships from the College Settlement Association and various women's groups to study women's unemployment in Chicago, Boston, and Philadelphia, which culminated in *Out of Work* (1904). Her first published work, however, was a five-part study of the environmental causes of black criminal behavior. See Fitzpatrick, *Endless Crusade,* 130–35. Why and how Kellor became involved in the selection of Wright Jr. is not clear, but it is likely that her fellowships with the College Settlement Association in Chicago and New York from 1902 to 1904 and her research in Philadelphia caused the College Settlement Association to ask her to assist them in identifying a prospective graduate student. See Kellor, "Criminal Negro"; Kellor, *Out of Work;* Fitzpatrick, *Endless Crusade,* 130–35; Lasch-Quinn, *Black Neighbors,* 17–19.

47. Du Bois to [Francis] Hoggan, Apr. 5, 1907, microfilm, Reel 2, F-0120–0121, Du Bois Papers, University of Massachusetts, Amherst.

48. Wright Jr., *Eighty-seven Years,* 115; *University of Pennsylvania Catalogue* for the years, *1905–1906,* and *1906–1907;* R. R. Wright Jr. transcript, in Wright Jr. Alumni Folder, University of Pennsylvania Archives.

49. R. R. Wright Jr. transcript, in Wright Jr. Alumni Folder, and Carl Kelsey Faculty Records, both at University of Pennsylvania Archives; Wright Jr. *Eighty-seven Years,* 48–49.

50. Wright Jr., *Eighty-seven Years,* 48–49. Presumably George Haynes would have different views on Kelsey's support for black education, calling on Kelsey to help identify students for the Urban League Fellows program. In one response to Haynes's request, Kelsey indicated that he had at the time "four negroes [*sic*] in my graduate work this year. They are unusually able men and women." However, this was a decade after Wright Jr. had been in Kelsey's classes. See Carl Kelsey to George E. Haynes, Feb. 16, 1915, Box 2, Folder 8, George Edmund Haynes Papers, Fisk University, Franklin Library Special Collections and Archives, Nashville, Tennessee (hereafter cited GEH-Fisk).

51. Wright Jr., *Eighty-seven Years,* 48–49.

52. Ibid., 48–49. In addition to the race problems course, Wright Jr. also took the graduate course Social Debtor Classes from Carl Kelsey both terms in 1905–6. Simon Patten, professor of economics, presented Wright Jr.'s dissertation and graduate work for certification. It is not clear whether this reflects Patten's more senior status than Kelsey's or reveals a break between Kelsey and Wright Jr. In addition to being a more senior faculty member at the University of Pennsylvania, Patten was past president of the American Economic Association. See Transcript of R. R. Wright Jr.; Odum, *American Sociology,* 7.

53. Despite Wright Jr.'s contention that Kelsey had never entered the home of a black person and never met a Negro farmer, a folder on Kelsey's career in the University of Pennsylvania Archives indicates that Kelsey spent the summer of 1902 in the South gathering data for his book. It is still possible that Kelsey had in fact never been in a black person's home. See Wright Jr. *Eighty-seven Years* 48–49; Carl Kelsey Folder, University of Pennsylvania Archives.

54. Wright Jr., *Eighty-seven Years,* 26–27, 48–49, 158–60; D. Ross, *Origins of American Social Science;* Bannister, *Sociology and Scientism.* For earlier analyses of American social scientists, see Haskell, *Emergence of Professional Social Science;* and Furner, *Advocacy and Objectivity.*

55. Kelsey, who completed his dissertation at the University of Pennsylvania in 1902 and began teaching there as an assistant professor in 1903, became a full professor in 1907. His major book, *The Negro Farmer,* conforms to stereotypes of the time about the inherent incompetency of black farmers. See Carl Kelsey Faculty Records, University of Pennsylvania Archives; Kelsey, *Negro Farmer.*

56. Perlman, "Stirring the White Conscience," 30–31.

57. Du Bois, *Autobiography,* 130.

58. Perlman, "Stirring the White Conscience," 28–31; Roberts, "Crucible for a Vision," 56; quotation in copy of letter dated Mar. 28, 1909, from William Graham Sumner, Division of Negro Economics Files, RG 174, NARA.

59. Roberts, "Crucible for a Vision," 56–58; Perlman, "Stirring the White Conscience," 30–31.

60. Frank Sanders was a member of the board of the International Committee of the YMCA. See Perlman, "Stirring the White Conscience," 30–31; G. E. Haynes, "Greatest Convention of Students Ever Held"; Houstoun, "YMCA Conference."

61. George E. Haynes to W. E. B. Du Bois, Apr. 4, 1905, and Du Bois's reply, n.d., Du Bois Papers, University of Massachusetts, Amherst; Hunton, *William Alphaeus Hunton,* 57–58.

62. Perlman, "Stirring the White Conscience," 46–49; I. B. Lindsay, s.v. "Haynes, George Edmund"; Roberts, "Crucible for a Vision," 77; Hunton, *William Alphaeus Hunton,* 57–58, 66.

63. Wright Jr., "Social Work and the Influence of the Negro Church."

64. Eva Bowles and Jessie Sleet worked in New York City and although both had been trained on the job in social work techniques, neither had a certificate or a degree in social work, which was not unusual for the period. Sleet was a nurse with

the Charities Organization Society that initiated the first formal schooling program in social work. Bowles, who worked for the Young Women's Christian Association, had taken courses at the New York School of Philanthropy, which was established in 1898, offering at first only a six-week summer course in social work; by 1903–4 the social work course was a one-year commitment, and in 1910 when it became the New York School of Social Work, it expanded to a two-year course of study. (This is now the Columbia University School of Social Work.) The Chicago School of Civics and Philanthropy was established in 1908; in 1920 it became the University of Chicago School of Social Service Administration. The Chicago school's first black graduate (1914) was Birdye Haynes, George Edmund Haynes's sister. See Wright Jr., "Social Work and the Influence of the Negro Church," 81; N. J. Weiss, *National Urban League, 1910–1940*, 72–73; Parris and Brooks, *Blacks in the City*, 30; Shaw, *What A Woman Ought to Be and to Do*, 142, passim; A. L. Jones, s.v. "Bowles, Eva Del Vakia"; Fitzpatrick, *Endless Crusade*, 166–200; Carlton-LaNey, "Career of Birdye Henrietta Haynes"; Obituary for Birdye H. Haynes.

65. Faculty members who were the most important to George Haynes were Edward T. Devine and Edwin R. Seligman as he indicated in the one-page memoir "Interracial Social Work Begins," Haynes Vertical File, microfiche, NYPLSC.

66. W. E. B. Du Bois to George Edmund Haynes, draft, Feb. 26, 1909, Du Bois Papers, University of Massachusetts, Amherst.

67. Following are the titles of the studies authored by R. R. Wright Jr.: "The Middle West, Ohio"; "The Negroes of Xenia, Ohio: A Social Study"; "Memorandum by R. R. Wright, Jr.: Mortality in Cities"; "Housing and Sanitation in Relation to Mortality of Negroes"; "The Migration of the Negro to the North"; "The Negro in Chicago"; "Forty Years of Negro Progress"; "Social Work and the Influence of the Negro Church"; "Homeownership and Savings among Negroes of Philadelphia"; "The Economic Condition of Negroes in the North," part II: "Rural Communities in Indiana," part III: "Negro Communities in New Jersey," part IV: "Negro Governments in the North," and part VI: "Negroes in Business in the North"; "Recent Improvements in Housing among Negroes in the North"; "The Skilled Mechanic in the North"; "The Northern Negro and Crime"; "Poverty among Northern Negroes"; *The Negro in Pennsylvania: A Study in Economic History*; "The Negro in Unskilled Labor"; and "One Hundred Negro Steel Workers."

68. The major professional association National Conference of Charities and Corrections changed its name in to National Conference of Social Work. *Charities* changed its name to *The Survey* several years after the special issue on blacks in the North. These name changes reflected the transformation of benevolent work into a profession and the attendant decreased emphasis on charity and focus on developing scientific methods of social work, including case work and social surveys.

69. Ovington, *Walls Came Tumbling Down*, 53. Other white social workers or academics who attended the Atlanta University conferences were Washington Gladden (eighth), Franz Boas (eleventh), and Jane Addams (thirteenth). In 1906, Boas served along with Du Bois and Wright Jr. as the resolutions committee. Du Bois,

Negro Church, 204; Du Bois, *Health and Physique of the Negro American,* 110; Du Bois, *Negro American Family,* 152.

70. *Charities* and *The Survey* mentioned social work among blacks in most of its issues after 1905 and published a number of articles by black authors. The *Annals* published articles by and about blacks much less frequently than *Charities* but devoted entire issues to blacks in 1913 and 1928: "The Negro's Progress in Fifty Years" and "The American Negro."

71. *Charities* 15 (Oct. 7, 1905): 1.

72. Lasch-Quinn, *Black Neighbors,* 11–13, situates the *Charities* issue in the mainstream of early twentieth-century progressive social reform.

73. Paul U. Kellogg to W. E. B. Du Bois, 15 May 1905, and Du Bois's reply, n.d., Du Bois Papers, University of Massachusetts, Amherst. At this time Hershaw and Du Bois were the publishers of the magazine *Horizon* and in the process of founding the Niagara Movement (Hershaw, "Negro Press in America").

74. F. B. Williams, "Social Bonds in the 'Black Belt' of Chicago," 44; Hendricks, s.v. "Williams, Fannie Barrier"; Spear, *Black Chicago,* 69–70; Harlan, *Booker T. Washington,* 10, 19, 98; Meier, *Negro Thought in America, 1880–1915,* 238–39.

75. Boas, "Negro and the Demands of Modern Life."

76. Ibid., 87.

77. "Opportunities and Responsibility."

78. *Charities* 15 (Oct. 7, 1905): 2.

79. See, for example, Bulkley, "Race Prejudice as Viewed from an Economic Standpoint"; Bulkley, "School as a Social Center"; Bulkley, "Industrial Conditions of Negroes in New York City"; Miller, "Professional and Skilled Occupations."

80. Ex-slave Bulkley's 1893 degree was in Ancient Languages.

81. Browne, "Training of the Negro Laborer in the North," 118; Harlan, *Booker T. Washington,* 63–83. Browne was the secretary of the Committee of Twelve for the Negro Race, a group led by Booker T. Washington after Du Bois resigned to form the more militant Niagara Movement. In the speech for the American Academy of Political and Social Science, Browne said that Washington had been sent by God to the colored race and described his school at Cheney, Pennsylvania, as a "Christian industrial Tuskegee." See Browne, "Training of the Negro Laborer in the North," 127. A biographer has asserted that although Browne was opposed to Du Bois's philosophy and maintained close ties to Washington, he was an independent conservative who was "no political and educational lackey of [Booker T.] Washington." See McGuire, s.v. "Browne, Hugh M."

82. Du Bois, "The Black North, A Social Study...."; Wright Jr., "Negro in Times of Industrial Unrest."

83. Miller, "Economic Handicap of the Negro in the North," 84; Ovington, "Negro in the Trade Unions in New York," 91.

84. Commons, *Races and Immigrants in America,* 145–49; Cherry, "Racial Thought and the Early Economics Profession," 149n. The most detailed account of Commons's views on so-called backward races, which included Chinese, Japanese, Russians, Mexicans, Bohemians, and others, as well as blacks, is contained in an

unpublished paper by Mark Aldrich entitled "Backward Races and the American Social Order." Mark Aldrich was kind enough to share his paper and tell me about Cherry's when I was a graduate student.

85. Walter Willcox presented "Negro Criminality" as an address at the 1899 American Social Science Association; it was then published in the *American Journal of Social Science* and reprinted in *Studies in the American Race Problem*; Du Bois, *Notes on Negro Crime*, 9–11; Du Bois to Walter Willcox, Mar. 29, 1904, in Du Bois, *Correspondence*, 1:75; Miller, "Crime among Negroes"; Booker T. Washington to Walter Willcox, Sept. 16, 1899, in *Washington Papers*, 5:205–6; "Letter from Mr. R. R. Wright, President of Georgia State Industrial College"; Aldrich, "Progressive Economists and Scientific Racism," 4–5, 10–11; Booker T. Washington to Jacob G. Schmidlapp, Jan. 12, 1910, in *Washington Papers*, 10:260–61.

86. Walter Willcox to Du Bois, Mar. 13, 1904, in Du Bois, *Correspondence*, 1:74–75.

87. Booker T. Washington to Walter Willcox, Nov. 9, 1904, and reply, and Washington to Schmidlapp, Jan. 12, 1910, in *Washington Papers*, 8:125–26, 131, and 10:260–61; Aldrich, "Progressive Economists and Scientific Racism."

88. Aldrich, "Progressive Economists and Scientific Racism," 3–4, 8, 12–13; Hoffman, "Race Traits and Tendencies of the American Negro"; Miller, "Review of Hoffman's 'Race Traits and Tendencies of the American Negro'"; Du Bois, review of "Race Traits and Tendencies of the American Negro"; Tillinghast, "Negro in Africa and America," esp. 402, 584–91.

89. Willcox to Du Bois, Mar. 13, 1904.

90. Du Bois, to Willcox, Mar. 29, 1904; in Du Bois, *Correspondence*, 1:75.

91. E. Harris, "Physical Condition of the Race; Whether Dependent Upon Social Conditions or Environment"; *Proceedings of the Hampton Negro Conference*, 27–40.

92. Booker T. Washington to Oswald Garrison Villard, Aug. 7, 1910, in *Washington Papers*, 9:614–15; Booker T. Washington to Carroll D. Wright, Mar. 26, 1907, in *Washington Papers*, 9:124.

93. Walter Willcox to W. E. B. Du Bois, Jan. 8, 1902, Du Bois Papers, University of Massachusetts, Amherst; Willcox et al., "Economic Position of the Negro."

94. Stone, "Economic Future of the Negro"; Washington to Carroll Wright, Mar. 26, 1907, and Washington to Villard, Aug. 7, 1910, in *Washington Papers*, 9:614–15, and 10:363–64; Harlan, *Booker T. Washington*, 259–60.

95. Du Bois, "Economic Future of the Negro"; Du Bois, *Autobiography*, 295–96; A. H. Stone, "Economic Future of the Negro."

96. [J. H. H.], "American Economic Association at Baltimore."

97. *Nation* (Feb. 1, 1906): 97.

98. Rudwick, "W. E. B. Du Bois as a Sociologist," 47–52.

99. Walter Willcox to Du Bois, Jan. 8, 1902, Apr. 9, 1902, Mar. 13, 1904, Du Bois Papers; Du Bois to Walter Willcox, Mar. 29, 1904, in Du Bois, *Correspondence*, 1:75; Du Bois to Willcox, reply to Nov. 5, 1904, n.d., Du Bois Papers; Walter Will-

cox to Booker T. Washington, Nov. 9, 1904, and reply, in *Washington Papers*, 8:125–26; Aldrich, "Progressive Economists and Scientific Racism," 6, 12–13.

100. By early 1907 Booker T. Washington had come to believe that Stone was unqualified, but his opposition to funding his research was also fueled by Washington's fear of Stone's pet project to replace black labor with Italians. See Booker T. Washington to Carroll D. Wright, Mar. 26, 1907, Washington to Oswald G. Villard, Aug. 7, 1910, Washington to Edgar G. Murphy, Aug. 29, 1908, in *Washington Papers*, 9:233–34, 614–15; Harlan, *Booker T. Washington*, 259–60; B. T. Washington, review of "The Negro in the New World," in *Washington Papers*, 10:364.

101. W. E. B. Du Bois to Andrew Carnegie, May 22, 1906, in Du Bois, *Correspondence*, 1:121–22; Du Bois, *Autobiography*, 225. Andrew Carnegie to William H. Baldwin Jr., Apr. 17, 1903, two letters, Harlan, *Booker T. Washington*, 133–37.

102. Aldrich, "Progressive Economists and Scientific Racism."

103. Du Bois, *Economic Cooperation among Negro Americans*; Du Bois, *Dusk of Dawn*, 84.

104. Du Bois, *Autobiography*, 225.

105. Du Bois, *Dusk of Dawn*, 85–86; Du Bois, *Autobiography*, 226–27; Wright Jr., *Eighty-seven Years*, 158. David L. Lewis lays out the potentially explosive content of the study. See D. L. Lewis, *W. E. B. Du Bois*, 354–56.

106. Du Bois, *Autobiography*, 228.

107. Ibid., 228–29; D. L. Lewis, *W. E. B. Du Bois*, 333.

108. Du Bois, *Autobiography*, 231–32, 252–53.

109. Wright Jr. was appointed pastor of a small church in nearby Conshohocken, Pennsylvania, in 1907, which allowed him to continue his research and remain active in Philadelphia reform circles. His doctoral thesis was accepted by Carl Kelsey on May 29, 1911, after Wright Jr. had submitted a certificate attesting to his reading ability of French on May 15, 1911. Wright Jr., *Eighty-seven Years*, 48, 159–61, 168, 213–24; Transcript of R. R. Wright Jr.

110. Perlman, "Stirring the White Conscience," 50–53.

111. Ibid., 53–61; N. J. Weiss, *National Urban League, 1910–1940*, 30–33; G. E. Haynes, *Negro at Work in New York City*, 3n124. Inabel Burns Lindsay identifies Haynes as "the first of his race to be awarded the Ph.D. degree (in economics): from Columbia University." See I. B. Lindsay, s.v. "Haynes, George Edmund," 298. Haynes's doctorate did include economics in the title, but his course work and research was primarily in sociology. Haynes never described himself as an economist; he did call himself a sociologist.

112. G. E. Haynes, *Negro at Work in New York City*, 7; N. J. Weiss, *National Urban League, 1910–1940*, 33–34, 40–41; Roberts, "Crucible for a Vision," 62–63; Parris and Brooks, *Blacks in the City*, 26. Bulkley also cofounded the NAACP.

113. N. J. Weiss, *National Urban League, 1910–1940*, 74–75.

114. G. E. Haynes, "Co-operation with Colleges in Securing and Training Negro Social Workers for Urban Centers."

115. Ibid.

116. N. J. Weiss, *National Urban League, 1910–1940*, 74–75; *Fisk University Catalogue, 1910–1911*, 39, 41–45.

117. N. J. Weiss, *National Urban League, 1910–1940*, 74–75, 77–79; National Urban League *Bulletin* (Nov. 1915): 12, 30; E. K. Jones, "The Way Opens"; National Urban League, *Thirty-Fifth Annual Report*, 11; National Urban League *Bulletin* (Jan. 1921): 1–6. Descriptions of courses and requirements can be found in *Fisk University Catalogue, 1910–1911*, 28–29, 39–45, and *Fisk University Catalogue, 1911–1912*, 31–34, 47–50.

118. C. S. Johnson, *Negro College Graduate*, 155–57, 312; Parris and Brooks, *Blacks in the City*, 191. Two of the first three directors of the Atlanta School of Social Work, Garrie Moore and Forrester B. Washington, were NUL fellows, as was Inabel Burns Lindsay, organizer and first director of the Howard University School of Social Work. E. Franklin Frazier, who was the second director of the Atlanta School of Social Work, had worked out of the New York City Urban League branch when undertaking a Russell Sage–funded study of black dock workers. Parris and Brooks, *Blacks in the City*, 192–93; E. L. Ross, "Black Heritage in Social Welfare," 304; R. W. Logan, *Howard University*, 367–70.

3. Black Women, Social Science, and Social Reform from the Turn of the Century to the Great Migration

1. S. E. Frazier, s.v. "Mrs. Wm. E. Matthews (Victoria Earle)."

2. E. A. Ross, "You Must Keep Up or Endure the Dust."

3. Cooper, *Voice from the South*. Cooper also argued that black people would not be free from discrimination until black women were placed on an equal footing with men. See Hadnott, "Mission of the Negro Woman," 7.

4. S. E. Frazier, s.v. "Mrs. Wm. E. Matthews (Victoria Earle)."

5. Arnold, s.v. "Women's Loyal Union of New York and Brooklyn"; F. B. Cash, s.v. "Matthews, Victoria Earle"; F. B. Cash, s.v. "White Rose Mission, New York City"; Terborg-Penn, s.v. "Mossell, Gertrude Bustill"; C. Brown, s.v. "Mossell, Gertrude E. H. Bustill"; Mayors, *Noted Negro Women*, 129–30; E. B. Brown, "Introduction."

6. Wells-Barnett, "Lynch Law in All Its Phases"; Hendricks, s.v. "Wells-Barnett, Ida B."; McMurry, *To Keep the Waters Troubled*, 143–70, 195–96, 213–21.

7. Wells-Barnett, *Red Record*; Wells-Barnett, "Lynch Law in All Its Phases"; Wells-Barnett, *Crusade for Justice*; Hendricks, s.v. "Wells-Barnett, Ida B."

8. Ruffin, "Address before First National Conference of Colored Women, July 29–31, 1895"; Lasch-Quinn, *Black Neighbors*, 119; Salem, s.v. "National Association of Colored Women."

9. E. B. Brown, "Womanist Consciousness"; F. R. Wilson, "'This Past Was Waiting for Me When I Came.'"

10. Forceful articles by the leaders of the National Association of Colored Women argued the merits of their social reforms. See F. B. Williams, "Club Movement among the Colored Women"; Terrell, "Club Work of Colored Women." The

July 1904 issue of *The Voice of the Negro* devoted most of the magazine to eight articles on black women's social activism, including Tuskegee Institute's Margaret M. Washington, the YWCA leader Addie Waites Hunton, and the school founder Nannie Helen Burroughs. Josephine Silone-Yates's article "The National Association of Colored Women" stressed seven years of uplift work directed by the national body that now had twenty-six state branches and claimed fifteen thousand members.

11. F. B. Williams, "Social Bonds in the 'Black Belt' of Chicago"; F. B. Williams, "Colored Women of Chicago."

12. T. W. Hunter, *To 'Joy My Freedom*, 136, 140–41; Shivery, "History of Organized Social Work among Atlanta Negroes, 1890–1935," 4–11; Bass, "Need of Kindergartens"; Butler, "Need of Day Nurseries." James B. Adams gives an account of the Neighborhood Union's "purely scientific" investigation of black schools in Atlanta in "Public Schools of Atlanta." See also Neverdon-Morton, *Afro-American Women of the South and the Advancement of the Race, 1895–1925*, 140–42; Salem, *To Better Our World*. The John and Lugenia Burns Hope Papers in the Atlanta University Archives contain Lugenia Hope's notebooks, research designs, and letters concerning surveys of black neighborhoods in Atlanta.

13. *Atlanta University Catalogue, 1894–1895*, "Alumni," 8; Patton, s.v. "Laney, Lucy Craft"; Logan, s.v. "Laney, Lucy Craft"; "Address before the Women's Meeting."

14. King, "Intemperance as a Cause of Mortality," 26–29.

15. Bass, "Poverty as a Cause of Mortality," 30–31.

16. Miller, "City Negro," 124; Miller, "Surplus Negro Women."

17. Laney, "General Conditions of Mortality," 35, 36.

18. Ibid., 35.

19. Higginbotham, *Righteous Discontent*, 14–15, 185–229. See also Higginbotham, "African-American Women's History and the Metalanguage of Race."

20. *Physical and Social Conditions of Negroes*, 33–34.

21. Gaines, *Uplifting the Race*, 128–51; Silone-Yates, "National Association of Colored Women"; Terrell, "Club Work of Southern Women"; Bruce, "What Education Has Done for Colored Women"; Miller, "Surplus Negro Women."

22. Cooper qtd. in Gaines, *Uplifting the Race*, 138.

23. Ibid.

24. *Social and Physical Condition of Negroes* 69, 31. "On the Campus" first reported that the January meeting of the First Sociological Club of Atlanta was "entertained in the teacher's parlor."

25. A. H. Logan, "Prenatal and Hereditary Influences"; Laney, "Address before the Women's Meeting"; Price, "Friendly Visiting"; King, "Mothers Meetings"; Butler, "Need of Day Nurseries"; Bass, "Need of Kindergartens." Laney's formal paper "Care of Children and Methods of Preventing Infant Mortality" was given during the concluding plenary session and was among several studies not reprinted in the report. See Neverdon-Morton, *Afro-American Women of the South and the Advancement of the Race, 1895–1925*, 141.

26. The experiences of white female social scientists are examined in Muncy, *Creating a Female Dominion in American Reform, 1890–1935*, and Fitzpatrick,

Endless Crusade. An exploration of early black women professionals is found in B. Aptheker, "Quest for Dignity." Wesley, *History of the National Association of Colored Women's Clubs*; E. H. Williams, "National Association of Colored Women"; Fuller, *Pictorial History of the American Negro,* 169, 187; Shaw, *What a Woman Ought to Be and to Do.*

27. Du Bois, *College-Bred Negro,* 54–56. The number of college graduates is from C. S. Johnson, *Negro College Graduate,* 8–9, 66–67, who adapted his from Du Bois, *College-Bred Negro,* 55–56. Breakdowns by gender for black college graduates are not easily available for the twentieth century. Perkins, s.v. "Education."

28. Du Bois, *College-Bred Negro,* 57–63. Du Bois's figure of 2,272 black male college graduates of roughly the same period forms the basis for Johnson's figures (see C. S. Johnson, *Negro College Graduate,* 8–9; also, Richardson, *History of Fisk University, 1865–1946,* 71). The sociologist Charles S. Johnson's 1938 study of black college graduates reported that 2,541 black men and women had earned bachelors degrees between 1826 and 1900. See R. W. Logan, *Howard University,* 370, 367–70, 491.

29. Du Bois, "Negro in the Black Belt." The five correspondents were two Atlanta University graduates, Aletha Howard, a schoolteacher in Dekalb County, Georgia; and Miss J. G. Childs, a native of Marion, Alabama; Miss T. B. Johnson, a native of Covington, Georgia; and two undergraduates, Mr. W. A. Rogers and Miss C. E. Byrdie, who reported on their respective hometowns of Marietta, Georgia, and Athens, Georgia. See Du Bois, *Contributions . . . in Government Publications and Proceedings,* 51a, 57a, 59a, 60a, 62a.

30. "Thesis in Economics." The students assigned these topics were L. I. Mack, class of 1900; C. E. Byrdie, 1899; and R. M. Harris, 1899. Other women's assignments included "Economics of the Plantation" by J. O. Wright, 1899, and "Effect of Indus. Competition on the Freedman" by A. T. Badger.

31. Neverdon-Morton, *Afro-American Women of the South and the Advancement of the Race, 1895–1925,* 38–41. Jessie Fauset to W. E. B. Du Bois, Dec. 26, 1903, Feb. 16, 1905, in Du Bois, *Correspondence,* 1:65–66, 95–96; *University of Pennsylvania Catalogue, 1918–1919,* 691.

32. "Commencement Week: . . . Quiz Club Prize Contest."

33. "Prize Contest" announcement in the form of a letter dated May 15, 1897, from George G. Bradford to M. W. Adams, Dean. There was one first prize of $35, two second prizes of $25, and two third prizes of $15. The third prizes were only open to persons who had not won in previous years. "Commencement Week: . . . Quiz Club Prize Contest." The 1897 program contestants and their topics are listed in *Scroll* (May 1897): 11. Du Bois's specific involvement in the 1897 and 1898 contest is not fully clear. He did not arrive at the university until after the 1897 contest was completed and the 1898 contest was underway. He was one of three faculty members who were designated to approve essay topics of students entering the 1899 contest. See *Atlanta University Bulletin* (Nov. 1898): 2. The topics for the years contests and the past years winners also appear in the *Atlanta University Catalogue, 1896–1899.*

34. *Atlanta University Bulletin* (June 1898): 2–3. George A. Towns, class of 1894, was later a popular faculty member and good friend of Du Bois.

35. *Atlanta University Bulletin* (Feb. 1898): 1; "Our Graduates"; E. R. Haynes, *Black Boy of Atlanta*, 37, 48; Patton, s.v. "Laney, Lucy Craft, 1:694; F. R. Wilson, "Introduction," xxx.

36. "Two Young Women," 2, original emphasis. It was unusual for the *Atlanta University Bulletin* not to mention the names of graduates. According to the catalogue, Mattie Freeman Childs of Marion, Alabama, and Georgia Louise Palmer of Augusta, Georgia, were the two women in the senior class of 1895. See *Atlanta University Catalogue, 1894–1895*, 14.

37. L. I. Mack, "College Woman." Mack was in Du Bois's economics class and wrote a term paper on the credit system. See *Scroll* (Feb. 1899): 8.

38. Howard University's first three women graduates dated from the 1870s when three daughters of a white faculty member graduated. According to Du Bois, eight black women earned bachelors degrees from Howard University between 1872 and 1898, the same total as Atlanta University but Howard's female graduates were spread out over the 25 year period while Atlanta's were concentrated in the last three years. Du Bois, *College-Bred Negro*, 53–57. "Fisk University"; Richardson, *Fisk University*, 49–51, 64–66; F. R. Wilson, "George Haynes."

39. "Fisk University."

40. Murray, "Education of Girls." Maggie J. Murray began to call herself Margaret after her marriage to Booker T. Washington in 1892.

41. E. A. Ross, "You Must Keep Up or Endure the Dust," 8.

42. Hadnott, "Mission of the Negro Woman," 6–7.

43. Childs, "Progress of the Colored Women since 1863," 5; Mary Steward, "Women in Public Life," 1888; Maria Anna Benson, "Thought: the Prime Condition of Progress"; Leonora A. Bowers, "The Anglo-Saxon Element in Modern Civilization," titles found in "Commencement Exercises, 1888," Program, Fisk University Archives.

44. Perkins, "African American Female Elite Sister"; Colson, "Home Work among Negro Women in Chicago." Terrell, "Graduates and Former Students of Washington Colored High School," 225. Terrell maintained that Cora Jackson had the high score on the University of Chicago examination "some years ago" and won a full scholarship.

45. Boris, "Elizabeth Ross Haynes"; F. R. Wilson, "Introduction"; F. R. Wilson, s.v. "Haynes, Elizabeth Ross"; Bogin, s.v. "Haynes, Elizabeth Ross."

46. J. D. Anderson, *Education of Blacks in the South*, 110–13. Alabama had 2,007 black students in private high schools. There were 273 black students in public high schools and 308 in private high schools in Arkansas in 1900, which had a much smaller black population. There were only 17,000 black high school students in the public and private high schools of sixteen southern and border states in 1900, three-quarters of whom were in private school. A large number of these persons enrolled above the elementary level never graduated.

47. Letter from Cornelious Wortendyke Morrow to George E. and Elizabeth R. Haynes, July 7, 1912, Box 3, Folder 29, GEH-Fisk.

48. Elizabeth A. Ross, application for the Graduate School of the University of Chicago, June 22, 1905, in the Office of the University Registrar, and correspondence between Maxine Hunsinger Sullivan, registrar, and the author, Dec. 8, 1995, Feb. 12, 1996.

49. Turner, "Outstanding Fisk Women, Who Have Contributed to the Advancement of the Negro Race."

50. Before her marriage in 1893, Addie Hunton had taught briefly at the vocational school that George Haynes had attended in Normal, Alabama. See Hutson, s.v. "Hunton, Addie D. Waites." I thank Adrienne Lash Jones for graciously sharing her unpublished work on black women in the YWCA with me.

51. "Haynes-Ross"; "Y.W.C.A."; "Notes"; George Edmund Haynes to Birdye Haynes, Mar. 12, 1915; GEH to Clifford Miller Feb. 23, 1915, discusses growing food and raising chickens. Haynes wrote his sister on Apr. 20, 1915, explaining that his wife and son could not visit because of the chickens and the garden. In Birdye Haynes to GEH, May 7, 1915, Haynes's sister agrees to loan him $100 of requested $250. GEH to Birdye Haynes, Oct. 30, 1915, describes plans to raise and sell pigs. Letter from Cornelious Wortendyke Morrow to GEH, July 2, 1912, mentions Elizabeth Ross Haynes's pregnancy, Box 3, Birdye Haynes Folder, Miller/Morrow Folder, GEH-Fisk.

52. C. S. Johnson, *Negro College Graduate*, 8–11; H. W. Greene, *Holders of Doctorates among American Negroes*; Bowles, "Opportunities for the Educated Colored Woman." There are no breakdowns by gender of black people who earned master's degrees before 1940.

53. Sadie Mosell Alexander, Georgiana Simpson, and Eva Dykes earned doctorates within eight days of one another in June 1921 (see "The Higher Education of Negroes," 105, cover; and "Achievement," 223). Both Simpson and Dykes were later hired, in 1931 and 1929, respectively, by Howard University president Mordecai Johnson (letter to author from Andrew Hannah, Associate Registrar, University of Chicago, Mar. 9, 1998). Anna Julia Cooper earned her degree in 1925 from the Sorbonne (see Hutchinson, s.v. "Cooper, Anna Julia"). For Dykes and Simpson, respectively, see also "Eva Beatrice Dykes," in the Black Women Oral History Project Records, Schlesinger Library, Radcliffe College; and D. S. Williams, *She Fulfilled the Impossible Dream*, 15.

54. Letter from Birdye H. Haynes to GEH, May 7, 1915, Box 3, Folders 26 and 27 contain correspondence with this wife and sister, respectively. Obituary for Birdye H. Haynes; Carlton-LaNey, "George and Birdye Haynes"; Carlton-LaNey, "Career of Birdye Henrietta Haynes." Letters to and from George Haynes's students concerning graduate school include Charles H. Wesley to GEH, May 8, 1911, Box 3, Folder 14; Aiken D. Pope to GEH, Mar. 12, Oct. 13, and 23, 1912, Box 3, Folder 3; GEH to Margurite Parks, Nov. 9, 1911, Box 3, Folder 2; Uxenia Scott to GEH, Sept. 28, 1913, Box 3, Folder 8, all in GEH-Fisk.

4. Mapping the Great Migration

1. C. S. Johnson, "How the Negro Fits in Northern Industries," 399. The actual estimates of the total numbers who migrated North between 1915 and 1920 vary between three hundred thousand and five hundred thousand and nearly the same numbers of black men and women filled the growing industrial cities of the South. The initial census figures were at the lower range but have subsequently been adjusted toward the higher numbers. See Kennedy, *Negro Peasant Turns Cityward*, 23–35. Marks, *Farewell—We're Good and Gone*, 1–2; M. E. Jones, *Black Migration in the United States*, 35. E. Lewis, "Beginnings of a Renaissance."

2. D. L. Lewis, *W. E. B. Du Bois, 1919–1963*, 544, 578; Gregg, *Sparks from the Anvil of Oppression*, 98–99, 194–199; A. L. Harris, "Negro Labor's Quarrel with White Workingmen"; Du Bois, "Hosts of Black Labor"; Daniel DeNoyelles, "Negro as Laborer"; Murdock, "Racial Differences Found in Two American Cities."

3. Locke, "New Negro," 6–7.

4. Trotter, "Introduction," 4–5, 10; N. J. Weiss, *National Urban League, 1910–1940*, 30–34; Goggin, *Carter G. Woodson*, 23–26; Wright, *Eighty-seven Years*, 47; Wright Jr., preface to *Negro in Pennsylvania*; Perlman, "Stirring the White Conscience," 53–61; G. E. Haynes, *Negro at Work in New York City*; Roberts, "Crucible for a Vision"; Richardson *History of Fisk University, 1865–1946*; C. S. Johnson, *Negro College Graduate*, 228–30.

5. Negro colleges did not have organized graduate programs until the twenties and white southern universities barred black graduate students in liberal arts until the 1960s. R. W. Logan, *Howard University*, 140, 275, 314–16. J. D. Anderson, *Education of Blacks in the South*, 258–60; C. S. Johnson, *Negro College Graduate*, 10–21, 294–95.

6. In 1920 the first black man to earn a doctorate in psychology was Francis Sumner, but the majority of black social scientists remained chiefly concerned with labor until the 1930s when studies of the black family by E. Franklin Frazier began to appear. Guthrie, *Even the Rat Was White*, 175–89.

7. Trotter, "Introduction," 5, 1–23.

8. Pickens, "Migrating to Fuller Life," 605.

9. Du Bois, "Hosts of Black Labor."

10. Gregg, *Sparks from the Anvil of Oppression*, 99, 103, 98–104. Spady, s.v. "Wright Sr., Richard Robert"; A. B. Henderson, "Richard R. Wright and the National Negro Bankers Association"; E. R. Haynes, *Black Boy of Atlanta*, 74–223.

11. G. E. Haynes, "Negroes Move North: I," G. E. Haynes, "Negroes Move North: II"; Woodson, *Century of Negro Migration*, 167–92.

12. Goggin, *Carter G. Woodson*, 202–5; G. E. Haynes, "Negroes Move North: I," G. E. Haynes, "Negroes Move North: II."

13. Goggin, *Carter G. Woodson*; E. J. Scott, "Letters of Negro Migrants of 1916–1918"; Woodson, *Negro Makers of History*, 323–27.

14. Donald, "Negro Migration of 1916–1918"; E. R. Haynes, "Negroes in Domestic Service in the United States."

15. Goggin, *Carter G. Woodson*, 203–4, Woodson, *Century of Negro Migration*, 168–75.

16. Woodson, *Century of Negro Migration*, 147–66, 174–76, quotations on 175, 165, 152.

17. Ibid., 161–66, 175; Woodson, *Miseducation of the Negro*; Goggin, *Carter G. Woodson*, 158–60.

18. G. E. Haynes, *Negro at Work in New York City*, 13–14.

19. Ibid., 13–33, quotation on 18.

20. G. E. Haynes, *Negro At Work in New York City*, 14. Haynes maintained life-long relationships with both W. E. B. Du Bois and Booker T. Washington, who served on the NUL board of directors. See Booker T. Washington to George E. Haynes, June 13, 1911, Box 3, Folder 13, GEH-Fisk.

21. "Purposes and accomplishments of Conferences on League's Work, and "Negro Labor in America," two-page typescript report of meetings in New York held on Jan. 29–31, 1918, of local affiliates of National Urban League, n.d., Box 7, GEH-Fisk; G. E. Haynes, "Negroes Move North: I," 118, 120; N. J. Weiss, *National Urban League, 1910–1940*, 89–90, 126–27, 66–68; Parris and Brooks, *Blacks in the City*, 34–35. An example of a card used appears in F. B. Washington, "Detroit Newcomers' Greeting."

22. G. E. Haynes, "Negroes Move North: I," 119, 118, 120.

23. Questions on Migration of Negroes to the North, completed questionnaires and correspondence; Migration of Negroes. Questionnaire List, three-page typescript, Box 4, Folder 17, GEH-Fisk; G. E. Haynes, *Negro Newcomers in Detroit, Michigan*.

24. G. E. Haynes, "Negroes Move North: I," 118.

25. G. E. Haynes, "Co-operation with Colleges in Securing and Training Negro Social Workers for Urban Centers," 384. N. J. Weiss, *National Urban League, 1910–1940*, 64; NUL stationery, DNE, RG 174, NARA; *The Survey* (Aug. 3, 1918): 513, has the NUL seal.

26. N. J. Weiss, *National Urban League, 1910–1940*, 129–135, and chapter 7 passim. Roberts, "Crucible for a Vision," 62–63. Haynes was rather unceremoniously eased out of the NUL in 1918 after years of conflict over his desire to work in Nashville and spend only part of the summer in New York.

27. G. B. Jackson and D. W. Davis, *Industrial History of the Negro Race of the United States*, 21–22. Finney, "Study of Negro Labor during and after World War I," 141–43; F. D. Dunlop to Giles B. Jackson, May 22, 1917, and "Extracts of Resolution Adopted by Executive Committee of Chamber of Commerce of City of Richmond," File 8/102, RG 174, NARA; J. R. Shillady to Butler R. Wilson, Apr. 9, 1920, Petition to Congress by National Civil Improvement Association, President Giles B. Jackson, n.d, General Labor Files, IC 319, NAACP Papers, LOC; *Messenger* (Jan. 1923): 561.

28. Card dated Mar. 29, 1907, Du Bois Papers, University of Massachusetts, Amherst. See also Du Bois to Frances Kellor, draft, c. 1906; Du Bois to the editor

of *The Appeal to Reason*, Girard Kansas, Apr. 8, 1907, Du Bois Papers, University of Massachusetts, Amherst.

29. William B. Wilson to Giles B. Jackson, Aug. 20, 1917; Giles Beecher Jackson to H. L. Kerwin, Jan. 14, 1918; Samuel Gompers to Woodrow Wilson, Jan. 23, 1918; Giles Beecher Jackson to Mr. Brahany, Assistant Secretary to the President, Feb. 12, 1918; Senator Thomas Martin to William G. McAdoo, Feb. 14, 1918; McAdoo to William B. Wilson, Feb. 14, 1918, Box 17, File 8/102, RG 174, NARA. Jackson first wanted the bureau to be funded publicly but privately run by himself.

30. *New York Times*, Jan. 21, 1918, editorial.

31. J. E. Johnson, Council of National Defense to Hon. J. P. Tumulty, Secretary to the President, Mar. 2, 1918, Chief Clerks Files, File 8/102a, RG 174, NARA.

32. George C. Clement to Woodrow Wilson, Mar. 16, 1918, File 8/102, RG 174, NARA.

33. Du Bois to Louis F. Post, Apr. 16, 1918, and Louis F. Post to Du Bois, Apr. 18, 1918, reply Du Bois to Post, Apr. 19, 1918, File 8/102, RG 174, NARA; Finney, "Study of Negro Labor during and after World War I," 147.

34. "Colored Labor Bureau," Washington *Bee*, n.d., Chief Clerks Files, Box 17, File 8/102a, RG 174, NARA.

35. Robert Russa Moton, James H. Dillard, L. Hollingsworth Wood, John R. Shillady, E. K. Jones, and Thomas J. Jones to William B. Wilson, Feb. 12, 1918, "Colored Labor Bureau," Washington *Bee*, n.d., Chief Clerks Files, Box 17, File 8/102a, RG 174, NARA.

36. Louis Post signed the Call for the 1909 National Negro Conference that led to the establishment of the NAACP and the United Mine Workers was one of the few major unions that admitted blacks. Henry Guzda, "Social Conscience of Woodrow Wilson's Administration: The U. S. Department of Labor," unpublished ms., n.d., Office of the Historian, DOL; Kellogg 297–99; Cuff, "Politics of Labor Administration during World War I."

37. In order not to offend the Virginia congressional delegation, however, Jackson was placed in the U.S. Employment Service in Richmond and given a title similar to Haynes's—Chief of the Negro Division. Jackson did not report to Haynes. The existing records of Jackson's official duties are sketchy. Ives, "Giles Beecher Jackson"; "Report of the Secretary of Labor, 1918," in *Reports of the U. S. Department of Labor,* 6:112, 698; Finney, "Study of Negro Labor during and after World War I," 150; *Handbook of Federal World War Agencies and Their Records, 1917–1921,* 382; Memorandum from the Director of DNE to the director general, USES, Mar. 8, 1919, 2 pages, File 8/102d, RG 174, NARA.

38. W. R. Manier, Commercial Club of Nashville to William B. Wilson, Mar. 15, 1918, File 8/102, RG 174, NARA; Press release announcing Haynes's appointment, n.d., 3 pages, and "Sketch of George Edmund Haynes," n.d., 6 pages, File 8/102, RG 174, NARA; G. E. Haynes, *Negro at Work during World War and during Reconstruction,* 12–19.

39. J. R. Shillady to Butler R. Wilson, Apr. 9, 1920, General Labor Files, IC 319, NAACP Papers, LOC.

40. DNE, "Matters of Record," DOL, Office of the Secretary, twelve-page typescript, n.d.; George E. Haynes, "Memorandum for the Secretary," through the assistant secretary, July 22, 1918, DNE, File 8/102, RG 174, NARA. The memorandum with Haynes's proposed program of action was initialed and approved by William B. Wilson on 24 July 1918. "Model Constitution for Local Negro Workers Advisory Committee," two-page typescript, n.d., DNE, File 1/H, RG 174, NARA.

41. DNE, "Matters of Record," memorandum, n.d., File 8/102, RG 174, NARA; Henry Guzda, "Social Conscience of Woodrow Wilson's Administration: The U. S. Department of Labor," 7, unpublished ms., n.d., Office of the Historian, DOL; Karl Phillips to GEH, memorandum, Oct. 30, 1920; Karl Phillips to GEH, Jan. 5, 1919 [1920], File 8/102, RG 174, NARA; G. E. Haynes, *Negro at Work during World War and during Reconstruction,* 20, 68; Guzman, *Negro Yearbook,* 84; E. L. Ross, "Black Heritage in Social Welfare," 307. Another member of Haynes's field staff, Jesse O. Thomas, became head of the NUL's southern office in Atlanta at the end of the war. See G. E. Haynes, *Negro at Work during World War and during Reconstruction,* 95. In Haynes's memo of Mar. 6, 1919, to the Director General of USES he listed seven supervisors of Negro Economics in eight states who were paid with funds from USES. See Finney, "Study of Negro Labor during and after World War I," 184–90.

42. "Function and Work of the Division of Negro Economics in the Office of the Secretary of Labor," Mar. 15, 1919, "Functions and Work of Negro Economics Advisory Service," Mar. 18, 1921, Monthly Reports, Division of Negro Economics, March 1919 to June 1929, and untitled seven-page statement of questions and answers concerning the Negro Workers Advisory Committee, n.d., Chief Clerks Files, File 8/102, RG 174, NARA; "Model Constitution for Local Negro Workers Advisory Committee," two-page typescript, n.d., Box A, RG 174, NARA; G. E. Haynes, *Negro at Work during World War and during Reconstruction,* 71.

43. "Testimony," 2, File 8/102, RG 174, NARA; G. E. Haynes, *Negro at Work during World War and during Reconstruction,* 19.

44. Louis F. Post, Memorandum For the Secretary, July 2, 1918; George Ramsey, Federal Director of USES in North Carolina to Louis F. Post, Assistant Secretary of Labor, June 20, 1918, RG 174, NARA; "Plan Promotion Negro Efficiency: Conference of Negro Leaders with Governor Plans to Increase Co-operation," newspaper clipping describing meeting with North Carolina governor Bickett, no source, n.d., with the notation, "This report was given out by the Governor's office"; DNE, "Matters of Record," 1–4, File 8/102, RG 174, NARA; G. E. Haynes, *Negro at Work during World War and during Reconstruction,* 14–15.

45. GEH to Dir. Gen. USES, "Activities of the Supervisor of Negro Economics for Florida," 3 Feb. 1919, memo, File 8/102, RG 174, NARA; Shofner, "Florida and the Black Migration"; G. E. Haynes, *Negro at Work during World War and during Reconstruction,* 64–66.

46. The NAACP suspected this episode might be a part of increased Ku Klux Klan activity in the South. Governor Sidney Catts to William B. Wilson, Apr. 7, 1919; Shofner, "Florida and the Black Migration," 274–83, 287; typescript of remarks of John H. Kirby, National Lumber Manufacturers Assn. in the *Washington Post,* Apr.

3, 1919, and "South Aroused Over Wilson's Labor Policies," clippings, IC 319, NAACP Papers, LOC; Louis Post, unpublished autobiography, Louis Post Papers, LOC, 393–94.

47. "Report of the Secretary of Labor, 1920," in *Reports of the Department of Labor*, 8:40–41; *Handbook of Federal World War Agencies and Their Records, 1917–1921*, 382; Henry Guzda, "Social Conscience of Woodrow Wilson's Administration: The U. S. Department of Labor," 37–41, unpublished ms., n.d., Office of the Historian, DOL; Finney, "Study of Negro Labor during and after World War I," 213–17.

48. The NAACP Papers, General Labor Files, IC 319, contain letters from black workers seeking the organization's intervention, LOC. See Finney, "Study of Negro Labor during and after World War I," 183, 194–95.

49. "W. E. B. Du Bois" (Who's Who column); "New Leadership for the Negro," 10.

50. "W. E. B. Du Bois" (Who's Who column).

51. Ibid.

52. "New Leadership for the Negro."

53. "George Haynes Compromises the Case of the Negro Again"; "New Leadership for the Negro," 10.

54. J. H. Harris, "Charles Harris Wesley, Educator and Historian, 1891–1947," 15–25; Winston, *Howard University Department of History, 1913–1973*, 17–25, 29; Meier and Rudwick, *Black History and the Historical Profession, 1915–1980*, 77; Robbins, *Sidelines Activist*, 18–29. I. Diggs, s.v. "Reid, Ira De Augustine"; B. A. Jones, "Tradition of Sociology Teaching in Black Colleges," 154–55; N. J. Weiss, *National Urban League, 1910–1940*, 217. Letter from the Reverend D. Augustine Reid to John Hope, Sept. 18, 1914, John and Lugenia Burns Hope Papers, Atlanta University. Greene, who grew up in a small New England town, was the only one of the five to attend integrated schools.

55. N. J. Weiss, *National Urban League, 1910–1940*, 31–34, 42–44; I. B. Lindsay, s.v. "Haynes, George Edmund"; B. A. Jones, "Tradition of Sociology Teaching in Black Colleges," 144–45. Parris and Brooks, *Blacks in the City*, 50, 78–79, 187–88, 200. "Interracial Social Work Begins," Haynes vertical file, microfiche, NYPLSC. G. E. Haynes, "Co-operation with Colleges in Securing and Training Negro Social Workers for Urban Centers"; "Work in Nashville Tennessee," one-page typescript, n.d., outlining activities of the second year of Bethlehem House settlement, Box 4, Folder 11; George Haynes to C. C. Poindexter at Fisk, July 17, 1911, Box 3, Folder 3, all in GEH-Fisk. Haynes's financial situation at Fisk can be seen in his letters to his sister, Birdye, describing raising chickens and asking for loans. George Haynes to Birdye H. Haynes, Mar. 12, 1915, Apr. 20, 1915, May 11, 1915, and reply May 17, 1915, Box 3, Folder 27, GEH-Fisk. See also the Jan. 23, 1915, Feb. 20, 1915, letters from Workman and Company Fire Insurance, Box 3, Folder 21, GEH-Fisk; Goggin, *Carter G. Woodson*, 66–77.

56. Goggin, *Carter G. Woodson*, 20–25, 29–30; Romero, "Carter G. Woodson," 70–75.

57. George E. Haynes to Eugene K. Jones, Jan. 3, 1914, Box 6, Folder 3; "Extract from the Report of the Director, For June, July, Aug., and to Sept. 22, 1913," five-page typescript, Oct. 25, 1913, Box 4, Folder 20, GEH-Fisk.

58. G. E. Haynes, "Co-operation with Colleges in Securing and Training Negro Social Workers for Urban Centers," 384; N. J. Weiss, *National Urban League, 1910–1940,* 41–44, 71–79. Richardson, *History of Fisk University, 1865–1946;* C. S. Johnson, *Negro College Graduate,* described Abram Harris as having "moved from social work into economics." See Boris, "Abram L. Harris" (1927), and contrast Elizabeth Ross Haynes's entries for 1927, 1931, and 1937–40.

59. Goggin, *Carter G. Woodson,* 34–36, 48–54; Winston, *Howard University Department of History, 1913–1973,* 18–25, 35–39; "George E. Haynes"; R. W. Logan, *Howard University,* 140, 171–72, 208.

60. Donald, "Negro Migration of 1916–1918"; E. R. Haynes, "Negroes in Domestic Service in the United States"; L. J. Greene and Colson Callis, *Employment of Negroes in the District of Columbia;* Woodson, "Annual Report of the Director." Woodson funded A. A. Taylor's studies of Reconstruction and his graduate program at Harvard University. See *Southern Workman* (Oct. 1925): 437. The topic of 1928 ASNLH annual meeting was the "Economic Condition of the Negro." See "Director's Report"; Meier and Rudwick, *Black History and the Historical Profession, 1915–1980,* 73–95; Goggin, *Carter G. Woodson,* 68–69, 72–75; Hemenway, *Zora Neale Hurston,* 95–101; J. H. Harris, "Charles Harris Wesley, Educator and Historian, 1891–1947," 122–45; L. J. Greene, *Selling Black History for Carter G. Woodson;* Weaver, "Negro Labor since 1929." This was an address given on Oct. 29, 1949. See "Proceedings of the Annual Meeting"; Browning, "Historical Sketch of the Association of Social Science Teachers at Negro Colleges."

61. This account is based on the author's interview with Charles H. Wesley, Jan. 23, 1983, and letters between Wesley and Haynes in the George E. Haynes Collection at Fisk University. See for example Charles H. Wesley to George Haynes, May 8, 1911, and others listed in this chapter. Charles H. Wesley Fisk University transcript, Box 3, Folder 14, GEH-Fisk.

62. Winston, *Howard University Department of History, 1913–1973,* 29, 17–29; J. H. Harris, "Charles Harris Wesley, Educator and Historian, 1891–1947," 26–28; Meier and Rudwick, *Black History and the Historical Profession, 1915–1980,* 77. F. R. Wilson, "Racial Consciousness and Black Scholarship." Studies of the Civil War by one of his Yale professor's, E. D. Fite, helped Wesley to confirm history as his choice of fields. George E. Haynes to Charles Wesley, carbon copy, n.d., GEH-Fisk.

63. Winston, *Howard University Department of History, 1913–1973,* 27–32. J. H. Harris, "Charles Harris Wesley, Educator and Historian, 1891–1947," 27–28. Lewis Baxter Moore Alumni Folder, University of Pennsylvania Archives. Haynes to Kelsey, Feb. 11, 1915, and reply, Feb. 16, 1915, GEH-Fisk.

64. Lewis B. Moore was a Congregational minister according to his alumni folder in the University of Pennsylvania Archives. Dyson, *Howard University,* 373–

75. According to Janette Harris, Wesley assumed a pastorate in Washington, D.C., in 1918 but was not fully ordained as an AME minister until 1921 (102–10).

65. J. H. Harris, "Charles Harris Wesley, Educator and Historian, 1891–1947," 80–177. Meier and Rudwick, *Black History and the Historical Profession, 1915–1980,* 77–80; Winston, *Howard University Department of History, 1913–1973,* 2–30.

66. Author's interview with Lorenzo J. Greene, Oct. 22, 1983, Detroit, Michigan; Strickland, "Editor's Introduction," 28–29; L. J. Greene, *Working with Carter G. Woodson,* 185–94; Reddick, "Carter G. Woodson"; "Phylon Profile VI: Carter G. Woodson"; Meier and Rudwick, *Black History and the Historical Profession, 1915–1980,* 78–83; Romero, "Carter G. Woodson," 186–88; J. H. Harris, "Charles Harris Wesley, Educator and Historian, 1891–1947," 134–40.

67. L. J. Greene, *Selling Black History for Carter G. Woodson,* 213–15, 255–56, 5–7, 221–22, 258, 266; Strickland, "Editor's Introduction," 3–7, quotation on 11; L. J. Greene and Woodson, *Negro Wage Earner,* vi; Meier and Rudwick, *Black History and the Historical Profession, 1915–1980,* 80–83, 94; L. J. Greene and Colson Callis, *Employment of Negroes in the District of Columbia.*

68. Strickland, "Editor's Introduction," 16–20; L. J. Greene, *Selling Black History for Carter G. Woodson,* 312. Meier and Rudwick, *Black History and the Historical Profession, 1915–1980,* 94–95, 77–119.

69. C. S. Johnson, *Negro College Graduate,* 131–58. The median salary for the male social worker was $2,075 and it was $1,993.75 for a male college professor but the median salary for black social work executives was $3,100. Male high school teachers earned a median salary of $1,300. The median income for all black college graduates male and female was $1,497 broken down to $1,881 for men and $972 for black women.

70. "Outstanding Fellows," 33, lists Ira Reid but not Abram Harris. Several years later E. Franklin Frazier had the same University of Chicago fellowship to work at the Chicago Urban League as Johnson had had. Robbins, *Sidelines Activist,* 31–33, 44–45; N. J. Weiss, *National Urban League, 1910–1940,* 142, 216–20.

71. Robbins, *Sidelines Activist,* 18–42; N. J. Weiss, *National Urban League, 1910–1940,* 142; Valien and Valien, s.v. "Johnson, Charles S."; Gilpin, "Charles S. Johnson," 5–6, 17. After Johnson became a professor at Fisk University his failure to earn an advanced degree would become a source of scornful commentary among the handful of black persons who had more degrees but far less power.

72. Gilpin, "Charles S. Johnson," 20–27, 43, 37–38, 59; N. J. Weiss, *National Urban League, 1910–1940,* 220–25; Robbins, *Sidelines Activist,* 34–37, 40–48; Chicago Commission on Race Relations, *Negro in Chicago: A Study of Race Relations and a Race Riot,* xviii; Strickland, *History of the Chicago Urban League,* 43–44, 67–68.

73. Parris and Brooks, *Blacks in the City,* 79, 167–70; N. J. Weiss, *National Urban League, 1910–1940,* 150–51.

74. R. Weiss, s.v. "Harris, Abram L."; I. Diggs, s.v. "Reid, Ira De Augustine"; A. L. Harris, "New Negro Worker in Pittsburgh."

75. N. J. Weiss, *National Urban League, 1910–1940,* 217; Parris and Brooks, *Blacks in the City,* 170, 215–16, 194–95; I. Diggs, s.v. "Reid, Ira De Augustine";

B. A. Jones, "Tradition of Sociology Teaching in Black Colleges," 154–55; Reid, "Negro in the Major Industries and the Building Trades of Pittsburgh"; the Reverend D. Augustine Reid to John Hope, Sept. 18, 1914, John and Lugenia Burns Hope Papers, Atlanta University. Ira Reid was only thirteen, so the family delayed his entrance for one year.

76. I. Diggs, s.v. "Reid, Ira De Augustine"; B. A. Jones, "Tradition of Sociology Teaching in Black Colleges," 154–55; Bacote, *Story of Atlanta University*. N. J. Weiss, *National Urban League, 1910–1940,* 151.

77. Neither Owen nor Harris are listed in the league's fortieth-anniversary book. See *National Urban League Fortieth Anniversary Book,* 32–33; Darity, "Introduction," 12–14.

78. Ibid.; Darity, "Soundings and Silences on Race and Social Change"; A. L. Harris, "Negro Problem as Viewed by Negro Leaders," 414.

79. Trotter, "Introduction," 5; U. S. Bureau of the Census, *Negroes in the United States,* tables 13, 12; "New Negro Migration," 752.

80. At the Federal Council of Churches (now National Council of Churches) Haynes developed programs that promoted interracial understanding among church groups. Amid the labor and migration articles Haynes published was "Negro Migration, Its Effects on Family and Community Life in the North."

81. Harry Washington Greene's *Negro Holders of Doctorates* states that a W. G. Peters earned a degree in economics in 1918 from Boston University, but I have been unable to confirm his racial identity.

82. Gregg, *Sparks from the Anvil of Oppression,* 63, 259n23.

83. Wright Jr. *Eighty-seven Years,* 178–79, 317–18.

84. Gilpin, "Charles S. Johnson," 20–25; F. R. Wilson, "Segregated Scholars," 358n26; Robbins, *Sidelines Activist,* 37. Johnson's salary was high for what was, after all, his first full-time job. George Haynes had earned $3,500 at the DNE. Eugene K. Jones, Johnson's superior at the NUL earned $2,500 in 1918 and $6,000 in 1928. See N. J. Weiss, *National Urban League, 1910–1940,* 247. Wesley received a salary raise in 1919 to $1,700 after six years of teaching. See F. R. Wilson, "Racial Consciousness and Black Scholarship," 75.

85. N. J. Weiss, *National Urban League, 1910–1940,* 217–16.

86. C. S. Johnson, "Negroes at Work in Baltimore, Maryland"; Robbins, "Charles S. Johnson," 60–62.

87. N. J. Weiss, *National Urban League, 1910–1940,* 216–20, 192, quotation on 217.

88. Trotter, "Introduction," 5, 3–6; N. J. Weiss, *National Urban League, 1910–1940,* 223–28.

89. Editorial, *Opportunity* 1, no. 1 (1923): 3.

90. D. L. Lewis, *When Harlem Was in Vogue,* 89–90, 45–49.

91. "Sense of Belonging."

92. "Sympathy without Understanding."

93. N. J. Weiss, *National Urban League, 1910–1940,* 220–27.

94. N. J. Weiss, *National Urban League, 1910–1940*, 181–90, 226; Strickland, *History of the Chicago Urban League*, 83, 262–63.

95. Hill, "Negro in Industry, 1926," 51–52.

96. C. S. Johnson, "How Much Is the Migration a Flight from Persecution?"

97. Ibid., 274.

98. Reid, "Mrs. Bailey Pays the Rent"; McKay, *Home to Harlem*, McKay, *Banjo*; Hughes, *Simple Speaks his Mind*. Hughes's Simple Stories began in 1943 as columns in the *Chicago Defender*. See Sullivan, *Not So Simple*.

99. *The Crisis* 35 (June 1928), 204; National Urban League, *Negro Membership in American Labor Unions*, frontispiece; McKay, *Home to Harlem*, 33–34, 31.

100. Darity, "Abram Harris," 13–14; A. L. Harris, "Negro Problem as Viewed by Negro Leaders," 414, 413; E. F. Frazier, "New Currents of Thought among the Colored People of America"; G. E. Harris, "Life and Work of E. Franklin Frazier," 231–34; E. F. Frazier, "Pathology of Race Prejudice"; Edwards, "Frazier, E. Franklin"; Edwards, s.v. "E. Franklin Frazier"; Platt, *E. Franklin Frazier Reconsidered*, 62–102, 133–36, 152–69.

101. Van Kleeck, "Foreword," v–xl.

102. E. F. Frazier, review of *Negro Membership in American Labor Unions*.

103. Du Bois, "Study of the Negro Problems"; Van Kleeck, "Foreword," viii, ix, quotation on ix.

104. Locke qtd. in *Negro in American Civilization*, 380–81; Van Kleeck, "Foreword," ix.

105. Stolberg qtd. in Darity, "Soundings and Silences on Race and Social Change," 245.

106. Darity, "Soundings and Silences on Race and Social Change," letter from Abram Harris to Benjamin Stolberg, Nov. 12, 1930, 243–44; Letter, quotations on 1, 2, also in Box 4b, Folder 2, Stolberg Papers, Columbia University Archives.

107. Feb. 8, 1928, letter from C. S. Johnson to T. E. Jones, qtd. in Robbins, "Charles S. Johnson," 62.

108. Work, review of *The Black Worker*; Work, review of *The Negro Wage Earner*; Du Bois, "Concerning the Negro"; Review (unsigned) of *The Negro Wage Earner*; Strickland, "Editor's Introduction," 31; Greene, *Working with Carter G. Woodson*, 210–14, 216–21, 208.

109. Woodson, "Introduction," vi; author's interview with Lorenzo J. Greene, Oct. 22, 1983, Detroit, Michigan; L. J. Greene, *Selling Black History for Carter G. Woodson*, 215, 222–23; Strickland, "Editor's Introduction," 31; Strickland, *History of the Chicago Urban League*, 5–6.

110. L. J. Greene, *Negro in Colonial New England*; Meier and Rudwick, *Black History and the Historical Profession, 1915–1980*, 78, 82–83; L. J. Greene and Colson Callis, *Employment of Negroes in the District of Columbia*; L. J. Greene, *Selling Black History for Carter G. Woodson*, 312–65; Woodson, "Introduction," vi; C. S. Johnson, "History of Negro Labor"; Frazier qtd. in Winston, *Howard University Department of History, 1913–1973*, 31. Greene's published diaries do not mention any joint research done with Myra Hill Colson Callis; her study of domestic

workers may have been added to the work after Lorenzo Greene finished his research.

111. L. J. Greene, *Selling Black History for Carter G. Woodson*, 313–15; Locke, "Where the Negro Worker Stands"; Work, review of *The Black Worker*; Work, review of *The Negro Wage Earner*; Du Bois, "Concerning the Negro"; Review (unsigned) of *The Negro Wage Earner*; Dorsey, review of *The Black Worker*; Review (unsigned) of *The Negro as a Capitalist*; Obituary for Abram L. Harris.

112. See F. R. Wilson, "Racial Consciousness and Black Scholarship," 72–74. Meier and Rudwick, *Black History and the Historical Profession*, 78; C. S. Johnson, "History of Negro Labor"; Frazier qtd. in Winston, *Howard University Department of History, 1913–1973*, 31. Other laudatory reviews of *Negro Labor in the United States* included Woodson, review of *Negro Labor in the United States, 1850–1925*; "Book Notes"; "Some Questions of Our Time"; "New Books."

113. Winston, *Howard University Department of History, 1913–1973*, 27–32, 58. See F. R. Wilson, "Racial Consciousness and Black Scholarship," 75–80. Wesley became chairman of the history department at Howard University after his return from Harvard in 1921. Wesley's early historiographical articles include Wesley, "Teacher's Point of View in the Study and Teaching of History"; Wesley, "Interest in A Neglected Phase of History"; Wesley, "Problems of Sources and Methods in History Teaching."

114. Curti qtd. in Robinson, "Charles H. Wesley," 9; F. R. Wilson, "Racial Consciousness and Black Scholarship," 76–78, passim; Joyce, *Edward Channing and the Great Work*, 27–30. In a letter to Wesley on May 29, 1927, Arthur Schlesinger Sr. characterized Wesley's performance on his special exam as "brilliant," qtd. in J. H. Harris, "Charles Harris Wesley, Educator and Historian, 1891–1947," 54, 201.

115. Wilson, "Racial Consciousness and Black Scholarship," 76. The late Armstead L. Robinson first directed my attention to this incident.

116. Wilson, "Racial Consciousness and Black Scholarship," 79.

117. Ibid., 78n22.

118. Wesley, *Negro Labor in the United States, 1850–1925*, 116–55, 238–48, quotations on v, 239.

119. Gutman, "Preface to the Atheneum Edition," viii–ix.

120. Darity, "Introduction," 10. Darity indicates that Harris was also funded by the Social Science Research Council from 1925 to 1930.

121. Spero and Harris, *The Black Worker*, 22–35; Wesley, *Negro Labor in the United States, 1850–1925*, 157–89, quotations on 306. Page xvi of the preface to *The Black Worker* indicates that Harris wrote this chapter.

122. For a detailed study of the Howard radicals, see Holloway, *Confronting the Veil*. Individual biographies include G. E. Harris, "Life and Work of E. Franklin Frazier," 231–34; and Darity, "Soundings and Silences on Race and Social Change"; and Platt, *E. Franklin Frazier Reconsidered*.

123. Letter to the author from Andrew Hannah, Associate Registrar, University of Chicago, Mar. 9, 1998. See "Achievement," which featured a photograph of Georgiana Simpson in her doctoral robes. Eva Beatrice Dykes's photo with a de-

scription of her accomplishment had appeared on page 105 in the same July 1921 issue of *The Crisis* that carried Mossell on the cover. Andrew Hannah, Associate Registrar, University of Chicago, to the author, Mar. 9, 1998; Eva Dykes, oral history interview by Merze Tate, Black Women Oral History Project, Schlesinger Library, Radcliffe College; D. S. Williams, *She Fulfilled the Impossible Dream,* 15; Hutchinson, s.v. "Cooper, Anna Julia."

124. Sadie Mossell Alexander, oral history interview by Walter M. Phillips, STMA Papers, Box 1, Folder 20, University of Pennsylvania Archives. See also the STMA oral history interview of the Black Women Oral History Project, Schlesinger Library, Radcliffe College.

125. *New Day for the Colored Woman Worker.*

5. "A New Day for the Colored Woman Worker"?

1. Eva Bowles, a black YWCA national board employee, reported that at the beginning of 1923 the YWCA had 107 black female secretaries, a position which required training and a college degree. Bowles, "Opportunities for the Educated Colored Woman." In 1920 there were 755 black women listed as either "religious and charity, or welfare workers." Figures for black men were 476 and 72, respectively, compared to 29,189 black female teachers and 6,319 male schoolteachers. See U.S. Bureau of the Census 1920, *Occupations,* 357.

2. T. W. Hunter, *To 'Joy My Freedom,* 136–42, quotation on 140. The Neighborhood Union Papers in the Atlanta University Center, Woodruff Library Archives, contain Lugenia Burns Hope's personal notebooks which contain her notes on sociological methods, her strategies for Neighborhood Union meetings, and her plans for community surveys.

3. Mrs. H. R. Watson, "Social Service Institute," [1919] Box 2, Folder 16; "Treating the Negro Problem at Basis," Box 2, Folder 18, Neighborhood Union Papers, John and Lugenia Hope Papers, Atlanta University Archives. Shivery, "History of Organized Social Work among Atlanta Negroes, 1890–1935," links Social Service Institutes in 1918 and 1919 to the founding of the Atlanta School of Social Work, saying that the AASW "used for its first class the students . . . the Faculty, the plant, and the Director," of the institute, 186–89, quotation on 186. See also Yabura, "Legacy of Forrester B. Washington"; E. L. Ross, "Black Heritage in Social Welfare." Frazier's studies for the Neighborhood Union include "A Survey of the Sanitary Conditions in the Neighborhood surrounding Leonard Street Orphanage" "directed by Professor E. F. Frazier, Executed and Analyzed by Neighborhood Union" [1925]; "A Survey of the Opinions of a Hundred Heads of Families Respecting Washington Park," "Made for the Neighborhood Union Under the direction of the Atlanta School of Social Work, E. Franklin Frazier, Director, Dec. 1924," all in Box 7, Folder 7, Neighborhood Union Papers, John and Lugenia Burns Hope Papers, Atlanta University Archives.

4. "Report of Mrs. L. E. Hope, Camp Upton, L.I., June 18, 1918," Box 1, Folder 28; "Our Staff Under the War Work Council, September 1918," Box 39,

Folder 13; *Bulletin of Circle for Negro War Relief* (July 1, 1918), *Colored American Women in War Work* (June 1918) pamphlet of the Committee on Work among Colored Girls and Women, War Work Council National Board YWCA, New York, Box 8, Folder 8, Neighborhood Union Papers, Atlanta University Archives. Hunton and Johnson, *Two Colored Women and the American Expeditionary Forces*; Chandler, "'That Biting, Stinging Thing Which Ever Shadows Us.'" Adrienne Lash Jones has graciously shared her unpublished work on black women in the YWCA with me.

5. Mary E. Jackson worked for the Department of Labor of Rhode Island before becoming industrial secretary for colored work for the YWCA. Salem, s.v. "World War I"; Neverdon-Morton, *Afro-American Women of the South and the Advancement of the Race, 1895–1925*, 219–22.

6. Mary Church Terrell's insights on her work for the War Camp Community Service are found in her papers. An interview and a memo that speak to white resistance in the North and the South to hiring black women to work as social workers is reprinted in Trotter and E. Lewis, *African Americans in the Industrial Age*, 92–97. See also "Negro Women in Industry" (Aug. 1924); Bethune, "Problems of the City Dweller"; A. D. Nelson, "Woman's Most Serious Problem."

7. *New Day for the Colored Woman Worker*; Holley, s.v. "Gertrude Elise Ayer."

8. *New Day for the Colored Woman Worker*, 6.

9. Ibid., 7, 9–11, 20–23, 34–35.

10. Ibid., 9–11, 25, 27–29, quotation on 11.

11. Ibid., 30.

12. Ibid., 31.

13. Phil Brown, commissioner of conciliation for the DOL to Mrs. Gertrude E. McDougald, Sept. 13, 1921; G. E. McDougald to U.S. Senator William Calder, Jan. 4, 1922; Gertrude E. McDougald, secretary North Harlem Vocational Guidance Committee, "The Survey of Colored Workers in New York City," two-page typescript, Jan. 3, 1922, Box 19, RG 174, NARA; "Negro and the Northern Public Schools"; E. J. McDougald, "Schools and the Vocational Life of Negroes." In her biographical sketch in *The New Negro*, McDougald is described as the "supervisor" of *New Day For the Colored Woman Worker*, 419. Gertrude McDougald (Ayer)'s participation in and some results from the Department of Labor New York study directed by Karl Phillips are mentioned in *The Negro in American Civilization*, vi, 82.

14. The research committee advised the research secretary, Charles S. Johnson who was loaned by the National Urban League to the National Interracial Conference. Other persons on the research committee included Robert Park, Broadus Mitchell, and Howard Odum. The other black members were Monroe Work and Forrester Washington. Margaret Mead and Eva Bowles of the YWCA were among eight women on the twenty-five-person executive committee. The National Interracial Conference was held Dec. 16–19, 1928; C. S. Johnson, *Negro in American Civilization*, vi, 519.

15. E. J. McDougald, "Double Task," E. J. McDougald, "Task of Negro Womanhood." Clark A. Chambers states that the *Survey Graphic* Harlem number sold

more than forty thousand copies, the most for this magazine until World War II. See *Paul U. Kellogg and the Survey,* 114.

16. E. J. McDougald, "Task of Negro Women," 370.

17. Ibid., 371–74.

18. Ibid., 377–38, quotation on 377. Also see her signature on a letter to Hugh Frayne, general organizer AF of L Feb. 1926, and mention of her position in *New Leader* (Jan. 16, 1926); and *Messenger* (Sept. 1926). See *The Black Worker,* 206–7, 230–32, 318–20. Also see J. Anderson, *A. Philip Randolph,* 12, 140; Clarke, *Harlem: A Community in Transition,* 252. I extend my thanks to M. Melinda Chateauvert for providing information on McDougald's relationship to A. Philip Randolph.

19. McDougald's memoir is reprinted as "The Women of the White Strain" in *Harlem's Glory: Black Women Writing: 1900–1950,* 519, quotation on 419.

20. Biographical details on McDougald Ayer's work as a teacher and principal are in Holley, s.v. "Gertrude Elise Ayer"; and Mabee, *Black Education in New York State,* 271–73, 279.

21. Mabee, *Black Education in New York State,* 271–73, 279.

22. E. J. McDougald, "Double Task," 689.

23. Ibid., 691.

24. Holley, s.v. "Gertrude Elise Ayer"; "Social Progress"; "Appointments."

25. The Women's Bureau was one of the few wartime labor bureaus to become a permanent part of the DOL. The Women's Bureau staff was made up almost entirely of white women from women's reform groups or trade union movement.

26. Forrester Washington, Illinois State director of Negro Economics succeeded E. Franklin Frazier as head of the Atlanta School of Social Work. Charles Hall returned to the Census Bureau where he supervised most of the special studies of black population for the next two decades.

27. E. R. Haynes, "Negroes in Domestic Service in the United States."

28. "Outline of work of the Department of Women and Children in Industry," n.d., Box 131, Folder 120/1-A, 1913–1918, RG 86, NARA. Breckinridge, the daughter of a U.S. congressman, was considered friendly to black people but was hardly a working-class black woman. Foreign-born white women were to represent themselves on another proposed committee.

29. "Report of the Secretary of Labor, 1918," in *Reports of the Department of Labor,* 6:121–22, 118–20.

30. Mary Van Kleeck to William B. Wilson, Sept. 3, 1918, Memo, Correspondence of the Director, 1918–1920, Secretary of Labor Folder, Box 1, WIIS, RG 86, NARA. See also minutes of Cabinet Meeting, Oct. 29, 1918, which refer to race riots. Van Kleeck was a member of the secretary's cabinet, while George Haynes reported to Louis Post, assistant director of Labor. As we saw in chapter 4, Haynes's salary was $3,500 a year.

31. Mary Van Kleeck, Biographical Data Folder; Memo to Chief Clerk, DOL from Chief Clerk, WIIS [Lillian Lewis], July 25, 1919; "The Woman in Industry Service," twenty-one-page history, no author, n.d., Correspondence of the Director, Box 3, WIIS, RG 86, NARA. See also Magat, *Unlikely Partners,* 13–16, 91–92.

32. "Negro Women in Industry in Fifteen States"; Letters from Mary Anderson, Women's Bureau to Lucy P. Garner YWCA, June 7, 1927; Ethel Best, Women's Bureau to Mary Anderson, Dec. 29, 1927, and Best to Anneta Dieckmann YWCA, Dec. 31, 1927, RG 86, NARA; reprinted in Trotter and E. Lewis, *African-Americans in the Industrial Age*, 122–25.

33. Letter to Mary Anderson from W. S. Carter Director U.S. Railroad, Aug. 28, 1918; Elizabeth Ross Haynes to Mary Anderson, Nov. 12, 1918, and replies, Box 3, WIIS, RG 86, NARA.

34. A study of black women workers compiled from fifteen state reports dating from 1918 to 1924 was published in 1929. Only four of these states—New Jersey, Ohio, Indiana, and Illinois—experienced a large increase in the numbers of black women or changes in occupational status as a result of the war or migration. See "Negro Women in Industry in Fifteen States."

35. Howard University *Forty-fifth Annual Commencement*, Wednesday, June 3, 1914, reproduced in the *Howard University Catalogue* for 1912–13 (no page nos.), and 1913–14 (p. 11). Dyson, *Howard University*, 182, mentions that Irvin (name "Irwin" in index) earned a master's degree in education in 1919. Dyson does not list Irvin in his list of the personnel of Howard University, 1867–1940, but he lists a Helen Irvin Grossley who was in the domestic science department from 1906 to 1914. See *Annual Report of the Director of the Women in Industry* (1919), 23; *Report of the Director of the Women's Bureau* (1921), 13–14. Helen Irvin is not listed in *Howard University Graduates, 1870–1980,* but Helen B. Grossley is listed as a "lost" graduate of the class of 1914 with a master's in 1919; carbon copy of memo listing names for the official register, July 25, 1919, from the Chief Clerk of the WIIS to the Chief Clerk of the Department of Labor; Mary Anderson to Mary Van Kleeck, June 10, 1919, "S-Z," Correspondence of the Director, Box 3, WIIS, RG 86, NARA.

36. Memorandum to the Secretary of Labor from Mary Van Kleeck, Apr. 18, 1919, Office of the Director, Box 1, WIIS, RG 86, NARA.

37. G. E. Haynes, *Negro at Work during World War and during Reconstruction*, 25–26, 124–33; *Monthly Labor Review* (Apr. 1924): 141–42; Memorandum from the Director of Negro Economics to the Director of the Women's Bureau Re: Draft of Report of Mrs. H. B. Irvin, Aug. 18, 1920, DNE, Chief Clerks Files, Box 2, RG 174, NARA; Karl Phillips to GEH, June 9, Aug. 19, 1920, File 8/102, RG 174, NARA.

38. "Colored Women Represent Their Race in State and Nation." Letter from Mary Van Kleeck to Mary Anderson, June 28, 1919, Correspondence of the Director, Box 3, WIIS, RG 86, NARA.

39. "Preliminary Program," Washington, D.C., Feb. 17–18, 1919, Auditorium of the Public Library 8th and K Streets, General Records of the Chief Clerks Files, Box 19, RG 174, NARA.

40. Neverdon-Morton, *Afro-American Women of the South and the Advancement of the Race, 1895–1925,* 74.

41. Mary Anderson to Mary Van Kleeck, June 10, 1919, and reply June 11, 1919, Box 3, WIIS, RG 86, NARA; quotation in Mary Van Kleeck to Mary Ander-

son, June 28, 1919; Finney, "Study of Negro Labor during and after World War I," 201–8. For an indication of black clubwomen's concerns for work workers, see "Conference of Negro Women."

42. Irvin, "Conditions in Industry as They Affect Negro Women," 522.

43. Ibid., 523, 524.

44. Irwin's work was chapter 19, "Negro Women in Industry," in G. E. Haynes, *The Negro at Work during World War II and during Reconstruction.*

45. Emma L. Shields Penn was also easier to follow because she moved from Washington to Harlem, where her activities were reported in national publications. Her close relationship to George Haynes is documented in his papers at Yale and Fisk Universities.

46. Emma L. Shields to GEH, Nov. 21, 1916, George Edmund Haynes Papers, Yale University, Beinecke Rare Book and Manuscript Library.

47. Ibid. In 1917 Shields sent Haynes a telegraph that stated: "Willing to come for living expenses plus incidental," Box 3/6, Folder 8, GEH-Fisk.

48. Memorandum from the Director of Negro Economics to the Director of the Women's Bureau Re: Draft of Report of Mrs. H. B. Irvin, Aug. 18, 1920; Karl Phillips to GEH, Aug. 19, 1920, DNE, Chief Clerks Files, Box 2, RG 174, NARA.

49. "Negro Women in Industry" (July 1922), 117, 118.

50. *Report of the Director of the Women's Bureau* (1921), 14. Mary Anderson acknowledged that Shields did the investigation and wrote the study.

51. Shields, "Half-Century in the Tobacco Industry," 420, 425; Shields, "Negro Women and the Tobacco Industry," 144; "Negro Women in Industry" (July 1922); J. Jones, *Labor of Love, Labor of Sorrow,* 138–40.

52. Shields, "Half-Century in the Tobacco Industry," 425.

53. Weisenfeld, "'More Abundant Life,'" 222–23; "Cover—Emma Shields Penn"; Penn, "Vocational Adjustment Problems of Negro Women in New York City."

54. John Riley, organizer AF of L to George E. Haynes, Aug. 25, 1918; Mary Anderson to GEH, Aug. 25, 1918; Anderson to W. S. Carter Chief of Labor Division of U.S. Railroad Administration, Aug. 23, 1918; Anderson to Riley, Aug. 24, 1918, Correspondence of the Director, Box 3, WIIS, RG 86, NARA.

55. "Efficiency Plus Spirit of Service: Bureau of Engraving," no author, n.d. [1918], one-page typescript on the stationery of the Office of the Secretary of the Department of Labor, Correspondence of the Director, Box 1, WIIS, RG 86, NARA.

56. Mrs. George E. Haynes to Mary Anderson, Sept. 12, 1918, and "Efficiency Plus Spirit of Service: Bureau of Engraving," no author, n.d. [1918], one-page typescript on the stationery of the Office of the Secretary of the Department of Labor, Correspondence of the Director, Box 1, WIIS, RG 86, NARA. The surviving correspondence of Elizabeth Ross Haynes so rarely uses her husband's name, contrary to the accepted practice of the time, that it is likely this was typed and signed by George Haynes's secretary, Mattie Campbell.

57. See F. R. Wilson's unpublished manuscript on black women in the Department of Labor, 1917–35: "Black Women's Labor Studies during the Great Migration." See also Mrs. George E. Haynes to Mary Anderson, Sept. 12, 1918, and reply

(apparently from Anderson), Oct. 3, 1918, Correspondence of the Director, Box 1, WIIS, RG 86, NARA. When George Haynes used a similar story of black male uncompensated extra work at the Hampton Roads shipyard, black socialists like A. Philip Randolph took exception to this model of undercompensated patriotism. See *Negro at Work during World War and during Reconstruction,* 62–63; "George Haynes Compromises the Case of the Negro Again."

58. E. R. Haynes, "Two Million Negro Women at Work." Memorial in behalf of Negro Women Laborers of the United States, Nov. 4, 1919, in the *Proceedings of the First International Congress of Working Women* in the National Women's Trade Union League Papers, LOC. See Boris, "Elizabeth Ross Haynes."

59. F. B. Washington, *Negro in Pennsylvania,* utilizes this method. See also F. R. Wilson, "Introduction," xxv–xxviii.

60. Du Bois, *Negro Artisan,* 20, 94–104, 179–87; F. R. Wilson, "Segregated Scholars," 79–84; E. R. Haynes, "Negroes in Domestic Service," 385–86.

61. E. R. Haynes, "Negroes in Domestic Service," 394–95, 414–15, 436–40.

62. Ibid., 391–93; Clark-Lewis, *Living In, Living Out.*

63. B. T. Dill, *Across the Boundaries of Race and Class,* 30; Katzman, *Seven Days a Week,* 247–48, 347.

64. F. R. Wilson, "Introduction," xx–xxv.

65. *Proceedings of the First International Congress of Working Women, 1919,* National Women's Trade Union Papers, LOC.

66. F. R. Wilson, "'You Must Keep Up or Endure the Dust.'"

67. E. R. Haynes, "Negroes in Domestic Service"; Woodson, "Negro Washerwoman, A Vanishing Figure"; Colson, "Negro Home Workers in Chicago"; L. J. Greene and Colson Callis, *Negro Employment in the District of Colombia*; R. W. Logan, *Howard University,* 367–70, 491.

68. "Negro Women in Industry in Fifteen States," 1.

69. An article by Eugene K. Jones, head of the National Urban League, uses a long quotation from "A New Day," on how black women's greater education and skills do not help them in the workplace but does not cite either the title of the report or the authors. E. K. Jones, "Problems of the Colored Child."

70. V. P. Franklin, s.v. "Alexander, Sadie Tanner Mossell"; F. R. Wilson, "'All of the Glory . . . Faded . . . Quickly,'" 167–75.

71. S. T. Mossell, "Standard of Living among One Hundred Negro Migrant Families in Philadelphia."

72. Sadie Mossell Alexander, oral history interview by Walter M. Phillips, STMA Papers, Box 1, Folder 20, University of Pennsylvania Archives; quote is on p. 5. See also F. R. Wilson, "All of the Glory . . . Faded . . . Quickly."

73. Carter G. Woodson to Eva Dykes, Apr. 7, 1921, Eva B. Dykes Papers, Series B, Box 63–1, J. E. Spingarn Papers, Moorland-Spingarn Research Center, Howard University (hereafter cited Howard University). Woodson offered to help Dykes get a job in a new field.

74. D. S. Williams, *She Fulfilled the Impossible Dream,* 50–53; Catherine John-

son, s.v. "Simpson, Georgiana"; F. R. Wilson, "'All of the Glory . . . Faded . . . Quickly,'" 177.

75. S. T. Mossell, *Study of the Negro Tuberculosis Problem in Philadelphia*. This study was used to justify the continued employment of black nurses and physicians in clinics serving black tuberculosis patients.

76. F. R. Wilson, "'All of the Glory . . . Faded . . . Quickly,'" 176–80.

77. S. T. M. Alexander, "Negro Women in Our Economic Life," was one of the few social science articles that she published after becoming a lawyer.

78. J. C. Brown, *The Negro Woman Worker*. Cythnia Neverdon-Morton has graciously let me read a part of her important forthcoming study on black women's work during World War II in Baltimore, in which she discusses the organizing activities of Jean Collier Brown.

79. The work of Mabel Smythe, an economist, was an exception. See M. M. Smythe, "Tipping Occupations as a Problem in the Administration of Protective Labor Legislation"; and M. M. Smythe, "Economics Teacher in the Post-War Period."

6. "A Corporal's Guard" for Negro Workers

1. M. M. Smythe, "Tipping Occupations as a Problem in the Administration of Protective Labor Legislation"; M. M. Smythe, "Economics Teacher in the Post-War Period"; Cayton and Mitchell, *Black Workers and the New Unions*; P. Valien, "Southern Negro Internal Migration between 1935 and 1940"; P. Valien, "Social and Economic Implications of Migration for the Negro in the Present Social Order"; Brazeal, *Brotherhood of Sleeping Car Porters*; Warren, "Negro in the American Labor Market"; Warren, "Partial Background for the Study of the Development of Negro Labor"; F. G. Davis, "War Economics and Negro Labor"; C. L. Franklin, *Negro Labor Unionist of New York*; C. L. Franklin, "Characteristics and Taxable Wages of Negro Workers, 13 Selected Southern States, 1938."

2. N. J. Weiss, *National Urban League, 1910–1940*, 181–91, 221, 322, 242–49, 250–79, 260–61; Du Bois, *Autobiography*, 191–99; W. Harris, *Harder We Run*, 109; Dancy, *Sand against the Wind*, 83; Lawrence, "Negro Organizations in Crisis," 8–10, 52–53, 123–27, 147. For examples of the NUL's fruitless negotiations with business executives, see "Great Atlantic and Pacific Tea, 1925–30"; and "Suggested Arguments to Use in Appealing to Employers for Jobs for Negroes," four-page typescript, n.d. (clipped to T. A. Hill to Helen R. Bryan, Jan. 7, 1930), NUL Papers, Box 4, Folder 3, LOC.

3. Rod Bush offers a survey of working-class involvement in communist, religious, and nationalist movements in *We Are not What We Seem*, 121–54. Cayton and Mitchell, *Black Workers and the New Unions*, include an early examination of the Congress of Industrial Organizations.

4. Reid, "Lack of Race Consciousness Responsible for Negligence in Raising Economic Status"; Reid, "Advertising Negro Labor"; Lawrence, "Negro Organizations in Crisis," 52–53; N. J. Weiss, *National Urban League, 1910–1940*, 209–15;

Report to Executive Secretary, 1930, 4–5, Box 3, Folder 3, NUL Papers, LOC; National Urban League, *Ever Widening Horizons*, 5–12.

5. Report to Executive Secretary, 1930, 4–5, Box 3, Folder 3, NUL Papers, LOC; National Urban League, *Ever Widening Horizons*, 1, 5–12. For a different assessment, see Parris and Brooks, *Blacks in the City*, 207–11.

6. N. J. Weiss, *National Urban League, 1910–1940*, 250–64. For a less critical view of the NUL's activities in 1929–34, see Parris and Brooks, *Blacks in the City*, 204–27.

7. Woodson, *Miseducation of the Negro*, 1; Goggin, *Carter G. Woodson*, 161–66.

8. Woodson, *Rural Negro*; Woodson, *Miseducation of the Negro*; Woodson, *Negro Professional Man and the Community*; L. J. Greene and Woodson, *Negro Wage Earner*; Harmon and A. G. Lindsay, *Negro as a Businessman*.

9. Goggin, *Carter G. Woodson*, 157–62; F. R. "Segregated Scholars," 178–88; Harley, "Nannie Helen Burroughs."

10. Woodson, *Miseducation of the Negro*, 116.

11. Ibid., 34.

12. Ibid., 116, 120, 52–54; Goggin, *Carter G. Woodson*, 166–67.

13. Woodson, *Miseducation of the Negro*, 29. Woodson attributed the "post-classic language" to John C. Dancy, who was the longtime executive secretary of the Detroit Urban League. Lorenzo Greene's diary entry of Oct. 29, 1930, attributed the same comment to Jesse O. Thomas of the Atlanta Urban League, so it is likely that this was a self-deprecating Urban League joke. See L. J. Greene, *Selling Black History for Carter G. Woodson*, 199.

14. L. J. Greene and Woodson, *Negro Wage Earner*, 191–97; Ralph J. Bunche, "Programs, Ideologies and Achievements of Negro Betterment and Interracial Organizations," *Research Memorandum II*, microfilm, 7–11, Carnegie-Myrdal Study, NYPLSC; J. P. Davis, "NRA Codifies Wage Slavery"; W. Harris, *Harder We Run*, 109–10; Lawrence, "Negro Organizations in Crisis," 250.

15. Wesley, "Organized Labor's Divided Front."

16. E. F. Frazier, *Black Bourgeoisie*; Cruse, *Crisis of the Negro Intellectual*.

17. Goggin, *Carter G. Woodson*, 162, 208–9.

18. Woodson, *Negro Professional Man and the Community*, ix. In the foreword, Woodson stated that this study was a part of a series that had begun with *The Negro Wage Earner* and *The Rural Negro*, which were "a part of the effort of the (ASNLH): to portray the social and economic conditions obtaining among Negroes in the United States since the Civil War." He also reported that "most of the tabulation was done by Myra Colson Callis," providing another piece of evidence on her research activities in the 1930s.

19. *Journal of Negro History* 13 (Oct. 1928): 400. The ASNLH was not a sponsor of the newly organized Joint Committee on Economic Recovery discussed later in this chapter.

20. The Association of Social Science Teachers in Negro Colleges had its own journal, *Quarterly Review of Higher Education among Negroes*.

21. Robert Weaver to Carter G. Woodson, Oct. 24, 1933, and Woodson to Weaver, Oct. 25, 1933, Weaver Papers, NYPLSC.

22. Weaver, "Negro Labor since 1929."

23. Meier and Rudwick, *Black History and the Historical Profession, 1915–1980*, 102–4. Woodson later published Bond's *Negro Education in Alabama*.

24. A. L. Harris, "Black and White World in American Labor and Politics"; A. L. Harris, *Negro as a Capitalist*.

25. Du Bois, *Autobiography*, 304–5.

26. Darity, "Introduction"; Review (unsigned) of *The Negro as a Capitalist*.

27. Woodson, *Negro Professional Man and the Community*, 333.

28. Robbins, *Sidelines Activist*, 122–24.

29. Woodson, *Miseducation of the Negro*, 1.

30. Ibid., 12–13, 116, 52–54.

31. Du Bois, "Negro's Industrial Plight."

32. Du Bois, "Education and Work," in *The Education of Black People*, 67, 61–82.

33. D. L. Lewis, *W. E. B. Du Bois, 1919–1963*, 313–14, 389, may understate the convergence of Du Bois's and Woodson's critiques of liberal arts colleges.

34. Du Bois, "Negro's Industrial Plight," 242. Du Bois made no mention of consumers or segregation in his October 1930 editorial entitled "Employment" in *The Crisis*.

35. Du Bois, "To Your Tents, Oh Israel?" 93–94.

36. "Segregation," 40.

37. Du Bois, "To Your Tents, Oh Israel?"; Du Bois, "Negro and Social Reconstruction"; "Segregation"; "Negro Nation within the Nation"; D. L. Lewis, *W. E. B. Du Bois, 1919–1963*, 302–48.

38. Du Bois, "Negro's Industrial Plight"; [W.] A. Davis, *Leadership, Love and Aggression*, 131–32.

39. E. F. Frazier, "Du Bois Program in the Present Crisis," 13; Platt, *E. Franklin Frazier Reconsidered*, 188–89.

40. E. F. Frazier, "Du Bois Program in the Present Crisis"; Bunche, "Triumph? or Fiasco." These two pieces appeared in *Race*, a publication of the Conference on Social and Economic Aspects of the Race Problem, an interracial group. See also "Letter to the Editor of *The Crisis*, June 14 [1934]," which was signed by Sterling A. Brown, Ralph J. Bunche, Emmett E. Dorsey, and E. Franklin Frazier.

41. Memo, Mar. 14, 1933, W. E. B. Du Bois to J. E. Spingarn, suggested the list of invitees, Folder 141; Emmett Dorsey to J. E. Spingarn, Sept. 6, 1933, Folder 135; Registration Blanks, Folder 523, J. E. Spingarn Papers, Howard University. Spingarn hosted two meetings at his estate in Amenia, New York. The first was in 1916 and the second in 1933. Du Bois selected most of the invitees for both meetings.

42. Abram Harris to Du Bois, Jan. 6, 1934, H. Aptheker, *Correspondence* 1:471–73.

43. Darity, "Soundings and Silences on Race and Social Change," 237.

44. Wilkins, *Standing Fast*, 152–55.

45. "Dr. Du Bois Resigns, The Board's Resolution," 245–46.

46. Abram Harris to Walter White, July 18, July 28, 1934, and replies, July 20, July 30, 1934, Walter White to Mary Ovington, July 12, 1934; William Hastie to Walter White, Sept. 24, 1934, Folder A29, NAACP Papers, LOC.

47. Ibid.; Kirby, *Black Americans in the Roosevelt Era*, 155–57, 159.

48. Program for 1935 NAACP Annual Conference in St. Louis, Missouri; John P. Davis Speech at NAACP 1935 conference, June 27, 1935; Press releases, June 28, June 30, 1935; Letter from Roy Wilkins to George Schuyler, June 29, 1935, Box 11, NAACP Papers, LOC.

49. H. V. Nelson, "Philadelphia NAACP."

50. Abram Harris to W. E. B. Du Bois, Nov. 21, 1925, in Du Bois, *Correspondence*, 1:327–38, quotation on 327.

51. W. E. B. Du Bois to Abram Harris, Dec. 15, 1925, Ibid., 1:328.

52. Abram Harris to W. E. B. Du Bois, Dec. 26, 1933, Du Bois Papers, University of Massachusetts, Amherst; reply W. E. B. Du Bois to Abram Harris, Jan. 3, 1934, in Du Bois, *Correspondence*, 1:470–71, quotation on 471.

53. Abram Harris to W. E. B. Du Bois, Jan. 6, 1934, in Du Bois, *Correspondence*, 1:471–72, quotation on 471. See also George Streator to W. E. B. Du Bois, Nov. 27, 1934, H. *Correspondence* 2:41.

54. W. E. B. Du Bois to Abram Harris, Jan. 3, 1934, ibid., 1:471.

55. Author's interview with Robert C. Weaver, July 17, 1981 (hereafter cited Weaver interview); A. Williams, "Robert C. Weaver," 1–2, 9. Weaver's maternal grandfather, Robert T. Freeman (c. 1847–73), was the first black graduate of Harvard Dental School (1869); and his mother's cousin the nineteenth-century Washington, D.C., high school principal Mary Jane Patterson (1840–94) had been the first black woman to earn a bachelor's degree from Oberlin College.

56. Weaver interview; A. Williams, "Robert C. Weaver," 1–2,5, 9. Panel discussions and interviews with Mae Miller (Kelly Miller's daughter), Laverne Gregory West, Montague Cobb, Sterling Brown, Anne Cooke Reid (widow of Ira Reid), and R. W. Logan, at a colloquium on segregation in Washington D.C., "In the Shadow of the Capitol," Apr. 12–13, 1981, Folger Library, Washington, D.C. Miller, West, and Brown were children of Howard University faculty members and grew up on or near the campus between 1900 and 1925.

57. Dunbar faculty with doctorates included Georgiana Simpson, Eva Dykes, and Anna Julia Cooper, who had earned their degrees in German, English, and French from the University of Chicago (1921), Radcliffe College (1921), and the Sorbonne (1925), respectively. See F. R. Wilson, "'All of the Glory . . . Faded . . . Quickly.'"

58. Sadie Mossell Alexander, oral history interview by Walter M. Phillips, p. 10, STMA Papers, Box 1, Folder 20, University of Pennsylvania Archives; West, "Dunbar High School Story, 1870–1926," used with the permission of Linda West Nickens. See also F. R. Wilson, "'All of the Glory . . . Faded . . . Quickly,'" 169–71.

59. West, "Dunbar High School Story, 1870–1926"; Weaver interview; "Higher

Training of Negroes." Houston was valedictorian of his class at Amherst College, Phi Beta Kappa, and the first black editor on the *Harvard Law Review*.

60. Letter from Robert C. Weaver to Francille Wilson, Nov. 6, 1981.

61. A. Williams, "Robert C. Weaver," 13; Weaver interview.

62. Ibid., 10–13; Ibid.

63. H. W. Greene, *Negro Holders of Doctorates*. They were Sadie T. M. Alexander, University of Pennsylvania, (1921), and Henderson Donald, Yale (1927).

64. Robert Weaver had applied to MIT to study engineering but was not admitted because he had not taken German. Mortimer Weaver was a Phi Beta Kappa graduate from Williams College. The Weavers planned to attend law school and set up a joint practice in Washington. Robert Weaver completed Harvard College in 1930, a year after his class, because of his brother's death. See Weaver interview; A. Williams, "Robert C. Weaver," 10–13.

65. Robert C. Weaver to W. E. B. Du Bois, Jan. 29, 1931, in Du Bois, *Correspondence*, 1:435.

66. Ibid., 434–35.

67. W. E. B. Du Bois to Robert Weaver, Feb. 10, 1931, in Du Bois, *Correspondence*, 1:435.

68. Weaver, "High Wage Theory of Prosperity"; Weaver interview.

69. A. Williams, "Robert C. Weaver," 17; Weaver interview.

70. W. Jones, "History and Appraisal of the Economic Consequences of Negro Trade Boycotts," 27–28, 36; G. J. Hunter, "'Don't Buy Where You Can't Work'"; J. A. Davis, "We Win the Right to Fight for Jobs." William Darity Jr. notes that Harris was hostile to the New Negro Alliance, and Jacqueline Goggin charts Woodson's warm support of it. John A. Davis was the brother of W. Allison Davis, anthropologist, and was not related to John P. Davis or to John W. Davis, historian. See Darity, "Soundings and Silences on Race and Social Change," 238–39.

71. "The Negro Industrial League—J. P. Davis Ex Sec 1932–33" n.d. [1937], carbon typescript, Box 1, National Negro Congress Papers, NYPLSC; Weaver interview.

72. Their testimony also led to the request for a statement for the record concerning black earnings in the structural clay products industry. See "Statement of the Negro Industrial League Concerning the Code of Fair Competition For the Cotton Textile Industry"; and "Statement of the Negro Industrial League Concerning the Code of the Fair Competition Proposed by the Structural Clay Products Industry," Box 1, NNC Papers, NYPLSC; "Summary of Work Already Accomplished and Suggested Next Steps in Program for the Joint Committee on National Recovery," Confidential Memorandum, no author, Sept. 15, 1933, 10 pages, Joint Committee Folder, NAACP Papers, LOC; Lawrence, "Negro Organizations in Crisis," 249–50; A. Williams, "Robert C. Weaver," 117–20.

73. "Statement of the Negro Industrial League Concerning the Code of Fair Competition For the Cotton Textile Industry," 5; and "Statement of the Negro Industrial League Concerning the Code of the Fair Competition Proposed by the Structural Clay Products Industry," Box 1, NNC Papers, NYPLSC; "Summary of

Work Already Accomplished and Suggested Next Steps in Program for the Joint Committee on National Recovery," Confidential Memorandum, no author, Sept. 15, 1933, 10 pages, Joint Committee Folder, NAACP Papers, LOC.

74. "Summary of Work Already Accomplished and Suggested Next Steps in Program for the Joint Committee on National Recovery," 3–4, Confidential Memorandum, Sept. 15, 1933, 10 pages, no author, Joint Committee Folder, NAACP Papers, LOC.

75. "Fair Play for Negro Miners Sought at the NRA Hearings: Dr. Robert C. Weaver of the Negro Industrial League, Makes Appeal at Hearings on Codes: Supported by Church and Fraternal Leaders," n.d., no place (Capital News Service), clipping, Box 7, NHB Papers, LOC. In addition to Burroughs, Weaver claimed the endorsement of the AME and AMEZ churches. His presentation was described as having been assisted by George Haynes and Mary Van Kleeck of the Russell Sage Foundation. See also Roberts, "Crucible for a Vision," 216–18.

76. John P. Davis, Executive Secretary NIL, to Miss Nannie Burroughs, Aug. 17, 1933, Box 7, NHB Papers, LOC.

77. "Fair Play for Negro Miners Sought at the NRA Hearings: Dr. Robert C. Weaver of the Negro Industrial League, Makes Appeal at Hearings on Codes: Supported by Church and Fraternal Leaders," n.d., no place (Capital News Service), clipping, Box 7, NHB Papers, LOC; G. E. Haynes, "The Negro and the National Recovery Act, II," n.d. [1933], GEH-Fisk.

78. "Summary of Work Already Accomplished and Suggested Next Steps in Program for the Joint Committee on National Recovery," Confidential Memorandum, no author, Sept. 15, 1933, 10 pages, Joint Committee Folder, NAACP Papers, LOC; Member Organizations of the Joint Committee on National Recovery (revised Sept. 17, 1934), NNC Papers, NYPLSC; Frances Williams to Walter White, Oct. 6, 1933; Frances Williams to Bishop William Fountain, Oct. 23, 1933; Frances Williams to Budget Chair for the Joint Committee and a Secretary of the Labor Division of the National YWCA Board, Neighborhood Union Papers, Atlanta University Archives.

79. "Summary of Work Already Accomplished and Suggested Next Steps in Program for the Joint Committee on National Recovery," 2–7, Confidential Memorandum, no author, Sept. 15, 1933, 10 pages, Joint Committee Folder, NAACP Papers, LOC; G. E. Haynes, "The Negro and the National Recovery Act, II," n.d. [1933], GEH-Fisk; Quotation in John P. Davis, Executive Secretary NIL, to Miss Nannie Burroughs, Aug. 17, 1933, Box 7, NHB Papers, LOC; William Hastie to Walter White, Dec. 7, 1933, Joint Committee Files, IC 311, NAACP Papers, LOC; Member Organizations of the Joint Committee on National Recovery (revised Sept. 17, 1934) lists 24 member organizations, their presidents and representatives on the JCER. "The Negro Market," 6, n.d. [1933], reported Weaver's formal report at the National Negro Business League Conferenece. See NNC Papers, NYPLSC.

80. Weaver interview. There were still hard feelings between league officials and Haynes fifteen years after his departure.

81. G. E. Haynes, "The Negro and the National Recovery Act, II," n.d. [1933], GEH-Fisk.

82. G. E. Haynes, "The Negro and the National Recovery Act, I," 1, Aug. 4 [1933], GEH-Fisk; four-page press release from the Federal Council of Churches, GEH-Fisk.

83. G. E. Haynes, "The Negro and the National Recovery Act, I," 1, Aug. 4 [1933], GEH-Fisk; four-page press release from the Federal Council of Churches, GEH-Fisk; G. E. Haynes, "The Negro and the National Recovery Act, II," 1, n.d. [1933], GEH-Fisk.

84. Copy of "Memorandum of Conference between Walter White, Abram Harris, John P. Davis and Charles H. Houston," Joint Committee Office, Saturday, Oct. 29, 1934, IC 311, NAACP Papers, LOC; Member Organizations of the Joint Committee on National Recovery (revised Sept. 17, 1934), NNC Papers, NYPLSC.

85. Frances Williams to John P. Davis, Sept. 15, 1933; William Hastie to Walter White, Dec. 7, 1933, Joint Committee Files, IC 311, NAACP Papers, LOC.

86. Weaver interview; Frances Williams to Walter White, Sept. 15, 29, 1933, NAACP Papers, LOC; A Williams, "Robert C. Weaver, 20–21."

87. "Summary of Work Already Accomplished and Suggested Next Steps in Program for the Joint Committee on National Recovery," Confidential Memorandum, no author, Sept. 15, 1933, 10 pages, Joint Committee Folder, NAACP Papers, LOC; Weaver interview; Williams, "Robert C. Weaver," 21; John P. Davis to Nannie Helen Burroughs, Sept. 19, 1933, GEH to NHB, Sept. 25, 1933, NHB Papers, LOC.

88. Weaver interview; Weaver to George Arthur, Oct. 26, 1933, Folder 1/3, Weaver to general managers of tobacco companies, 28 Oct. 1933; John P. Davis to Weaver, Nov. 4, 1933, Folder 1/5; C. C. Spaulding to Weaver, Oct. 9, 1933, reply, Oct. 23, 1933, Folder 2/6; Weaver Papers, NYPLSC; A. Williams, "Robert C. Weaver," 21; Kirby, *Black Americans in the Roosevelt Era*, 106–7, 121; Spaulding, "Is the Negro Meeting the Test in Business." Weaver also wrote speeches and articles for Spaulding, who was one of the National Negro Business League representatives on the JCER, and Weaver certainly met with him when he addressed the National Negro Business League in August 1933.

89. Kirby, *Black Americans in the Roosevelt Era*, 106–7; Roberts, "Crucible for a Vision," 217; George E. Haynes to the Members of the Joint Committee on National Recovery, Oct. 4, 1933, NHB Papers, LOC.

90. Kirby, *Black Americans in the Roosevelt Era*. The fact that the white advisors on Negro affairs sometimes went to segregated country clubs was also offensive to many blacks, although liberal whites used this as part of their rationale for having white rather than black advisors.

91. Kirby, *Black Americans in the Roosevelt Era*; Robert C. Weaver to John P. Davis, Nov. 6, 1933, Folder 1/5, Weaver Papers, NYPLSC; A. Williams, "Robert C. Weaver," 23.

92. John P. Davis to Weaver, Nov. 7, Nov. 11, 1933, Davis to Harold Ickes, Nov. 7, 1933, and Davis to Clark Foreman, Nov. 7, 1933, Weaver Papers, NYPLSC.

93. A. Williams, "Robert C. Weaver," chap. 4; Buni, *Robert L. Vann of the Pitts-*

burgh Courier, 206–7; Weaver, "Impact of the New Deal upon Blacks and Their Participation in World War II Production," 10; Kirby, *Black Americans in the Roosevelt Era,* 131–34. Most of the Black Cabinet were young black intellectuals in their twenties and thirties, and only Mrs. Bethune, who was in her sixties, had a sizable political base in the black community or direct access to President Roosevelt.

94. Curriculum vitae of Robert C. Weaver, n.d. (c. 1978), in the possession of the author. Weaver's published social scientific writings stretched in a steady progression from 1934 to 1965. These include Weaver, *Negro Labor;* Weaver, *Negro Ghetto;* Weaver, *Male Negro Skilled Workers in the United States, 1930–1936;* Weaver, "Efficiency of Negro Labor"; Weaver, "New Deal and the Negro"; Weaver, "Defense Industries and the Negro"; Weaver, "Negro Employment in the Aircraft Industry."

95. Weaver ranked George Haynes's studies as far superior to the social analyses of the NUL executives Eugene K. Jones and T. Arnold Hill but slightly below the brilliance of W. E. B. Bois or E. Franklin Frazier. Weaver interview; Robert C. Weaver to Francille Wilson, Nov. 6, 1981.

96. Darity, "Soundings and Silences on Race and Social Change," 243–44; letter from Abram Harris to Benjamin Stolberg, Nov. 12, 1930; letter, quotations on pp. 1, 2; see also in Box 4b, Folder 2, Stolberg Papers, Columbia University Archives.

97. Reid, Valien, and Johnson, *Statistics by Regions;* Reid, *Negro Immigrant;* Reid, *In A Minor Key;* Raper and Reid, *Sharecroppers All;* Weaver, *Male Negro Skilled Workers in the United States, 1930–1936;* Gilpin, "Charles S. Johnson," 439; B. A. Jones, "Tradition of Sociology Teaching in Black Colleges," 154–55.

98. Weaver, "Employment of Negroes in the United States War Industries." The employment study was a small part of Weaver's overall portfolio, and Ira Reid was teaching at Atlanta University and consulting with a number of federal agencies.

99. See Robert C. Weaver to Walter White, Aug. 1, 1941, Weaver Papers, NYPLSC; "National Defense Labor Problems."

100. Ickes dramatically bolstered Weaver's and William Hastie's efforts to integrate the cafeteria in the Interior Department simply by eating lunch with them. After that occasion the cafeteria was open to all employees, black as well as white.

101. Weaver, "Employment in Federal Projects"; Weaver interview.

102. Kruman, "Quotas for Blacks"; Weaver, "Public Works Administration and School Building–Aid Program and Separate Negro School"; Weaver, "Impact of the New Deal upon Blacks and Their Participation in World War II Production," 9–12; Weaver, *Negro Labor,* 12; Weaver, "Experiment in Negro Labor"; Weaver interview; McNeil, *Groundwork,* 132; A. Williams, "Robert C. Weaver," 64–65, 67–68; Kirby, *Black Americans in the Roosevelt Era,* 145–47; Conrad and Sherer, "From the New Deal to the Great Society."

103. Weaver, "Negro in a Program of Public Housing"; Weaver interview; Weaver, "Impact of the New Deal upon Blacks and Their Participation in World War II Production," 9–12; Kruman, "Quotas for Blacks"; Conrad and Sherer, "From the New Deal to the Great Society," 293–94.

104. Weaver, "Impact of the New Deal upon Blacks and Their Participation in World War II Production," 9–10.

105. Weaver, "Employment in Federal Projects," 515.

106. Weaver, "Negro Labor since 1929"; "Proceedings of the Annual Meeting." The speech was given on Oct. 29, 1949.

107. Weaver, "Employment in Federal Projects"; Weaver, "Negro Comes of Age in Industry"; Weaver interview.

108. Weaver, "Wither Northern Race Relations Committees?"

109. Weaver interview; Weaver, "Impact of the New Deal upon Blacks and Their Participation in World War II Production," 16–17.

110. Weaver, *Negro Labor*; Weaver, "Negro Labor since 1929."

111. Philip Foner began teaching at historically black Lincoln University in Pennsylvania in 1967, after being fired from City University of New York in 1941 for being a communist. F. Ray Marshall's black labor studies stressed the exclusion of blacks from unions. He became secretary of labor in 1977 under President Jimmy Carter. Beginning in the late sixties Herbert R. Northrup edited two series on black employment selected industries that were published by the Wharton School of the University of Pennsylvania. Racial Policies of American Industry had twenty-three reports, and Studies in Negro Employment had at least eight. One of Northrup's black graduate students, Bernard E. Anderson, went on to a distinguished career at the University of Pennsylvania and as assistant secretary of labor at the Employment Standards Administration, 1994–2001. Anderson has been very supportive of my efforts to study early black labor scholars. See Foner, *Organized Labor and the Black Worker, 1619–1973*; Marshall, *Negro and Organized Labor*; Northrup, *Organized Labor and the Negro*; Northrup, *Will Negroes Get Jobs Now?* Northrup, *Negro in the Automobile Industry*; B. E. Anderson, *Negro Employment in Public Utilities*; Anderson, "Faculty Profile"; McLemee, "Seeing Red"; Reynolds, "Labor Unions."

112. F. R. Wilson, "Going, Going, Gone."

113. F. G. Davis, "War Economics and Negro Labor"; M. M. Smythe, "Economics Teacher in the Post-War Period"; C. L. Franklin, "Characteristics and Taxable Wages of Negro Workers, 13 Selected Southern States, 1938"; P. Valien, "Social and Economic Implications of Migration for the Negro in the Present Social Order"; Warren, "Partial Background for the Study of the Development of Negro Labor."

114. Du Bois, assisted by H. M. Smythe, *Report of the Second Conference of Negro Land Grant Colleges for Coordinating a Program of Cooperative Social Studies*. This study offers a small glimpse at the social and economic research that was taking place at black colleges at the time. It contained L. P. Jackson, "Labor and Land Tenure among Negroes in Southern Agriculture." The University of Chicago hired Abram Harris and the anthropologist Allison Davis. The addition of blacks to the faculty of the University of Chicago was not completely successful and met considerable resistance. The Rosenwald Foundation paid both men's salaries, but neither was able to join the academic department of their specialty. See Belles, "College Faculty, the Negro Scholar, and the Julius Rosenwald Fund." Darity's "Sound-

ings and Silences on Race and Social Change" probes the underlying reasons for Harris's transformation from a radical to a moderate. See D. L. Lewis, *W. E. B. Du Bois, 1919–1963*, 490–93. L. P. Jackson died early in 1950.

115. Weaver interview; Curriculum vitae of Robert C. Weaver, n.d. (c. 1978), in the possession of the author; *Negro Ghetto*; Weaver, "Recent Developments in Urban Housing and Their Implications for Minorities"; Weaver, "Integration in Public and Private Housing."

116. Meier and Rudwick, *Black History and the Historical Profession, 1915–1980*, 280–81, 79, 82–83, 85–88, 91–92; Goggin, *Carter G. Woodson*, 176–78; Egerton, *Speak Now Against the Day*, 304–5, 311–12, 435–36; F. R. Wilson, s.v. "Johnson, Charles S."; F. R. Wilson, "Sadie T. Alexander's Construction of a Public Persona"; F. R. Wilson, "Shaping American and International Protections for Blacks and Women: Sadie T. M. Alexander's Crusade in the U.S. and U.N., 1944–1964."

117. R. R. Wright Jr.'s first assignment as an AME bishop was to South Africa. George Haynes took two study missions to Africa for the YMCA in the 1940s and 1950s and wrote a book, *Africa, Continent of the Future*. Charles S. Johnson and Charles H. Wesley both supported African studies at Fisk, Howard, and Central State. Woodson had long been interested in Africa. The economists Mabel Smythe and her husband, Hugh Smythe, a political scientist, successfully turned their interests to Africa and international affairs. Both were appointed as U.S. ambassadors, Hugh to Syria and Malta, 1965–67, and Mabel to Cameroon and Equatorial Guinea, 1977–79. Black social scientists who began to study Africa in the 1950s included the political scientist Martin Kilson and the anthropologists James Gibbs and Elliot Skinner. These men spent most of their careers at the prestigious, historically white institutions Harvard, Stanford, and Columbia, respectively. See H. H. Smythe and M. M. Smythe, *New Nigerian Elite*.

118. Bond, *Black American Scholars*, 27–28; Meier and Rudwick, *Black History and the Historical Profession, 1915–1980*, 123–36.

Bibliography

Archives and Special Collections

Atlanta University Center, Woodruff Library Archives
Atlanta School of Social Work Papers
Horace Bumstead Papers
Financial Records of Atlanta University
John and Lugenia Burns Hope Papers
Neighborhood Union Papers

Columbia University Archives
Benjamim Stolberg Papers

Fisk University, Franklin Library Special Collections and Archives
George E. Haynes Papers
Charles S. Johnson Papers

Harvard University Archives
Student Records

Howard University, Moorland-Spingarn Research Center
Eva B. Dykes Papers
T. M. Gregory Papers
Abram Harris Papers
Howard University Archives
Arthur B. Spingarn Papers
J. E. Spingarn Paperss

Library of Congress
Sophonisba Breckinridge Papers
Breckinridge Family Papers
Nannie Helen Burroughs Papers
NAACP Papers
National Urban League Papers

National Women's Trade Union League Papers
Louis Post Papers
Mary Church Terrell Papers
Booker T. Washington Papers
Carter G. Woodson Papers

National Archives, Washington, D.C.
RG 86: Records of the Women's Bureau
RG 174: General Records of the Department of Labor
RG 257: Records of the Bureau of Labor Statistics

New York Public Library, Schomburg Center for Research on Black Culture
Carnegie-Myrdal Study
Clippings File
John P. Davis Papers
George E. Haynes, Vertical File
National Negro Congress Papers
Negro Industrial League Papers
Robert C. Weaver Papers

Radcliffe College, Schlesinger Library
Black Women Oral History Project Records

Temple University
Urban History Archives

University of Massachusetts, Amherst
W. E. B. Du Bois Papers

University of Pennsylvania Archives
Raymond Pace Alexander Papers
Sadie Tanner Mossell Alexander Papers
Alexander Family Papers
Alumni Folders
Faculty Records
University Archives

Yale University, Beinecke Rare Book
and Manuscript Library
Elizabeth Ross Haynes Papers
George E. Haynes Papers
James Weldon Johnson Papers
Anson Phelps Stokes Papers

Journals and Newspapers

A.M.E. Church Review
American Historical Review
American Journal of Sociology
American Quarterly
American Sociologist
*Annals of the American Academy of
    Political and Social Science*
Arena
Athenaeum
Atlanta University Bulletin
The Bee
Boston Herald
Bulletin of the Department of Labor
Century Magazine
Charities
Chronicle of Higher Education
The Crimson and Gray
The Crisis
Fisk Herald
Fisk News
Florida Historical Quarterly
Journal of Black Studies

Journal of Negro Education
Journal of Negro History
Journal of Political Economy
Monthly Labor Review
The Nation
Negro History Bulletin
New York Times
Ohio History
Opportunity
Our Day
Outlook
Philadelphia Public Ledger
Phylon
Pittsburgh Courier
*Quarterly Review of Higher Education
    among Negroes*
Scroll
South Atlantic Quarterly
Southern Workman
The Survey
Voice of the Negro
William & Mary Quarterly

Other Sources

"Achievement." *The Crisis* 22, no. 5 (Sept. 1921): 223.

Adams, James B. "The Public Schools of Atlanta." *Athenaeum* 16, no. 5 (Mar. 1914): 6–7.

Adams, Myron W. *A History of Atlanta University*. Atlanta, 1930.

"Address of President R. R. Wright." *Supplement to Atlanta University Bulletin* (Mar. 1896): 3.

Aldrich, Mark. "The Backward Races and the American Social Order: Race and Ethnicity in the Thought of John R. Commons." Unpublished paper.

————. "Progressive Economists and Scientific Racism: Walter Willcox and Black Americans, 1895–1910." *Phylon* 40, no. 1 (Spring 1979): 1–14.

Alexander, Adele Logan. s.v. "Logan, Adella Hunt." In *Black Women in America: An Historical Encyclopedia,* ed. Darlene Clark Hine, Elsa Barkley Brown, and Rosalyn Terborg-Penn, 1:729–31. Brooklyn, 1993.

Alexander, Sadie T. M. "Negro Women in Our Economic Life." *Opportunity* 8 (July 1930): 201–3.

Allan, Henry Christopher. "History of the Non-residential Degree Program at Illinois Wesleyan University, 1873–1910: A Study of a Pioneer External Degree Program in the United States." Ph.D. diss., University of Chicago, 1984.

"The American Negro." Special issue, *Annals of the American Academy of Political and Social Science* 140 (Nov. 1928).

Anderson, Bernard E. "Faculty Profile." Wharton School of the University of Pennsylvania. Available online at http://www.wharton.upenn.edu/faculty/anderson.html.

————. *Negro Employment in Public Utilities: A Study of Racial Policies in the Electric Power, Gas, and Telephone Industries.* Studies in Negro Employment, no. 3. Philadelphia, 1970.

Anderson, James D. *The Education of Blacks in the South, 1860–1935.* Chapel Hill, N.C., 1988.

Anderson, Jervis. *A. Philip Randolph: A Biographical Portrait.* New York, 1973.

Anderson, Margo J. *The American Census: A Social History.* New Haven, Conn., 1988.

Anderson, Pauline Relylea. "Gustav von Schmoller, 1828–1917." In *Some Historians of Modern Europe,* ed. Bernadette E. Schmidt, 415–43. 1942. Reprint, Port Washington, N.Y., 1966.

"Announcement of Summer School at Fisk." *Fisk Herald* 20, no. 5 (Mar. 1903): 11.

Annual Register of the University of Chicago. 1897–1898. 1898–1899.

Annual Report of the Director of the Women in Industry Service, Washington, D.C., 1919.

Appiah, Kwame Anthony. *In My Father's House: Africa in the Philosophy of Culture.* New York, 1992.

————. "The Uncompleted Argument: Du Bois and the Illusion of Race." *Critical Inquiry* 12 (Autumn 1985): 21–37.

"Appointments." *Opportunity* 8 (Mar. 1935): 93.

Aptheker, Bettina. "Quest for Dignity: Black Women in the Professions, 1865–1900." In her *Woman's Legacy: Essays on Race, Sex, and Class in American History,* 89–110. Amherst, Mass., 1982.

Aptheker, Herbert, ed. *A Documentary History of the Negro People of the United States.* 1951. Reprint, New York, 1979.

Arnold, Thea. "Women's Loyal Union of New York and Brooklyn." In *Black Women in America: An Historical Encyclopedia,* ed. Darlene Clark Hine, Elsa Barkley Brown, and Rosalyn Terborg-Penn, 2:1278–79. Brooklyn, 1993.

Avery, Sheldon. *Up from Washington: William Pickens and the Negro Struggle for Equality, 1900–1954*. Newark, Del., 1989.

Baird, Carol. "Albert Bushnell Hart: The Rise of the Professional Historian." In *Social Sciences at Harvard, 1860–1920: From Inculcation to the Open Mind*, ed. Paul S. Buck, 129–74. Cambridge, Mass., 1965.

Baltzell, Digby. "Introduction." In *The Philadelphia Negro*, by W. E. B. Du Bois. 1899. Reprint, New York, 1967.

Banks, William M. *Black Intellectuals: Race and Responsibility in American Life*. New York, 1996.

Bannister, Robert C. *Sociology and Scientism: The American Quest for Objectivity, 1880–1940*. Chapel Hill, N.C., 1987.

"Baptist College." *Athenaeum* 13, no. 3 (Jan. 1910): 11.

Bardolph, Richard. "Bowen, John Wesley Edward." In *Dictionary of American Negro Biography*, ed. Rayford W. Logan and Michael R. Winston, 52–53. New York, 1982.

Bass, Rosa Morehead. "Need of Kindergartens." In *Social and Physical Condition of Negroes in Cities: Report of an Investigation under the Direction of Atlanta University and Proceedings of the Second Conference for the Study of Problems Concerning Negro City Life held at Atlanta University, May 25–26, 1897*, 66–68. Atlanta University Publications, no. 2. Atlanta, 1897.

———. "Poverty as a Cause of Mortality." In *Mortality among Negroes in Cities: Proceedings of the Conference for Investigation of City Problems held at Atlanta University, May 26–27, 1896*, 30–31. Atlanta University Publications, no. 1. Atlanta, 1896.

Bay, Mia. "'The World Was Thinking Wrong about Race': *The Philadelphia Negro* and Nineteenth-Century Science." In *W. E. B. Du Bois, Race, and the City: The Philadelphia Negro and Its Legacy*, ed. Michael B. Katz and Thomas J. Sugrue, 40–59. Philadelphia, 1998.

Belles, A. Gilbert. "The College Faculty, the Negro Scholar, and the Julius Rosenwald Fund." *Journal of Negro History* 54, no. 4 (May 1969): 383–92.

Bethune, Mary McLeod. "The Problems of the City Dweller." *Opportunity* 3 (Feb. 1925): 54–55.

The Black Worker: A Documentary History from Colonial Times to the Present. Ed. Philip S. Foner and Ronald L. Lewis. 8 vols. Philadelphia, 1978–85.

Blackwell, James E., and Morris Janowitz, eds. *Black Sociologists: Historical and Contemporary Perspectives*. Chicago, 1974.

Boas, Franz. "The Negro and the Demands of Modern Life." *Charities* 15 (Oct. 7, 1905): 86–87.

Bogin, Ruth. "Haynes, Elizabeth Ross." In *Notable American Women: The Modern Period, A Biographical Dictionary*, ed. Barbara Sicherman et al., 324–25. Cambridge, Mass., 1980.

Bond, Horace Mann. *Black America Scholars: A Study of Their Beginnings*. Detroit, 1972.

————. *Negro Education in Alabama: A Study of Iron and Steel.* Washington, D.C., 1939.

"Book Notes." *Historical Outlook* 18 (Oct. 1927): 285.

Booth, Charles. *Life and Labour of the People in London.* London, 1899–1902.

Boris, Joseph J., ed. "Abram L. Harris." In *Who's Who in Colored America.* New York, 1927.

————. "Elizabeth Ross Haynes." In *Who's Who in Colored America.* New York, 1927, 1931, 1937–40.

Boston, Thomas D., ed. *A Different Vision: African American Economic Thought.* New York, 1997.

Bowles, Eva. "Opportunities for the Educated Colored Woman." *Opportunity* 1 (Mar. 1923): 8–10.

Bradford, George G. "Report from the City of Washington." In *Mortality among Negroes in Cities: Proceedings of the Conference for Investigation of City Problems, held at Atlanta University, May 26–27, 1896,* 13–16. Atlanta University Publications, no. 1. Atlanta, 1896.

Brazeal, Brailsford R. *The Brotherhood of Sleeping Car Porters: Its Origin and Development.* New York, 1946.

Broderick, Francis L. "German Influence on the Scholarship of W. E. B. Du Bois." *Phylon* 14, no. 4 (Winter 1958): 367–71.

————. "W. E. B. Du Bois: History of an Intellectual." In *Black Sociologists: Historical and Contemporary Perspectives,* ed. James E. Blackwell and Morris Janowitz, 3–24. Chicago, 1974.

Brown, Claudette. "Mossell, Gertrude E. H. Bustill." In *Dictionary of American Negro Biography,* ed. Rayford W. Logan and Michael R. Winston, 457. New York, 1982.

Brown, Elsa Barkley. "Introduction." In *The Negro Trail Blazers of California,* by Delilah Beasley. 1919. African American Women Writers Series, 1910–1940, ed. Henry Louis Gates, xv–iii. New York, 1997.

————. "Womanist Consciousness: Maggie Lena Walker and the Independent Order of Saint Luke." *Signs* 14, no. 3 (1989): 610–33.

Brown, Jean Collier. "The Negro Woman Worker." *Women's Bureau Bulletin* 165 (1938).

Browne, Hugh M. "The Training of the Negro Laborer in the North." *Annals of the American Academy of Political and Social Science* 27 (May 1906): 117–27.

Browning, James A. "A Historical Sketch of the Association of Social Science Teachers at Negro Colleges." *Quarterly Review of Higher Education among Negroes* 12 (Apr. 1944): 143–45.

Bruce, Josephine B. "What Education Has Done for Colored Women." *Voice of the Negro* 1, no. 7 (1904): 294–300.

Buck, Paul S., ed. "Introduction." In his *Social Sciences at Harvard, 1860–1920: From Inculcation to the Open Mind,* 1–18. Cambridge, Mass., 1965.

Bulkley, William L. "The Industrial Conditions of Negroes in New York City."

Annals of the American Academy of Political and Social Science 27, no. 3 (May 1906): 128–34.

———. "Race Prejudice as Viewed from an Economic Standpoint." In Proceedings of the National Negro Conference 1909, 89–97. 1909. Reprint, New York, 1969.

———. "The School as a Social Center." Charities 15 (Oct. 7, 1905): 76–78.

Bullock, Henry Allen. A History of Negro Education in the South: From 1619 to the Present. New York, 1970.

Bulmer, Martin. The Chicago School of Sociology. Chicago, 1984.

Bunche, Ralph J. "Triumph? or Fiasco." Race 1 (Summer 1936): 93–96.

Buni, Andrew. Robert L. Vann of the Pittsburgh Courier. Pittsburgh, 1974.

Burkett, Randall K. Black Redemption: Churchmen Speak for Garvey Movement. Philadelphia, 1978.

Burkett, Randall K., and Richard Newman, eds. Black Apostles: Afro-American Clergy Confront the Twentieth Century. Boston, 1978.

Bush, Rod. We Are not What We Seem: Black Nationalism and Class Struggle in the American Century. New York, 1999.

Butler, Selena Sloan. "Need of Day Nurseries." In Social and Physical Condition of Negroes in Cities: Report of an Investigation under the Direction of Atlanta University and Proceedings of the Second Conference for the Study of Problems Concerning Negro City Life held at Atlanta University, May 25–26, 1897, 63–65. Atlanta University Publications, no. 2. Atlanta, 1897.

Carlton-LaNey, Iris. "The Career of Birdye Henrietta Haynes: A Pioneer Settlement House Worker." Social Service Review 68, no. 2 (1994): 254–73.

———. "George and Birdye Haynes: Legacy to Community Practice." In African American Community Practice Models: Historical and Contemporary Responses, ed. Iris Carlton-LaNey and N. Yolanda Burwell, 27–48. New York, 1996.

Carlton-LaNey, Iris, and N. Yolanda Burwell, eds. African American Community Practice Models: Historical and Contemporary Responses. New York, 1996.

Cash, Floris Barnett. "Matthews, Victoria Earle." In Black Women in America: An Historical Encyclopedia, ed. Darlene Clark Hine, Elsa Barkley Brown, and Rosalyn Terborg-Penn, 1:759–61. Brooklyn, 1993.

———. "White Rose Mission, New York City." In Black Women in America: An Historical Encyclopedia, ed. Darlene Clark Hine, Elsa Barkley Brown, and Rosalyn Terborg-Penn, 2:1258–59. Brooklyn, 1993.

Cash, William L. "A Study of Sociology." Fisk Herald 20, no. 3 (1902): 3–5.

Cayton, Horace R., and George S. Mitchell. Black Workers and the New Unions. 1939. Reprint, College Park, Md., 1969.

Chambers, Clark A. Paul U. Kellogg and the Survey: Voices for Social Welfare and Social Justice. Minneapolis, 1971.

Chandler, Susan Kerr. "'That Biting, Stinging Thing Which Ever Shadows Us': African-American Social Workers in France during World War I." Social Service Review 69 (Sept. 1995): 498–514.

Chateauvert, Melinda. Marching Together: Women of the Brotherhood of Sleeping Car Porters. Urbana, Ill., 1998.

Cherry, Robert. "Racial Thought and the Early Economics Profession." *Review of Social Economy* 34, no. 2 (Oct. 1976): 147–62.

Chicago Commission on Race Relations. *The Negro in Chicago: A Study of Race Relations and a Race Riot.* Chicago, 1922.

Childs, Mattie F. "The Progress of the Colored Women since 1863." Emancipation Day Oration, Jan. 1, 1894. In *Atlanta University Bulletin* (Jan. 1894): 5–6.

Church, Robert L. "The Economists Study Society: Sociology at Harvard, 1891–1902." In *Social Sciences at Harvard, 1860–1920: From Inculcation to the Open Mind,* ed. Paul S. Buck, 19–90. Cambridge, Mass., 1965.

"City Problem Studies." *Atlanta University Bulletin* 74 (May 1896): 2.

Clarke, John Henrik. *Harlem: A Community in Transition.* New York, 1969.

Clark-Lewis, Elizabeth. *Living In, Living Out: African American Domestics in Washington, D.C., 1910–1940.* Washington, D.C., 1994.

"Colored Women Represent Their Race in State and Nation." *New York City Tribune,* Mar. 23, 1919. In *Afro-American Women of the South and the Advancement of the Race, 1895–1925,* by Cynthia Neverdon-Morton, 74–75. Knoxville, Tenn., 1989.

Colson, Myra Hill. "Home Work among Negro Women in Chicago." Master's thesis, University of Chicago, 1927.

———. "Negro Home Workers in Chicago." *Social Service Review* 2, no. 3 (Sept. 1923): 385–413.

"Commencement Week: . . . Quiz Club Prize Contest." *Atlanta University Bulletin* 93 (June 1898): 1–2.

Commons, John R. *Races and Immigrants in America.* New York, 1908.

———, ed. *Trade Unionism and Labor Problems.* New York, 1905.

"Conditions of the Negro in Various Cities." *Bulletin of the Department of Labor* 10 (May 1897): 257–369.

"Conference of City Problem Studies." *Atlanta University Bulletin* 75 (June 1896): 1.

"Conference of Negro Women." *Survey* 4 (Aug. 30, 1918): 513–14.

Conrad, Celilia A., and George Sherer. "From the New Deal to the Great Society: The Economic Activism of Robert C. Weaver." In *A Different Vision,* ed. Thomas D. Boston, 290–301. New York, 1997.

Cooper, Anna J. "The American Negro Academy." *Southern Workman* 27 (Feb. 1898): 35–36.

———. *A Voice from the South.* Introduction by Mary Helen Washington. 1892. Reprint, New York, 1988.

"Cover—Emma Shields Penn." *Opportunity* 16, no. 2 (1938): 59–60.

Crummell, Alexander. "The Attitude of the American Mind Toward the Negro Intellect." *American Negro Academy Occasional Papers,* no. 3. New York, 1969.

———. *Destiny and Race: Selected Writings, 1840–1898,* ed. Wilson J. Moses. Amherst, Mass., 1992.

———. "No. 2 Character: The Great Thing." In *Some Efforts of American Negroes for Their Own Social Betterment,* ed. W. E. B. Du Bois, 36–40. Washington, D.C., 1897.

Cruse, Harold. *The Crisis of the Negro Intellectual.* New York, 1967.

Cuff, Robert D. "The Politics of Labor Administration during World War I." *Labor History* 21 (Fall 1980): 548–69.

Dancy, John A. *Sand against the Wind.* Detroit, 1966.

Darity, William, Jr. "Abram Harris: An Odyssey from Howard to Chicago." *Review of Black Political Economy* 15 (Winter 1987): 13–14.

———. "Introduction: The Odyssey of Abram Harris from Howard to Chicago." In *Race, Radicalism, and Reform: Selected Papers of Abram L. Harris,* ed. William Darity Jr., 1–34. New Brunswick, N.J., 1989.

———. "Soundings and Silences on Race and Social Change: Abram Harris, Jr. In the Great Depression." In *A Different Vision: African American Economic Thought,* ed. Thomas D. Boston, 230–49. New York, 1997.

Davis, [W.] Allison. *Leadership, Love and Aggression, as the Twig Is Bent: The Psychological Factors in the Making of Four Black Leaders, Frederick Douglass, W. E. B. Du Bois, Richard Wright, Martin Luther King, Jr.* San Diego, 1983.

Davis, Frank G. "War Economics and Negro Labor." *Quarterly Review of Higher Education among Negroes* 10 (July 1942): 133–68.

Davis, John A. "We Win the Right to Fight for Jobs." *Opportunity* 16 (Aug. 1938): 230–37.

Davis, John P. "NRA Codifies Wage Slavery." *The Crisis* 41 (Oct. 1934): 298–99.

Davis, Katherine Bement. "The Condition of the Negro in Philadelphia." *Journal of Political Economy* 8 (Dec. 1899–Sept. 1900): 248–60.

Deegan, Mary Jo. *Jane Addams and the Men of the Chicago School, 1892–1918.* New Brunswick, N.J., 1988.

———. "W. E. B. Du Bois and the Women of Hull-House, 1895–1899." *American Sociologist* 19, no. 4 (Winter 1988): 301–11.

Dennis, Rutledge M., ed. *Research in Race and Ethnic Relations: The Black Intellectuals.* Vol. 10. Greenwich, Conn., 1997.

DeNoyelles, Daniel. "The Negro as Laborer." *Industrial Psychology* 1 (Feb. 1926): 91–93.

Diggs, Irene. "Reid, Ira De Augustine." In *Dictionary of American Negro Biography,* ed. Rayford W. Logan and Michael R. Winston, 519–20. New York, 1982.

Dill, Bonnie Thornton. *Across the Boundaries of Race and Class: An Exploration of Work and Family among Black Female Domestic Servants.* New York, 1994.

"Director's Report." *Journal of Negro History* 13 (Oct. 1928): 400.

Donald, Henderson. "The Negro Migration of 1916–1918." *Journal of Negro History* 6, no. 4 (Oct. 1921): 383–92.

Dorsey, Emmett E. Review of *The Black Worker,* by Sterling D. Spero and Abram L. Harris. *Journal of Negro History* 16 (July 1931): 340.

Drake, St. Clair. "In the Mirror of Black Scholarship: W. Allison Davis and *Deep South.*" In *Education and Black Struggle: Notes From the Colonized World,* ed.

Institute of the Black World (Harvard Educational Review monograph, no. 2), 42–54. Cambridge, Mass., 1974.

Drake, St. Clair, and Horace R. Cayton. *Black Metropolis: A Study of Negro Life in a Northern City*. 1945. 2 vols. Revised and enlarged ed., New York, 1962.

"Dr. Du Bois Resigns, The Board's Resolution." *The Crisis* 31 (Aug. 1934): 254–46.

Du Bois, W. E. B. *Against Racism: Unpublished Essays, Papers, Adresses, 1887–1961*, ed. Herbert Aptheker. Amherst, Mass., 1985.

———. "The Atlanta Conferences." *Voice of the Negro* 1 (Mar. 1904): 85–89. Reprint, *W. E. B. Du Bois on Sociology and the Black Community*, ed. Dan S. Green and Edwin D. Driver, 58–59. Chicago, 1978.

———. *The Autobiography of W. E. B. Du Bois: A Soliloquy on Viewing My Life from the Last Decade of its First Century*. New York, 1968.

———. "The Black North, A Social Study . . ." Pts. 1–4, 6 (pt. 5 does not exist). *New York Times Sunday Magazine Supplement*, November 17, 1901, p. 10; November 24, 1901, p. 11; December 1, 1901, p. 11; December 8, 1901, p. 20; December 15, 1901, p. 20.

———. *Black Reconstruction: An essay towards a history of the part which black folk played in the attempt to reconstruct democracy in America, 1860–1880*. Philadelphia, 1935.

———, ed. *The College-Bred Negro, Report of a Social Study Made under the Direction of Atlanta University; together with the Proceedings of the Fifth Conference for the Study of the Negro Problems, held at Atlanta University, May 29–30, 1900*. Atlanta University Publications, no. 5. Atlanta, 1900.

———. "Concerning the Negro." Review of *The Black Worker*, by Sterling D. Spero and Abram L. Harris, and of *The Negro Wage Earner*, by L. J. Greene and Carter G. Woodson. *Nation* 132 (Apr. 1931): 385.

———. "The Conservation of Races." American Negro Academy Occasional Papers, no. 2. Washington, D.C., 1897.

———. *Contributions by W. E. B. Du Bois in Government Publications and Proceedings*. Comp. and ed. Herbert Aptheker. Millwood, N.Y., 1980.

———. *The Correspondence of W. E. B. Du Bois*. Ed. Herbert Aptheker. 3 vols. Amherst, Mass., 1997.

———. *Darkwater: Voices from Within the Veil*. 1920. Reprint, New York, 1969.

———. *Dusk of Dawn: An Essay toward an Autobiography of a Race Concept*. 1940. Reprint, New York, 1968.

———. ed. *Economic Cooperation among Negro Americans*. Atlanta University Publications, no. 12. Atlanta, 1907.

———. "The Economic Future of the Negro." *AEA Publications*, 3d ser., 7 (Feb. 1906): 219–42.

———. *The Education of Black People: Ten Critiques, 1906–1960*. Ed. Herbert Aptheker. New York, 1973.

———. "The Evolution of Negro Leadership." *Dial* 31 (July 16, 1901): 53–55.

———. "The Freedmen's Bureau." *Atlantic Monthly* 87 (Mar. 1901): 354–65.

———. ed. *The Health and Physique of the Negro American: Report of a Social*

Study Made under the Direction of Atlanta University; together with the Proceedings of the Eleventh Conference for the Study of the Negro Problems, held at Atlanta University, on May 29th, 1906. Atlanta University Publications, no. 11. Atlanta, 1906.

———. "The Hosts of Black Labor." *Nation* 116, no. 3018 (May 9, 1924): 539–41.

———. ed., *The Negro American Family: Report of a Social Study Made Principally by the College Classes of 1909 and 1910 of Atlanta University, under the Patronage of the Trustees of the John F. Slater Fund; together with the Proceedings of the 13th Annual Conference for the Study of the Negro Problems, held at Atlanta University on Tuesday, May the 26th, 1908.* Atlanta University Publications, no. 13. Atlanta, 1908.

———. *The Negro Artisan: Report of a Social Study Made under the Direction of Atlanta University; together with the Proceedings of the Seventh Conference for the Study of Negro Problems, held at Atlanta University, on May 27, 1902.* Atlanta University Publications, no. 7. Atlanta, 1902.

———. "The Negro as He Really Is." *World's Work* (June 1901).

———. *The Negro Common School: Report of a Social Study Made under the Direction of Atlanta University; together with the Proceedings of the Sixth Conference for the Study of the Negro Problems, held at Atlanta University, on May 28th, 1901,* Atlanta University Publications, no. 6. Atlanta, 1901.

———. "The Negro Farmer." *Bulletin of the Bureau of the Census* 8 (1904): 69–98. Reprinted in U.S. Bureau of the Census, Special Reports, *Supplementary Analysis and Derivative Tables. Twelfth Census of the United States, 1900,* 511–79 (Washington D.C., 1906).

———, ed. *The Negro in Business: Report of a Social Study Made under the Direction of Atlanta University; together with the Proceedings of the Fourth Conference for the Study of the Negro Problems, held at Atlanta University, May 30–31, 1899.* Atlanta University Publications, no. 4. Atlanta, 1899.

———. "The Negro in the Black Belt: Some Social Sketches." *Bulletin of the Department of Labor* 4, no. 22 (1899): 401–17. Reprinted in *Contributions by W. E. B. Du Bois in Government Publications and Proceedings,* ed. Herbert Aptheker, 45–63 (Millwood, N.Y., 1980).

———. "The Negroes of Farmville, Virginia: A Social Study." *Bulletin of the Department of Labor* 14 (Jan. 1898): 1–38.

———. "The Negro Landholder of Georgia." *Bulletin of the Department of Labor* 6, no. 35 (1901): 647–77.

———. "A Negro Schoolmaster in the New South." *Atlantic Monthly* 82 (Jan. 1899): 99–104.

———. "The Negro's Industrial Plight." *The Crisis* 40 (July 1931): 241–42.

———. "Of the Training of Black Men," *Atlantic Monthly* 90 (Sept. 1902): 289–97.

———. *The Philadelphia Negro: A Social Study together with a Special Report on Domestic Service by Isabel Eaton.* 1899. Reprint, New York, 1967.

———. "The Relation of the Negro to the Whites in the South." *Annals of the American Academy of Political and Social Science* 18 (July 1901): 121–40.

———. "The Religion of the American Negro." *New World* 9 (Dec. 1900): 614–25.

———. ed., assisted by Hugh H. Smythe. *Report of the Second Conference of Negro Land Grant Colleges for Coordinating a Program of Cooperative Social Studies.* Atlanta University Publications, no. 23. Atlanta, 1944.

———. Review of "Race Traits and Tendencies of the American Negro." *Annals of the American Academy of Political and Social Science* 9 (1897): 127–33.

———, ed. *Some Efforts of American Negroes for Their Own Social Betterment: Report of an Investigation under the Direction of Atlanta University; together with the Proceedings of the Third Conference for the Study of the Negro Problems, held at Atlanta University, May 25–26, 1898.* Atlanta University Publications, no. 3. Atlanta, 1898.

———, ed. *Some Notes on Negro Crime, Particularly in Georgia: Report of a Social Study Made under the Direction of Atlanta University; together with the Proceedings of the Ninth Conference for the Study of the Negro Problems, held at Atlanta University, May 24, 1904.* Atlanta University Publications, no. 9. Atlanta, 1904.

———. *The Souls of Black Folk.* 1903. Reprint, New York, 1966.

———. "Strivings of the Negro People." *Atlantic Monthly* 80 (Aug. 1897): 194–98.

———. "The Study of the Negro Problems." *Annals of the American Academy of Political and Social Science* 11 (Jan. 1898): 1–23. Reprinted in *W. E. B. Du Bois On Sociology and the Black Community*, ed. Dan S. Green and Edwin D. Driver, 71–84 (Chicago, 1978).

———. *The Suppression of the African Slave-Trade to the United States of America, 1638–1870.* 1896. Reprint, New York, 1969.

———. "To Your Tents, Oh Israel?" *The Crisis* 39 (Mar. 1932): 93–94.

Du Bois, W. E. B., and Augustus Granville Dill, eds. *The College-Bred Negro American: Report of a Social Study Made by Atlanta University under the Patronage of the Trustees of the John F. Slater Fund; with the Proceedings of the Fifteenth Annual Conference for the Study of the Negro Problems, held at Atlanta University, on Tuesday, May 24th, 1910.* Atlanta University Publications, no. 15. Atlanta, 1910.

———. *The Negro American Artisan: Report of a Social Study Made by Atlanta University under the Patronage of the Trustees of the John F. Slater Fund, Atlanta University; with the Proceedings of the Seventeenth Annual Conference for the Study of Negro Problems, held at Atlanta University, on Monday, May 27th, 1912.* Atlanta University Publications, no. 7. Atlanta, 1912.

Dykes, Eva. "Alexander Pope's Influence on America, 1710–1850." Ph.D. diss., Radcliffe College, 1921.

Dyson, Walter. *Howard University: The Capstone of Negro Education, A History, 1867–1940.* Washington, D.C., 1941.

Eagles, Charles W. "From Shotguns to Umbrellas: The Civil Rights Movement in Lowndes County, Alabama." In *The Adaptable South*, ed. Elizabeth Jacoway, 212–36. Baton Rouge, La., 1991.

Eaton, Isabel. "Special Report on Negro Domestic Service in the Seventh Ward,

Philadelphia." In *The Philadelphia Negro,* by W. E. B. Du Bois, 425–509. 1899. Reprint, New York, 1967.

Edwards, G. Franklin. "E. Franklin Frazier." In *Black Sociologists: Historical and Contemporary Perspectives,* ed. James E. Blackwell and Morris Janowitz. Chicago, 1974.

———. "Frazier, E. Franklin." In *Dictionary of American Negro Biography,* ed. Rayford W. Logan and Michael R. Winston, 241–44. New York, 1982.

Egerton, John. *Speak Now Against the Day: The Generation before the Civil Rights Movement in the South.* Chapel Hill, N.C., 1995.

"Employment." *The Crisis* 37 (Oct. 1930): 353–54.

Finney, John D., Jr. "A Study of Negro Labor during and after World War I." Ph.D. diss., Georgetown University, 1967.

"The Fisk Club of Chicago." *Fisk Herald* (Mar. 1899), 7.

"Fisk University: Facilities for the Education of Young Women." *Fisk Herald* 3, no. 6 (Feb. 1886): 1.

Fitzpatrick, Ellen. *Endless Crusade: Women Social Scientists and Progressive Reform.* New York, 1990.

Folbre, Nancy. "The 'Sphere of Women' in Early-Twentieth-Century Economics." In *Gender and American Social Science: The Formative Years,* ed. Helene Silverberg, 35–60. Princeton, N.J., 1998.

Foner, Philip. *Organized Labor and the Black Worker, 1619–1973.* New York, 1974.

Franklin, Charles L. "Characteristics and Taxable Wages of Negro Workers, 13 Selected Southern States, 1938." *Quarterly Review of Higher Education among Negroes* 11 (Apr. 1943): 66–72.

———. *The Negro Labor Unionist of New York.* New York, 1936.

Franklin, John Hope. "The Dilemma of the American Negro Scholar." In *Soon, One Morning,* ed. Herbert Hill, 60–76. New York, 1963.

———. *George Washington Williams: A Biography.* Chicago, 1984.

———. *Race and History: Selected Essays, 1938–1988.* Baton Rouge, La., 1989.

Franklin, V. P. "Alexander, Sadie Tanner Mossell." In *Black Women in America: An Historical Encyclopedia,* ed. Darlene Clark Hine, Elsa Barkley Brown, and Rosalyn Terborg-Penn, 1:17–19. Brooklyn, 1993.

———. *Black Self-Determination: A Cultural History of African-American Resistance.* New York, 1992.

———. "Black Social Scientists and the Mental Testing Movement, 1920–1940." In *Black Psychology,* ed. Reginald L. Jones. New York, 1980.

———. *The Education of Black Philadelphia.* Philadelphia, 1979.

Frazier, E. Franklin. *Black Bourgeoisie.* New York, 1957.

———. "The Du Bois Program in the Present Crisis." *Race* 1 (Fall 1935): 11–13.

———. "A Negro Industrial Group." *Howard University Review,* nos. 2–3 (June 1924): 196–223.

———. "New Currents of Thought among the Colored People of America." Master's thesis, Clark University, 1920.

———. "The Pathology of Race Prejudice." *Forum* 70 (June 1927): 856–62.

———. Review of *Negro Membership in American Labor Unions,* by Ira Reid. *Journal of American Sociology* 37 (Sept. 1931): 310.

Frazier, S. Elizabeth. "Mrs. Wm. E. Matthews (Victoria Earle)." *Women's Era* 1, no. 2 (May 1, 1894). Reprinted in Anne Ruggles Gere and Sarah R. Robbins, "Gendered Literacy in Black and White: Turn-of-the-Century African American and European American Club Women's Printed Texts," *Signs* 21, no. 3 (1996): 643–78.

Fuller, Thomas O., ed. *Pictorial History of the American Negro.* Memphis, 1933.

Furner, Mary O. *Advocacy and Objectivity: A Crisis in the Professionalization of American Social Science, 1865–1905.* Lexington, Ky., 1975.

Gaines, Kevin K. *Uplifting the Race: Black Leadership, Politics, and Culture in the Twentieth Century.* Chapel Hill, N.C., 1996.

"George E. Haynes." *Negro History Bulletin* 23, no. 1 (Oct. 1959): 2, 12.

"George Haynes Compromises the Case of the Negro Again." *Messenger* 2 (July 1919): 7–8.

Gilpin, Patrick J. "Charles S. Johnson: An Intellectual Biography." Ph.D. diss., Vanderbilt University, 1973.

Goggin, Jacqueline. *Carter G. Woodson: A Life in Black History.* Baton Rouge, La., 1997.

Goodard, Terrell Dale. "The Black Social Gospel in Chicago, 1896–1906: The Ministries of Reverdy C. Ransom and Richard R. Wright Jr. *Journal of Negro History* 83, no. 3 (Summer 1999): 227–46.

Goodspeed, Thomas Wakefield. *A History of the University of Chicago: The First Quarter Century.* Chicago, 1972.

Greene, Harry Washington. *Negro Holders of Doctorates: An Educational and Social Study of Negroes Who Have Earned Doctoral Degrees in Course, 1876–1943.* Boston, 1946.

Greene, Lorenzo J. *The Negro in Colonial New England.* New York, 1942.

———. *Selling Black History for Carter G. Woodson: A Diary, 1930–1933.* Ed. Arvarh E. Strickland. Columbia, Mo., 1996.

———. *Working with Carter G. Woodson, the Father of Black History: A Diary, 1928–1930.* Ed. Arvarh E. Strickland. Baton Rouge, La., 1989.

Greene, Lorenzo J., and Carter G. Woodson. *The Negro Wage Earner.* Washington, D.C., 1930.

Greene, Lorenzo J., and Myra Colson Callis. *The Employment of Negroes in the District of Columbia.* Washington D.C., 1931.

Gregg, Robert. *Sparks from the Anvil of Oppression: Philadelphia's African Methodists and Southern Migrants, 1890–1940.* Philadelphia, 1993.

Griffler, Keith. *What Price Alliance? Black Radicals Confront White Labor, 1918–1938.* New York, 1995.

Grossman, James R. *Land of Hope: Chicago, Black Southerners, and the Great Migration.* Chicago, 1989.

Grossman, Jonathan. "Black Studies in the Department of Labor, 1897–1907." *Monthly Labor Review* 97 (June 1974): 17–27.

————. "The Origin of the U.S. Department of Labor." *Monthly Labor Review* 96 (Mar. 1973): 3–7.

Guthrie, Robert V. *Even the Rat Was White: A Historical View of Psychology*. New York, 1976.

Gutman, Herbert G. "Preface to the Atheneum Edition." In *The Black Worker*, by Sterling D. Spero and Abram L. Harris. New York, 1974.

Guzman, Jessie P. "Monroe Nathan Work and His Contributions." *Journal of Negro History* 34 (Oct. 1949): 428–61.

————, ed. *Negro Yearbook*. Tuskegee, Ala., 1948.

Haber, Samuel. *The Quest for Authority and Honor in the American Professions, 1750–1900*. Chicago, 1991.

Hadnott, Grace. "The Mission of the Negro Woman." *Fisk Herald* 17, no. 6 (1900): 6–7.

"Hampton Incidents." *Southern Workman* 53 (Oct. 1906): 566.

Handbook of Federal World War Agencies and Their Records, 1917–1921. Washington, D.C., 1943.

Harlan, Louis R. *Booker T. Washington: The Wizard of Tuskegee*. 2 vols. New York, 1983.

Harley, Sharon. "Nannie Helen Burroughs: Black Goddess of Liberty." *Journal of Negro History* 81, nos. 1–4 (1996): 62–71.

————. "Reclaiming Public Voice and the Study of Black Women's Work." In *Gender, Families, and Close Relationships: Feminist Research Journeys*, ed. Donna L. Sollie and Leigh A. Leslie. Thousand Oaks, Calif., 1994.

Harmon, James H., and Arnett G. Lindsay, *The Negro as a Businessman*. Washington, D.C., 1929.

Harris, Abram L. "A Black and White World in American Labor and Politics." *Social Forces* 4, no. 2 (Dec. 1925): 376–83.

————. *The Negro as a Capitalist: A Study of Banking and Business among American Negroes*. Philadelphia, 1936.

————. "Negro Labor's Quarrel with White Workingmen." *Current History* 24 (Sept. 1924): 410–18.

————. "The Negro Problem as Viewed by Negro Leaders." *Current History* 18 (June 1923): 410–18.

————. "New Negro Worker in Pittsburgh." Master's thesis, University of Pittsburgh, 1924.

————. *Race, Radicalism, and Reform: Selected Papers of Abram L. Harris*. Ed. William Darity Jr. New Brunswick, N.J., 1989.

Harris, Eugene. "The Physical Condition of the Race; Whether Dependent Upon Social Conditions or Environment." In *Social and Physical Condition of Negroes in Cities: Report of an Investigation under the Direction of Atlanta University and proceedings of the Second Conference for the Study of Problems Concerning Negro City Life, held at Atlanta University, May 25–26, 1897*, 20–28. Atlanta University Publications, no. 2. Atlanta, 1897.

Harris, Grace E. "The Life and Work of E. Franklin Frazier." Ph.D. diss., University of Virginia, 1975.

Harris, Janette Hoston. "Charles Harris Wesley, Educator and Historian, 1891–1947." Ph.D. diss., Howard University, 1975.

Harris, William. *The Harder We Run: Black Workers since the Civil War.* New York, 1982.

Haskell, Thomas L. *The Emergence of Professional Social Science: The American Social Science Association and the Nineteenth-Century Crisis of Authority.* Urbana, Ill., 1977.

Haynes, Elizabeth Ross. *The Black Boy of Atlanta.* 1952. Reprint, New York, 1996.

———. "Negroes in Domestic Service in the United States." *Journal of Negro History* 8, no. 4 (Oct. 1923): 384–442.

———. "Two Million Negro Women at Work." *Southern Workman* 51, no. 2 (1922): 64–72.

———. *Unsung Heroes.* New York, 1921.

Haynes, George Edmund. "Co-operation with Colleges in Securing and Training Negro Social Workers for Urban Centers." *Proceedings of the National Conference of Charities and Corrections* 38 (1911): 384–87.

———. "The Greatest Convention of Students Ever Held." *Fisk Herald* 19, no. 6 (Apr. 1902): 11–15.

———. "The Lamp of Sacrifice." *Fisk Herald* 20, no. 5 (1903): 8–13.

———. *The Negro at Work during World War and during Reconstruction: Statistics, Problems, and Policies Relative to the Greater Inclusion of Negro Wage Earners in American Industry and Agriculture.* Washington, D.C., 1921.

———. *The Negro at Work in New York City: A Study in Economic Progress.* 1912. Reprint, New York, 1968.

———. "Negroes Move North: I. Their Departure from the South." *Survey* 40, no. 5 (May 4, 1918): 115–21.

———. Negroes Move North: II. Their Arrival in the North." *Survey* 41, no. 4 (Jan. 4, 1919): 455–61.

———. "Negro Migration, Its Effects on Family and Community Life in the North." *Opportunity* 2 (Sept. 1924): 271.

———. *Negro Newcomers in Detroit, Michigan: A Challenge to Christian Statesmanship, A Preliminary Survey.* New York, 1918.

"Haynes-Ross." "*Fisk Herald* 28, no. 3 (Jan. 1911): 4–5.

"To Help the Negroes." *Philadelphia Public Ledger* 15 (Feb. 1897).

Hemenway, Robert. *Zora Neale Hurston: A Literary Biography.* Urbana, Ill., 1978.

Henderson, Alexa Benson. "Richard R. Wright and the National Negro Bankers Association: Early Organizing Efforts among Black Bankers, 1924–1942." *Pennsylvania Magazine of History and Biography* 117, nos. 1–2 (Jan.–Apr. 1993): 51–81.

Hendricks, Wanda. "Wells-Barnett, Ida B." In *Black Women in America: An Historical Encyclopedia,* ed. Darlene Clark Hine, Elsa Barkley Brown, and Rosalyn Terborg-Penn, 2:1242–46. Brooklyn, 1993.

———. "Williams, Fannie Barrier." In *Black Women in America: An Historical Encyclopedia,* ed. Darlene Clark Hine, Elsa Barkley Brown, and Rosalyn Terborg-Penn, 2:1259–61. Brooklyn, 1993.

Hershaw, LaFayette M. "The Negro Press in America." *Charities* 15, no. 1 (Oct. 7, 1905): 66-68.

———. "Social and Physical Progress: A Comparative Analysis of the Reports of the Boards of Health of Atlanta, Baltimore, Charleston, Memphis and Richmond." In *The Social and Physical Condition of Negroes in Cities: Report of an Investigation under the Direction of Atlanta University and Proceedings of the Second Conference for the Study of Problems Concerning Negro City Life held at Atlanta University, May 25–26, 1897,* 10–19. Atlanta University Publications, no. 2. Atlanta, 1897.

Higginbotham, Evelyn Brooks. "African-American Women's History and the Metalanguage of Race." *Signs* 14, no. 1 (1992): 251–74.

———. *Righteous Discontent: The Women's Movement in the Black Baptist Church, 1880–1920.* Cambridge, Mass., 1993.

"The Higher Education of Negroes." *The Crisis* 22 (June 1921): 105–6.

"The Higher Training of Negroes." *The Crisis* 22 (July 1921): 105–13.

Hill, T. Arnold. "The Negro in Industry, 1926." *Opportunity* 4 (Feb. 1927): 51–52.

Hine, Darlene Clark. *Hine Sight: Black Women and the Re-Construction of American History.* Brooklyn, 1994.

Hine, Darlene Clark, Elsa Barkley Brown, and Rosalyn Terborg-Penn, eds. *Black Women in America: An Historical Encyclopedia.* 2 Vols. Brooklyn, 1993.

Hoffman, Frederick L. "Race Traits and Tendencies of the American Negro." *Publications of the American Economics Association* 11, nos. 1–3 (1896): 1–329.

Holley, Mary R. "Gertrude Elise Ayer." In *Notable Black American Women,* ed. Jessie Carney Smith, 29–31. Detroit, 1992.

Holloway, Jonathan. "Confronting the Veil: New Deal African-American Intellectuals and the Evolution of a Radical Voice." Ph.D. diss., Yale University, 1995.

———. *Confronting the Veil: Abram Harris Jr., E. Franklin Frazier, Ralph Bunche, 1919–1941.* Chapel Hill, N.C., 2002.

Holt, Thomas C. "W. E. B. Du Bois's Archaeology of Race: Re-Reading 'The Conservation of Races.'" In *W. E. B. Du Bois, Race, and the City: The Philadelphia Negro and Its Legacy,* ed. Michael B. Katz and Thomas J. Sugrue, 61–76. Philadelphia, 1998.

Horne, Gerald. *Black and Red: W. E. B. Du Bois and the Afro-American Response to the Cold War, 1944–1963.* Albany, N.Y., 1986.

Houstoun, E. W. "The YMCA Conference," *Scroll* (Jan. 1903): 36–37.

Hughes, Langston. *Simple Speaks His Mind.* New York, 1950.

Hunter, Gary J. "'Don't Buy Where You Can't Work': Black Urban Boycott Movements during the Depression, 1929–1941." Ph. D. diss., University of Michigan, 1977.

Hunter, Tera W. *To 'Joy My Freedom: Southern Black Women's Lives and Labors after the Civil War.* Cambridge, Mass., 1997.

Hunton, Addie Waites. *William Alphaeus Hunton: A Pioneer Prophet of Young Men.* New York, 1938.

Hunton, Addie W., and Kathryn Johnson. *Two Colored Women and the American Expeditionary Forces.* Brooklyn, 1920.

Hutchinson, Louis Daniel. "Cooper, Anna Julia." *Black Women in America: An Historical Encyclopedia,* ed. Darlene Clark Hine, Elsa Barkley Brown, and Rosalyn Terborg-Penn, 1:275–81. Brooklyn, 1993.

Hutson, Jean Blackwell. "Hunton, Addie D. Waites." In *Dictionary of American Negro Biography,* ed. Rayford W. Logan and Michael R. Winston, 337–38. New York, 1982.

"If You Are a Woman Don't Read This." *Athenaeum* 1, no. 5 (Jan. 1899): 11.

"The Industrial Conditions of the Negro in the North." *Annals of the American Academy of Political and Social Science* 27, no. 3 (May 1906): part 3, 81–134.

Irvin, Helen Brooks. "Conditions in Industry as They Affect Negro Women." In *National Conference of Social Work Proceedings, 1919,* 521–24. Chicago, 1920.

Ives, Patricia C. "Giles Beecher Jackson: Director-General of the Negro Development and Exposition Commission of the United States for the Jamestown Tercentennial Exposition of 1907." *Negro History Bulletin* 38, no. 7 (Dec. 1975): 480–83.

Jackson, Giles B., and D. W. Jackson Webster Davis. *Industrial History of the Negro Race of the United States.* Richmond, 1911.

Jackson, Henry. *From the Congo to Soweto: U.S. Foreign Policy toward Africa since 1960.* New York, 1982.

Jackson, Luther Porter. "Labor and Land Tenure among Negroes in Southern Agriculture." In *Report of the Second Conference of Negro Land Grant Colleges,* ed. W. E. B. Du Bois, assisted by H. H. Smythe, 52–67. Atlanta University Publications, no. 23. Atlanta, 1944.

Jackson, Walter A. *Gunnar Myrdal and America's Conscience: Social Engineering and Racial Liberalism, 1938–1987.* Chapel Hill, N.C., 1990.

James, Joy. *Transcending the Talented Tenth: Black Leaders and American Intellectuals.* New York, 1997.

Janken, Kenneth Robert. *Rayford W. Logan and the Dilemma of the African-American Intellectual.* Amherst, Mass., 1993.

[J. H. H.] "American Economic Association at Baltimore." *Nation* 82, no. 2116 (Jan. 18, 1906): 51–52.

Johnson, Catherine. "Simpson, Georgiana." In *Black Women in America: An Historical Encyclopedia,* ed. Darlene Clark Hine, Elsa Barkley Brown, and Rosalyn Terborg-Penn, 2:1038–39. Brooklyn, 1993.

Johnson, Charles S. *Economic Status of Negroes.* Nashville, 1933.

———. "A History of Negro Labor." Review of *Negro Labor in the United States, 1850–1925,* by Charles Wesley. *New York Herald Tribune,* June 12, 1927, 10.

———. "How Much Is the Migration a Flight from Persecution?" *Opportunity* 1 (Sept. 1923): 272–74.

———. "How the Negro Fits in Northern Industries." *Industrial Psychology* 1 (June 1926): 399–412.

———, ed. *The Negro in American Civilization: A Study of Negro Life and Race Relations in the Light of Social Research.* New York, 1930.

———. *The Negro College Graduate.* Chapel Hill, N.C., 1938.

———. "Negroes at Work in Baltimore, Maryland." *Opportunity* 1 (June 1923): 12–19.

Jones, Adrienne Lash. "Bowles, Eva Del Vakia." In *Black Women in America: An Historical Encyclopedia,* ed. Darlene Clark Hine, Elsa Barkley Brown, and Rosalyn Terborg-Penn, 1:152–53. Brooklyn, 1993.

Jones, Butler A. "The Tradition of Sociology Teaching in Black Colleges: The Unheralded Professionals." In *Black Sociologists: Historical and Contemporary Perspectives,* ed. James E. Blackwell and Morris Janowitz, 121–63. Chicago, 1974.

Jones, Eugene K. "Problems of the Colored Child." *Annals of the American Academy of Political and Social Science* 98, no. 187 (Nov. 1921): 142–47.

———. "The Way Opens." *Opportunity* 2 (Mar. 1924): 69–71.

Jones, Jacqueline. *Labor of Love, Labor of Sorrow: Black Women, Work, and the Family, from Slavery to the Present.* New York, 1986.

Jones, Marcus E. *Black Migration in the United States, with Emphasis on Selected Central Cities.* Saratoga, Calif., 1980.

Jones, Reginald L., ed. *Black Psychology.* 2nd ed. New York, 1980.

Jones, William. "A History and Appraisal of the Economic Consequences of Negro Trade Boycotts." Master's thesis, Atlanta University, 1940.

Joyce, Davis D. *Edward Channing and the Great Work.* The Hague, 1974.

Katz, Michael B., and Thomas J. Sugrue, eds. "Introduction." In *W. E. B. Du Bois, Race, and the City: The Philadelphia Negro and Its Legacy,* 4–22. Philadelphia, 1998.

Katzman, David. *Seven Days a Week: Women and Domestic Service in Industrializing America.* Urbana, Ill., 1978.

"Keeping it Up." *The Crimson and Gray* 2 (Apr. 1912).

Kellor, Frances. "The Criminal Negro: A Sociological Study." *Arena* 25 (Jan.–May 1901).

———. *Out of Work: A Study of Employment Agencies.* New York, 1904.

Kelsey, Carl. *The Negro Farmer.* 1903. Reprint, New York, 1977.

Kennedy, Louise Venable. *The Negro Peasant Turns Cityward.* College Park, Md., 1930.

King, Georgia Swift. "Intemperance as a Cause of Mortality." In *Mortality among Negroes in Cities: Proceedings of the Conference for Investigation of City Problems held at Atlanta University, May 26–27, 1896,* 26–29. Atlanta University Publications, no. 1. Atlanta, 1896.

———. "Mothers Meetings." In *The Social and Physical Condition of Negroes in Cities: Report of an Investigation under the Direction of Atlanta University and Proceedings of the Second Conference for the Study of Problems Concerning*

Negro City Life held at Atlanta University, May 25–26, 1897, 29–30. Atlanta University Publications, no. 2. Atlanta, 1897.

Kirby, John B. *Black Americans in the Roosevelt Era: Liberalism and Race.* Knoxville, Tenn., 1980.

Kluger, Richard. *Simple Justice: The History of Brown v. Board of Education and Black America's Struggle for Equality.* New York, 1976.

Kruman, Marc. "Quotas for Blacks: The Public Works Administration and the Black Construction Worker." *Labor History* 16, no. 1 (1975): 37–51.

Kuklick, Henrietta. "The Organization of Social Sciences in the United States." *American Quarterly* 28 (Spring 1976): 124–41.

Laney, Lucy C. "Address before the Women's Meeting." In *The Social and Physical Condition of Negroes in Cities: Report of an Investigation under the Direction of Atlanta University and Proceedings of the Second Conference for the Study of Problems Concerning Negro City Life held at Atlanta University, May 25–26, 1897*, 55–57. Atlanta University Publications, no. 2. Atlanta, 1897.

———. "General Conditions of Mortality." In *Mortality Among Negroes in Cities: Proceedings of the Conference for Investigation of City Problems held at Atlanta University, May 26–27, 1896*, 35–37. Atlanta, Atlanta University Publications, no. 1, 1896.

Lasch-Quinn, Elisabeth. *Black Neighbors: Race and the Limits of Reform in the American Settlement House Movement, 1890–1945.* Chapel Hill, N.C., 1993.

Lawrence, Charles R. "Negro Organizations in Crisis: Depression, New Deal, World War II." Ph.D. diss., Columbia University, 1953.

Leiby, James. *Carroll Wright and Labor Reform: The Origins of Labor Statistics.* Cambridge, Mass., 1960.

"Letter from Mr. R. R. Wright, President of Georgia State Industrial College." In *Mortality among Negroes in Cities. Proceedings of the Conference for Investigation of City Problems, held at Atlanta University, May 26–27, 1896*, 48–49. Atlanta University Publications, no. 1. Atlanta, 1896.

"Letter to the Editor of *The Crisis*, June 14, [1934]." *Nation* (July 3, 1934): 657.

Lewis, David Levering. *W. E. B. Du Bois: A Biography of a Race, 1868–1919.* New York, 1994.

———. *W. E. B. Du Bois: The Fight for Equality and the American Century, 1919–1963.* New York, 2000.

———. *When Harlem Was in Vogue.* New York, 1981.

Lewis, Earl. "The Beginnings of a Renaissance: Black Migration, the Industrial Order, and the Search for Power." *Urban History* 17, no. 3 (May 1991): 296–302.

Linden, Marcel, ed. "The End of Labour History?" *International Review of Social History* 38 (1993).

Lindley, Susan H. "Neglected Voices and Praxis in the Social Gospel." *A.M.E. Church Review* 109, no. 353 (Jan.–Mar. 1994): 16–30.

Lindsay, Inabel Burns. "Haynes, George Edmund." In *Dictionary of American Negro Biography*, ed. Rayford W. Logan and Michael R. Winston, 297–300. New York, 1982.

Lindsay, Samuel McCune. "The Charity Problem in Philadelphia." *Citizen* 2, no. 8 (Oct. 1896): 263–66.

Locke, Alain. "The New Negro." In *The New Negro,* ed. Alain Locke, 3–16. 1925. Reprint, New York, 1969.

———. "Where the Negro Worker Stands." Review of *The Black Worker,* by Sterling D. Spero and Abram L. Harris. *Survey* 65 (Mar. 1931): 679.

Logan, Adella Hunt. "Prenatal and Hereditary Influences." In *Social and Physical Condition of Negroes in Cities: Report of an Investigation under the Direction of Atlanta University: and Proceedings of the Second Conference for the Study of Problems Concerning Negro City Life, held at Atlanta University, May 25–26, 1897,* 37–41. Atlanta University Publications, no. 2. Atlanta, 1897.

Logan, Rayford W. "Hope, John." In *Dictionary of American Negro Biography,* ed. Rayford W. Logan and Michael R. Winston, 321–25. New York, 1982.

———. *Howard University: The First Hundred Years, 1867–1967.* New York, 1969.

———. "Laney, Lucy Craft." In *Dictionary of American Negro Biography,* ed. Rayford W. Logan and Michael R. Winston, 380. New York, 1982.

Lyman, Stanford M. *The Black American in Sociological Thought.* New York, 1972.

Mabee, Carleton. *Black Education in New York State: From Colonial to Modern Times.* Syracuse, N.Y., 1979.

Mack, L. I. "The College Woman." *Scroll* 4, no. 2 (Jan. 1900): 12–14.

Magat, Richard. *Unlikely Partners: Philanthropic Foundations and the Labor Movement.* Ithaca, N.Y., 1999.

Malveaux, Julianne. "Missed Opportunity: Sadie Tanner Mossell Alexander and the Economics Profession." *American Economic Review: Papers and Proceedings* 81, no. 2 (May 1991): 307–10.

Marks, Carole. *Farewell—We're Good and Gone: The Great Black Migration.* Bloomington, Ind., 1989.

Marshall, F. Ray. *The Negro and Organized Labor.* New York, 1967.

Mayors, M. M. *Noted Negro Women: Their Triumphs and Activities.* Chicago, 1893.

McCuistion, Fred. *Graduate Instruction for Negroes in the United States.* Nashville, 1939.

———. *Higher Education of Negroes.* Nashville, 1933.

McDougald, Elise Johnson. "The Double Task: The Struggle of Negro Women for Sex and Race Emancipation." *Survey Graphic* 6, no. 6 (Mar. 1925): 689–91.

———. "The Schools and the Vocational Life of Negroes." *Opportunity* 1 (June 1923): 8–11.

———. "The Task of Negro Womanhood." In *The New Negro,* ed. Alain Locke, 369–82. 1925. Reprint, New York, 1969.

———. "The Women of the White Strain." In *Harlem's Glory: Black Women Writing, 1900–1950,* ed. Lorraine Elena Roses and Ruth Elizabeth Randolph, 411–22. Cambridge, Mass., 1996.

McDowell, Deborah E. *"The Changing Same": Black Women's Literature, Criticism, and Theory.* Bloomington, Ind., 1995.

McGuire, Robert M., III. "Browne, Hugh M." In *Dictionary of American Negro Biography,* ed. Rayford W. Logan and Michael R. Winston, 73–74. New York, 1982.

McKay, Claude. *Banjo: A Story without a Plot.* New York, 1929.

———. *Home to Harlem.* New York, 1928.

McLemee, Scott. "Seeing Red." *Chronicle of Higher Education* 49, no. 42 (June 27, 2003).

McMurry, Linda O. *Recorder of the Black Experience: A Biography of Monroe Nathan Work.* Baton Rouge, La., 1985.

———. *To Keep the Waters Troubled: The Life of Ida B. Wells.* New York, 1998.

McNeil, Genna Rae. *Groundwork: Charles Hamilton Houston and the Struggle for Civil Rights.* Philadelphia, 1983.

Means, Rev. F. H. "A Review of the Atlanta University Conferences and Social Studies." In *Select Discussions of Race Problems: A Collection of Papers of Especial Use in the Study of Negro American Problems, with the Proceedings of the Twentieth Annual Conference for the Study of Negro Problems, held at Atlanta University, May 24, 1915,* ed. J. A. Bigham, 9–16. Atlanta University Publications, no. 20. Atlanta, 1916.

Meier, August. *Negro Thought in America, 1880–1915: Racial Ideologies in the Age of Booker T. Washington.* Ann Arbor, Mich., 1963.

Meier, August, and Elliot Rudwick. *Black History and the Historical Profession, 1915–1980.* Urbana, Ill., 1986.

Miller, Kelly. "The City Negro." In *Race Adjustment: Essays on the Negro in America,* 119–31. 1908. Reprint, New York, 1968.

———. "Crime among Negroes." In *Out of the House of Bondage: A Discussion of the Race Problem,* 95–98. New York, 1914.

———. "The Economic Handicap of the Negro in the North." *Annals of the American Academy of Political and Social Science* 27, no. 3 (May 1906): 81–88.

———. "Professional and Skilled Occupations." *Annals of the American Academy of Political and Social Science* 49 (Sept. 1913): 10–18.

———. *Race Adjustment: Essays on the Negro in America.* 1908. Reprint, New York, 1968.

———. "Radicals and Conservatives." In *Race Adjustment: Essays on the Negro in America.* 1908. Reprint, New York, 1968.

———. "A Review of Hoffman's 'Race Traits and Tendencies of the American Negro.'" *American Negro Academy Occasional Papers,* no. 1, 1–36. Washington, D.C., 1897.

———. "Surplus Negro Women." *The New York Independent,* Jan. 1905. Reprinted in *Race Adjustment: Essays on the Negro in America,* by Kelly Miler, 168–78 (1908; reprint, New York, 1968).

Morris, Calvin S. "Black Advocates of the Social Gospel." Paper presented at the meeting of the Southern Historical Association, Houston, Tex., 1985.

———. "Richard R. Wright Jr.: Scholar-Activist of the Social Gospel." *A.M.E. Church Review* 105, no. 335 (July–Sept. 1989): 22–31.

Mortality among Negroes in Cities: Proceedings of the Conference for Investigation of City Problems, held at Atlanta University, May 26–27, 1896. Atlanta University Publications, no. 1. Atlanta, 1896.

Moses, Wilson J., ed. *Alexander Crummell, Destiny and Race: Selected Writings, 1840–1898*. Amherst, Mass., 1992.

———. *Alexander Crummell: A Study of Civilization and Discontent*. New York, 1989.

———. *The Golden Age of Black Nationalism, 1850–1925*. New York, 1988.

Moss, Alfred A., Jr. *The American Negro Academy: Voice of the Talented Tenth*. Baton Rouge, La., 1981.

Mossell, Sadie Tanner. "The Standard of Living among One Hundred Negro Migrant Families in Philadelphia." *Annals of the American Academy of Political and Social Science* 98, no. 187 (Nov. 1921): 169–218.

———. *A Study of the Negro Tuberculosis Problem in Philadelphia*. Philadelphia, 1923.

Moynihan, Kenneth James. "History as a Weapon for Social Advancement: Group History as Told by Jewish, Irish, and Black Americans, 1892–1950." Ph.D. diss., Clark University, 1973.

Muncy, Robyn. *Creating a Female Dominion in American Reform, 1890–1935*. New York, 1991.

Murdock, Kathleen. "Racial Differences Found in Two American Cities." *Industrial Psychology* 1 (Feb. 1926): 99–104.

Murray, Maggie J. "Education of Girls." *Fisk Herald* (June 1883): 3.

Myers, Gerald E. *William James: His Life and Thought*. New Haven, Conn., 1986.

National Academy of Sciences. *A Century of Doctorates: Data Analyses of Growth and Change*. Washington, D.C., 1978.

"National Defense Labor Problems: The Weaver Appointment." *The Crisis* 47 (Oct. 1940): 319–22.

National Urban League. *Ever Widening Horizons: The Story of the Vocational Opportunity Campaign*. New York, 1951.

———. *Negro Membership in American Labor Unions*. New York, 1930.

———. *Thirty-fifth Annual Report*. New York, 1945.

"The Negro and the Northern Public Schools." *The Crisis* 25 (Mar. 1923): 205–8.

"The Negro Girl in the Rural Districts." *Atlanta University Bulletin* Nov. 1898): 4.

"The Negro in the Cities of the North." Special issue, *Charities* 15 (Oct. 7, 1905).

"A Negro Nation within the Nation." *Current History* 42 (June 1935): 265–70.

"The Negro Problem in the North." *Nation* 69 (Oct. 16, 1899): 310.

"The Negro's Progress in Fifty Years." Special issue, *Annals of the American Academy of Political and Social Science* 49 (Sept. 1913).

"Negro Women in Industry." *Women's Bureau Bulletin* 20 (1922): 55–65.

"Negro Women in Industry." *Monthly Labor Review* 15 (July 1922): 116–18.

"Negro Women in Industry." *Opportunity* 2 (Aug. 1924): 242–44.

"Negro Women in Industry in Fifteen States." *Women's Bureau Bulletin* 70 (1929).

Nelson, Alice Dunbar. "Woman's Most Serious Problem." *Messenger* (Mar. 1927).

Reprinted in *Speech and Power* 2, ed. Gerald Early, 224–27 (Hopewood, N.J., 1993).

Nelson, H. Viscount. "The Philadelphia NAACP: Race versus Class Consciousness during the 1930s." *Journal of Black Studies* 5, no. 3 (1975): 255–76.

Neverdon-Morton, Cynthia. *Afro-American Women of the South and the Advancement of the Race.* Knoxville, 1989.

"New Books." *American Economic Review* 17 (Sept. 1927): 546–47.

A New Day for the Colored Woman Worker. New York, 1919.

New Jersey Bureau of Statistics of Labor and Industries. "The Negro in Manufacturing and Mechanical Industries." *Twenty-sixth Annual Report, 1903,* 163–215. Somerville, N.J., 1904.

New Leadership for the Negro," *Messenger* 2 (May–June 1919): 9–10.

"A New Negro Migration." *Survey* (Feb. 26, 1921).

Newman, Richard. *Words Like Freedom: Essays on African-American Culture and History.* West Cornwall, Conn., 1996.

Northrup, Herbert Roof. *The Negro in the Automobile Industry.* Racial Policies of American Industry Report, no. 1. Philadelphia, [1968].

———. *Organized Labor and the Negro.* New York, 1944.

———. *Will Negroes Get Jobs Now?* New York, 1945.

"Notes." *Fisk Herald* 28, no. 3 (Jan. 1911): 12–13.

Novick, Peter. *That Noble Dream: The "Objectivity Question" and the American Historical Profession.* Cambridge, 1988.

Obituary for Abram L. Harris. *Journal of Negro History* 49 (Feb. 1964): 149.

Obituary for Birdye H. Haynes. *The Crisis* 24, no. 5 (Sept. 1922): 223.

Odum, Howard. *American Sociology: The Story of Sociology in the United States through 1950.* New York, 1951.

"On the Campus." *Atlanta University Bulletin* 89 (Feb. 1898).

"Opportunities and Responsibility." *Charities* 15 (Oct. 7, 1905): 2.

Ovington, Mary White. *Half a Man: The Status of the Negro in New York.* New York, 1911.

———. "The Negro in the Trade Unions in New York." *Annals of the American Academy of Political and Social Science* 27 (May 1906): 86–96.

———. *The Walls Came Tumbling Down.* 1947. Reprint, New York, 1969.

"Our Graduates." *Scroll* (Feb. 1899): 8–9.

"Outstanding Fellows." *National Urban League Fortieth Anniversary Book.* New York, 1950.

Painter, Nell Irvin. *The Exodusters.* 1976. Reprint, Lawrence, Kans., 1986.

Parris, Guichard, and Lester Brooks, *Blacks in the City: A History of the National Urban League.* Boston, 1971.

Patton, June Odessa. "Laney, Lucy Craft." In *Black Women in America: An Historical Encyclopedia,* ed. Darlene Clark Hine, Elsa Barkley Brown, and Rosalyn Terborg-Penn, 1:693–95. Brooklyn, 1993.

———. "Major Richard Robert Wright, Sr., and Black Higher Education in Georgia, 1880–1920." Ph.D. diss., University of Chicago, 1980.

Penn, Emma Shields. "Vocational Adjustment Problems of Negro Women in New York City." Master's thesis, New York University, 1932.

Perkins, Linda M. "The African American Female Elite Sister: The Early History of African American Women in the Seven Sister Colleges, 1880–1960." *Harvard Educational Review* 67, no. 4 (Winter 1997): 718–56.

———. "Education." In *Black Women in America: An Historical Encyclopedia,* ed. Darlene Clark Hine, Elsa Barkley Brown, and Rosalyn Terborg-Penn, 1:380–87. Brooklyn, 1993.

Perlman, Daniel. "Stirring the White Conscience: The Life of George Edmund Haynes," Ph.D. diss., New York University, 1972.

Pettigrew, Thomas F., ed. *The Sociology of Race Relations: Reflection and Reform.* New York, 1980.

"The Philadelphia Negro." *Southern Workman* 29 (Feb. 1900): 121.

Phillips, Henry L. Review of *The Philadelphia Negro,* by W. E. B. Du Bois. *Charities Review* 12 (Feb. 1900): 575–78.

Philpot, Thomas J. *The Slum and the Ghetto: Immigrants, Blacks, and Reformers in Chicago, 1880–1930.* Belmont, Calif., 1991.

"Phylon Profile VI: Carter G. Woodson," *Phylon* 6 (1945): 315–21.

Pickens, William. "Migrating to Fuller Life." *Forum,* 600–607.

Platt, Anthony M. *E. Franklin Frazier Reconsidered.* New Brunswick, N.J., 1991.

Potts, David B. "Social Ethics at Harvard, 1881–1931: A Study in Academic Activism." In *Social Sciences at Harvard, 1860–1920: From Inculcation to the Open Mind,* ed. Paul S. Buck, 91–128. Cambridge, Mass., 1965.

Price, Minnie. "Friendly Visiting." In *The Social and Physical Condition of Negroes in Cities: Report of an Investigation under the Direction of Atlanta University and Proceedings of the Second Conference for the Study of Problems Concerning Negro City Life held at Atlanta University, May 25–26, 1897,* 58–62. Atlanta University Publications, no. 2. Atlanta, 1897.

"Prize Contest." *Scroll* (May 1897): 4–5.

"Proceedings of the Annual Meeting." *Journal of Negro History* 35 (Jan. 1950): 3.

Proceedings of the Hampton Negro Conference. Vol. 2. Hampton, Va., 1898.

Proctor, H. H., and M. N. Work. "Atlanta and Savannah." In *Some Notes on Negro Crime Particularly in Georgia: Report of a Social Study Made under the Direction of Atlanta University; together with the Proceedings of the Ninth Conference for the Study of the Negro Problems, held at Atlanta University, May 24, 1904,* ed. W. E. B. Du Bois, 49–52. Atlanta University Publications, no. 9. Atlanta, 1904.

Rampersad, Arnold. *The Art and Imagination of W. E. B. Du Bois.* Cambridge, Mass., 1976.

Raper, Arthur, and Ira Reid. *Sharecroppers All.* Chapel Hill, N.C., 1941.

Read, Florence. *The Story of Spelman College.* Atlanta, 1964.

Reddick, L. D. "Carter G. Woodson (1875–1950): An Appreciation." *Phylon* 11, no. 2 (1950): 177–79.

Reed, Adolph L., Jr. *W. E. B. Du Bois and American Political Thought: Fabianism and the Color Line.* New York, 1997.

Reed, Christopher R. *"All the World Is Here": The Black Presence at White City.* Bloomington, Ind., 2000.

Reid, Ira De A. "Advertising Negro Labor." *Pittsburgh Courier* (May 28, 1927): 28.

———. "Lack of Race Consciousness Responsible for Negligence in Raising Economic Status." *Pittsburgh Courier,* Aug. 20, 1927, 20.

———. *In a Minor Key: Negro Youth in Story and Fact.* Washington, D.C., 1940.

———. "Mrs. Bailey Pays the Rent." In *Ebony and Topaz: A Collectanea,* ed. Charles S. Johnson, 144–48. New York, 1927.

———. *The Negro Immigrant: His Background, Characteristics and Social Adjustment, 1899–1937.* New York, 1939.

———. "The Negro in the Major Industries and the Building Trades of Pittsburgh." Master's thesis, University of Pittsburgh, 1925.

Reid, Ira De A., with Preston Valien and Charles S. Johnson. *Statistics by Regions.* Vol. 1 of *The Urban Negro Worker in the United States, 1925–1936: An Analysis of the Training, Types, and Conditions of Employment and Earnings of 200,000 Skilled and White Collar Negroes.* Washington, D.C., 1938.

Report of the Director of the Women's Bureau. Department of Labor. Washington, D.C., 1921.

Residents of Hull-House. In *Hull-House Maps and Papers: A Presentation of Nationalities and Wages in a Congested District of Chicago together with Comments and Essays on Problems Growing Out of the Social Conditions.* New York, 1895.

"Resolutions Adopted by the Conference." In *Social and Physical Condition of Negroes in Cities: Report of an Investigation under the Direction of Atlanta University and Proceedings of the Second Conference for the Study of Problems Concerning Negro City Life held at Atlanta University, May 25–26, 1897,* 32–34. Atlanta University Publications, no. 2. Atlanta, 1897.

Review (unsigned) of *The Negro as a Capitalist,* by Abram L. Harris. *Journal of Negro History* 21 (July 1937): 237.

Review (unsigned) of *The Negro Wage Earner,* by L. J. Greene and Carter G. Woodson. *Journal of Negro History* 1 (July 1931): 341.

Reynolds, Morgan O. "Labor Unions." *The Concise Encyclopedia of Economics,* ed. David R. Henderson. Indianapolis, 2002. Available online at http://www.econlib.org/library/Enc/LaborUnions.html.

Richardson, Joe M. *A History of Fisk University, 1865–1946.* Tuscaloosa, Ala., 1980.

Robbins, Richard. "Charles S. Johnson." In *Black Sociologists: Historical and Contemporary Perspectives,* ed. James E. Blackwell and Morris Janowitz, 56–84. Chicago, 1974.

———. *Sidelines Activist: Charles S. Johnson and the Struggle for Civil Rights.* Jackson, Miss., 1996.

Roberts, Samuel Kelton. "Crucible for a Vision: The Work of George E. Haynes and the Commission on Race Relations, 1922–1947." Ph.D. diss., Columbia University, 1974.

———. "George Edmund Haynes: Advocate for Interracial Cooperation." In *Black*

Apostles: Afro-American Clergy Confront the Twentieth Century, ed. Randall K. Burkett and Richard Newman, 97–127. Boston, 1978.

Robinson, Armstead L. "Charles H. Wesley: Pioneer Social Historian." Paper presented at the annual meeting of the Organization of American Historians, Apr. 20, 1985.

Romero, Patricia W. "Carter G. Woodson: A Biography." Ph.D. diss., Ohio State University, 1971.

Ross, Dorothy. *The Origins of American Social Science.* New York, 1991.

Ross, Edyth L., ed. "Black Heritage in Social Welfare: A Case Study of Atlanta." *Phylon* 37, no. 4 (Winter 1976): 305–7.

———. *Black Heritage in Social Welfare, 1860–1930.* Metuchen, N.J., 1978.

Ross, Elizabeth A. "You Must Keep Up or Endure the Dust." *Fisk Herald* 15 (Feb. 1899): 7–9.

Rouse, Jacqueline. *Lugenia Burns Hope, Black Southern Reformer.* Athens, Ga., 1989.

Rudwick, Elliot. "W. E. B. Du Bois as a Sociologist." In *Black Sociologists: Historical and Contemporary Perspectives,* ed. James E. Blackwell and Morris Janowitz, 25–52. Chicago, 1974.

Ruffin, Josephine St. Pierre. "Address before National Conference of Colored Women, July 29–31, 1895." Reprinted in *Black Women in White America: A Documentary History,* by Gerda Lerner, 441–43. New York, 1973.

Salem, Dorothy. *To Better Our World: Black Women in Organized Reform, 1890–1920.* New York, 1990.

———. "National Association of Colored Women." In *Black Women in America: An Historical Encyclopedia,* ed. Darlene Clark Hine, Elsa Barkley Brown, and Rosalyn Terborg-Penn, 1:842–45. Brooklyn, 1993.

———. "World War I." In *Black Women in America: An Historical Encyclopedia,* ed. Darlene Clark Hine, Elsa Barkley Brown, and Rosalyn Terborg-Penn, 2:1284–90. Brooklyn, 1993.

Scarborough, William. "The Educated Negro and His Mission." American Negro Academy Occasional Papers, no. 8. Washington, D.C., 1903.

Schrager, Cynthia. "Both Sides of the Veil: Race, Science, and Mysticism in W. E. B. Du Bois." *American Quarterly* 48, no. 4 (1996): 551–86.

Scott, Daryl Michael. *Contempt and Pity: Social Policy and the Image of the Damaged Black Psyche, 1880–1996.* Chapel Hill, N.C., 1997.

Scott, Emmett J., ed. "Letters of Negro Migrants of 1916–1918." *Journal of Negro History* 4, no. 3 (July 1919): 290–340.

———. *Negro Migration during the War.* Preliminary Economic Studies of the War, no. 16. 1920. Reprint, New York, 1969.

Scruggs, Otey M. "Crummell, Alexander." In *Dictionary of American Negro Biography,* ed. Rayford W. Logan and Michael R. Winston, 145–47. New York, 1982.

"Segregation." *The Crisis* 41 (Jan. 1934): 20.

"The Sense of Belonging," *Opportunity* 1, no. 1 (1923): 4.

Shaw, Stephanie J. *What a Women Ought to Be and to Do: Black Professional Women Workers during the Jim Crow Era.* Chicago, 1996.

Shields, Emma L. "A Half-Century in the Tobacco Industry." *Southern Workman* 51 (Sept. 1922): 419–25.

———. "Negro Women and the Tobacco Industry." *Life and Labor* (May 1921): 142–44.

Shivery, Louie D. "The History of Organized Social Work among Atlanta Negroes, 1890–1935." Master's thesis, Atlanta University, 1936.

Shofner, Jerrell H. "Florida and the Black Migration." *Florida Historical Quarterly* 57 (Jan. 1979): 267–88.

Sicherman, Barbara, et al., eds. *Notable American Women: The Modern Period, A Biographical Dictionary.* Cambridge, Mass., 1980.

Silone-Yates, Josephine. "The National Association of Colored Women." *Voice of the Negro* 1 (July 1904): 283–87.

Skinner, Elliot. *African Americans and U.S. Policy toward Africa, 1850–1924: In Defense of Black Nationality.* Washington, D.C., 1992.

Skotheim, Robert Allen. *American Intellectual Histories and Historians.* Princeton, N.J., 1966.

Smythe, Hugh H., and Mabel M. Smythe. *The New Nigerian Elite.* Stanford, Calif., 1960.

Smythe, Mabel M. "The Economics Teacher in the Post-War Period." *Quarterly Review of Higher Education among Negroes* 12, no. 3 (July 1944): 173–76.

———. "Tipping Occupations as a Problem in the Administration of Protective Labor Legislation." Ph.D. diss., University of Wisconsin, 1944.

The Social and Economic Status of the Black Population in the United States: An Historical View, 1790–1978. U.S. Bureau of the Census, Current Population Reports, Special Studies Series P-23, no. 80. Washington, D.C., n.d.

The Social and Physical Condition of Negroes in Cities: Report of an Investigation under the Direction of Atlanta University and Proceedings of the Second Conference for the Study of Problems Concerning Negro City Life held at Atlanta University, May 25–26, 1897. Atlanta University Publications, no. 2. Atlanta, 1897.

"Social Progress." *Opportunity* 3, no. 25 (Jan. 1925): 28–29.

"Sociology in Southern Colleges." *Scroll* (Nov. 1900): 3–4.

Sollie, Donna L., and Leigh A. Leslie, eds. *Gender, Families, and Close Relationships: Feminist Research Journeys.* Thousand Oaks, Calif., 1994.

"Some Questions of Our Time." *American Review of Reviews* 75 (May 1927).

Spady, James G. "Wright, Richard Robert, Sr." In *Dictionary of American Negro Biography,* ed. Rayford W. Logan and Michael R. Winston, 674–75. New York, 1982.

Spaulding, C. C. "Is the Negro Meeting the Test in Business?" *Journal of Negro History* 18 (Jan. 1933): 66–70.

Spear, Alan. *Black Chicago: The Making of a Negro Ghetto, 1890–1920.* 1967. Reprint, Chicago, 2003.

Spero, Sterling D., and Abram L. Harris. *The Black Worker: The Negro and the American Labor Movement.* 1931. Reprint, New York, 1974.

Stern, Sheldon M. "William James and the New Psychology." In *Social Sciences at Harvard, 1860–1920: From Inculcation to the Open Mind*, ed. Paul S. Buck, 175–222. Cambridge, Mass., 1965.

Stolberg, Benjamin. Review of *The Negro in American Civilization*, by Charles S. Johnson. Originally published in the *Herald Tribune*, June 22, 1930. Reprinted in William Darity, Jr., "Soundings and Silences on Race and Social Change," in *A Different Vision: African American Economic Thought*, ed. Thomas D. Boston, 230–49 (New York, 1997).

Stone, Alfred Holt. "The Economic Future of the Negro: The Factor of White Competition." *AEA Publications*, 3rd ser., 7 (Feb. 1906): 243–79.

Storr, Richard J. *Harper's University: The Beginnings, a History of the University of Chicago*, 10–19. Chicago, 1966.

Strickland, Arvarh E. "Editor's Introduction." In *Working with Carter G. Woodson, the Father of Black History: A Diary, 1928–1930*, by Lorenzo J. Greene. Baton Rouge, La., 1989.

———. *The History of the Chicago Urban League*. Urbana, Ill., 1966.

Stuckey, Sterling. *The Ideological Origins of Black Nationalism*. Boston, 1972.

———. *Slave Culture: Nationalist Theory and the Foundations of Black America*. New York, 1989.

"Student Life at Chicago." *Athenaeum* 1, no. 4 (Dec. 15, 1898): 4–5.

Sullivan, Donna Akiba Harper. *Not So Simple: The "Simple" Stories by Langston Hughes*. Columbia, Mo., 1995.

"Sympathy without Understanding." *Opportunity* 1 (Jan. 1923): 4.

Synott, Marcia C. *The Half-Opened Door: Discrimination and Admission at Harvard, Yale, and Princeton, 1900–1970*. Westport, Conn., 1979.

Terborg-Penn, Rosalyn. "Mossell, Gertrude Bustill." In *Black Women in America: An Historical Encyclopedia*, ed. Darlene Clark Hine, Elsa Barkley Brown, and Rosalyn Terborg-Penn, 1:820–21. Brooklyn, 1993.

Terrell, Mary Church. "The Club Work of Southern Women." *Southern Workman* 30 (1901): 435–38.

———. "Graduates and Former Students of Washington Colored High School." *Voices of the Negro* 1 (June 1904): 225.

"Thesis in Economics." *Scroll* (1899).

Thorpe, Earl E. *Black Historians: A Critique*. New York, 1971.

———. *The Central Theme of Black History*. Durham, N.C., 1969.

Tillinghast, Joseph A. "The Negro in Africa and America." *Publications of the American Economics Association*, 3rd ser., 3 (June 1902): 401–638.

Toll, William. *The Resurgence of Race: Black Social Theory from Reconstruction to the Pan-African Conferences*. Philadelphia, 1979.

Tollman, Frank. "The Study of Sociology in Institutions of Learning in the United States II." *American Journal of Sociology* 8 (1902–3): 85–121, 531–88.

Torrence, Ridgely. *The Story of John Hope*. New York, 1948.

Trotter, Joe William, Jr. "African-American Workers: New Directions in U.S. Labor Historiography." *Labor History* 35 (1994): 495–523.

————, ed. *The Great Migration in Historical Perspective: New Dimensions of Race, Class, and Gender.* Bloomington, Ind., 1991.

————. "Introduction: Black Migration in Historical Perspective: A Review of the Literature." In his *The Great Migration in Historical Perspective: New Dimension of Race, Class, and Gender,* 1–23. Bloomington, Ind., 1991.

Trotter, Joe William, Jr., and Earl Lewis, eds. *African Americans in the Industrial Age: A Documentary History, 1915–1945.* Boston, 1996.

Turner, Mamie A. "Outstanding Fisk Women, Who Have Contributed to the Advancement of the Negro Race." *Fisk News* 10 (Jan.–Feb. 1937): 6–7.

"Two Young Women." *Atlanta University Bulletin* 66 (June 1895): 2.

Urban, Wayne J. *Black Scholar: Horace Mann Bond, 1904–1972.* Athens, Ga., 1992.

Urquhart, Brian. *Ralph Bunche: An American Life.* New York, 1993.

United States. Bureau of the Census. *Negroes in the United States, 1920–32.* Prepared under the supervision of Z. R. Pettet, chief statistician for agriculture, by Charles E. Hall, specialist in Negro statistics. 1935. Reprint, New York, 1969.

————. *Occupations.* Washington, D.C., 1920.

————. Department of Labor. *The Anvil and the Plow: A History of the United States Department of Labor [1913–1963],* comp. and ed. O. L. Harvey. Washington, D.C., 1963.

————. *Reports of the Department of Labor.* 8 vols. Washington, D.C., 1914–1921.

Valien, Preston, and Bonita Valien. "Johnson, Charles S." In *Dictionary of American Negro Biography,* ed. Rayford W. Logan and Michael R. Winston, 347–49. New York, 1982.

Valien, Preston. "Social and Economic Implications of Migration for the Negro in the Present Social Order." *Quarterly Review of Higher Education among Negroes* 10 (Apr. 1942): 74–84.

————. "Southern Negro Internal Migration between 1935 and 1940." Ph.D. diss., University of Wisconsin, 1946.

Van Kleeck, Mary. "Foreword." In *The Negro in American Civilization: A Study of Negro Life and Race Relations in the Light of Social Research,* ed. Charles S. Johnson, v–ix. New York, 1930.

Walters, Ronald. *The Formulation of United States Foreign Policy toward Africa, 1938–1963.* Ann Arbor, Mich., 1973.

————. *Pan-Africanism in the African Diaspora: An Analysis of Modern Afrocentric Political Movements.* Detroit, 1993.

Warren, Samuel. "The Negro in the American Labor Market." Ph.D. diss., University of Wisconsin, 1941.

————. "A Partial Background for the Study of the Development of Negro Labor." *Journal of Negro History* 25 (Jan. 1940): 45–59.

Washington, Booker T. *The Booker T. Washington Papers.* 14 vols. Ed. Louis R. Harlan (vols. 1–14), and Louise R. Harlan and Raymond W. Smock (vols. 5–14). Urbana, Ill., [1927]–1989.

————. "Signs of Progress among the Negroes." *Century Magazine* 59 (Jan. 1900): 472–78.

Washington, Forrester B. "The Detroit Newcomers' Greeting." *Survey* 38 (July 14, 1917): 334–35.

———. *The Negro in Pennsylvania.* Harrisburg: Pennsylvania Department of Labor, 1927.

Watts, Jerry Gafio. *Heroism and the Black Intellectual: Ralph Ellison, Politics, and Afro-American Intellectual Life.* Chapel Hill, N.C., 1994.

Weaver, Robert C. "Defense Industries and the Negro." *Annals of the American Academy of Political and Social Science* (Sept. 1942): 60–66.

———. "The Efficiency of Negro Labor." *American Federationist* (Dec. 1934): 1327–31.

———. "Employment in Federal Projects." *Occupations* 14 (Mar. 1936): 515–19.

———. "The Employment of Negroes in the United States War Industries." *International Labor Review* 50 (Aug. 1944): 144–45.

———. "An Experiment in Negro Labor." *Opportunity* 14 (Oct. 1935): 295–98.

———. "The High Wage Theory of Prosperity." Ph.D. diss., Harvard University, 1934.

———. "The Higher Training of Negroes." *The Crisis* 22, no. 3 (July 1921): 105–13.

———. "The Impact of the New Deal upon Blacks and Their Participation in World War II Production." Speech delivered to American Association for the Advancement of Science, Feb. 15, 1978.

———. "Integration in Public and Private Housing." *Annals of the American Academy of Political and Social Science* (Mar. 1956): 86–97.

———. *Male Negro Skilled Workers in the United States, 1930–1936.* Vol. 2 of *The Urban Negro Worker in the United States, 1925–1936: An Analysis of the Training, Types, and Conditions of Employment and Earnings of 200,000 Skilled and White Collar Negroes.* Washington, D.C., 1939.

———. "Negro Comes of Age in Industry." *Atlantic Monthly* (Sept. 1943): 54–55.

———. "Negro Employment in the Aircraft Industry." *Quarterly Journal of Economics* 59, no. 4 (Aug. 1945): 597–625.

———. *The Negro Ghetto.* New York, 1948.

———. "The Negro in a Program of Public Housing." *Opportunity* 16 (July 1938): 198–202.

———. *Negro Labor: A National Problem.* 1946. Reprint, New York, 1969.

———. "Negro Labor since 1929." *Journal of Negro History* 35 (Jan. 1950): 29–38.

———. "The New Deal and the Negro." *Opportunity* 12 (Oct. 1935): 200–202.

———. "The Public Works Administration and School Building-Aid Program and Separate Negro School." *Journal of Negro Education* 7, no. 3 (July 1938): 366–74.

———. "Recent Developments in Urban Housing and Their Implications for Minorities." *Phylon* 16, no. 3 (1955): 1275–82.

———. "Wither Northern Race Relations Committees?" *Phylon* 5, no. 3 (1944): 205–18.

"W. E. B. Du Bois." Who's Who column. *Messenger* 2 (Mar. 1919): 21–22.

Weisenburger, Francis P. "Scarborough, Scholarship, The Negro, Religion, and Politics." *Ohio History* 72 (Jan. 1963): 25–50.

———. "William Sanders Scarborough: Early Life and Years at Wilberforce." *Ohio History* 71 (Oct. 1962): 203–26.

Weisenfeld, Judith. *African American Women and Christian Activism: New York's Black YWCA, 1905–1945.* Cambridge, Mass., 1997.

———. "'The More Abundant Life': The Harlem Branch of the New York City Young Women's Christian Association, 1905–1945." Ph.D. diss., Princeton University, 1992.

Weiss, Nancy J. *The National Urban League, 1910–1940.* New York, 1974.

Weiss, Roger. "Harris, Abram L." In *Dictionary of American Negro Biography,* ed. Rayford W. Logan and Michael R. Winston, 1091–92. New York, 1982.

Wells-Barnett, Ida B. *Crusade for Justice: The Autobiography of Ida B. Wells.* Ed. Alfreda M. Duster. Chicago, 1970.

———. "Lynch Law in All Its Phases." *Our Day* (May 1893).

———. *On Lynchings: Southern Horrors.* 1892. Reprint, New York, 1969.

———. *The Memphis Diary of Ida B. Wells: An Intimate Portrait of the Activist as a Young Woman.* Ed. Miriam DeCosta-Willis. Boston, 1995.

———. *A Red Record: Tabulated Statistics and Alleged Causes of Lynching in the United States, 1892–1893–1894.* 1895. Reprint, Amherst, N.Y., 2002.

Wesley, Charles Harris. *The Collapse of the Confederacy.* Washington, D.C., 1937.

———. *The History of the National Association of Colored Women's Clubs: A Legacy of Service.* Washington, D.C., 1984.

———. "Interest in a Neglected Phase of History." *A.M.E. Church Review* 32, no. 4 (Apr. 1916).

———. *Negro Labor in the United States, 1850–1925: A Study in American Economic History.* 1927. Reprint, New York, 1967.

———. "Organized Labor's Divided Front." *The Crisis* 45 (July 1938): 223–26.

———. "Problems of Sources and Methods in History Teaching." *School Review* 24 (May 1916): 329–41.

———. "Racial Historical Societies and the American Heritage." *Journal of Negro History* 37 (Jan. 1952): 11–35.

———. "Teacher's Point of View in the Study and Teaching of History." *Education* 34 (Apr. 1914): 509–13.

West, Laverne Gregory. "The Dunbar High School Story, 1870–1926." In *Dunbar High School Class of 1926, Fiftieth Anniversary Program,* 8–12. Washington, D.C., 1976.

Whittier, John Greenleaf. "Howard at Atlanta." In *The Complete Poetical Works of John Greenleaf Whittier,* 353. Boston, 1892.

———. "Howard at Atlanta." In *The Complete Writings of John Greenleaf Whittier.* Amesbury edition. Boston, 1894.

Wilkins, Roy. *Standing Fast: The Autobiography of Roy Wilkins.* New York, 1984.

Willcox, Walter F. "Negro Criminality." In *Studies in the American Race Problem,* ed. Alfred H. Stone. New York, 1908.

————. "The Negro Population." In *Negroes in the United States*, by U.S. Bureau of the Census, 232. Washington, D.C., 1904.

Willcox, Walter F., W. E. B. Du Bois, H. T. Newcomb, W. Z. Ripley, and A. H. Stone. "The Economic Position of the Negro." *AEA Publications*, 3rd ser., 6 (Feb. 1905): 212–21.

Williams, Alma. "Robert C. Weaver: From the Black Cabinet to the President's Cabinet." Ph.D. diss., Washington University, 1978.

Williams, DeWitt S. *She Fulfilled the Impossible Dream: The Story of Eva B. Dykes.* Washington, D.C., 1985.

Williams, Emily H. "The National Association of Colored Women." *Southern Workman* 43 (1914): 481–83.

Williams, Fannie Barrier. "The Club Movement among the Colored Women." *Voice of the Negro* 1 (Mar. 1904): 99–102.

————. "Colored Women of Chicago." *Southern Workman* 43 (Oct. 1914): 564–66.

————. "Social Bonds in the 'Black Belt' of Chicago." *Charities* 15 (Oct. 7, 1905): 41–44.

Williams, Vernon J., Jr. *From a Caste to a Minority: Changing Attitudes of American Sociologists toward Afro-Americans, 1986–1945.* New York, 1989.

————. *Rethinking Race: Franz Boas and His Contemporaries.* Lexington, Ky., 1996.

Wills, David. "Reverdy C. Ransom: The Making of an AME Bishop." In *Black Apostles: Afro-American Clergy Confront the Twentieth Century*, ed. Randall K. Burkett and Richard Newman, 196–97. Boston, 1978.

Wilson, Butler R. "General Summary." In *Social and Physical Condition of Negroes in Cities: Report of an Investigation under the Direction of Atlanta University and Proceedings of the Second Conference for the Study of Problems Concerning Negro City Life held at Atlanta University, May 25–26, 1897*, 5–19. Atlanta University Publications, no. 2. Atlanta, 1897.

Wilson, Francille Rusan. "'All of the Glory . . . Faded . . . Quickly': Sadie T. M. Alexander and Black Professional Women, 1920–1950." In *Sister Circle: Black Women and Work*, ed. Sharon Harley and the Black Women and Work Collective, 164–83. New Brunswick, N.J., 2002.

————. "Black Women's Labor Studies during the Great Migration: Recovering the Lost Generation of Black Female Social Scientists, 1915–1940." Paper presented at the annual meeting of the North American Labor History Conference, Detroit, Mich., Oct. 19, 2001.

————. "Haynes, Elizabeth Ross." In *Black Women in America: An Historical Encyclopedia*, ed. Darlene Clark Hine, Elsa Barkley Brown, and Rosalyn Terborg-Penn, 1:548–49. Brooklyn, 1993.

————. "George Haynes: The Scholar as a Professional Advocate." Unpublished paper.

————. "Going, Going, Gone: Social Research, Public Policy, and Black Industrial Workers." *Black Renaissance, Renaissance Noire* 1, no. 2 (1997): 66–75.

————. "Introduction." In *Unsung Heroes; The Black Boy of Atlanta; and "Negroes in Domestic Service in the United States,"* by Elizabeth Ross Haynes, xv–xxxviii. New York, 1997.

———. "Johnson, Charles S." *Encyclopedia of Southern Culture,* ed. Charles R. Wilson and William Ferris, 214–15. Chapel Hill, N.C., 1989.

———. "Racial Consciousness and Black Scholarship: Charles H. Wesley and the Construction of *Negro Labor in the United States." Journal of Negro History* 81, nos. 1–4 (1997): 72–88.

———. "Sadie T. Alexander's Construction of a Public Persona." Keynote address delivered at the annual meeting of the Association of Black Women Historians, Orlando, Fla., 2003.

———. "The Segregated Scholars: Black Labor Historians, 1895–1950." Ph.D. diss., University of Pennsylvania, 1988.

———. "Shaping American and International Protections for Blacks and Women: Sadie T. M. Alexander's Crusade in the U.S. and U.N., 1944–1964." Paper presented at the Collegium for African American Research, Sardinia, Italy, Mar. 23, 2001.

———. "'This Past Was Waiting for Me When I Came': The Contextualization of Black Women"s History," *Feminist Studies* 22, no. 2 (1996): 345–61.

———. "Wright, R. R., Sr." *Encyclopedia of African-American Civil Rights,* ed. Charles Lowery and John Marszalek, 595–94. Westport, Conn., 1992.

———. "'You Must Keep Up or Endure the Dust'": New Negro Women in a New Century, Theorizing the Life of Elizabeth Ross Haynes." Paper presented at the Ford Foundation Seminar on the Meanings and Representations of Black Women's Work, 1997.

Winston, Michael R. *The Howard University Department of History, 1913–1973.* Washington, D.C., 1973.

———. "Miller, Kelly." In *Dictionary of American Negro Biography,* ed. Rayford W. Logan and Michael R. Winston, 435–39. New York, 1982.

———. "Through the Back Door: Academic Racism and the Negro Scholar in Historical Perspective." *Daedalus* 100, no. 3 (1971): 678–719.

Wood, Peter H. "'I Did the Best I Could for My Day': The Study of Early Black History during the Second Reconstruction, 1960 to 1976." *William & Mary Quarterly* 35, no. 2 (Apr. 1978): 185–225.

Woodruff, C. R. Review of *The Philadelphia Negro. City and State,* Jan. 4, 1900.

Woodson, Carter G. "Annual Report of the Director." *Journal of Negro History* 9, no. 1 (Oct. 1924): 469–70.

———. *A Century of Negro Migration.* New York, 1918.

———. *The History of the Negro Church.* Washington, D.C., 1921.

———. "Introduction." In *The Negro Wage Earner,* by Lorenzo J. Greene and Carter G. Woodson. Washington, D.C., 1930.

———. *The Miseducation of the Negro.* Washington, D.C., 1933.

———. *Negro Makers of History.* Washington, D.C., 1928.

———. *The Negro Professional Man and the Community: With Special Emphasis on the Physician and the Lawyer.* 1934. Reprint, New York, 1969.

————. "The Negro Washerwoman, A Vanishing Figure." *Journal of Negro History* 15, no. 3 (July 1930): 269–77.

————. Review of *Negro Labor in the United States, 1850–1925*, by Charles Wesley. *American Historical Review* 33 (Oct. 1927): 154–56.

————. Review of *Negro Labor in the United States, 1850–1925*, by Charles Wesley. *New York Times*, Apr. 17, 1927, 20.

————. *The Rural Negro.* Washington, D.C., 1930.

Work, Monroe N. "Additional Information and Corrections in Reconstruction Records." *Journal of Negro History* (Apr. 1920): 235–48.

————. "African Agriculture." *Southern Workman* 39 (Nov.–Dec. 1910): 613–18, and 40 (Jan.–Feb. 1911): 37–42, 79–87.

————. "The African Family as an Institution." Parts 1–3. *Southern Workman* 38 (June 1909): 343–53; (July 1909): 319–97; (Aug. 1909): 433–40.

————. "The African Medicine Man." *Southern Workman* 36 (Oct. 1907): 561–64.

————. "An African System of Writing." *Southern Workman* 37 (Oct. 1908): 518–26.

————. *A Bibliography of the Negro in Africa and America.* New York, 1928.

————. "Crime among the Negroes of Chicago." *American Journal of Sociology* 6 (Sept. 1900): 204–23.

————. "Crime in Cities." In *Some Notes on Negro Crime Particularly in Georgia: Report of a Social Study Made under the Direction of Atlanta University; together with the Proceedings of the Ninth Conference for the Study of the Negro Problems, held at Atlanta University, May 24, 1904*, ed. W. E. B. Du Bois, 18–31. Atlanta University Publications, no. 9. Atlanta,1904.

————. "Crime in Savannah as Compared with Chicago, Illinois." Conference presentation. N.p., n.d.

————. "Effects of the War on Southern Labor." *Southern Workman* 47 (Aug. 1918): 381–84.

————. "Folk Tales from Students in the Georgia State College." *Journal of American Folklore* 32 (July–Sept. 1919): 402–5.

————. "Folk Tales from Students in Tuskegee Institute, Alabama." *Journal of American Folklore* 34 (July–Sept. 1919): 397–401.

————. "The Negro Church and the Community." *Southern Workman* 37 (Aug. 1908): 428–32.

————. "The Negroes of Warsaw, Georgia." *Southern Workman* 37 (Jan. 1908): 29–40.

————. "The Negro in Business and the Professions." *Annals of the American Academy of Political and Social Science* (Nov. 1928): 138–44.

————. "Negro Migration Changes in Rural Organization and Population of the Cotton Belt." *Southern Workman* 50 (Sept. 1921).

————. "Negro Migration in 1916–1917." *Southern Workman* 47 (Nov. 1918): 614–15.

————. "The Negro Real Estate Owners of Chicago." Master's thesis, University of Chicago, 1903.

————. "The Negro's Industrial Problem." *Southern Workman* 43 (Aug.–Sept. 1914): 428–39.

————. "The Ninth Atlanta Conference." In *Some Notes on Negro Crime Particularly in Georgia: Report of a Social Study Made under the Direction of Atlanta University; together with the Proceedings of the Ninth Conference for the Study of the Negro Problems, held at Atlanta University, May 24, 1904,* ed. W. E. B. Du Bois, 64. Atlanta University Publications, no. 9. Atlanta, 1904.

————. "Problems of Adjustment of Race and Class in the South." *Social Forces* 16 (Oct. 1937): 108–17.

————. "Racial Factors and Economic Forces in Land Tenure in the South, 1860–1930." *Social Forces* 15 (Dec. 1936): 205–15.

————. Review of *The Black Worker,* by Sterling D. Spero and Abram L. Harris. *American Journal of Sociology* 37 (Sept. 1931): 307.

————. Review of *The Negro Wage Earner,* by Lorenzo J. Greene and Carter G. Woodson. *American Journal of Sociology* 37 (Sept. 1931): 307.

————. "Secret Societies as Factors in the Social and Economic Life of the Negro." In *Proceedings of the Southern Sociological Congress.* 1916.

————. "Sociology in the Common Schools." *Proceedings of the American Sociological Society* 13 (Dec. 1918): 95–97.

————. "Some Geechee Folklore." *Southern Workman* 34 (Nov.–Dec. 1905): 633–34, 696–97.

————. "Some Negro Members of Reconstruction Conventions and Legislatures and of Congress." *Journal of Negro History* (Jan. 1920): 63–119.

————. "Some Parallelisms in the Development of Africans and Other Races." Parts 1–4. *Southern Workman* 35 (Nov. 1906), 36 (Jan. 1907, Feb. 1907, Mar. 1907).

————. "The South's Labor Problem." *South Atlantic Quarterly* 19 (Jan. 1920): 1–8.

Work, Monroe N., and the Editor, "Middle West, Illinois." In *The Negro Church, Report of a Social Study Made under the Direction of Atlanta University; together with the Proceedings of the Eighth Conference for the Study of the Negro Problems, held at Atlanta university, May 26th, 1903,* 83–92. Atlanta University Publications, no. 8. Atlanta, 1903.

Wright, Carroll D. "The Growth and Purposes of Bureaus of Statistics of Labor." Address before the American Social Science Association, Sept. 3, 1888. Reprinted in Jonathan Grossman, "Black Studies in the Department of Labor," *Monthly Labor Review* 97 (June 1974): 17–27.

Wright, I. B. "The Higher Education of Women." *The Athenaeum* 14, no. 7 (Apr. 1908): 2–4.

Wright, John S. "Intellectual Life." In *Encyclopedia of African American Culture and History,* 4:1369–90. New York, 1996.

Wright, Richard R., Jr. "The Economic Condition of Negroes in the North, II: Rural Communities in Indiana." *Southern Workman* 37 (Mar. 1908): 158–72.

———. "The Economic Condition of Negroes in the North, III: Negro Communities in New Jersey." *Southern Workman* 37 (July 1908): 385–93.

———. "The Economic Condition of Negroes in the North, IV: Negro Governments in the North." *Southern Workman* 37 (Sept. 1908): 486–98.

———. "The Economic Condition of Negroes in the North, VI: Negroes in Business in the North." *Southern Workman* 38 (Jan. 1909): 36–44.

———. *Eighty-seven Years Behind the Black Curtain: An Autobiography.* Philadelphia, 1965.

———. "Forty Years of Negro Progress." *Southern Workman* 36 (Mar. 1907): 157–63.

———. "The Historicity of the Acts of the Apostles." Master's thesis, University of Chicago, 1904.

———. "Homeownership and Savings among Negroes of Philadelphia." *Southern Workman* 36 (Dec. 1907): 665–76.

———. "Housing and Sanitation in Relation to Mortality of Negroes." Report, Hampton Institute Conference, 1906. *Southern Workman* 35 (Sept. 1906): 475–80.

———. "Memorandum by R. R. Wright, Jr.: Mortality in Cities." In *The Health and Physique of the Negro American; Report of a Social Study Made under the Direction of Atlanta University; together with the Proceedings of the Eleventh Conference for the Study of the Negro Problems, held at Atlanta University, on May the 29th, 1906,* ed. W. E. B. Du Bois, 82–90. Atlanta University Publications, no. 11. Atlanta, 1906.

———. "The Middle West, Ohio." In *The Negro Church: Report of a Social Study Made under the Direction of Atlanta University; together with the Proceedings of the Eighth Conference for the Study of the Negro Problems, held at Atlanta University, May 26th, 1903,* 92–110. Atlanta University Publications, no. 8. Atlanta, 1903.

———. "The Migration of the Negro to the North." *Annals of the American Academy of Political and Social Science* 27, no. 3 (May 1906): 97–116.

———. "The Industrial Condition of Negroes in Chicago." Bachelor's thesis, University of Chicago, 1901.

———. "The Negro in Chicago." *Southern Workman* 35 (Oct. 1906): 553–66.

———. *The Negro in Pennsylvania: A Study in Economic History.* 1912. Reprint, New York, 1969.

———. "The Negro in Times of Industrial Unrest." *Charities* 15 (Oct. 7, 1905): 69–73.

———. "The Negro in Unskilled Labor." *Annals of the American Academy of Political and Social Science* 49 (Sept. 1913): 19–27.

———. "The Negroes of Xenia, Ohio: A Social Study." *Bulletin of the Department of Labor* 48 (1903): 1006–44.

———. "The Northern Negro and Crime." *Southern Workman* 39 (Mar. 1910): 137–42.

———. "One Hundred Negro Steel Workers." In *Pittsburgh Survey* 6, ed. Paul U. Kellogg, 97–112. New York, 1914.

———. "Poverty among Northern Negroes." *Southern Workman* 40 (Dec. 1911): 699–709.

———. "Recent Improvements in Housing among Negroes in the North." *Southern Workman* 37 (Nov. 1908).

———. "The Skilled Mechanic in the North." *Southern Workman* 38 (Mar. 1909): 155–68.

———. "Social Work and the Influence of the Negro Church." *Annals of the American Academy of Political and Social Science* 30 (Nov. 1907): 81–93.

Wright, Richard R., Sr. *A Brief Historical Sketch of Negro Education in Georgia.* Savannah, 1894.

———. "The Colored Farm Laborers and Farmers of Georgia." Remarks given at Augusta, Georgia, Nov. 23, 1883. In *Report of the Education and Labor Committee of the Senate Upon the Relations between Labor and Capital, and Testimony Taken by the Committee*, 3:811–19. Washington, D.C., 1885. Reprinted in *The Black Worker: A Documentary History from Colonial Times to the Present*, ed. Philip S. Foner and Ronald L. Lewis, 3:25–32. Philadelphia, 1978.

———. "The Negro as an Inventor." *A.M.E. Church Review* (Apr. 1886): 392–411.

———. "Negro Companions of the Spanish Explorers." *American Anthropologist* (Apr.–June 1902): 217–29.

Wright, W. D. *Black Intellectuals, Black Cognition, and a Black Aesthetic.* Westport, Conn., 1997.

Yabura, Lloyd. "The Legacy of Forrester B. Washington: Black Social Work Educator and Nation Builder." In *Proceedings: Fiftieth Anniversary at Atlanta School of Social Work*, ed. Charles L. Sanders, 28–30. Atlanta, 1970.

"Y.W.C.A." *Fisk Herald* 28, no. 3 (Jan. 1911): 5–6.

Index

Page numbers in italics refer to photographs in the text.

Childs, J. G., 277n29
Childs, Mattie Freeman, 109, 278n36
Christian Recorder, 116, 120
Christian sociology movement, 47, 48
CIICN. *See* Committee for Improving the Industrial Conditions among Negroes
Circle for Negro War Relief, 177
Civil Rights Committee. *See* U.S. Civil Rights Committee
civil rights movement, 249, 250, 251, 253
Clark, Jessie, 180–81
Clark-Lewis, Elizabeth, 205
Clement, George C., 129
clubwomen, 90, 91–96, 99, 102, 174
coal industry, 157, 236, 237, 239
Code of Fair Competition hearings, 235–36, 239–41
Coffin, A. O., 267n22
Colored Protective Association, 151
Colored Women's Congress (1895), 93, 95
Colson, Myra Hill. *See* Callis, Myra Hill Colson
Columbia University, 43, 65, 109
Commission on Race Relations (Chicago), 146
Committee for Improving the Industrial Conditions among Negroes (CIICN), 84, 221
Committee on the Economic Condition of the Negro (American Economics Association), 79
Committee on Urban Conditions among Negroes (CUCAN), 84
Commons, John R., 38, 72
Communist Party, 169, 217
construction industry, 246–47
Consumers League (New York City), 179–80
Cooper, Anna Julia, 91, 100–101, 113
Coopers International Union, 34–35
Cornell University, 109
Cotton States Exposition (1895), 24, 93, 95

cotton textile industry, 235–36
Cox, Oliver Cromwell, 6
crime, studies of, 25, 50, 72
Crisis, The, 116, 120, 216, 224, 226
Crummell, Alexander, 14, 17–19, 28–30
Cruse, Harold, 221
CUCAN. See Committee on Urban Conditions among Negroes
Cummings, Edward, 13, 20–21
Current History, 157

Dancy, John C., 297n13
Darity, William, 161, 169
Davis, John A., 217, 235
Davis, John P., 228, 233, 234–39, 243
Davis, John W., 45
day-care services, 56, 96, 101, 205
defense industry, 249
Department of Labor. *See* U.S. Department of Labor
Depression (1930s), 207–8, 216–18, 225
Detroit (Mich.), studies of, 126
Devine, Edward T., 66–67, 83
Diggs, Irene, 102
Diggs, James Robert Lincoln, 47–48
Dill, Augustus, 104
Dillard, James H., 130
disease. *See* mortality and disease
Divison of Negro Economics. *See under* U.S. Department of Labor
DOL. *See* U.S. Department of Labor
domestic workers, 122, 179, 200, 203–5, 208, 241
Donald, Henderson, 122, 151
"Don't Buy Where You Can't Work" campaigns, 216–17, 235
Dorsey, Emmett E., 171, 225
Drake, St. Clair, 7
dual wage systems, 220, 234, 236–37, 240–41
Du Bois, Nina Gomer, 14
Du Bois, W. E. B., 2, 6–7, 9–39, 12, 148, 227, 250; AEA and, 76–79; assessments

Du Bois, W. E. B. (*continued*)
of, 134–35, 158, 225, 232; beginnings as
social scientist, 11–23; break from
Washington, 29–30, 37–38, 75, 81;
Charities special issue and, 67; economic strategies of, 5, 34, 77, 215, 218,
222, 223–27; education of, 11–14, 42;
employment of, 13–14, 22, 27, 79, 80–
81, 117, 148, 226; funding for research
of, 79, 88; intellectual philosophy of,
169; Inter-Collegiate Banquet and, 49–
50; on G. Jackson, 129; Jamestown
exposition and, 128; on labor unions,
224; land-grant college research program of, 251; maturation of thought of,
28–31; mentoring by, 4–5, 42, 50, 57–
58, 61, 102, 104, 230, 233–34; migration studies of, 120, 151; on racial
progress, 9, 40; research methodology
of, 21–22, 197, 204; on social class roles,
16–17, 35–36, 168; on social disorganization and Social Darwinism, 16, 17–
18, 29–31; voting rights and, 171; on
Willcox, 73–74. Works: "The Black
North," 71; "The Economic Future of
the Negro," 77; "Education and Work,"
223–24; "The Hosts of Black Labor,"
120, 151; *The Negro Artisan*, 11, 30–39,
105, 197; "The Negro in the Black
Belt," 91, 104; "The Negro's Industrial
Plight," 224; *The Philadelphia Negro*,
11, 14–17, 35, 100, 135; *The Souls of
Black Folk*, 28, 30, 38, 39, 258n9,
264n77; "The Study of Negro Problems," 22, 160. *See also* Atlanta University Conferences; National Association
for the Advancement of Colored
People
Dykes, Eva Beatrice, 112–14, 210–11

Eastman, Elizabeth, 240
Eaton, Isabel, 259n17
Elks (fraternal organization), 238
Embree, Edwin, 242–43

Employment Service, U. S. *See* U.S.
Employment Service

Farmville (Va.), studies of, 22
farm workers, 32, 51, 205, 270n55
Fauset, Jessie, 102
Federal Council of Churches, 117, 151,
161, 238, 239
Federal Employment Practices
Commission, 249
Fisk University, 11; social science pro-
grams at, 4, 66, 85–87, 138, 162;
women's education and, 103, 107–8
Foner, Philip, 249
Ford, Henry, 154
Foreman, Clark, 242–43
Fortune, T. Thomas, 67
Frankfurter, Felix, 129
Franklin, Vincent P., 7, 10
fraternal organizations, 238
Frazier, E. Franklin, 6; community stud-
ies and other publications of, 171, 177,
280n6; economic strategies of, 225;
employment of, 211, 275n118, 286n70;
land-grant college research program
of, 251; reviews by, 160. Works: *Black
Bourgeoisie*, 221
Freedmen's Bureau, 36

Gaines, Kevin K., 100
Garvey, Marcus, 128
Garveyism, 222
Gate City Free Kindergarten Association,
96
gender discrimination, 175, 210, 213
Gibbs, James, 305n117
Gladden, Washington, 271n69
Goggin, Jacqueline, 122
Gomer, Nina, 14
Gompers, Samuel, 128
Grant, Anna R., 202–3
Great Migration, 115–17, 170–71. *See
also* migration, studies of
Greene, Lorenzo J., 4, 6, 117, 143, 250;

civil rights movement and, 251; education of, 136, 144, 163; employment of, 144, 163; mentors of, 5, 139, 142–44. Works: *The Negro in Colonial New England,* 164; *The Negro Wage Earner,* 119, 144, 159, 163–64

Gregg, Robert, 120

Gutman, Herbert, 168

Hadnott, Grace, 90, 91, 108

Hall, Charles, 131, 292n26

Hampton Institute, 37, 64

Hampton Institute Conferences, 75

Harding, Warren, 154

Harlem Renaissance, 153, 183

Harper, William Rainey, 51

Harris, Abram L., 4, 7, 117, *149*; ASNLH and, 139; coal miner studies of, 157; economic strategies of, 225–26; education of, 86, 136, 145, 147, 149, 152, 157, 169; employment of, 149–50, 152, 157, 161, 171, 250; labor philosophy of, 157–58, 169–70, 215, 222; mentors of, 5, 145, 146; migration studies of, 119, 157; NAACP reorganization and, 5, 226–30; National Interracial Conference and, 161–62; NIL-JCER support and, 238; reviews by, 164; on social class roles, 170. Works: *The Black Worker,* 160, 164–65, 168–70; *The Negro as a Capitalist,* 164, 222; "The Negro Problem as Viewed by Negro Leaders," 157

Harris, Eugene, 25, 75

Harris, Ruth Marion, 104–5

Harrison, Charles C., 15

Hart, Albert Bushnell, 12, 14, 166

Harvard University, 12, 109, 232–33, 265n8

Hastie, William, 228, 233, 247, 303n100

Haynes, Birdye H., 63, 110, 114, 271n64

Haynes, Elizabeth Ross, 4, 6–7, 202; education of, 44, 91, 107–8, 110–12, 203, 206; employment of, 110–13, 174,

188–89, 191, 200–201, 206–7; JCER support and, 240; on racial progress, 91, 108. Works: "Negroes in Domestic Service," 122, 151, 179, 200, 203–5, 208; "Two Million Negro Women at Work," 203; *Unsung Heroes,* 206

Haynes, George Edmund, 3–5, 6, 62, 250; African studies and, 305n117; assessments of, 157, 163, 244; Division of Negro Economics and, 117, 119, 127–35, 188, 189–90, 197, 244; dual wage system and, 220; employment of, 56, 63–64, 85, 113–14, 136, 151, 206, 287n84; graduate education of, 4, 45, 47, 56, 61–65, 83–84, 91, 111; institutionalizing mentorship and, 4–5, 83–87, 115, 135–40; migration studies of, 65, 83–84, 115, 117, 119–21, 123–27, 151; National Interracial Conference and, 160; NIL-JCER support and, 237–40, 242, 244; on racial progress, 40–41. Works: *The Negro at Work in New York City,* 84, 124, 135, 244; *The Negro at Work in World War and Reconstruction,* 131, 151, 195–96. See also Fisk University; National Urban League

Henderson, Charles Richmond, 52–54, 58

Hershaw, LaFayette M., 28, 33, 67, 94

Higginbotham, Evelyn Brooks, 10, 99

Hill, T. Arnold, 154–55, 217, 244

Hoffman, Frederick L., 18, 73, 76

Hope, John, 28, 44, 46, 265n7

Hope, Lugenia Burns, 44, 96, 176–77, 179

housing, 45, 97, 99, 246–47

Housing and Urban Development. *See* U.S. Department of Housing and Urban Development

Houston, Charles H., 228, 247, 300n59

Howard, Aletha, 277n29

Howard University: history programs at, 139, 140–41; "radical" professors of, 171; social science/sociology programs

Kester, Howard, 228
Kilson, Martin, 305n117
kindergarten programs, 26, 96, 205
King, Georgia Swift, 25–26, 97, 101, 105

Labor Advisory Board (National Recov-
ery Administration), 242
Labor Bureau. *See* U.S. Department of
Labor
labor unions: affirmative action plans
and, 247; NIL support by, 237; racial
discrimination by, 34–35, 72, 131–32;
strikebreakers and, 157, 170; studies
of, 32, 34, 156, 159–60, 168–69;
women and, 184, 195, 201–2, 206
Lamar, Lucius Q. C., 21
Laney, Lucy Craft, 25–26, 44, 90, 96–99,
101, 105
laundry workers, 190
Lee, Henry, 33
Lehman, Herbert, 207
Leland, W. G., 78
Lewis, David Levering, 153
Lewis, John L., 237
Lindsay, Inabel Burns, 274n111, 275n118
Lindsay, Samuel McCune, 27, 58, 261n38
living conditions, studies of, 24–25, 67,
98
Locke, Alain, 117, 161, 162
Logan, Adella Hunt, 25, 101
Logan, Rayford, 103, 171, 233, 250, 251
Lowell, Abbott, 154, 233
Lowndes County (Ala.) study, 80–81
lynchings, 79–80, 94, 121, 155
Lyons, Marchita, 259n27

Mabee, Carleton, 185
Mack, Lula Iola, 104, 106
Marshall, F. Ray, 249
Mathews, Shailer, 51, 53, 54
Matthews, Victoria Earle, 90, 93–95
McDougald, Gertrude E. J., 4, 7,
182–87, *184*, 208. Works: *A New Day
for the Colored Woman*, 179–81

McKay, Claude, 156
Mead, Margaret, 183
Meier, August, 165, 221
Memphis (Tenn), studies of, 33
Messenger, 134–35, 149, 157–58
migration, studies of, 41, 51, 71, 83–84,
118–27, 152–53
Miller, Kelly, 17–18, 31, 67, 70–71, 75–
76, 98, 100
minimum wage plans, 204–5, 220
Monthly Labor Review, 197–98
Moore, Garrie, 275n118
Moore, Lewis Baxter, 140, *140*, 211
Moorland, Jesse, 63
Morehouse College, 177
Morrow, Cornelious Wortendyke, 110
mortality and disease, 24–25, 75, 97–99,
212
Mossell, Sadie Tanner. *See* Alexander,
Sadie Tanner Mossell
Moton, Robert Russa, 36, 37, 135, 157,
237
Muncy, Robyn, 102
Murray, Maggie J., 107

NAACP. *See* National Association for the
Advancement of Colored People
NACW. *See* National Association of Colored Women
Nation, The, 77–78
National Association for the Advancement of Colored People (NAACP):
founding/administration of, 66, 81,
225–26, 282n36; as mentoring institution, 6, 117; NIL-JCER support and,
238, 240; reorganization of, 5, 7, 226–
30; strategies of, 134, 216
National Association of Colored Women
(NACW), 7, 95, 96, 100, 102, 174, 190,
205
National Baptist Convention, 238
National Conference of Social Work,
271n68
National Interracial Conference, 160–61

---

racial prejudice and discrimination:
among white academics, 59, 72, 167;
data collection, difficulty of, on, 21;
migration and, 121, 155; social disorganization and, 68; studies of, 16;
toward black women, 175, 181, 196,
197–98; working-class whites and, 35,
38, 169, 220. *See also* black inferiority
stereotypes
Radcliffe College, 109
Randolph, A. Philip, 134–35, 184, 242,
249
Ransom, Reverdy C., 46, 49–50, 142, 238
real-estate ownership, studies of, 50
Records and Research Department,
Tuskegee Institute, 50–51
Reid, Ira De A., 4, 6–7, 117, *148*; civil
rights movement and, 251; education
of, 86, 136, 145, 147, 152; employment
of, 146, 148, 155, 227, 250; mentors of,
5, 145, 146; migration studies of, 119;
NUL research program and, 155–57,
159, 217; voting rights/civil rights and,
171, 251. Works: *Male Negro Skilled
Workers in the United States, 1930–
1936*, 245; *Negro Membership in
American Labor Unions*, 156, 159; *Sta-
tistics by Regions*, 245
rent parties, 155–56
Rogers, W. A., 277n29
Roosevelt, Franklin D., 236, 249
Rosenwald Fund, 51, 60, 242
Ross, Dorothy, 60
Ross, Elizabeth. *See* Haynes, Elizabeth
Ross
Rouse, Jacqueline, 176
Royce, Josiah, 12
Rudwick, Elliott, 165, 221
Ruffin, Josephine St. Pierre, 94–95
rural industries and conditions, 22, 205
Russell Sage Foundation, 60, 160

Salem, Dorothy, 95
Saunders, Frank, 63

Sayre, Helen, 178
Scarborough, William, 28
Schlesinger, Arthur, Sr., 166–67
Schmoller, Gustav von, 13, 15
Schuyler, George, 169
scientific racism. *See* black inferiority
stereotypes
Scott, Emmett J., 51
"segregated scholars," definition of, 2
self-hatred, 221, 223
self-help philosophy, 26, 29, 217, 218
Seligmann, Herbert, 161
Sexton, S. M., 34
Shadd, F. J., 75
Shields, Emma L., 4, 7, 114, 179, 188,
196–200, 208. Works: "Vocational
Adjustment Problems of Negro
Women in New York City," 200
Shillady, John R., 130
Shivery, Louie D., 96
Simpson, Georgianna, 45, 113–14,
210–11
Skinner, Elliot, 305n117
Slater (John F.) Fund, 13, 37, 264n80
slavery, 30, 35–36, 73, 97, 199
Sleet, Jessie, 270n64
Small, Albion, 42, 47, 52, 55, 58
Smith, Joseph, 24
Smythe, Hugh, 171, 305n117
Smythe, Mabel, 251, 305n117
social class: categorizations of, 16–17,
35–36, 71, 98–99, 183; intraclass con-
flicts, 122; leadership roles and, 122–
23, 168, 170, 218; as methodological
approach, 158; self-hatred and, 221,
223. *See also* social disorganization
Social Darwinism, 11, 16, 17–18, 62, 94
social disorganization, 18, 25, 29–30, 68,
75, 99–100
Social Gospel movement, 47
Social Science Research Council, 160–
61, 289n120
social sciences and sociology: as academic
disciplines, 12, 19; attitudes toward,

social sciences and sociology (*continued*)
44; censuses and, 21; Christian sociol-
ogy movement, 47, 48; professionaliza-
tion of, 87, 271n68; as racial uplift tool,
2, 10, 18–19, 253; research methods
of, 13, 17, 72, 93, 197, 204
Sociological Club of Atlanta, 101
sociology. *See* social sciences and
sociology
Southern politics and attitudes, 3, 18, 21,
24, 34, 35, 67, 72, 76, 118, 125
Spaulding, C. C., 211, 241
Spear, Alan, 44
Spencer, Herbert, 15
Spero, Sterling D., 160, 164–65, 168–69
Spingarn, Joel E., 225
Steward, Mary, 109
Stolberg, Benjamin, 161, 225
Stone, Alfred Holt, 76–80, 82
Straus, Nathan, 245–46
Sumner, Francis, 171, 229, 280n6
Sumner, William Graham, 61–62
Sunday Men's Club, 49–50
Survey, The, 67, 121, 126
Survey Graphic (special issue on
Harlem), 183

Talbert, Mary, 194
Tanner, Benjamin Tucker, 53, 211
Taussig, Frank W., 233
Taylor, A. A., 139
Taylor, Graham, 48
temperance ideology, 97
Temporary Commission on the Status of
the Urban Colored Population (N.Y.),
207–8
Terrell, Mary Church, 178
textile industry, 236
Thomas, Jesse O., 283n41, 297n13
Thomas, William I., 48, 58
Thompson, Charles H., 171
Tillinghast, Joseph A., 73–74, 76
timber industry, 132, 236–37
tobacco industry, 198–99, 241

Towns, George A., 105
Treitschke, Heinrich von, 13
Trinity Mission (Chicago), 55–56
Trotter, Joe William, Jr., 118, 150, 152–53
Truman, Harry, 251
tuberculosis, 25, 98, 212
Tuskegee Institute, 37, 50–51

unemployment, 25, 68, 73, 155, 216
United Mine Workers, 34, 282n36
University of Chicago, 3, 12, 43–47, 109–
10, 265n8
University of Pennsylvania, 43, 109
University of Pittsburgh, 145
urban conditions, 24–25, 101, 118
Urban League. *See* National Urban
League
Urban League Fellows Program, 86, 138,
145, 211, 269n50
U.S. Bureau of the Census, 21, 79–80, 83
U.S. Civil Rights Committee, 251
U.S. Department of Housing and Urban
Development, 251
U.S. Department of Labor (DOL):
Atlanta University Conferences and,
20–22; Division of Negro Economics
of, 117, 119, 127–35, 187–88, 191,
201–2, 211; Du Bois's studies for, 11,
22, 57, 80–81, 91, 104; U. S. Employment Service and, 132–33, 190–91,
282n37; Labor Advisory Board of, 242;
women researchers in, 178, 179, 187–
92; Women's Bureau of, 133, 187–92,
201–2
U.S. Department of the Interior, 242–43,
245–46, 303n100
U.S. Employment Service (USES),
132–33, 190–91, 282n37

Valien, Preston, 251
Van Kleeck, Mary, 133, 160–61, 188,
190–91, 193–94
Vann, Robert, 243
Vardaman, James K., 73

Virginia: congressional delegation of, 128, 282n37; studies of, 22, 198–99

vocational education. *See* industrial education

voting rights, 18, 36, 171

wage differentials. *See* dual wage systems

Wagner, Adolf, 13

Washington (D.C.): boycotts in, 217, 221; studies of, 163, 205, 208

Washington, Booker T.: on black crime, 72–73; on black-owned businesses, 34; break from Du Bois, 29–30, 37–38, 75, 81; *Charities* special issue and, 67–68; critiques of, 70–71; funding for projects of, 79, 87; Inter-Collegiate Banquet and, 49–50; materialism of, 30; mentoring by, 68; on skilled professional opportunities, 33–34; Stone's economic views and, 76–77, 79

Washington, Forrester B., 211, 275n118, 292n26

Washington, Margaret Murray, 107

Weaver, Mortimer, 233

Weaver, Robert C., 1, 7, 232; affirmative action programs and, 244, 246–47; ASNLH and, 221, 248; dual wage system, opposition to, by, 5, 220, 234, 235–37; education of, 231–33; employment of, 230, 241, 242–46, 251; labor philosophy of, 215, 248–49; mentors of, 139, 230, 233; NIL-JCER and, 235–43; publications and studies of, 244–45, 251. Works: *Negro Labor*, 216, 249, 250

Weber, Max, 13

Weiss, Nancy J., 152–53, 218

Wells-Barnett, Ida B., 46, 94–95. Works: *On Lynchings*, 10, 79

Wendell, Barrett, 12

Wesley, A. A., 50

Wesley, Charles H., 7, 117, *141*; African studies and, 305n117; education of, 4, 114, 136, 139–40, 165–67; employment of, 140–41, 171, 250, 287n84; labor phi-

losophy of, 170; mentors of, 5, 139, 142, 143–44; migration studies of, 119; ministry of, 49, 141–42; NIL-JCER support and, 238. Works: *Negro Labor in the United States*, 6, 164–65, 167–68, 220

West Virginia Collegiate Institute (later West Virginia State College for Negroes), 266n15

Wharton, Susan P., 15

White, Walter, 228, 229

white advisors on black issues, 59, 242

White Rose Mission, 93–94

Whittier, John Greenleaf, 26

Wilberforce University, 13–14, 54

Wilkins, Roy, 238

Willcox, Walter, 72–74, 78–80

Williams, Fannie Barrier, 46, 68, 95

Williams, Frances, 240

Williams, Mary Louise, 178

Williams, S. Laing, 46, 50, 68

Williams, William T. B., 33

Wilson, Butler R., 24, 130

Wilson, William B., 129, 189

Wilson, Woodrow, 194

women: Atlanta University Conference and, 25–26, 90, 96–103, 105; career opportunities for, 91–92, 103, 110; equal workplace/home treatment for, 100, 186; gender discrimination and, 210, 213; higher education for, 4, 103–13, 118, 265n8; labor unions and, 184, 195, 201–2, 206; mentoring of, 91, 102, 175, 259n27; racial prejudice/discrimination toward, 181, 196, 197–98; social class categorizations of, 183; social disorganization and, 99–100; as social scientists, 3–4, 26, 60, 118, 171–76, 188, 259n27; stereotypes of, 198, 201; war work and, 173, 177–78, 189, 201; as workers, studies of, 93–94, 179–81, 190, 193, 195–97. *See also* clubwomen

Women in Industry Service (WIIS). *See* Women's Bureau (U.S. Dept. of Labor)